Language Learners in Study Abroad Contexts

SECOND LANGUAGE ACQUISITION
Series Editor: Professor David Singleton, *Trinity College, Dublin, Ireland*

This new series will bring together titles dealing with a variety of aspects of language acquisition and processing in situations where a language or languages other than the native language is involved. Second language will thus be interpreted in its broadest possible sense. The volumes included in the series will all in their different ways offer, on the one hand, exposition and discussion of empirical findings and, on the other, some degree of theoretical reflection. In this latter connection, no particular theoretical stance will be privileged in the series; nor will any relevant perspective – sociolinguistic, psycholinguistic, neurolinguistic, etc. – be deemed out of place. The intended readership of the series will be final-year undergraduates working on second language acquisition projects, postgraduate students involved in second language acquisition research, and researchers and teachers in general whose interests include a second language acquisition component.

Other Books in the Series
Learning to Request in a Second Language: A Study of Child Interlanguage Pragmatics
    Machiko Achiba
Effects of Second Language on the First
    Vivian Cook (ed.)
Age and the Acquisition of English as a Foreign Language
    María del Pilar García Mayo and Maria Luisa García Lecumberri (eds)
Fossilization in Adult Second Language Acquisition
    ZhaoHong Han
Silence in Second Language Learning: A Psychoanalytic Reading
    Colette A. Granger
Age, Accent and Experience in Second Language Acquisition
    Alene Moyer
Studying Speaking to Inform Second Language Learning
    Diana Boxer and Andrew D. Cohen (eds)
Language Acquisition: The Age Factor (2nd Edition)
    David Singleton and Lisa Ryan
Focus on French as a Foreign Language: Multidisciplinary Approaches
    Jean-Marc Dewaele (ed.)
Second Language Writing Systems
    Vivian Cook and Benedetta Bassetti (eds)
Third Language Learners: Pragmatic Production and Awareness
    Maria Pilar Safont Jordà
Artificial Intelligence in Second Language Learning: Raising Error Awareness
    Marina Dodigovic
Studies of Fossilization in Second Language Acquisition
    ZhaoHong Han and Terence Odlin (eds)
Early Trilingualism: a Focus on Questions
    Julia D. Barnes

For more details of these or any other of our publications, please contact:
Multilingual Matters, Frankfurt Lodge, Clevedon Hall,
Victoria Road, Clevedon, BS21 7HH, England
http://www.multilingual-matters.com

SECOND LANGUAGE ACQUISITION 15
Series Editor: David Singleton, *Trinity College, Dublin, Ireland*

Language Learners in Study Abroad Contexts

Edited by
Margaret A. DuFon and Eton Churchill

MULTILINGUAL MATTERS LTD
Clevedon • Buffalo • Toronto

Library of Congress Cataloging in Publication Data
Language Learners in Study Abroad Contexts
Edited by Margaret A. DuFon and Eton Churchill.
Second Language Acquisition: 15
Includes bibliographical references and index.
1. Second language acquisition. 2. Language and languages–Study and
teaching–Foreign speakers. 3. Language and culture. 4. Intercultural communication.
5. Sociolinguistics. I. DuFon, Margaret A. II. Churchill, Eton.
III. Second Language Acquisition (Clevedon, England): 15.
P118.2.L3645 2006
418–dc22   2005014690

British Library Cataloguing in Publication Data
A catalogue entry for this book is available from the British Library.

ISBN 1-85359-851-8 / EAN 978-1-85359-851-7 (pbk)
ISBN 1-85359-852-6 / EAN 978-1-85359-852-4 (hbk)

Multilingual Matters Ltd
UK: Frankfurt Lodge, Clevedon Hall, Victoria Road, Clevedon BS21 7HH.
USA: UTP, 2250 Military Road, Tonawanda, NY 14150, USA.
Canada: UTP, 5201 Dufferin Street, North York, Ontario M3H 5T8, Canada.

Typeset by Techset Composition Ltd.
Printed and bound in Great Britain by MPG Books Ltd.

Contents

Preface

As the number of study abroad programs has continued to increase into the 21st century, so has the interest in and breadth of research on language learning in these contexts. Following trends in the field of second language acquisition, the research agenda has expanded from a focus on global linguistic gains to include investigations into learning processes, individual differences, dimensions of sociolinguistic competence, the development of specific skills and the role that the host context plays in shaping opportunities for interaction and learning. Accordingly, situated studies employing qualitative research methods (e.g. videotapes of table talk, interviews, learner journals) have come to play an important role in furthering our understanding and in supplementing data collected through quantitative measures.

The chapters in this volume – selected for their contextual diversity and methodological approaches – contribute to this evolving body of research. *Language Learners in Study Abroad Contexts* features nine studies that address specific calls for research by previous authors (e.g. Freed, 1995a; Huebner, 1995b) and engage in theoretical discussions in the field of second language acquisition. The volume opens with a review that outlines primary areas of research on study abroad in the last 10 years and situates subsequent chapters within this work.

Part 1 follows with two studies that investigate the acquisition of pragmatic competence. First, 'Learning to take leave in social conversation' documents the case study of an adult learner attempting to acquire native-like proficiency in leave-taking in Indonesia. Diary data drawn from two sojourns in Indonesia are analyzed for leave-taking and applied to the theoretical claims made by Schmidt (1993), Bialystok (1993) and Schumann (1997) regarding SLA processes and the acquisition of pragmatic knowledge. Touching on similar theoretical issues, 'Learning to say "you" in German' examines the development of sociolinguistic competence of 33 Irish learners of German in their use of second person pronouns (e.g. *Sie, du*) on three administrations of a free discourse completion task over a 14-month span.

Part 2 focuses on interaction at the host dinner table to look at socialization processes, the sharing of folk beliefs through stories and the co-construction of identity and interactional norms. 'The socialization of taste' applies a language socialization framework (Schieffelin & Ochs, 1986b) to investigate how Indonesians, through their discourse moves, socialize learners into the Indonesian world of food, which includes themes such as food as pleasure and as an ethnic identity marker. Adopting a similar theoretical framework, 'Joint construction of cultural folk beliefs' examines the dynamic process of joint storytelling between JFL learners and their hosts and presents evidence that co-telling provides an opportunity for transforming and negotiating one's stereotypical cultural beliefs and social identity. Continuing with the theme of a bi-directional flow of linguistic and cultural resources, 'Norms of interaction' illustrates how the interactional dynamics in the Japanese host family are mutually negotiated providing opportunities for language learning and the co-construction of identity.

Part 3 begins with 'Negotiation in a Japanese study abroad setting' comparing interaction between American students and Japanese interlocutors at home and in the classroom for frequency and type of negotiation, modified output and focus on form. Within the framework of negotiation studies (e.g. Long, 1981a; Pica, 1993), the data are also analyzed to illustrate the opportunities and processes of language learning in the two contexts. Also focusing on instructional contexts, 'Variable learner competence in the study abroad classroom' draws on learner journals and classroom observations to investigate how Japanese learners of English were differentially incorporated into the classroom during their time in the United States. It is suggested that interactions between program-wide decisions, the reception received at the school level and dynamics specific to individual classroom cultures contribute to how learners' competence is locally co-constructed.

The concluding two studies in Part 4 investigate the relationship between contextual and learner factors and gains in linguistic proficiency. Based on learner diaries, informal and oral proficiency interviews, 'Study-abroad social networks, motivation and attitudes' explores the relationship between the ability of learners to create social networks (Milroy, 1987), their motivation towards learning, attitudes toward the host culture and ultimate acquisition as measured by oral proficiency interviews. Program variables (e.g. volunteer work, host family involvement) and learner investment are shown to interact in influencing ultimate gains in proficiency. Also touching on the role of program design, 'Language learning strategies in the study abroad context' reports on the effects of program variables, personal variables and self-reported changes in proficiency on the development of learning strategies (Oxford, 1990). The findings of this multi-program study suggest that students who increase their strategy use abroad are more likely to experience gains in language skills and that specific program-related factors could influence the development of learning strategies.

While each of these studies offers a privileged window into learner experiences in a variety of contexts and addresses important theoretical issues current in the field of second language acquisition, read together they help portray the wonderfully complex experience that study abroad constitutes. Together, the studies in this volume paint a picture of the individual learner struggling with choices at the micro-level which are shaped by sociolinguistic concerns (e.g. how to take leave in the target language and which second person pronoun to use). They document the socialization processes collaboratively constructed at the host dinner table and provide insight into how the conversational dynamics in both the home and classroom support language acquisition, while also acknowledging that both individual and program variables can play an instrumental role in facilitating, and sometimes restricting, opportunities to engage in negotiation, to improve one's learning strategies and to increase investment in learning processes.

In terms of theory and praxis, these studies bring a wide range of perspectives and invite readers to interrogate with the contributors the degree to which learner competence is constructed, to which motivation (or investment) is a fixed trait or shaped by interactions in the host context, and to which the acquisition of pragmatics is a cognitive or social process. The chapters suggest directions for further research, include implications for language teaching and provide recommendations for program development. Indeed, because of the various methodological and theoretical approaches, *Language Learners in Study Abroad Contexts* is intended primarily for graduate students and advanced researchers investigating second language acquisition and socialization both in study abroad and in other contexts. In addition, this volume also promises to be a useful reference for educators involved in study abroad programs as it contributes to our understanding of the overseas sojourn.

Acknowledgements

This volume is the result of the support and collaboration of many mentors, colleagues, students and friends. Credit goes to Gabriele Kasper for originally inspiring this volume and for encouraging the editors, providing useful guidance, particularly in the early phases of the project. California State University-Chico afforded working time and assistance through a California State University Faculty Development grant. As editors, we would like to thank the contributors for their patience with the process and for the enriching experience of working together. We would also like to note the assistance of Cindy Jorth, who helped us acquire some of the reference material, and of Lyn Churchill, who carefully edited the chapters in the final phases of the project. In addition, our gratitude goes to David Singleton, the SLA series editor, and Marjukka Grover at Multilingual Matters for taking on the volume and to the editors and staff who helped bring the volume to its finished form.

Finally, on behalf of all the contributors, we would like to express our appreciation to all those who participated in the studies presented in this volume – as program administrators, teachers, members of the host communities or the language learners themselves – who allowed us to closely scrutinize them in the interest of advancing our knowledge of second language acquisition particularly as it pertains to study abroad.

Contributors

Rebecca Adams received her PhD at Georgetown University and is a Lecturer in the School of Linguistics and Applied Language Studies at Victoria University of Wellington. Her current research interests include interaction-driven second language learning, instructed SLA, the role of individual differences in language acquisition, and the role of context in language learning.

Anne Barron is Associate Professor in the English Department at the University of Bonn. She is author of *Acquisition in Interlanguage Pragmatics* (Benjamins, 2003). Research interests are in pragmatics, second language acquisition and genre analysis. Recent work focuses on intra-lingual pragmatic variation, the pragmatics of Irish English, and cross-cultural advertising.

Eton Churchill is currently teaching in the Faculty of Foreign Languages at Kanagawa University. He earned his EdD from Temple University and his current research interests include sociolinguistics and the role of context in language learning.

Haruko Minegishi Cook is Associate Professor of Japanese at the University of Hawai'i. Her main research interests include language socialization, discourse analysis and pragmatics. She has published a number of articles on the Japanese sentence-final particles and honorifics. Currently, she is working on JFL learners' speech-style shifts from the language socialization perspective.

Margaret A. DuFon is an Assistant Professor of Linguistics at California State University-Chico. She received her PhD in Second Language Acquisition from the University of Hawai'i. Her current research interests include interlanguage pragmatics, second language socialization, and issues of language and identity in Indonesian.

Tim Hassall teaches Indonesian Language and Linguistics in the Faculty of Asian Studies at the Australian National University. He holds a Masters and a PhD degree in Applied Linguistics, and his main research interest is the pragmatics of second language learners.

Masakazu Iino is a Professor of Sociolinguistics at Waseda University, Tokyo. He received his PhD in Educational Linguistics and MS in Intercultural Communication from the University of Pennsylvania, and BA in Political Science from Waseda University. His research interests include sociolinguistics, language planning and intercultural communication.

Christina Isabelli-García received her PhD from the University of Texas at Austin, and is an associate professor in the Department of Hispanic Studies at Illinois Wesleyan University where she teaches courses in Spanish, Linguistics and Second Language Acquisition. Currently, she researches second language acquisition in the foreign language classroom and in study abroad contexts.

Abigail McMeekin received her Master's degree in Japanese Linguistics from the University or Iowa and her PhD in Japanese second language acquisition from the University of Hawai'i. Her research interests include Japanese second language acquisition, NS-NNS communication breakdowns, and study abroad. She currently teaches at the University of Hawai'i.

Transcription Conventions

[	overlapped speech
=	latching
(0.5)	the number indicates the length of a pause in seconds
(.)	unmeasured micropause
( )	unclear utterance or (xxx), where each *x* indicates one unclear syllable
(( ))	commentary
::	sound stretch
WORD	loudness
° °	portions which are delivered in a quieter voice
-	cut-off
?	rising intonation
.	falling intonation (full stop)
@word@	word said with laughter
. . .	skipped turns

Chapter 1
Evolving Threads in Study Abroad Research

ETON CHURCHILL and MARGARET A. DuFON

Introduction

For the second language acquisition (SLA) researcher, there are perhaps few contexts as potentially rich and complex as study abroad. On the one hand, concentrated time enjoyed by learners in the host context would appear to facilitate significant linguistic gains. On the other hand, pre-departure individual differences interact in complex ways and are affected by the study abroad context, itself conditioned by cultural norms and factors related to program design. Adding to these dynamics, patterns of acquisition of skills and specific forms are far from linear and have proven difficult to consistently record based on pre–post tests. Given these interactions, it is not surprising that within-group differences are just as frequently reported as between-group differences and that these findings are supported by accounts in qualitative studies (see Coleman, 1995, 1996, 1997, 1998; Freed, 1995a, 1998 for overviews; Huebner 1995b, 1998; Pellegrino, 1998 for discussions of research methods; and Regan, 1998; Pellegrino, 1998 respectively for reviews concentrating on sociolinguistics and conditions of learning experienced by the SA student).

In the present chapter, drawing primarily from studies published subsequent to the reviews cited above, we will focus on what is learned, how individual differences interact with proficiency gains, and how cultural and program related factors shape opportunities for contact with native speakers. We begin with the literature on gains in linguistic skills and then turn our attention to the area of pragmatics. We then address the research on individual differences concentrating on motivation, learning strategies and anxiety. Finally, we focus on the dynamics of language learning highlighting learner involvement in the host context, and on how engagement with native speakers can be enhanced or mitigated by cultural norms and program design. Thus, we hope to delineate what is known regarding the formal aspects of acquisition in the SA context while drawing reader attention to the social conditions in which this learning takes place. Concurrently, we intend to introduce potential directions for future research.

Acquisition of Linguistic Abilities

Reflecting the predominant interest in SLA, the bulk of study abroad research has focused on what is acquired (e.g. forms and skills) by the learner. The majority of these studies have concentrated on gains in specific skills in individual programs. However, returning to an earlier approach taken by DeKeyser (1986) and Lafford (1995), the research agenda has recently expanded to include studies comparing gains in SA contexts with those attained in domestic programs (Bradley, 2003; Collentine, 2004; Dewey, 2004a, 2004b; Díaz-Campos, 2004; Freed *et al.*, 2004; Hoffman-Hicks, 2000; Howard, 2001; Matsumura, 2001; Rodriguez, 2002; Segalowitz & Freed, 2004; Stevens, 2001; Torres, 2003). In the discussion below, we outline the acquisition of linguistic abilities in terms of literacy, listening, speaking (oral proficiency, fluency and pronunciation) and grammar. In each section, we first address the results from single program studies and then review the comparative studies.

Literacy

Relatively few studies of language learners within SA contexts have focused on the acquisition of literacy skills, reflecting a bias in programs themselves and in expectations for gains in the aural/oral skills. To wit, Allen (2002) found that students preferred to obtain information by talking to others (either NSs of their L1 or the L2) rather than by reading or listening to the radio. Although the emphasis has been on oral rather than written language, evidence from both quantitative and qualitative studies suggests that the area of literacy merits more attention.

Researchers have taken different methodological approaches depending on their view of literacy. Some, such as Fraser (2002), who compared the ability of learners to match anaphora and cataphora to their referents, have taken a skills-based approach. Meanwhile, Dewey (2004a, 2004b) used both quantitative (vocabulary tests) and qualitative measures to examine increased word knowledge, improved comprehension, reading processes, habits, strategies and learner perceptions. Elsewhere, Kline (1998) investigated how learners' literacy-related identities affected literacy behaviors and text-related interaction over time.

Despite the varied methodologies employed, the consistent finding is that SA learners develop their reading skills (Dewey, 2004a, 2004b; Fraser, 2002; Waldbaum, 1997) and literacy (Kline, 1998). For example, Dewey (2004a) reported that his American learners of Japanese became stronger in vocabulary recognition and text comprehension, and developed more confidence in their reading ability. This seemed to be due to the frequency and range of experiences in interacting with text in a naturalistic environment, a claim qualitatively supported by other studies (see Churchill, 2003a: 286–289; Huebner, 1995b: 185; Wilkinson, 1995). Adding further evidence to Dewey's observations on reader confidence, Kline reported that over the course of a year in France, students gained greater independence in reading texts, learned to look for a 'deeper meaning' and began to discuss reading material with their host families. Meanwhile in terms of specific reading skills, learners of German typically advanced in their ability to match anaphora and cataphora to their referents, though the amount of gain depended on pre-program levels and effort expended.

Of these studies, Dewey (2004a, 2004b) is the only one to have compared SA students with those studying at home. SA learners in Japan gained greater confidence than the intensive at-home (AH) group; yet despite increased confidence, there were no significant differences between groups in gains in vocabulary or ability to recall the reading passage. However, there were differences in the way the two groups approached the task of reading. The SA group monitored their understanding of what they were reading more than the AH group, while the AH group more often responded affectively to the text. Dewey concludes that because of the nature of the AH groups' interaction with their teachers (e.g. more comprehension checks and requests for affective responses), they were able to develop their reading skills as much as their overseas counterparts.

Given the scant attention that literacy has received in SA research and the positive findings summarized above, this would appear to be a rich area for further investigation. In particular, it would be interesting to document the extent to which oral interaction in the host context either supports literacy activities (e.g. reading with younger siblings, sharing of the daily news), or indirectly facilitates reading through increased lexical breadth and grammatical development.

Listening

As with literacy, research on of the acquisition of listening skills in the SA literature has also been scant. However, several studies (Allen, 2002;

Kinginger & Whitworth, 2005; Waldbaum, 1997) have found that SA students make improvements in this area, and Tanaka and Ellis (2003) reported minor gains on the listening component of the TOEFL taken by Japanese learners studying in the United States. Investigating the development of listening comprehension during a six-week summer program in France, Allen (2002) reported a significant ($p < 0.001$) improvement based on a 14-item listening skills test. In a self-assessment questionnaire on listening and speaking tasks, Allen's learners claimed they made significant gains in listening, but felt they had more success in mastering complicated speaking tasks. Interestingly, at the time of the pre-test, three of the 25 learners reported that they could easily perform certain listening tasks, but on the post-test, they reported that they could not easily perform at least one of those same tasks. Allen attributed this change to a greater awareness of the challenges of interacting with native speakers.

Speaking

Most studies of language acquisition during study abroad have focused on speaking. Below, we begin with a discussion of proficiency and fluency, then turn to pronunciation.

Oral proficiency and fluency

Investigations into gains in oral proficiency have relied heavily on the Oral Proficiency Interview (OPI) or similar interviews. Studies of gains in oral proficiency made by SA learners have revealed that they improve their proficiency over the course of a semester or more abroad (Isabelli-García, 2003; Segalowitz & Freed, 2004). Even learners who go abroad for only a few weeks have been found to improve their oral proficiency, although their gains are not necessarily enough to advance to a higher level on the ACTFL scale (Simões, 1996).

Fluency has also typically been measured using the OPI or another interview format. The learners' speech in the interview has then been examined with respect to various temporal and hesitation phenomena. Research using pre- post test designs has revealed that SA learners improve their fluency as a result of an increase in rate and length of fluent runs (Segalowitz & Freed, 2004) and reductions in the number of pauses, fillers, dysfluencies and struggles (Freed *et al.*, 2004; Isabelli-García, 2003; Segalowitz & Freed, 2004; Simões, 1996; Woodman, 1999). However, it was noted in several of these studies (Segalowitz & Freed, 2004; Simões, 1996) that not all learners in these SA groups improved in their fluency; rather individual learner differences accounted for considerable variation.

Several studies investigating fluency and proficiency (Isabelli-García, 2003) and grammatical features (Collentine, 2004; Lopez Ortega, 2003; Schell, 2001, Torres, 2003) reported improvements in narrative ability. Collentine (2004), examining language acquisition in Spain, found that learners improved their narrative abilities. By the end of the program, students were able to relate more narrative events and do so with fewer words. In addition, Isabelli-García (2003) reported that two of three L2 learners of Argentine Spanish, unable to produce complex narratives at the beginning of the program, could do so by the end.

In comparative studies on fluency and proficiency, results have been mixed, depending largely on the type of program at home and initial proficiency level. Bradley (2003) compared two groups of Intermediate and Advanced learners of German – an at-home (AH) group in the United States and a SA group – with respect to formulaic speech using a simulated oral proficiency interview. The two groups performed similarly in terms of rate of speech and number of fillers. However, the SA group outperformed the AH group in terms of total number of words and non-filler formulas. Qualitatively, the SA group employed a wider repertoire of fillers for a greater range of functions. Furthermore, in linguistically challenging situations, the SA students were better able to benefit from formulaic language, appearing linguistically more competent than they actually were.

However, Freed *et al.* (2004) argue that learners might be able to gain just as much – if not more – from an intensive language program at home. Comparing gains in oral fluency and oral proficiency in learners of French in three learning contexts: (1) at home (AH) in formal language classrooms, (2) at home in an intensive all French language summer immersion (IM) program, and (3) abroad in France, Freed and her associates found that gains were related to both learning context and time spent speaking French outside of class. The AH group made no significant progress in any area, while the SA group made significant gains only in speech fluidity. However, the gains of the IM group were greater, attributed in part to the fact that IM students both spoke and wrote significantly more than the other two groups. As a result, Freed and her associates concluded that it is not the learning context *per se* which determines language gain, but rather the nature and intensity of contact within that context. Segalowitz and Freed (2004) came to similar conclusions based on their investigation of learners of Spanish. Generally, greater gains were made by the SA students both in fluency and in oral proficiency (as measured by the OPI) than the AH group. However, the SA advantage could not be accounted for by out-of-class contact with NSs of the target language alone. At best, this relationship was weak and indirect. Rather, the learners' initial language abilities played a role in influencing the nature and intensity of out-of-class contact they engaged in, and their ability to quickly and efficiently connect words to meaning affected gains in oral performance.

From these studies on fluency and proficiency, one may posit that the SA experience leads to significant gains in both areas and that these gains tend to be larger than those found in most traditional at-home programs. However, this work also illustrates the importance of the quality and quantity of language use and the fact that initial learner proficiency may be a variable that plays a role in shaping intensity and quality of contact with NSs.

Pronunciation

Recent studies that have examined the effect of SA on the acquisition of pronunciation (Díaz-Campos, 2004; Simões, 1996; Stevens, 2001) have focused on Spanish pronunciation by native speakers of English. In these studies, the SA learners were able to make changes toward the target norm in terms of vowel quality (Simões, 1996), tongue placement in word final laterals (Díaz-Campos, 2004), reduced voice onset time for voiceless stops (Díaz-Campos, 2004; Stevens, 2001), and linking between words (Simões, 1996).

However, there were some inconsistencies in the findings. The subjects in Stevens' (2001) study improved their pronunciation of voiced intervocalic fricatives while those in the Díaz-Campos' (2004) study did not. In Stevens' study, the two groups of learners in Spain improved in their ability to produce the tap and the trill from pre-test to post-test, however these differences were not significant. Simões (1996) found his learners actually moved away from the target, overgeneralizing the trilled r in contexts where a single tap in Spanish was correct. Problems were also noted with prosodic features. Simões found that all his students continued to exhibit American English rhythm and intonation patterns in Spanish, though some students indicated awareness of this problem by modulating their intensity (but not their pitch) in order to address this issue.

Of these studies, two (Díaz-Campos, 2004; Stevens, 2001) compared SA learners with those in domestic learning contexts. Stevens (2001) compared the acquisition of Spanish phonology of three groups of learners: one at-home (AH) group in the United States and two SA groups in

Madrid, Spain (one summer study group and one semester study group). An acoustic analysis of pre- and post-test phonetic data revealed that the SA groups made significantly greater progress overall than the AH group in acquiring more target-like pronunciation. Both the SA and AH groups improved their pronunciation of sounds that were more similar to English, but only the SA groups demonstrated significant gains in producing phonemes that were less similar to those in English.

Unlike Stevens (2001), Díaz-Campos (2004) found no advantage for the SA group. The discrepancy in these conclusions might be attributable to differences at the outset of the study. In Steven's study, the AH group had approximately two years of prior Spanish instruction, the summer group three years and the semester group four years. Díaz-Campos does not mention the proficiency level of his students; however, the number of years of prior language instruction was found to affect phonological gain in his study. Thus, Stevens' SA learners may have had an advantage, not only because of the context they were in, but also because of their additional years of formal language instruction.

Factors that might account for differences in pronunciation performance between and within learner groups include not only the learning context, but also the length of time abroad, years of formal language instruction (Díaz-Campos, 2004), proficiency level at the outset of the program (Díaz-Campos, 2004; Simões, 1996; Stevens, 2001), time spent using the target language prior to and during the SA period or opportunities for input (Díaz-Campos, 2004; Stevens, 2001) and gender (i.e. females using a more careful pronunciation than males) (Díaz-Campos, 2004). Thus, as we concluded from the studies on oral proficiency and fluency, it is not just learning context, but individual learner factors and the nature and intensity of contact with target language speakers which combine to shape linguistic development.

Grammar

Much of the work on grammar acquisition has been done on learners of Spanish or French. Several methods have been used to collect grammatical data to examine the acquisition of features such as subject expression (null subject vs. pronoun vs. full NP), clitics, tense and aspect. Methods used to date include analysis of oral proficiency interview data (Collentine, 2004; Howard, 2001; Isabelli, 2002), written language samples from narrative essays (Schell, 2001), learners' performance on a worksheet of grammatical exercises (Schell, 2001) and grammaticality judgment tasks (Isabelli, 2002).

In these studies, the consistent finding is that learners move toward target norms, but sometimes their paths of development vary and they do not acquire native proficiency during a semester or even a year abroad. In her examination of the null subject parameter, Isabelli (2002) found that while L2 Spanish learners improved their abilities on all three syntactic properties of the null subject parameter, *that*-trace violations particularly remained a problem. She concluded that the parameter was not reset. Lopez Ortega (2003) found that whether or not the subject was overtly expressed depended upon a range of discourse conditions. Not only did the traditional aspects of contrast, emphasis, and disambiguation affect subject expression but so did factors such as the speaker's identity and topic involvement, semantic features of the referents, inter-linguistic narrative structures, type of verb, conjunctions and adverbials. Also illustrating the complex dynamics of grammar acquisition, Torres (2003) investigated the acquisition of Spanish clitics (e.g. direct and indirect object pronouns, reflexives) by 10 novice-high to advanced-low SA learners of Spanish over the course of one semester. The lower proficiency learners rarely used clitics and preferred zero marking. In contrast, the intermediate learners had begun to use clitics, but their contexts of use were quite restricted when compared with NS use due to learner overuse of full NPs as objects and obliques, and limited use and variety of transitive verbs. Finally, in Schell's (2001) study on the acquisition of Spanish aspect (preterit vs. imperfect) in a nine-month SA program in Spain, all five intermediate to advanced learners demonstrated improved accuracy in morphology and grammatical aspect, revealing that they had basically acquired the preterit–imperfect distinction. While initially the less advanced learners displayed a preference for the preterit over the imperfect, by the end no learners displayed preference for one aspect over another. All subjects were able to identify and correctly mark for aspect habitual events, but variation existed for future/intention events, and events in progress. Moreover, the paths were not quite identical across learners.

Studies to date that compare learning at home and abroad have found little to indicate that the SA context is more advantageous for the acquisition of grammar. Comparing language learning prior to, during, and following study abroad, Longcope (2003) reported that learners of English made gains in fluency but not necessarily in grammatical accuracy or syntactic complexity during their time abroad. Torres (2003) found that the SA context did not seem to be more advantageous than the AH context as far as the acquisition of clitics was concerned; however, the SA learners had an advantage over the AH group in terms of discourse and pragmatics, and were able to use language more effectively. Investigating the performance of two groups on oral proficiency interviews, Collentine (2004) concluded that the AH group in fact demonstrated greater development on discrete grammatical and lexical features than the SA group in Spain. However, the SA group outperformed the AH group in terms of narrative ability and semantic density. In contrast, the SA group in Howard's (2001) study achieved higher levels of accuracy in their use of aspect marking (i.e. passé composé vs. imparfait) in French across a wider range of contexts than the two AH groups. In terms of patterns of contextual use, the three groups performed similarly, but there was a quantitative difference in level of accuracy across contexts. Discrepancies in these findings should not be regarded as conflicting results, but rather further evidence that grammatical development patterns are tremendously complex, vary considerably depending on the linguistic feature highlighted in the research (and quite probably the method used to collect the data) and are undoubtedly confounded by learner initial proficiency.

Acquisition of Pragmatic Abilities

The research on pragmatics has examined the acquisition of routines, register, terms of address, and speech acts. The primary method used has been the collection of ethnographic data – typically including recorded conversations in naturalistic contexts, learner journals, interviews, and field notes. However, some studies focusing on speech acts have elicited data through role plays, production questionnaires and meta-pragmatic assessments. We will now summarize the findings on routines and register, then turn towards terms of address and speech acts.

Routines

Two studies examining routines include a diary study of the acquisition of the Javanese Indonesian tea routine (DuFon, 1998), and a learner journal study of gift-giving routines in Indonesia (DuFon, 2003). For each study, DuFon used *rich* points (Agar, 1994) or critical incidents from diaries/journals to identify these routines, then analyzed them using a frame analysis (Goffman, 1974).

In her diary study, DuFon (1998) found that the high value she placed on personal choice (e.g. what and when she ate and drank) conflicted with Javanese Indonesian cultural routines of serving refreshments, which conformed with their values of respect, acceptance, humility, co-operation and harmony over personal choice. Therefore she struggled to find appropriate ways to let her choice be known without violating Javanese norms. In DuFon's (2003) study of the acquisition of gift-giving routines, learners' knowledge of local norms was not sufficient to bring about conformity to them. Learners sometimes deliberately violated these norms because they preferred their own ways of doing things. However, they did not always get the responses they expected, which provided them with salient input encouraging them to conform in future realizations of the routine. In other cases, when learners did follow native-speaker norms using appropriate pragmalinguistic expressions, and native speakers were not expecting this from a non-native, they misinterpreted the learners' intentions (cf. Hassall, 2004), which led to both failed communication and confusion for the learner. Consequently, routines required repeated experience and the gathering of often conflicting data in order for learners to correctly interpret the pragmalinguistic expressions of NSs used in them.

While placing the analytical focus on routines and socialization processes is a relatively novel approach to the study abroad context (see also DuFon, this volume), further work in this area has the potential to reveal not only pragmatic development but also processes by which learners acquire a specific lexicon and grammar.

Register

Studies on the use of register have relied primarily on the analysis of transcripts of recorded data. The earliest studies in this area were conducted by Siegal (1995a, 1995b), who examined the acquisition of Japanese by Western women. All four learners in Siegal's (1995b) study attempted to speak Japanese politely, but the progress they made varied considerably, and the behavior of participants often did not conform to native speaker norms. In many cases this was due to their lack of knowledge of the norms in all their complexities; however, some learners actively resisted native speaker norms. For example, some learners avoided the use of the polite style and/or honorific markers and pragmatic particles because they associated them with a Japanese female conversational style, which they negatively evaluated, finding it to be too humble or too silly. The difficulty in acquiring native speaker norms was compounded by the use of foreigner talk by Japanese interlocutors, which provided learners with faulty input, leading to confusion regarding what was appropriate. The role of foreigner talk in native speaker-study abroad student interaction has also been discussed at length by Iino (1996) and has been mentioned in the research on terms of address (see below).

Studies on the acquisition of colloquial words in French (Dewaele & Regan, 2001; Kinginger & Farrell, 2004) found that the frequency of colloquial words significantly increased during the time abroad, though they still fell considerably short of NS frequencies (Dewaele & Regan, 2001) and the degree of improvement varied considerably among learners. Engagement with French native speakers was a better predictor of acquisition of colloquial vocabulary (Kinginger & Whitworth, 2005) than formal classroom instruction, which had no predictive value with respect to the use of colloquial words (Dewaele & Regan, 2001). Dewaele and Regan concluded that the implicit, proceduralized, socio-pragmatic knowledge needed to incorporate colloquial words into the learners' productive vocabulary can only be obtained through 'prolonged, authentic contact with the TL community' (p. 63).

Terms of address

The acquisition of terms of address has been examined in Japanese by Siegal (1995b) and Iino (1996), in Indonesian by DuFon (2000a; in press), and in French by Kinginger and Farrell (2004). These studies have all drawn on multiple methods in their data collection, the first three using a qualitative ethnographic approach, the last combining pre- and post-program measures with qualitative data. In the first three studies, the learners were studying languages in non-Western societies where recognition of hierarchy and proper place occupancy are highly valued, and a range of terms of address are available to choose from. In the fourth study, learners had to learn the complexities of the *tu/vous* distinction in French. While some learners progressed in their use of address terms during the term abroad, their use did not reach native-like norms.

In the case of the non-Western languages, many learners tended to overuse the pronoun that most closely resembled the English *you* (e.g. the generic *anata* in Japanese, and *Anda* in Indonesian), which frequently appeared in the input. While Japanese and Indonesians rarely use these pronouns when speaking to each other, they use them frequently when speaking to foreigners. By using these pronouns, the American learners reinforced their egalitarian values and made the task less cognitively demanding. Although the learners may have assumed this was acceptable, the reciprocal use of these terms in asymmetrical relationships is not appropriate. In spite of this, native speakers were reluctant to provide negative feedback as they appeared to consider the errors to be social rather than linguistic. Thus the learners typically remained unaware that they had offended their interlocutors and, in the absence of correction, continued to make these errors.

Advancement toward native speaker norms was not found to be related to grammatical competence as some lower level learners used terms of address more appropriately than advanced learners because they focused their attention on them (DuFon, 2000a), and some advanced learners who were aware of the native norms deliberately chose not to conform to them (Kinginger & Farrell, 2004). Kinginger and Farrell concluded that in addition to examining changes that take place in pronoun use, investigating the rationale underlying pronoun choices can provide insights into selection strategies and the attention devoted to their choices. For a treatment of terms of address in the German context, we refer you to Anne Barron's study in this volume.

Speech acts

Research on speech acts has been investigated in a variety of SA contexts including: greetings by Japanese and American English learners of Indonesian (DuFon, 2000a); greetings, leave-taking and complimenting by American learners of French (Hoffman-Hicks, 2000); requests by Japanese learners of English (Churchill, 2003b), and English speaking learners of Russian (Owen, 2002) and Spanish (Rodriguez, 2002); requests, offers and refusal of offers by Irish learners of German (Barron, 2003); and apologies (Kondo, 1997b) and advice giving (Matsumura, 2001) by Japanese learners of English. Questionnaires have been the most common type of data collection instrument. However, other methods of data collection have been employed including OPI role plays (Owen, 2002), learner journals (DuFon, 2000a) and notebook data (Churchill, 2002). In addition to this research, we refer you to the diary study by Hassall in this volume on leave-taking in Indonesian.

Consistent with the findings in other areas, learner speech act behavior became more native-like over time, but learner progress was quite limited when compared to NS norms. With respect to comprehension, learners may initially misinterpret the illocutionary force of certain pragmatic routines, understanding only their literal meaning, particularly if their direct translations carry a different force in the learners' native language. Later they learn their extended (and more frequently used) meaning (DuFon, 2000b).

With respect to production, some speech acts were easier to acquire than others, perhaps due to their frequency in daily conversation. For example, learners made more progress in greeting and leave-taking than in complimenting (Hoffman-Hicks, 2000), and appropriate requests developed sooner than offers and refusal of offers (Barron, 2003). Learners also tended to increase the number of pragmatic features (e.g. greeting formulas, discourse particles) they used over time. For example, requests increased in frequency and appropriateness even prior to departure on a SA program as they helped learners express their needs and concerns (Churchill, 2002). As learners improved their understanding of how pragmatic features functioned, they used them more frequently in an expanding range of contexts (DuFon, 2000a; Hoffman-Hicks, 2000).

Generally, learners increased their use of formulaic pragmatic expressions and concomitantly decreased their use of non-L2 like interlanguage specific routines, thus enhancing the native-like quality of their speech (Barron, 2003; Hoffman-Hicks, 2000; Kondo, 1997a; Owen, 2002). For example, in Russian, the use of speaker-oriented requests decreased and unspecified agent-oriented requests increased (Owen, 2002). In making apologies, Japanese learners of English decreased their use of features transferred from their native language, used more explanatory utterances, offered repair more frequently and gave fewer direct apologies (Kondo, 1997a).

Furthermore, learners became aware of some of the socio-cultural norms of linguistic behavior. For example, they discerned some contexts in which it was inappropriate to perform a particular speech act [e.g. greeting a stranger in a café in France (Hoffman-Hicks, 2000), or re-offering something to the hearer following a refusal in German (Barron, 2003)]. Japanese learners of English also better appreciated the weight of contextual variables (other than power relations) in determining the politeness level to be employed in giving advice (Matsumura, 2001) and changed their perceptions regarding distance between speakers, power relationships and the severity of offenses in judging the appropriateness of apology strategies (Kondo, 1997b).

Although learners made significant progress in their pragmatic development in some areas, it must be noted that their pragmatic behavior remained in many ways quite non-native like. In some cases, they even moved away from the target norm. For example, while learners improved their command over formulaic pragmatic expressions, they also tended to increase their verbosity and to use expressions in contexts where they were not appropriate. Hoffman-Hicks (2000) found, for instance, that her SA learners of French added semantic formulas such as expressions of gratitude, words of advice and requests to their leave-taking routines in French, whereas native speakers rarely ever did. This non-native like behavior resulted from a variety of sources including lack of awareness of the norm and inability to control output to conform to the norm (Barron, 2003; Hoffman-Hicks, 2000) as has been found to be the case with the acquisition of grammar. However, in the case of pragmatic acquisition, another element comes into play. That is, in some cases conformity was not seen as a necessity (Barron, 2003) and in others the norms conflicted with learner personality and/or identity (DuFon, 2000a, 2004; Siegal, 1995a, 1995b).

As mentioned above, pragmatic development appears to be an area where SA students have the advantage over AH learners, at least in terms of production. Hoffman-Hicks (2000) found that the SA learners outperformed her AH group, making advancements in a number of areas. Likewise, Owen (2002) found that the SA intermediate-mid learners of Russian made requests that were much more target-like than those produced by comparable AH learners.

With respect to receptive abilities, the results have been mixed. Rodriguez (2002), who investigated the ability to judge the appropriateness of Spanish requests, reported no difference between the SA group and the AH control group in their assessments of request forms. Rodriguez reasoned that this surprising finding might be attributable to the high frequency of requests; that is, knowledge of the appropriateness of request forms can be acquired in the foreign language classroom and does not require interaction in a target language environment. In contrast to Rodriguez, Matsumura (2001) found an advantage for SA learners in his nine-month comparative study of Japanese learners of English. Employing a multiple choice questionnaire to determine learner perceptions of social status and its impact on language use when giving advice, Matsumura revealed that the SA group initially performed at significantly lower levels than the AH group, but by the end of the program the SA group performed significantly higher. Thus, with the exception of Rodriguez's study, the evidence to date suggests that SA students improve in their pragmatic development more than AH learners, but they fall short of native norms in most areas.

Individual Differences

Aside from linguistic forms, skills and pragmatics, recent research on SA has also begun to focus on individual differences, most notably on factors related to learner motivation and strategy use. In this section, we review the literature on motivation, anxiety, and learning strategies.

Motivation and willingness to communicate

Motivation enjoys continued attention as an important variable in the language acquisition process. Of particular interest in the area of SA have been the constructs of integrative motivation and the willingness to communicate (cf. MacIntyre *et al.*, 1998) with studies investigating both the effect of pre-departure motivation on the SA experience (e.g. Yashima, 1999; Yashima *et al.*, 2004) and the effect of time abroad on learner motivation (e.g. Allen, 2002; Hoffman-Hicks, 2000; Simões, 1996). Based on a study of Japanese learners studying in the United States, Yashima *et al.* (2004) hypothesize that a SA student's willingness to communicate might result in behaviors that invite the hosts to interact more extensively with him or her, thereby facilitating the acquisition process. Similarly, in a German SA program, students who actively positioned themselves in situations that required participation in communicative interactions (e.g. community involvement in sports and the arts) were the ones most likely to demonstrate gains in language proficiency (Fraser, 2002). However, even when reported levels of integrative motivation were quite strong before the SA experience, they have not always resulted in active learner integration into the target community. For example, learners in several studies (Allen, 2002; Hoffman-Hicks, 2000; Kinginger & Farrell, 2004; Wilkinson, 1998a, 1998b) expressed disappointment at the end of their programs that they had not met more people and established friendships within the host community.

As in studies on the acquisition of specific language skills and forms, two factors that may mitigate the interaction between motivation and language learning overseas are the length of stay and previous language learning experience. While some studies have reported that a short stay can increase learner motivation, the findings have not been consistent. For example, Simões (1996) reported that spending as little as five weeks abroad resulted in a higher level of self-confidence and higher motivation, and Campbell (1996), an already highly motivated and sophisticated learner at the outset, related that she was able to integrate with the host culture during a short summer session. However, Allen (2002), finding that some of her learners had not integrated into French culture and consequently had yet to develop a positive attitude toward native speakers after six weeks abroad, questioned the value of short-term immersion programs for increasing positive attitudes towards the target culture. However, challenging the assumption that a longer program will lead to greater integration, Hoffman-Hicks (2000) reported that some learners did not develop a positive attitude towards the host community even after a year abroad.

A probable intervening variable in these studies may be the previous experience of language learners. For example, Allen (2002) teased out the learning histories of her participants to reveal that those with more than two years of college French prior to their sojourn showed significant gains in their integrative motivation, whereas those with less experience exhibited lower integrative motivation following the program. Allen concluded that it was likely that the more advanced students were better prepared both linguistically and culturally to benefit from interaction with native speakers. In a similar vein, in Yashima's (1999) study of the effect of extroversion and competence on sojourner adjustment, the Japanese learners with more previous experience abroad and higher levels of proficiency were considered by their American families to have adjusted more easily to the host context. In a later study, Yashima *et al.* (2004) found that students who scored higher on a measure of willingness to communicate prior to their departure did in fact spend more time communicating with host families during their early weeks abroad. Interestingly, learner willingness to communicate was not affected by differences in proficiency, but rather by differences in their perceived communicative competence. In other words, many students reporting that they wanted to take the initiative did not do so because they perceived their L2 English competence to be too low. In this way, it may not be the previous language learning experiences and the resulting proficiency levels in themselves that interact with motivation, but rather the learner's perception of their abilities once they find themselves in the host culture.

Anxiety

Related to these self-perceptions is learner anxiety. In contrast to learners in a traditional foreign language classroom, SA sojourners usually do not share a common cultural background with their interlocutors and failing to communicate has real-world consequences. Two studies involving learner anxiety in SA contexts (Allen, 2002; Tanaka & Ellis, 2003) found that anxiety decreased during the stay abroad. However, Allen (2002) found that initially learners experienced little reduction, with anxiety levels remaining high during the first two weeks of a six-week program. Allen also concluded that anxiety was situationally dependent. While anxiety was reduced in short controlled interactions (e.g. service encounters), anxiety and discomfort levels remained high in more complex and less controlled interactions involving misunderstandings resulting from cultural differences, and cases where the learners did not have the linguistic tools needed to present their point of view. This finding suggests that some time is needed initially to adjust to communicating in the target language. This adjustment, and the resulting consequences for motivation and anxiety, can be susceptible to both the learner's strategies for socially integrating into the host culture and to the ways in which the learner is received.

Learning strategies

Studies of learning strategies have investigated a number of questions. (1) Which strategies most likely lead to successful SLA abroad? (2) How does strategy use by SA learners compare with that of AH learners? (3) How does strategy use change over time? (4) What is the effect of strategy training on subsequent strategy use by SA learners?

Addressing the question of which strategies lead to greater success in SLA, Golonka (2001) examined the metacognitive strategy of self-monitoring and found that the learners of Russian who made self-repairs of their errors in grammar, vocabulary, pronunciation and pragmatics were those who made the greatest and fastest gains linguistically. In contrast, Tanaka and Ellis (2003) reported no correlation between changes in learner strategies – categorized as analytic and experiential learning – and gains as measured by the TOEFL. While they observed changes in the strategies learners used, gain scores did not appear to be related to specific strategy use.

Because the demands of the SA and AH contexts are different, some researchers have hypothesized that the preferred strategies might vary according to context. For example, Calvin (1999) found that her SA learners made frequent use of compensation strategies but low use of memory strategies and speculated that this pattern might differ from learners studying at home. Several studies have actually compared SA and AH learners and found differences in strategy use between these groups. Lafford (2004) found that both groups preferred strategies – self-repairs and accuracy checks – that addressed problems in their own production, though this may have been an artifact of collecting data under test conditions. Smartt (1998), who specifically focused on self-repair strategies, found that the while the SA learners used 'language switch' significantly less than the AH controls, they used 'word form search' more. Lafford (2004), in contrast, found that the SA learners used far fewer strategies than the AH group in all categories by the post-test. Both groups decreased their strategy use over time; however the SA group decreased more dramatically. The decrease was particularly great for those SA learners who spent more time speaking Spanish outside of class with their host families and others. Presumably these behaviors resulted in improved fluency and discursive skills, which reduced the frequency of communication gaps, and thus decreased the need for strategies. Paige *et al.* (2004) similarly postulated a decreased need, due to increased exposure to vocabulary, to explain the decrease in word attack strategies and flashcard practice during study abroad.

To examine the effects of strategy training on strategy use while abroad, Paige *et al.* (2004) used a pre–post test control group design supplemented by qualitative data. While no significant differences were detected between the experimental and control groups on either the language or the cultural learning strategies instruments as a whole, an item analysis revealed that significant differences between the two groups did exist, and that in some cases gains by the experimental group could be attributed to explicit teaching through course materials.[1] Moreover, qualitative data based on feedback from e-journals indicated that the experimental participants felt they had benefited from the strategy training. For further work on learning strategies, we refer you to the chapter by Rebecca Adams in this volume.

Learner Involvement in the Host Context

Both the comparative studies (AH vs. SA) and the literature on individual differences suggest that the quality of interaction with NSs is of prime importance in the acquisition process. It also indicates that the approach taken by L2 learners to this interaction can be mediated by their actual, or perceived, level of proficiency as well as situationally determined levels of anxiety and overall motivation. As noted above, however, the relationship between learners' engagement with the host context on the one hand, and increased motivation and proficiency and lower levels of anxiety on the other is not unidirectional, but rather mutually constituted. It is perhaps for this reason that stakeholders at all levels in SA programs place a high importance on learner involvement in the host context. What learners do to enhance their opportunities for language use and therefore opportunities for acquisition is sometimes emphasized in SA orientations prior to and throughout the duration of programs.

The approach that learners take to interacting with their host families and communities can both facilitate and restrict opportunities for interaction. For example, host mothers interviewed in Knight and Schmidt-Rinehart's (2002) study reported that the ability of the learners to be *abierta*, or open, and mature was more important to their initial adjustment than their language aptitude. In particular, the host mothers argued that participants with close ties to home spent an inordinate amount of time communicating with their friends and family back home, and this limited their available time to engage in activities with their hosts, a finding supported by Li (2000) and Kinginger and Whitworth (2005). Outside of the home, students who remained open to the target culture despite some unpleasant contacts and who developed close relationships with NS peers (cf. Campbell, 1996; Kinginger, 2004; Kinginger & Farrell, 2004; Kinginger & Whitworth, 2005; Levin, 2001; Schumann, 1997) were able to create social networks (cf. Isabelli-García, this volume) thus increasing their exposure to various situations and registers and advancing their language development.

However, even when the learner develops a social network in the host community, practicing the target language can still be difficult in some learning environments, and only the most tenacious and persistent language learners can succeed in attaining opportunities for practice. For example, in diglossic Wales, where English is the *lingua franca* and outgroup code, Trosset (1986) only succeeded in getting her interlocutors to switch to Welsh by persisting to speak the language for several minutes while her interlocutors responded in English and by carefully selecting interlocutors who were willing to speak Welsh (e.g. extreme nationalists, children and Welsh language teachers).

Supporting Trosset, Campbell (1996) also noted the importance of interacting with teachers in social situations outside of class; she worked her way into their inner circle by making herself socially salient so that she stood apart from the other students. By socializing with teachers, she gained access to unmodified input, which challenged her and improved her listening comprehension.

The importance of access to unmodified input was also noted by Calvin (1999). In her study of an English language school in Wales, she reported that when the learners were able to communicate with the native community, who often did not speak to them with foreigner talk, their self-confidence and motivation increased and their attitudes toward learning English shifted in a favorable direction.

These studies indicate that gains in proficiency, fluency and accuracy may be related to exposing oneself to some combination of modified and unmodified input, either with individual interlocutors or in groups. The importance of interacting both with individuals and groups was evident in a study of L2 learners of Russian abroad by Mathews (2001), who discovered that, for female learners, both time spent with one interlocutor and with groups of Russians correlated positively with gains in speaking and listening. She also noted that those females with higher pre-program speaking scores were the ones who were more likely to engage in these behaviors. However, no such correlations were evident in the data on males.[2]

20

When examining data on individual learners, it appears that some prefer one-on-one interaction, where they receive input that is finely tuned to their level of proficiency (Warden *et al.*, 1995), while others prefer group interactions (Campbell, 1996; Schmidt & Frota, 1986; Warden *et al.*, 1995). The reasons for preferring group interactions, however, vary across learners. For example, one learner in Warden *et al.*'s study preferred group interactions so that he could tune out if he did not want to participate in the conversation. In contrast, both Schmidt and Campbell remained active listeners in a group even when the input was a bit beyond them, believing that this helped both their language acquisition and their integration into the target community.

While interaction with hosts appears to be generally facilitative, building a social network is more easily achieved by some learners than others. Success in this endeavor is related to learner characteristics such as openness, ability to make oneself socially salient, persistence in working to gain access, and tolerance for and attention to unmodified input. The last trait appears to be related not only to personality, but also to the learner's level of proficiency. Additional research is needed to sort out these variables.

The Role of the Host Culture in Mitigating Interaction

Although a great deal of emphasis is placed on what learners can and should do to promote their opportunities for language acquisition, research is increasingly focusing on how learning opportunities are affected by practices in the host culture and program designs. In spite of the benefits found with respect to females interacting with the host culture (Mathews, 2001), much of the research has pointed to unfortunate circumstances faced by female learners and how these influence learning attitudes. Other studies highlight interactional dynamics specific to certain cultures, challenges in adjusting to different cultural norms and how these can interact to affect access to NSs and the quality of input learners receive.

Following on the work of Polanyi (1995), several articles and dissertations have reported on the challenges faced by females in SA contexts in responding to unwelcomed remarks by NS males. Talburt and Stewart (1999) document how an African-American female student in Spain was harassed on a daily basis with name calling, sexual remarks and insults, which resulted in her developing negative attitudes toward the host community. Similarly, Twombly's (1995) interview study relates how a large number of females participating in a SA program in Costa

Rica were also negatively affected, in terms of motivation and desire to interact with NSs, after experiencing frequent catcalling. Likewise, Isabelli-García (2003, this volume) found that Jennifer, the only female learner in her study, also reported gendered experiences and felt a sense of rejection by the host culture. She responded by withdrawing, reducing her active participation in interactions with NSs and consequently limited her opportunities for language development. Accordingly, she made less progress than the male learners in terms of proficiency gains and narrative development.

Kinginer and Whitworth (2005) similarly reported that L2 French learners' success depended on their perceptions of their host culture, which in turn influenced their willingness to continue to interact and invest in learning French. Focusing on gender-related experiences, these researchers noted that these dynamics were not confined to females, but touched males as well. While all the learners experienced negative gender-related encounters, the way in which they responded to them was different and so affected their continued investment in language learning. Only one of three learners investigated, Jada, was able to shift her views of and abilities to perform gender (cf. Pavlenko, 2001) in the host culture. The least successful learner, Dierdre, like Jennifer in Isabelli-García's studies above, used her negative experiences to justify her withdrawal from investment in learning French.

These studies and others reveal that SA learners often feel rejected by their host culture (Hoffman-Hicks, 2000; Wilkinson 1998a, 1998b) or at least feel a shallowness in their relationship with host members (Burns, 1997). These perceptions can result in withdrawal and consequently reduce success in language acquisition. At the same time, it is clear that learners themselves may play a role in creating this perception. Cross-cultural misunderstandings or an inability or unwillingness to conform to local norms in terms of dress, appearance, ways of speaking, and other ways of expressing gender (cf. Kinginer & Whitworth, 2005), of participating in host family interactions (e.g. taking the initiative as opposed to waiting to be invited to join in family activities) (Knight & Schmidt-Rinehart, 2002) and of participating in the larger host community (Hoffman-Hicks, 2000; Li, 2000) may contribute to this sense of rejection, reduced contact, and disappointment with the SA experience as a result. It is also clear that different learners respond to the same types of experiences in very different ways. While some withdraw after experiencing rejection, others only redouble their efforts to improve their proficiency (Calvin, 1999), their pragmatic abilities and their non-linguistic behavior (Kinginer, 2004; Kinginer & Whitworth, 2005), thus making themselves more appealing to their hosts and reducing their chances of being rejected.

Expanding on the notion of cultural differences, recent studies have also pointed to culturally specific ways of responding to outsiders and how these behaviors can restrict or facilitate learner access to NSs. As mentioned earlier, in Wales, where English is the outgroup code, the burden of effort for communicating in Welsh falls upon the learner, who must be persistent in using Welsh in spite of responses in English (Trosset, 1986). Folk linguistic beliefs of the target community have also reportedly affected learner-native speaker interaction in Indonesia and Japan. In Indonesia, Hassall (2004), whose employment of native strategies of vagueness and *etok-etok* or proper lying (Geertz, 1960: 245–246) was not recognized as a refusal to answer personal questions, concluded that because Indonesians expect Westerners to be direct and explicit, they do not recognize such responses as indirect refusals and persist in their questioning for more explicit information, something they would not do with another native. In Japan, as Cook (this volume) discusses, the Japanese discourse on their uniqueness (*nihonjinron*) includes the belief that outsiders are incapable of learning their language. Consequently, Japanese who do not feel confident in their English eschew interaction with non-Japanese. When a NS is approached by a non-Japanese, the Japanese may signal nonverbally that they cannot speak and do not wish to be approached (Seigal, 1995b). However, once they realize that the learner can speak some Japanese, they are typically willing to communicate in standard Japanese, but avoid using non-standard codes with foreigners (Iino, 1996, this volume). In contrast, in Spain and Mexico (Knight & Schmidt-Rinehart, 2002) and in Indonesia (Hassall, this volume), where Spanish and Indonesian respectively are the languages of intergroup communication, NSs are typically quite willing to initiate conversations with foreigners – taking on the burden of effort for communicating – and even to draw them out when their language proficiency is minimal.

Program (Structural) Variables

In addition to the studies focusing on the effect of cultural differences on interaction, an increasing amount of research has concentrated on how the explicit – and sometimes unintended – design of programs shapes the quality and quantity of learner contact with NSs. The focus of these studies has been on the effect of program length and the degree to which different program features (e.g. housing, classroom arrangements, excursions) shape language learning opportunities.

A question of interest to administrators and consumers alike is 'How does length of program affect gains in SLA?' Unfortunately, the research of the effect of program length is relatively scarce and inconclusive. Those who have measured or tracked language acquisition after only a few weeks abroad have found that some learners have been able to improve their language abilities in listening (Allen, 2002; Campbell, 1996), speaking (Campbell, 1996; Woodman, 1999), pronunciation (Simões, 1996; Stevens, 2001) and pragmatics (Campbell, 1996; Matsumura, 2001). Given these short-term gains, it is widely acknowledged that remaining for longer periods allows learners to advance further. For example, in Hoffman-Hicks' (2000) longitudinal study of learners in France, after only two to three months abroad, subjects had already increased their use of votive expressions in leave-taking, and they continued to develop this ability and were near native-like by the end of 10 months. In comparing two groups of SA learners in Germany – one in a semester-long program and one in a year-long program – on their reading and writing abilities, Fraser (2002) found that both groups made impressive gains, but the year-long group outperformed the semester group. Thus, while a longer period of stay is generally perceived as preferable, the question of how long is needed to make significant gains in specific skills still remains unanswered.

In addition to program length, researcher attention has focused on the degree to which programs promote the grouping of learners and how different arrangements shape language learning opportunities. SA programs, by their very nature, bring large groups of learners together. Depending on residential and classroom arrangements and the ways in which excursions are organized, programs can promote a grouping of learners that actually restricts opportunities for interaction with NSs. For example, in explaining the marginal improvements made by Japanese learners in their study, Tanaka and Ellis (2003) characterized the program as a 'Japanese College Overseas' because students were in homogeneous classes and lived together in dormitories. As a result, they questioned whether the SA program was substantially different from the learners' university in Japan. In situations such as these, it can be considerably more challenging even for motivated and advanced learners to create language learning opportunities. Learners who are encouraged to group together are more likely to interact with each other in their native language thus decreasing the time they can spend with NSs (Allen, 2002; Churchill, 2003a, 2003b; Kinoshita, 2001; Li, 2000; Wilkinson, 1998a, 1998b). This tends to have an adverse affect on language development (Allen, 2002; Freed _et al._, 2004; Kinginger & Farrell, 2004; Tanaka and

Ellis, 2003), but a positive social and emotional effect as it provides a buffer space between learners and the host culture (Calvin, 1999; Talburt & Stewart, 1999; Wilkinson, 1998b).

In terms of residence, a few studies have compared the dormitory experience and life in the host family and research has begun to document the complex dynamics that can arise within host families. In a comparative study, Rivers (1998) – while acknowledging some pre-program group differences – found that students living with other American L2 learners of Russian in a dorm actually outperformed homestay students in terms of gains made in speaking. Surprisingly, the homestay students outperformed the dorm students in reading gains, which suggests that they spent more time reading Russian than interacting with their hosts. In contrast, data from Allen's (2002) study based on the perceptions of learners in France does not point to any advantage for group residence. Students who elected to stay in a *pension de famille*, where several students boarded with a hostess, reported that while they felt satisfied with their living arrangements, they believed it was disadvantageous to their language development when compared to life in a host family.

While these comparative studies are of some interest, it is important to remember that their results depend a great deal on what transpires in each residential arrangement. For one, the success of the homestay experience appears to have a lot to do with how hosts and students perceive their respective roles. For example, the Spanish and Mexican host mothers in Knight and Schmidt-Rinehart's (2002) study viewed themselves as surrogate mothers to the learners and took on the roles of conversation partner and teacher (for specifics on this dynamic in a Japanese setting, see McMeekin, this volume). Also in the Mexican context, students in Law's (2003) study reported spending hours conversing with their host mothers, thereby generating ample input, practice and feedback. In contrast, some of the host mothers in other studies (Kinoshita, 2001; Wilkinson, 1998a, 1998b) have been characterized by learners as mere landladies. In some cases, hosts took on simultaneous roles as landlord and parent, making the learner both a tenant and host child. This worked to the disadvantage of the learner who took on household responsibilities in order to establish themselves as a member of the family, yet in other ways continued to be treated like a tenant excluded from family events and privileges (Kinoshita, 2001).

Secondly, research has also revealed that interaction with NS hosts may be affected by dynamics within the families or by multiple placement of learners within a single family. For example, dialog between students and their hosts has been found to be minimal, particularly when the hosts do not have the patience to communicate with less than fluent learners (Wilkinson, 1998a) or when the busy schedules of academically and professionally driven families do not allow time for it (Churchill, 2003a). Frank (cited in Rivers, 1998) also noted that time spent with Russian homestay families – in quotidian dialog or while watching TV – was not particularly conducive to the negotiation of input. Related to learner placement, studies by both Allen (2002) and Churchill (2003a, 2003b) revealed that students who lived in a host family with other learners spent a great deal more time with their peers than with their host families and that students who had their own families expressed higher degrees of satisfaction. Churchill illustrated how such living arrangements led to competition, leaving learners with the impression that their peers were dominating the interaction. In addition, some learners in Churchill's (2003a, 2003b) study felt that dual placement of learners negatively affected their access to social networks extending from the family. However, despite the reported disadvantages of some living arrangements, it is important to note that the host family may still provide opportunities for interaction otherwise unavailable to the learner. While confirming Wilkinson's findings regarding the potential of homestay placements to result in negative experiences, Allen (2002) noted that despite learner dissatisfaction, 90% of her participants still viewed the host family environment as culturally or linguistically advantageous, and almost half reported that interacting with members of their host family was a key factor in their language improvement.

In terms of program implementation, the research indicates that the more successful programs include orientations on life in the host family, extensive interviews with prospective hosts and regular monitoring of families already in the program (Law, 2003) whereas less successful programs have lacked such features (e.g. Kinoshita, 2001). Additionally, it is recommended that students be given pre-departure information on what they can realistically expect to achieve linguistically during their time abroad, that they be carefully matched with study abroad programs and host families (Kinoshita, 2001; Wilkinson, 2001), that students be taught strategies for integrating themselves into the host family (Knight & Schmidt-Rinehart, 2002; Rivers, 1998), that the schools hold ongoing discussions with host families regarding their roles (Knight & Schmidt-Rinehart, 2002), and that contracts might be written for students and host families defining those roles and delineating their rights and obligations (Kinoshita, 2001). While such administrative arrangements may be ideal, it is equally important for programs to be flexibly responsive to unexpected changes (e.g. withdrawal of a host family, a change in

available classes) in ways that keep the interests of the learners at the fore-
front of the decision-making process. After all, the ability of learners to
take the initiative to promote their own learning opportunities is deli-
neated to some extent by the very design of SA programs. For additional
information on how program variables affect language learning in the SA
experience, see Churchill (this volume).

Conclusion

While there have been considerable contributions to our understanding of study abroad in the past 10 years, the research – having largely followed the trail cleared by studies in SLA – is still in its infancy. The
research agenda continues to interrogate the popular assumption that
the study abroad experience leads to language acquisition. Accordingly,
the analytical focus has expanded (e.g. from oral/aural skills to literacy,
from speech acts to register, routines and terms of address, from
general proficiency to a more fine-grained analysis of specific grammatical forms and prosodic features). With the renewed interest in comparative studies (AH vs. SA) and as studies parse out developmental
differences related to gender, pre-program proficiency levels, and individual differences such as motivation, strategies and anxiety, greater attention is also being devoted to who learns what. Finally, following the
social turn in second language acquisition, with more qualitative
studies documenting what the learner does to promote language acquisition and the ways in which learning opportunities are mediated by
the host environment, there is a greater appreciation for the markedly
different experiences of learners, sometimes even between those within
the same program.

Although the research supports the most popularly held beliefs about
study abroad programs in some respects, it also calls for these assumptions to be qualified. Overall, the studies summarized in this review
suggest that (a) even short programs can lead to gains, (b) longer programs have the potential to benefit learners more – particularly in the
areas of pragmatics, pronunciation and fluency, and (c) at best, learner
development only approaches native-like norms. However, the quality
and quantity of language learning opportunities varies considerably
between programs. Moreover, while lower-level learners have the most
to gain by definition, more advanced learners may be more likely to
find themselves in contact situations facilitative to language acquisition
– through initiatives of their own or by the ways they are received by
NSs, or most likely because of some interaction between the two.

Finally, linguistic development is further mediated by the complex inter-action between initial abilities, individual differences and changes in these factors that occur in the host context.

At this point in time, the generalizations that may be made across pro-grams are disappointingly few, but opportunities for future projects abound. In particular, in this review we have highlighted new directions being taken in the area of literacy and pragmatics, the renewed interest in comparative studies and a consideration of the role that learner strategies play in shaping learner experience. In addition, research on grammar and pronunciation has begun to look at discrete features, but this research has been largely restricted to a few study abroad contexts and to relatively few target languages. Furthermore, findings from quantitative and quali-tative studies on individual programs point to the need to document lin-guistic development, learning opportunities and their interaction over time. While such repeated measures studies supplemented by ethno-graphic data present methodological challenges not addressed to date, a series of such studies conducted in different programs and target language contexts could go a long way towards improving our under-standing of what is learned, by whom and under what conditions. Undoubtedly, research along these lines will aid in furthering our under-standing of second language acquisition. Indeed, research on study abroad is potentially as rich as ever and we are only beginning to reveal its complexities. The chapters included in this volume help further our understanding and it is our hope that they also inspire others to investigate the dynamic and multifaceted experiences of lear-ners in study abroad contexts.

Notes

1. The course materials were *Maximizing Study Abroad: A Student's Guide to Strategies for Language and Culture Learning and Use* by Paige *et al.* (2002).
2. These differences were perhaps due to an artifact of the data collection method; males gave less detailed responses than females. Also, intensity and quality of the interactions were not examined and individual differences were not examined.

Part 1: The Acquisition of Pragmatic Competence During Study Abroad

Chapter 2

Learning to Take Leave in Social Conversations: A Diary Study

TIM HASSALL

This is a study of one learner's acquisition of the speech act of leave-taking in social conversations in Indonesian, over a three-month period.[1] Its main purpose is to identify the stages by which he developed the ability to take leave; a secondary aim is to identify key factors that influenced his learning. This will add to the scant body of research on how pragmatic ability is acquired in a second language.

Background

Acquisition of second language pragmatics

Longitudinal studies with the goal of discovering how learners acquire pragmatic ability are still scarce and few trends emerge from findings to date (for a recent review of developmental findings see Kasper & Rose, 2002: chap. 4). However, some important theoretical claims have been made about how learners acquire second language (L2) pragmatics.

Schmidt (1993) claims that learners acquire pragmatic knowledge in the second language by consciously noting input, that is, noticing pragmatic features in the target language environment. He asserts that it is only by conscious noticings of this type that new knowledge becomes available for uptake by learners to become part of their own pragmatic knowledge (cf. Schmidt's similar claim about acquisition of L2 grammatical knowledge in Schmidt & Frota, 1986). Two studies of L2 pragmatic development that find support for Schmidt's claim are Barron (this volume) and DuFon (2000a: 510–511, 530–531).

Bialystok (1993) argues that acquiring knowledge is of relatively minor importance for adult L2 learners of pragmatics. She acknowledges that they must acquire a certain amount of knowledge, in the form of an increasingly explicit understanding of L2 pragmatic features. However, she asserts that the crucial process for them is acquiring *control* over attention to their knowledge. They generally produce inappropriate utterances not because their knowledge is deviant but because they cannot access it rapidly enough to use it when they need it.

Schumann (1997) makes relevant claims about second language acquisition more broadly, in his theory of 'stimulus appraisal'. Observing that learners constantly appraise the myriad stimuli that make up the learning experience, he claims that they must in general appraise these stimuli positively. If not, 'sustained deep learning' cannot occur; the learner cannot become proficient in the language (see Schumann, 1997: chap. 1). However, he is led by his reading of the autobiography of one learner, Eva Hoffman (discussed in Schumann, 1997: chap. 4) to speculate that learners need not assess stimuli as pleasant. Even unpleasant experiences may be assessed as desirable by some learners because they are so relevant to the paramount goal of learning the language that these experiences will still be appraised positively in terms of Schumann's theory (Schumann, 1997: 138).

Study abroad for advanced learners

How much study abroad with its potential for informal, out-of-class learning helps learners at an advanced level of proficiency is doubtful (see e.g. Lapkin *et al.*, 1995: 68). Advanced learners do seem to improve more in pragmatic (i.e. sociolinguistic) aspects of language during study abroad than they do in structural aspects such as syntax (see Regan, 1995: 246). But several detailed studies reveal advanced learners make only modest progress in pragmatics even over long sojourns (Barron, this volume; Hoffman-Hicks, 2000; Regan, 1995). In all those studies, advanced learners remain non-native in even quite basic pragmatic knowledge and aspects of pragmatic performance after a sojourn of one year's length or more. Hoffman-Hicks, in fact, sums up the pragmatic progress of her American learners of French over 16 months as 'generally slight and limited in scope' (Hoffman-Hicks, 2000: 256). So as regards the learning of pragmatics, advanced learners consistently appear to make only modest progress even over long periods of study abroad.

Amount of interaction during study abroad

It is often assumed that study abroad learners have a rich environment for interaction with native speakers of the target language. But in fact learners during study abroad often do not interact much with native speakers – often much less than they intended to before departing (see e.g. Pellegrino, 1998; Wilkinson, 2000).

Such behavior is often seen by researchers as indicative of students who are lazy and lack discipline. However this explanation is inadequate (Pellegrino, 1998; Wilkinson, 2000: 39). Learners may reject opportunities for social interaction in the target language for a wide range of social, cultural or psychological reasons. Wilkinson (2000) cites the example of two of her American learners of French who chose to spend most of their out-of-class time socializing with each other in English instead of with native speakers. These learners chose to do so because for them 'the benefits of being able to express their feelings freely outweighed the potential costs of not achieving personal and programmatic goals' (Wilkinson, 2000: 39). Wilkinson suggests that this type of conscious decision to choose activities other than interaction with native speakers in order to achieve other legitimate goals is common among learners in study abroad.

In such cases can we attribute the learners' behavior to low motivation? Both Pellegrino (1998) and Wilkinson (2000: 39) explicitly reject this interpretation, apparently regarding a verdict of low motivation as tantamount to an accusation of laziness. But in fact motivation is the key. Leaving aside pejorative labels such as 'poor' to describe level of motivation, it can fairly be said that study abroad learners who reject opportunities for interaction lack a sufficiently strong motivation to learn the language. In Schumann's (1997) terms, they do not desire to learn strongly enough to make them desire interactions for the sake of learning; to make them appraise interactions positively for their value in attaining that goal alone.

Learner strategies

Two learner strategies are important for this study. Cohen (1998) terms them 'metacognitive' strategies as they allow students to control their own cognition during the learning process. One is the learning strategy of post-evaluation, that is, of evaluating one's own utterance after saying it. Another strategy for learning (as well as language use) is that of pre-planning an utterance. Pre-planning can take various forms. One type apparently common among learners is rehearsal of the utterance before producing it; for example, rehearsing it mentally by running through it silently in your head (Ortega, 1999: 27). Pre-planning can enhance learning of material by enabling it to be integrated into the learner's active repertoire.

The speech act of leave-taking

Leave-taking can be defined for the purposes of this study as an act intended by the speaker to convey to the hearer that the speaker regards the encounter as at an end. As such, this speech act has a clear politeness function. Ferguson (1976) classifies leave-taking formulas as 'politeness formulas', whose main function is to smooth social interaction. This speech act is also closely linked to the management of conversation. Thus Scarcella (1983a) calls leave-taking a 'conversational device' rather than a speech act, while Kasper (1992) acknowledges its dual status, observing that leave-takings 'are illocutions and hence pragmatics, but since they happen in patterned exchanges and particular phases of encounters, conversations and the like, they are matters of discourse' (Kasper, 1992: 206).

Several studies have investigated leave-taking by second language learners. These reveal it to be a fairly difficult speech act. Learners may not know the right formulas to take leave (Hoffman-Hicks, 2000) or may not know how to vary choice of formula according to the social context (Cook, 1985). And in particular, learners may not be able to manage leave-taking as conversation; to cooperate with the interlocutor in bringing the interaction to a close (Omar, 1993; Scarcella, 1983a; and Schmidt, 1993: 29–30).

Leave-taking in Indonesian

No published empirical descriptions exist of leave-taking in Indonesian. But many politeness formulas to perform this function can be commonly observed. Two are of special importance to this study. One, routinely taught to learners of Indonesian, is the self-excusing formula *Permisi* 'Excuse me'. This formula is suitable for taking leave in many contexts but is somewhat formal and slightly deferential in tone and so tends not to be suitable for taking leave of familiar equals (e.g. friends or close acquaintances the same age).

The other formula, not in the writer's experience routinely taught to learners, is a formula that I shall call the *'dulu* statement'. Here the speaker makes a statement expressing his intention to leave (cf. Omar, 1993: 105) then adds the word *dulu* 'for now, for the time being'. So one can say, for example, *Mau beristirahat dulu* 'I'm going to have a rest for now' (literally 'Will rest for-now'), or *Saya keluar dulu* 'I'm going out for now' (literally 'I go-out for-now'). This formula is suitable in a very wide range of contexts but does not explicitly convey deference and so is less appropriate than *permisi* in contexts where that effect is desired. So there is a large overlap in the social contexts where the two formulas *permisi* and the *dulu* statement can be used, but there are also certain contexts where one is more appropriate.

Other common Indonesian leave-taking formulas mentioned in this paper are *Mari* and *Ayo* (both meaning roughly 'Bye'), and *Sampai jumpa* 'See you later' (literally 'Until meet').

Method

The subject

The subject of this study, the writer, is a 42-year-old Australian. I had started studying Indonesian as a hobby 15 years earlier and had been learning it ever since; mostly in Australia, mostly by self-study, plus by doing an undergraduate major in Indonesian. For the previous seven years I had also been teaching Indonesian at university, mainly to students in their second year of an undergraduate major in Indonesian. I had also visited Indonesia for six short trips of three to eight weeks duration: all holidays with a strong informal language learning focus except for one study trip to do a one-month intensive Indonesian course at the advanced level (in 1992). My proficiency at the start of the sojourn can be characterized as advanced but with uneven ability in different skills, for example, reading was very advanced but my speaking, while lexico-grammatically advanced, was not highly fluent. This was due probably to lack of practice; outside my classroom teaching and my short trips to Indonesia I rarely spoke Indonesian to anyone.

Apart from once learning Spanish informally for eight months during a sojourn in Madrid some 15 years before this study began, I had also formally studied four other foreign languages at various times: French and Latin at high school and then Italian, Mandarin and French (again) by intensive self-study for one to two years each in Australia, for enjoyment. Although I had greatly liked learning those languages at the time I had long ago stopped studying any of them, and so at the time of the sojourn I spoke no foreign languages besides Indonesian.

The sojourn

The main period examined is a three-month sojourn in Indonesia, from the end of 2001 to early 2002. My main purpose for embarking on the sojourn was twofold: to find a quiet spot to work on my own academic reading and writing and to learn Indonesian informally by exposing myself to the linguistic and cultural environment. I stayed in three different places for about one month each: firstly in a city in West Sumatra (Padang), then in a large town nearby (Bukittinggi), and lastly in the capital city (Jakarta) on the island of Java. In each place I stayed in a guest house/boarding house. My typical daily routine was similar in each place: wake up early and spend some hours working on my own reading and writing; go out into town by myself to explore for the rest of the day, and come home in the early evening and then study Indonesian by listening to radio and reading novels or newspapers.

So this learning experience was not study abroad in the classic sense of immersion in the native speech community combined with learning in a formal setting (Freed, 1995a: 5). Rather, it was immersion in the native speech community for the deliberate purpose of language learning.

Data collection method

The study uses a diary method, whereby I kept a journal of my own language learning experience. This method has been employed in many studies of second language acquisition, including several of pragmatic acquisition specifically (e.g. Cohen, 1997; DuFon, 1998, 2000a). For discussion of the strengths and weaknesses of the diary method see, for example, Bailey (1991) and Bailey and Ochsner (1983).

Procedure

The diary was written long-hand in exercise books. I wrote in it most days, about five days a week. In total the diary consisted of 272 pages of entries, although the number and length of my entries varied greatly from day to day. The time lapse between the episode and the diary entry also varied. I usually recorded an entry that night, that is, some hours after it occurred, or else the morning of the next day; but I sometimes recorded it straight away and occasionally did not record it until several days afterwards.

I started the study by formulating two broad research questions: (1) *What* did I do with respect to pragmatics? and (2) *How* did I learn pragmatics? Guided by these two questions, I made a list of categories and sub-categories to code the diary data. My coding of data was tested for intra-rater reliability at the end of the sojourn, by re-coding all entries for one randomly chosen week (Week 5). This test yielded a reliability rating of 91.6%.

As recommended by Miles and Huberman (1994), analysis of the data was started early. Starting in Week 2, each day's entries were coded the following day. At the start of Week 9, I re-read the entire diary up to that point, and made a 'time-ordered matrix' (Miles & Huberman, 1994) to display all the data visually. Based on that display, I identified three pragmatic issues as salient: leave-taking, greeting, and terms of address; and started to narrow the focus of my study, collecting data on these three features almost to the exclusion of others for the remaining weeks of the sojourn. As a result, most of the entries on leave-taking were collected in the last four weeks (61 of the total 81 entries).

When the sojourn was over, I made a very short summary of each leave-taking entry listed in a time sequence. By studying that list,

I isolated strands and patterns in my learning of leave-taking, discarded some leave-taking entries as irrelevant to the emerging narrative, rewrote all relevant entries, changing names as I did so; and began to take extended notes for a draft of the paper.

Supplementary data

The data from the sojourn diary are supplemented by a small number of data from another source: a diary that I kept on my learning of pragmatics during a three-week holiday trip to Indonesia one year before the sojourn (during which my daily routine was not greatly different from that during the sojourn). That diary consisted of 35 pages of handwritten entries, with 16 entries on leave-taking, mostly made during the last two weeks. That earlier diary was kept less rigorously as no research questions were set and no coding of data was done, but it still yields some useful data on my leave-taking ability prior to the sojourn.

Findings

From pre-sojourn until late into the sojourn, two distinct developmental issues can be identified. The first is a vying for place as my main leave-taking formula between _permisi_ and the _dulu_ statement. The second is the question of whether my leave-taking formula should be preceded by a _preliminary_ formula, henceforth called a 'pre-closing' (cf. Schegloff & Sacks, 1973), to signal my intention to take leave before I actually do so.[2] For clarity, I will outline the path of development of these two issues separately as far as possible.

Formulas: Pre-sojourn to Week 7

During my pre-sojourn trip to Indonesia in 2001, I sometimes took leave with _permisi_. I selected it in appropriate contexts only, using formulas other than _permisi_ (e.g. _ayo_ or _mari_) to end casual conversations with familiar equals where _permisi_ would not be appropriate. On one occasion, I considered _permisi_ then explicitly rejected it as a way to end a long and friendly chat with a café owner around my age because 'it felt too formal' (Diary entry from pre-sojourn trip, Parangtritis, Week 3, 13/1/01). As for the _dulu_ statement formula, it seems clear that this formula was not in my active repertoire during that earlier trip. In the last week I had a painful awakening encounter with it:

(1) I didn't understand a polite remark by a fellow guest in my guesthouse here. I was sitting on the verandah outside my room when she passed by; she stopped and we exchanged a couple of small-talk

social questions. Then, she said, to take leave, *'Mau keluar dulu'* 'I'm going out for now' (literally, 'Will go-out for-now'). I completely misunderstood it: thought *dulu* meant 'formerly' (which it can, though not in this context) and took it for another social question and answered irrelevantly. She looked displeased and said shortly, *'Tidak'* 'No'. When she'd gone I realized what she'd meant. I felt very incompetent for misunderstanding a simple polite move. It was the *dulu* that threw me – I feel more sensitized to that meaning of it now. (Diary entry from presojourn trip, Parangtritis, Week 3, 17/1/01)

So one year before the sojourn began I was using *permisi* appropriately and was not using *dulu* statements at all.

The earliest part of the sojourn itself marks a new stage where I use both of these formulas. In Week 1, I use *permisi* to take leave on one occasion (adding a *dulu* statement to it as a supportive move), and evaluate it as successful:

(2)   I was sitting in the post office and a woman (28ish) on the same bench struck up a conversation... Eventually I felt it was time to go, and said, *'Permisi, mau belanja dulu.'* She looked pretty blank, and didn't say anything back, but I think that was just her, she had been remarkably slow right through the conversation. I think there was nothing wrong with it as a way to take leave. (Diary entry, Week 1, Padang, 31/12/01)

On another occasion soon afterwards I use a *dulu* statement instead and evaluate it as successful. In adding the *dulu* statement formula to my repertoire at this time, I consciously draw on my painful learning experience of it (see Sample 1) that had occurred a year earlier.

(3)   Parting with a friendly hotel employee after he'd come to chat with me while I was sitting outside my room yesterday: eventually, knowing I'd just got home from a long walk, he said: I'll let you go, you want to rest, and I said, *'Ya, saya mandi dulu'* 'Yes, I'll have a wash for now' (literally 'I bathe for-now'), and got up to leave. In using this *dulu* statement formula I was consciously drawing on that episode in my last trip when I misunderstood it – it was still vivid in my mind. It got a good response here: pleased, relaxed, which reinforces my feeling that it's a good gambit to use in taking leave. (Diary entry, Padang, Week 2, 5/1/02)

The number of instances on which I posit a 'stage' here is very small: one with *permisi* and one with a *dulu* statement. Nevertheless, it can be said that at this time I use the two formulas: the *dulu* statement has now entered my repertoire, alongside *permisi*. While I do not state the precise notion I hold of the relative social contexts for the two, I clearly regard the *dulu* statement as appropriate for many situations ('a good gambit to use in taking leave') and regard *permisi* as appropriate for some situations too.

But now something happens that prompts a re-thinking about the relative appropriateness of the two formulas. I use my new *dulu* statement formula once again but this time I evaluate it as a failure, and so start to lose faith in it.

(4)   As I was trudging home on the final stretch after a long hot walk, I was called over to chat by two women in the yard of a house nearby... We chatted amiably enough, but I suddenly got the impression that I'd overstayed my welcome – one of them seemed to be casting around rather awkwardly for further questions to ask me. So I rather hastily took my leave, with a dulu statement: *'Pulang dulu ya'* 'I'm going home for now, okay' (literally, 'Go-home for-now, yes'). I said it a bit tensely and unsmilingly and it felt a bit abrupt as I said it. As I then turned to go, one of them said softly, in English, 'Excuse me'. I turned around in puzzlement. She then repeated it in Indonesian: *'Permisi'*, and laughed. So her 'excuse me' had been a gentle correction; a supplying of what I'd omitted to say. (Diary entry, Padang Week 2, 9/1/02)

I took this correction to heart, noting in the same journal entry how useful it had been and how true it was that a *dulu* statement by itself will often be inadequately polite. About two weeks later, when after a long and casual chat with a boarding-house mate I am about to take leave solely with a *dulu* statement, I remember that earlier correction and decide to use *permisi* after all – saying to him *'Permisi, mau mandi dulu'* 'Excuse me, I want to wash for now' (Diary entry, Padang, Week 4, 21/1/02).

For the next two weeks, as several more entries bear out, I dutifully use *permisi* (with a *dulu* statement tacked onto it as a supportive move) and do not use a *dulu* statement by itself again. During this stage I overuse *permisi* in fact by using it on several occasions to end conversations of a markedly informal nature as well. For example, once I use it to end a long and very casual chat sitting on the side of the road with the young manager of my regular Internet café and several of his young friends (Diary entry, Padang, Week 6, 1/2/02). I evidently regard all my leave-takings with *permisi* during this stage as appropriate, making no criticisms of them in the relevant diary entries.

So for the time being, the question of choice of formula is resolved to my satisfaction. But soon afterwards I once again start to revise my knowledge of what my staple leave-taking formula should be – this time away from *permisi* and towards the *dulu* statement. The trigger seems to be when I hear my *dulu* statement formula in a drama on TV and am very struck by it. For the first time, I analyze its form explicitly:

(5) I watched a TV drama last night with Udin, a worker here at my new lodgings, and noticed a nice leave-taking. A glamorous pro-fessional woman said to a colleague at a social function: *'Saya pulang dulu ya'* 'I'm going home for now, right?' (literally 'I go-home for-now, yes'). I liked that one. The *ya* at the end struck me as a nice soft-ener. And the way she started it with *'Saya* pulang' 'I'm going home' instead of with *Mau* '(I) *will* go home' is a nice variant. (Diary entry, Bukittinggi, Week 7, 11/2/02)

This episode clearly makes an impression on me. Soon afterwards I use a *dulu* statement twice myself – both times noting in my diary that I am consciously imitating this TV leave-taking. So I am clearly starting to shift allegiance to the *dulu* statement. However, before examining this development any further we must shift focus to the other strand of my development: the question of pre-closings.

Pre-closing: Pre-sojourn to Week 8

During my short pre-sojourn trip to Indonesia I apparently did not think of using pre-closing formulas at first. I make three entries about leave-taking in the first week and never mention it. But from Week 2 of that trip, I start to feel the need to preface my leave-takings with a pre-closing formula. Several entries demonstrate this. One example: after a long chat with a restaurant owner after my meal, I deliberately do a non-verbal pre-closing by conspicuously gathering my belongings together 'because I felt stuck for something to say as a preliminary, to pave the way to take leave' (Diary entry from pre-sojourn trip, Parangtritis, Week 3, 13/1/01). Another example is when taking leave after a chat with two workers in a café on my last day, I lapse into English to pre-close:

(6) To leave I switched to English first, saying, 'It was good to meet you'. They cheerfully said *'Ya'* 'Yes', then I closed with *'Sampai jumpa'* 'See you later', and left. It felt smooth, friendly, and successful. I *needed* that initial pre-closing move of 'Good to meet you' in English. (Diary entry from pre-sojourn trip, Yogyakarta, Week 3, 17/1/01)

So during this period I implicitly believe that pre-closings are appropriate and try to use them. But now, right at the end of this short trip, I explicitly question for the first time whether pre-closings are even appropriate. I add as an afterthought to the entry in (6) above: 'Hey, I just thought: possibly Indonesians don't do that step! I'll have to observe'.

That was the last diary entry of that earlier trip. After that trip was over, I apparently forgot this sudden skepticism about the appropriateness of pre-closings. This is evident from an episode back in Australia, eight months after that short trip, and before the present sojourn begins:

(7)   Hadi, an Indonesian postgraduate student I knew, came to my office on campus to report on his progress in finding friends of his to be subjects for a research study of mine. Then we chatted socially for a bit. Eventually he said '*Oke deh*' 'Oke then', in a tone of finality, signaling that he was ready to go. I immediately noticed it, thought, 'Hey, that's a pre-closing – that's what I've been looking for!' and made a mental note to remember it for my own use... He then stood up and we took leave at the door. (Field note, Padang, 21/1/02)

So before the sojourn began I had felt the lack of a pre-closing formula in taking leave, then momentarily doubted whether such formulas were common, then apparently forgotten that doubt again.

As for during the sojourn itself: I apparently did not think of using pre-closings for some time. None of my leave-taking entries in the first three weeks refer to it at all. But this changes distinctly in Week 4. The trigger seems to be when I notice a radio DJ use one:

(8)   I heard *Oke deh* 'Okay then' by a DJ to a telephone caller last night. He used as a pre-closing, to show that he wanted to end the conversation. Just like Hadi's! [see Sample 7]. I feel ready to try it out. (Diary entry, Padang, Week 4, 21/1/02)

Two days later I notice another radio DJ use the same *Oke deh* formula for the same function and reflect: 'At this rate it will become automatic for me, hopefully' (Diary entry, Padang, Week 5, 24/1/02). And later that week I use it twice myself, and both times I evaluate it as successful. One example:

(9)   I popped in at the travel agent, Rina, who had asked me in for a chat when I was passing by a week or so ago. I asked a few questions about buses to Bukittinggi, then we started chatting in general. She served me a cup of mineral water. When I was ready to leave, I said: '*Oke deh*' 'Okay then', to which she said, '*Ya*' 'yes'. Then as I was

going out we exchanged *Mari* 'Bye'. It all felt quite smooth and natural. (Diary entry, Padang, Week 5, 25/1/02)

My preoccupation with preliminaries continues that week. I notice yet another one by a radio DJ: this time a bare *Oke* 'Okay'. I still feel that my repertoire of formulas for pre-closing is limited. On two occasions that week I consider using *Oke (deh)* but decide it is a bit too businesslike in tone for the situation; cannot think of how else to pre-close and do it non-verbally, by gathering together my shopping bags to show I am ready to leave.

One night soon afterwards (in Week 7) I notice a new pre-closing formula used in a TV drama three times by the glamorous female star, namely, *Udah or Udah deh* 'That's it' or 'That's it then' (literally 'already' + optional modal particle). The next day I try it out tentatively myself ('*Udah*') to close a social chat with vendors at a market stall, and evaluate it as quite successful.

So now I am using pre-closings and trying to expand my repertoire of formulas for them. But then an important thing happens: all my attempts to use pre-closings start to go wrong. Repeatedly, on four occasions (in Week 8/8+), I use one and produce a bungled leave-taking. An example is this:

(10)   Today I passed by the bookshop and out the front on the footpath was Dewi, the 19-year-old bookshop assistant. A few days earlier we had had a long chat, in which she confided about her boyfriend problems, while I was browsing in the shop. We greeted each other, and I asked her if there were any developments with the boyfriend problem; she told me the latest good news, to which I responded happily. I couldn't think of anything else to talk about, and to end, I said briskly, automatically, '*Oke deh*' 'Okay then' – but then couldn't think of what to say to actually take leave; my mind was a blank. I said '*Mari*' 'Bye', but a bit nervously and uncertainly. It felt quite clumsy and probably didn't seem friendly; she didn't look very happy with it either. After I left I immediately thought, that was stupid, that *Oke deh* sounded too curt and businesslike ... Although it wasn't a disastrous blunder or anything, it's a nuisance'. (Diary entry, Bukittinggi, Week 8, 14/2/02)

Formulas and pre-closings: Weeks 8–12

At this point, where I am trying to pre-close and cannot do it gracefully, the two issues of pre-closing and choice of formula collide. For at this point in the sojourn I have also begun to switch allegiance to the *dulu* statement as my customary way of taking leave. Having heard someone say it on TV (see Sample 5), I use it twice myself in imitation. But on both occasions I am thwarted by this notion of a pre-closing. Even though that TV character had used her *dulu* statement with no pre-closing, I evidently feel the need to improve on her performance by using one. This produces leave-takings that I find awkward and unsatisfactory.

In the first of these, I end a long chat with a shopkeeper by producing the *dulu* statement formula that I had heard on TV, '*Saya pulang dulu ya?*' 'I'm going home for now, okay?' But then, as I start to leave the shop, I 'felt stuck for a final closing formula... My mind was a blank. I just made a faint strangled-sounding noise and nodded mutely' (Diary entry, Bukit-tinggi, Week 8, 16/2/02). By trying to add a 'real' leave-taking formula to my *dulu* statement I thus turn it into a mere pre-closing.

A few days later I try to *precede* my *dulu* statement with a pre-closing move: similarly ill-fated. I end a chat with two young boys on the roadside by first saying '*oke deh*', and then adding '*Saya jalan dulu ya?*' 'I'm walking on for now, okay?' But immediately I feel that 'it had been clumsy on my part: the initial *oke deh* had been blatantly superfluous and made a big deal of the leave-taking' (Diary entry, Bukittinggi, Week 8+, 21/2/02). So my determination to take leave in two moves is foiling my attempts to use my *dulu* statement. I am trying to use that formula within a two-part sequence of pre-closing plus leave-taking and am not happy with the results.

Now, however, comes a rapid sequence of events that leads to a resolution of the pre-closing issue. First, at lunch later the same day, in a café, I notice the *dulu* statement formula again, and am once again struck by it.

(11)   One of the café workers, a nice guy (early 30s, confident, impress-ive) came and sat at my table and we chatted in a desultory way until my meal came ... After I'd finished the meal and was reading the paper, he came back out and we chatted again for a while. He took leave by saying briskly, cheerily '*Saya turun dulu ya*' 'I'm going out for now, okay?' (literally 'I'm going down', i.e. down the stairs). Another *dulu* statement! I thought about that one. (Diary entry, Bukit-tinggi, Week 8+, 21/2/02)

And then I imitate him:

(12)   Later in the day I copied him twice, first saying '*Jalan-jalan dulu ya*' 'I'm going for a walk for now, okay?' to close a conversation with

two chatty fruit vendors at a stall, and shortly after, '*Saya ke kantor pos dulu ya*' 'I'm going to the post office for now, okay?' to close a conversation with a chatty magazine seller. (Diary entry, Bukittinggi, Week 8+, 21/2/02)

I do not consciously decide to eschew a pre-closing when imitating this person on these occasions; I simply do what he did. But the events of the day do seem to produce a re-thinking about pre-closings. That night, I write: 'As for how to take leave, I'm now (a) confused, but (b) feeling better about it. I'm not even sure any more that you have two distinct steps of pre-closing formula and then real formula' (Diary entry, Bukittinggi, Week 8+, 21/2/02). So finally, late in the sojourn, I have come to explicitly question whether pre-closings are appropriate in social conversations.

The same sequence of events also marks a resolution of the question of which formula to favor: the *dulu* statement or *permisi*. In the same diary entry I proclaim my faith in the *dulu* statement:

(13)   I'm struck by the identicalness of the form that that woman used on the TV drama recently [see Sample 5] and the form that this café guy used to me today. It's the exact same form *Saya ... dulu ya?* 'I'm ...ing for now, okay?' It gives me a lot of confidence in this one... It looks like a *dulu* statement, alone, is a good way to end a lot of social conversations. (Diary entry, Bukittinggi, Week 8+, 21/2/02)

I now leave Indonesia for one week. When I get back, these elements of my leave-taking become firmly established. In the first week after my return (Week 9) I notice the *dulu* statement several more times and use it several times – never with a pre-closing.

I also vary my selection between *dulu* statement and *permisi* appropriately during this stage. This is evident from the one time I use *permisi*. I use it in a situation where considerable deference was called for, so that a *dulu* statement would have been inappropriate. This is when I have just re-entered Indonesia after the one-week break in my sojourn and am at a small provincial airport from which I am about to fly to Jakarta:

(14)   I was walking through the airport and went past an official sitting at a baggage X-ray belt that wasn't being used. He cheerily called out and stopped me. In order to put an end to a jovial but rather insulting social grilling at the hands of this official (and four of his idle colleagues), who was apparently relishing his power, I finally ventured a *permisi* formula, deliberately making it extra deferential by adding modifiers to it: *Permisi Pak ya* 'Excuse me, Sir, yes'. To my relief he

responded well to it and graciously waved me on. (Diary entry, Batam, Week 9, 5/3/03)

Nothing in that diary entry indicates that I even contemplated using a *dulu* statement to take leave of the official. But otherwise at this stage of the sojourn, I am consistently using *dulu* statements instead of *permisi* in a wide range of appropriate social contexts.

I reflect explicitly on these developments in my learning of leave-taking:

(15) I just looked back on a couple of early entries (Weeks 3 and 4) and realize that I've changed my mind about how to take leave quite a bit. I still thought back then that I should make a pre-closing move before I actually take leave – I don't any more. And I thought that *permisi* was the best formula for leave-taking – now I think that a *dulu* statement is more normal. I think I'd been confused by that correction I once got to use *permisi* (see Sample 4). (Diary entry, Jakarta, Week 9, 7/3/02)

So the issues of key formula and pre-closings are now settled to my satisfaction. From now until the end of the sojourn I use *dulu* statements frequently (and use a range of other formulas too including *mari, ayo* and *sampai jumpa*). I no longer use *permisi* except for the solitary instance with the airport official in Sample 14 above, and no longer use pre-closing formulas. I mention the latter only once again during the sojourn, in Week 12, to remark that I have not even thought of them for weeks and reiterate my rejection of them.

Before going any further, it is useful to take stock of what I learned about these elements of leave-taking. For *permisi* versus *dulu* statement, my learning path is summed up in Table 2.1. Table 2.1 shows a complex path of learning about *permisi* and the *dulu* statement. For both formulas, I replace basically native-like knowledge with explicit and *deviant* knowledge, before acquiring native-like knowledge once again. At the last stage, I finally possess native-like and fairly detailed knowledge about the relative frequency and the appropriate social contexts for both. I also change my action patterns largely in accordance with my changing states of knowledge about the two formulas.

As for pre-closing, my path of learning is summarized in Table 2.2. While it remains largely an open question how native-like my knowledge was at any stage, Table 2.2 reveals a complex path of learning about pre-closings. I repeatedly revise my knowledge of whether pre-closings are normally used in social conversations, with my knowledge on this issue

Table 2.1 Stages in acquiring *permisi* versus *dulu* statement as my main formula

Stage	Features
Stage 1: pre-sojourn	I sometimes use *permisi*. I implicitly know the key social constraints on its use. I never use the *dulu* statement and apparently do not know it.
Stage 2: weeks 1–2	I use both *permisi* and the *dulu* statement. I believe the *dulu* statement to be 'a good gambit'. I have no clear knowledge of the relative frequency or relative social contexts for the two formulas.
Stage 3: weeks 2–6	I use *permisi* but not the *dulu* statement. I believe the former to be appropriate in virtually any context and the latter to be widely unsuitable.
Stage 4: weeks 7–12	I use the *dulu* statement much more often than *permisi*. I believe it to be more widely appropriate than *permisi* and also know the key social constraints on its use.

becoming explicit at several stages, including the last two stages. I also change my action patterns to a large degree to suit my changing stages of knowledge.

Table 2.2 Stages in my learning to use a pre-closing formula (PCF) in taking leave

Stage	Features
Stage 1: pre-sojourn trip (1st week)	I do not use or attempt to use a PCF. I implicitly believe that 'zero pre-closing' is appropriate.
Stage 2: pre-sojourn trip (2nd–3rd week)	I regularly attempt to use a PCF. I do not know the requisite forms and compensate by e.g. using an English PCF. I explicitly believe that using a PCF is appropriate.
Stage 3: weeks 1–3 of sojourn	I do not use or attempt to use a PCF. I implicitly believe that zero pre-closing is appropriate.
Stage 4: weeks 4–8 + [a]	I regularly use a PCF. I explicitly believe that using one is appropriate.
Stage 5: weeks 8 + –12	I never use a PCF. I explicitly believe that zero pre-closing is appropriate.

[a]*Week 8+* refers to the period of four extra days straight after Week 8, just before I break the sojourn for a week in Singapore.

Beyond formulas: Weeks 10–12

A final stage in my learning of leave-taking begins. I come to reject what I see as my preoccupation with learning formulas. I form two explicit and related notions: that taking leave is mainly a matter of managing conversation and that it is often best done without a formula. I change my leave-taking behavior accordingly.

The apparent trigger for this new stage is an episode in Week 10. During that week I had been regularly taking leave with *dulu* statements and assessing these leave-takings as satisfactory. But now, on the last day of that week, I report:

> (16) I just had my regular morning chat with *Pak* Samsul (Mr Samsul) the owner of this place, while hanging up my washing … Eventually I felt it was time to go back to my room and I moved subtly towards the door to show I was ready to go back inside, while forming in my mind a *dulu* statement, namely, *Belajar dulu ya?* 'I'm going to study for now, okay?' But then he started to move towards the door, too, so we were closing the conversation tacitly, by mutual consent. I felt a bit cheated of a chance to practice a leave-taking formula and, as we walked back in, stupidly murmured my pre-planned formula: *Belajar dulu ya?* I felt even as I said it that it was awkward – why spell out that I want to end the conversation when we're ending it already? Fortunately he said something just as I spoke, and so didn't even hear it. (Diary entry, Jakarta, Week 10, 16/2/02)

This makes me reflect that it is probably common to take leave without saying anything in Indonesian. I go on to note, 'this kind of taking leave without words is probably a common, natural way to do it. Perhaps I've been too concerned to explicitly say something, to trot out a formula, even when it would have been better not to' (Diary entry, Jakarta, Week 10, 16/2/02).

The next day I reflect explicitly that leave-taking is something that you do together with someone else.

> (17) I've been looking through old entries where I obsess over finding a magic formula and I've been thinking, there's no such thing as The Right Way to take leave in a social conversation. The problem is that you have to take leave together with the other person. That adds a whole host of subtle complications. What they say or do become all-important, and you have to respond to that on the run – that episode with Pak Samsul yesterday made that clear. (Diary entry, Jakarta, Week 11, 17/3/02)

This idea makes me feel pessimistic about how well I can learn to take leave in Indonesian. In the same entry, I go on to reflect:

(18) I think leave-taking will always be hard for me, mainly because participating in conversation is hard for me. I'll be able to learn an impressive stock of formulas. But as for the conversation-related stuff: making what you say fit with what they say, handling the myriad permutations for bringing a conversation to an end together – I expect I'll be slow to learn to handle conversation in that sense... Not being sociable, I simply don't have many Indonesian conversations, even when I'm in Indonesia, so it will take me ages to accumulate 'flying time'. Come to think of it, maybe you need a certain *intensity* of immersion too, to learn that sort of stuff well. And if so I'll probably never get it. My conversations will be too spaced out from each other, no matter over how many years I learn the language. (Diary entry, Jakarta, Week 11, 17/3/02)

My malaise seems to deepen as I sense the daunting task ahead. The next day I say: 'I feel as if I've plateaued with leave-takings for the time being. I don't expect to learn anything much during the last couple of weeks, and don't feel enthusiastic about trying to' (Diary entry, Jakarta, Week 11, 18/3/02).

However, my leave-taking now starts to change markedly in line with my new insights. I exhibit two new traits: I regularly try to take leave without a formula if I can, and choose my way of leave-taking based on how the conversation develops instead of pre-planning how to do it. One strategy I use that illustrates both these traits is that I deliberately restrain myself from saying a formula to see what happens. Here is the one such episode – the first of four in Weeks 11 and 12:

(19) I had a nice chat this afternoon with Sari, a fellow lodger (30ish, female) while I was outside gathering my laundry off the line... The conversation ended on a humorous note, we just parted, chuckling... I deliberately didn't trot out a formula as we were parting; waited to see if it was needed. Then *she* said '*Ayo*' 'Bye' casually, as if as an after-thought, as she was going into her room, and I just grunted 'Ya' 'yes' in a friendly tone. That's more like it. That's probably something I don't do often enough: wait for the other person to say a formula first, if they want. I probably tend to blurt out a formula too quickly, and sometimes superfluously. (Diary entry, Jakarta, Week 11, 18/3/02)

In the episodes like this one when I delay saying anything, each time the other person initiates the leave-taking and I just respond with a short rejoinder. I am pleased each time this happens, and so on two other occasions I even try deliberately to get the other person to initiate, so that I can just respond. Once I'm successful; once I am not – below:

(20)   This evening as I was going out of our gate into the alley, the manager was at the gate and we chatted for a little while about various things... I tried to take my leave without a formula: when a pause came I said nothing for a moment and made movements of turning slightly towards the gate, hoping he'd pick up on it and say something to close the conversation himself, but he just said nothing, too. I hastily came up with a *dulu* statement: said '*Nelpon dulu ya*' 'I'm going to make a phone call for now, okay'. (Diary entry, Jakarta, Week 12, 26/12/02)

Another way I avoid formulas on several occasions during this period is to deliberately say something *non*-formulaic to take leave. All three episodes are conversations with fellow lodgers in my boarding house; here is one:

(21)   I just had a bit of a chat with a fellow lodger who I hadn't really spoken to before: Atdi, a 35ish, guileless, pleasant guy from Medan. After we'd been talking in a desultory way for a while, I had my head out the window eyeing my washing and the gathering storm clouds, and I said in a low-key way that I'd better rescue my washing if it's going to rain again – he agreeably grunted something back (just a short syllable or two that I didn't catch), and I went out. That felt all right to me. I deliberately didn't use any of my precious stock of formulas. I think I've been so obsessed with them that I've been neglecting other ordinary, low-key ways of ending conversations. So I want to try not to use one whenever I can, for a while, and find out what other ways I can do it. (Diary entry, Jakarta, Week 11, 20/3/02)

I did not totally dispense with formulas during this period. On four occasions I decided, after assessing things, that I *did* need to say a formula in order to be adequately polite. Each time I was pleased with the outcome. One example:

(22)   I came out of my room this morning to go out and get something to eat up the road. Iwan, a fellow lodger, was at the table; we had a bit of a chat. The old owner of our lodgings came along and said something to him – the two of them spoke for a bit. Then the owner left, which seemed a good point to take my leave of Iwan too. I weighed up the idea of leaving without saying anything but decided I did need to say something to be adequately polite, ran through a couple of formulas

in my head . . . and just said '*Ayo*' 'Bye' casually and softly, he said 'Ya' 'Yes'. It felt fine: low-key, minimalist: I'd done the least that I assessed I decently could. (Diary entry, Jakarta, Week 12, 30/3/02)

As for my former practice of pre-planning how I would take leave, I reflected now it was inherently flawed. I note 'you have to be really attuned to subtle cues from the other person . . . And that means that if you pre-plan how to take leave it can become inappropriate an instant later!' (Diary entry, Jakarta, Week 11, 18/3/02). For example, I sternly rebuke myself for pre-planning once (in Week 12), when I store up a *dulu* statement formula early in a conversation and then blurt it out later when it is no longer needed. In another conversation some days after that I consciously resist pre-planning how I will take leave. This feels to me like something new:

(23)   When I came back from town, the old owner was in the boarding house, and he struck up a conversation with me about my impending move to Bandung. We talked for a long time . . . I once started to cast around mentally for a formula to take leave, just to store it for later, but consciously stopped myself and directed my attention back to the conversation, and just chatted. . . It felt quite daring letting the conversation go on with no idea of how I was going to end it. (Diary entry, Jakarta, Week 12, 30/3/02)

And I go on in that entry to reflect how important it is not to pre-plan:

(24)   I'm sure I'm on the right track by not planning a formula in advance, and instead staying with the conversation all the way through – so I can pick up . . . cues and so decide on the run how to take leave. It's a scary thought, but actually the reality is not so scary, and it seems to go well: feels natural, and makes leave-taking not such a big deal. (Diary entry, Jakarta, Week 12, 30/3/02)

As I persevere with my new approaches, my recent pessimism about learning largely vanishes. A few days before the end of the sojourn, I report:

(25)   I'm feeling a lot better about leave-takings lately, since adopting my minimalist approach to them, that is, doing the least I assess that I can do at that point in the conversation. It feels a lot better; more natural and spontaneous. And I feel calmer now, under less pressure to perform well. (Diary entry, Jakarta, Week 12, 26/3/02)

To let us take stock of what I learned in this last leg of the sojourn, my path of learning is summed up in Table 2.3.

Table 2.3 Stages in learning to take leave according to how the conversation develops

Stage	Features
Stage 1: weeks 1–9	I implicitly regard leave-taking as a solo act. I often pre-plan how to take leave. I always use a verbal formula.
Stage 2: weeks 10–12	I explicitly believe that leave-taking is done together and that the right way to take leave depends on the development of the conversation up to that point. I consciously restrain myself from pre-planning. I experiment with ways to take leave without a formula.

Table 2.3 shows that late in the sojourn, learning of a more subtle type took place. I acquired explicit knowledge that the best way to take leave depends on how the conversation has developed up to that point and that leave-taking can be done without formulas. I changed my behavior in line with these notions, including deliberately not pre-planning how I would take leave and taking leave in non-formulaic ways.

Discussion

Learning of sociopragmatics

Before anything else, an obvious bias of the study needs to be pointed out. The diary data focus almost entirely on the learning of linguistic forms and the pragmatic force they convey (and in the later stages, on the learning of discourse). This linguistic form – pragmatic force relationship is what Thomas (1983) terms 'pragmalinguistics'. As for the learning of 'sociopragmatics', that is, the weighting of the *social* factors that determine choice of linguistic form (Thomas, 1983), the diary entries are totally silent. This bias was a blind spot. Despite my commencing the data analysis early, re-reading entries, and trying to fill gaps in the data; I never realized till long after the sojourn was finished that I had overlooked sociopragmatic aspects of my leave-taking.

Obviously I drew constantly on sociopragmatic knowledge. An example is my regular use of *dulu* statements to take leave of strangers in public places who have struck up a conversation with me. This draws not only on the knowledge that a *dulu* statement conveys a moderately high degree of politeness by its provision of a ritual explanation for leaving (e.g. *I'm going home* for now), but also on the sociopragmatic knowledge that people in Indonesia have a strong right to initiate social conversations with a stranger in public so that the interlocutor is obliged to end the conversation with such a level of politeness. A second example is my use of *permisi* in Sample 14 to take leave of a uniformed airport official who had initiated a social chat with me. This draws not only on the knowledge that *permisi* conveys deference and formality but also on the sociopragmatic knowledge that the official here holds such high status and power relative to mine that a high degree of deference should be conveyed.

I happen to believe that those two particular pieces of sociopragmatic knowledge were well-established even before the sojourn began. It stands to reason, though, that I was also acquiring sociopragmatic knowledge throughout the sojourn and that the state of that knowledge affected my leave-taking. But to try to trace a path of sociopragmatic learning in the face of a total lack of explicit data about it would be frustratingly speculative. I can only acknowledge that sociopragmatic factors do influence how I took leave, observe that some basic sociopragmatic knowledge is apparently not transferable from my first language and culture, and acknowledge the lack of explicit data about this aspect of learning as a limitation of the study.

Implications of amount of learning for study abroad

There is no doubt that I learned a lot. I especially learned a good deal about the two formulas *permisi* and the *dulu statement*, as well as a good deal about pre-closings, and changed my behavior accordingly. In the last leg of the sojourn, I acquired explicit knowledge about the importance of aligning my leave-taking with the conversation and of ways to do it, and a degree of ability to do it as well.

This demonstrates the high value of the informal, out-of-class interaction offered by study abroad for the learning of pragmatics at an advanced level. Previous studies of study abroad tend to suggest only modest gains for advanced learners in learning pragmatics. However, the insights into my changing states of knowledge revealed by the diary data demonstrate that the informal learning environment can be a powerful stimulus for the acquisition of pragmatic knowledge. A good deal of shaping and re-shaping of pragmatic knowledge with many corresponding changes in behavior may evidently take place during even a short sojourn.

What remains to be learned?

Here, despite the difficulty in judging objectively, the answer clearly seems to be: a great deal. My ability to take leave as evidenced in journal entries was, even in the last weeks, quite low. Although I usually managed to produce leave-takings that I assessed as acceptable, these took conscious effort to produce – rarely did I find it easy to take leave in a social conversation. Furthermore, right up to the end of the sojourn, quite a few of my leave-takings felt awkward and inappropriate.

The main thing that remained to be learned, as I saw it, was the ability to manage conversation. I needed to learn to align my own leave-taking contributions to the development of the interaction. But in fact I probably also had a lot to learn even about aspects of leave-taking that I considered settled at the end of the sojourn. A telling example is my pre-closing formulas. As a postscript to this study: after this three-month sojourn period had ended I remained in Indonesia for some time, and in later months noticed pre-closing formulas used twice in social conversations and concluded that they probably *are* useful after all.[3] So a lot of re-forming knowledge about even the most basic aspects of leave-taking probably lies ahead of me.

Implications for Bialystok's theory

The above has obvious implications for Bialystok's (1993) theory of how adults learn L2 pragmatics. Certainly, the last weeks of the sojourn lend some support to Bialystok's contention that the crucial process is that of gaining control over attention to knowledge. During those weeks I came to regard leave-taking as mainly a matter of gaining skill in managing conversation, in responding on the run to the cues that determine how I should best take leave. But other aspects of the learning process challenge Bialystok's (1993) claim. My acquisition of leave-taking formulas and of pre-closings is primarily a tale of acquiring knowledge itself. I repeatedly revise and firm up my knowledge about both these aspects of leave-taking, as well as learning new forms: the *dulu* statement for leave-taking and *okay (deh)* and *udah (deh)* for pre-closing. So this study confirms the findings of Barron (this volume) and Hassall (2001) in providing only partial support for Bialystok's (1993) model of L2 pragmatic acquisition. It confirms the importance of acquiring control over existing pragmatic knowledge but demonstrates that acquiring knowledge is also a major task for adult learners.

Cognitive and affective factors influencing learning

While we must be cautious in making claims about the relative importance of learning variables from a diary of one learner's experience (cf. Schmidt & Frota, 1986), it is worthwhile pointing out what factors seem crucial in my own case. Both cognitive and affective factors played a large role.

Noticing

Most striking is the key role of conscious noticing. Certain noticings of leave-taking formulas strike me as landmark events in my own learning of formulas (see Samples 1, 5 and 11). Moreover, my noticing of certain pre-closings seems vital in forming my own notions of when I should use a pre-closing (see Samples 7 and 8). My late epiphany that leave-taking can be done without words, too, is apparently triggered by my noticing someone do just that (see Sample 16). So this study affirms the central place asserted by Schmidt (1993) for conscious noticing in the learning of pragmatics.

Post-evaluation

Another key factor is the learning strategy of evaluating my own leave-takings after I have done them. Each time I use a *dulu* statement I assess how successful it was and adjust my knowledge of its appropriateness accordingly. Similarly, I assess each pre-closing I produce as successful or not, and change my notions of whether pre-closings are a good idea largely on the basis of these assessments. In the last leg of the sojourn I decide to avoid formulas when I can after evaluating one of mine as blatantly superfluous. So this learning strategy of post-evaluation is one that I rely on heavily and that strongly shapes my learning path.

Pre-planning

Pre-planning in the form of mentally rehearsing my utterances before saying them is a strategy that greatly influences my learning and my performance. To a degree that strategy is very helpful to me. Mentally rehearsing my leave-takings is sometimes the only way that I can actually produce forms that I have previously noticed and hence integrate them into my active repertoire. However, the strategy also impedes my learning of leave-taking. I come to see it as a curse in some respects, because it locks me prematurely into taking leave in a certain way. Evidently pre-planning can be a seductive habit, one that lends a sense of psychological security but that some learners must learn to abandon in order to acquire certain aspects of pragmatics.

Motivation and aversion

Affective factors influenced my learning greatly. Such factors are always important for second language acquisition but will probably affect the learning of pragmatics and discourse especially since these aspects of language are linked so closely with expression of personality (Schmidt, 1993: 36).

Motivation is one of these factors. I did have some degree of motivation, reflecting early in the sojourn:

(26) I'm conscious of two main reasons for wanting to get better at pragmatics: so I can teach it better back in Australia, and to improve my ability to have social conversations with Indonesians I know back in Australia and ones I meet on visits here. (Diary entry, Padang, Week 3, 11/1/02)

But my motivation was, quite simply, never very strong. I note this at various points in the sojourn. Here is a typical entry:

(27) At the moment I'm not concerned very much whether I learn pragmatics or not. My conscious priorities are elsewhere; my own academic writing especially. I largely measure the success of a day by how much of that I get done. (Diary entry, Padang, Week 5, 28/1/02)

Throughout the sojourn my motivation engages in a tug-of-war with another affective factor: a mild aversion to interaction in Indonesian. I seem to experience a great many social conversations during the sojourn as mildly unpleasant. This is demonstrated by the scattering through diary entries of negative adjectives like 'tense', 'anxious', 'worried' and 'annoyed' to describe my experiences. And I note it explicitly too:

(28) It seems that exercising my skill in pragmatics – which is so intimately bound up with establishing and maintaining social relations – will always be an anxious business, marked by relief when it goes well and by excessive guilt and self-recrimination when it goes badly. (Diary entry, Bukttinggi, Week 7, 12/2/02)

And so my desire to get better at pragmatics battles my dislike of interaction itself. Occasionally my motivation wins out over my aversion. Thus, on two occasions I strike up conversations when I do not feel like it, purely for the practice. But much more often, my aversion wins out. It leads me to avoid interactions even though I know I need them in order to learn. So I observe:

(29) Where I'm consciously a bit slack in learning pragmatics is in range and type of interactions. I know that if I actively tried to build up a social circle, went out socially with people more, lived in a place with a more active social scene ... I'd learn a lot more pragmatics.

> But that sort of life doesn't appeal ... I'm willing to sacrifice my learn-
> ing for my peace of mind. (Diary entry, Padang, Week 3, 11/1/02)

At every place I stay during the sojourn, I repeat this observation that
I am largely avoiding social interaction.

This tug-of-war between competing affective factors confirms
Schumann's (1997) assertion that a learner may appraise a learning
experience as desirable even if unpleasant. Like the learner Eva
Hoffman whom Schumann (1997) discusses in this regard, I desire
social interactions because they are highly relevant to my goal of learning
the language. On the other hand, my case demonstrates quite a different
outcome. While that learner's desire to engage with target language users
consistently triumphed over her dislike of the actual experience, my own
desire to do so consistently yields. So unlike her, I do not manage to
appraise the learning experience positively despite its intrinsic unplea-
santness. This leads us to Schumann's (1997) claim that positive apprai-
sals are essential for sustained deep learning to occur. This study is
certainly consistent with that claim. Sustained deep learning has not
occurred; I have not yet become expert in this basic feature of Indonesian
pragmatics in 15 years of studying the language, and it seems likely that I
will not while I continue to appraise interactions negatively and avoid
them accordingly.

It is significant that I do not see my avoidance of interaction as something to overcome and resolve to change my ways in the future. Rather,
I simply observe my deliberate choice not to interact much. This has
implications for the behavior of learners during study abroad. It confirms
findings that they frequently reject opportunities for interaction in the L2
environment and supports Wilkinson's (2000) contention that this often
reflects a conscious and deliberate decision not to spend time interacting
with native speakers due to a placing of other priorities higher than their
language learning goals.

Influence of learning perspective

A related factor that influences my path of acquisition is my view of
the process as a highly cognitive one. This view is well captured by
Atkinson's (2002) image of 'a single cactus in the middle of a lonely
desert'. Just as the cactus sits and waits for rain, so the L2 learner seems
to 'sit in the middle of a lonely scene and ... wait there for [input] to
come pouring in' (Atkinson, 2002: 525). A sociocognitive view of acquisition evokes the contrasting image of a tropical rainforest: 'a lush
ecology in which every organism operates in complex relationship with

every other organism ... developing continuously and being sustained through its involvement in the whole ecology' (Atkinson, 2002: 526).

I implicitly but strongly hold the former, 'lonely cactus' view of acquisition during the sojourn and this affects my path of learning. For example, until the last month of the sojourn I lacked any explicit awareness that I needed to align my leave-takings with the development of the conversation and made no conscious effort to do so. In other words I ignored a truth that I had known with the force of an axiom since my first postgraduate study in the field of Conversation Analysis; namely, that leave-taking is cooperative. This could not have happened if I had conceived of my learning of leave-taking as a largely social process. In that case I would probably have regarded my task from the outset as one of learning to align my own contributions with those of the other person. This suggests that a strongly cognitive perspective by a learner might make it harder to acquire those features that are at the discourse-end of pragmatics, such as leave-taking.

The observer's paradox

A final factor that affected my learning of leave-taking is the very fact that I was trying to observe how I learned it (the 'observer's paradox' pointed out by Labov, 1972b). Leave-taking loomed a lot larger in my mind during some social conversations than it would have if I had not been keeping a diary. I put pressure on myself to learn it well for reasons of face, wanting to show that I was a capable learner of pragmatics and uneasily conscious that any blunders I made would become in a small way public.

How all this changed my leave-taking in concrete terms is hard to say for certain. But some or all of these are likely effects: I pre-planned my leave-takings more often and further in advance, I performed some of them more awkwardly, and I evaluated them more carefully and anxiously after performing them.

The implications of this for the diary method in investigating language learning are obvious. It shows that for all the advantages of diary data and their unparalleled richness in some respects, the process of collecting diary data can substantially alter the process of learning itself.

Conclusions

This study identifies the stages by which an advanced level learner acquired the speech act of leave-taking during a period of in-country study. It highlights a potential key role for several factors in the process of acquisition: conscious noticing of input, the strategies of pre-planning and post-evaluation, and affective factors such as motivation and aversion.

The study thus confirms Schmidt's (1993) claim that conscious noticing of pragmatic input is crucial for acquiring second language pragmatic knowledge. It challenges Bialystok's (1993) model of pragmatic acquisition by showing that acquiring knowledge can be a major task for the adult learner, and confirms Schumann's (1997) theory of stimulus appraisal in two respects. It illustrates the possible tension between desire for and dislike of learning experiences and, most importantly, seems to confirm that learners must appraise the learning experience positively if they are to learn successfully.

The study also has implications for the learning of pragmatics by advanced learners during study abroad, specifically through the informal exposure to the target language environment that it offers. It reveals that a large amount of learning of pragmatics took place during a short sojourn. This is a useful complement to the findings of studies based mainly on performance data that show progress by advanced learners during much longer sojourns to be only modest or even slight.

In addition, the study sheds light on the observation that learners during study abroad often do not interact much with native speakers. It supports Wilkinson's (2000) contention that these learners may make a conscious and deliberate decision to not spend their time interacting with native speakers due to a placing of other priorities higher than their language learning goals.

Notes

1. The term 'social conversation' is used broadly here to include semi-social conversations that begin as service encounters and then turn into social chat. But it excludes purely transactional service encounters.
2. Schegloff and Sacks (1973) actually use the term 'pre-closing' to refer to a *sequence* of moves, but I have borrowed it to refer to a single move by the one speaker.
3. At that time I was immersed in an English-speaking work environment and was no longer keeping a pragmatic diary beyond sporadic notes. On the first occasion, when a fellow lodger used a pre-closing formula (*Ya deh* 'Right then') to me, I tried to explain it away to myself as a gauche leave-taking on his part but then admitted 'maybe I'm just trying to avoid having to reshape my mental map of how to take leave yet again ... I'd rather just dismiss the idea of pre-closings' (Field note, Bandung, 13/4/02). And the second time, when I heard one (*Udah deh*) used attractively on a TV drama to pre-close a chat with friends, I admitted to myself, 'so pre-closings do have a place in purely social conversations after all' (Field note, Bandung, 30/6/02).

Chapter 3

Learning to Say 'You' in German: The Acquisition of Sociolinguistic Competence in a Study Abroad Context[1]

ANNE BARRON

Introduction

Learning to say 'you' in a foreign language may seem a rather straight-forward and tedious task to the layperson. Many foreign language learners, however, know differently. Indeed, depending on the language in question, mastery of the address system of a language may represent a source of considerable difficulty.

Time spent in the target speech community would appear to represent an ideal opportunity to acquire sociolinguistic competence in aspects of the second language (L2) such as the address system, given the accessibility of authentic input and the potentially extensive opportunities to use the target language. However, in the light of a dearth of interlanguage sociolinguistic and – until recently – study abroad research, it is hardly surprisingly that little is known of the acquisition of L2 sociolinguistic competence during a sojourn in the target speech community.[2] This is especially so for the case of German as a foreign language.

The present study reports on an investigation designed to address this need for interlanguage research in L2 sociolinguistics. Specifically, the study concerns a longitudinal report of the development of the L2 socio-linguistic competence of 33 Irish learners of German in their use of the address system over ten months (termed 'a year abroad' in an Anglo-Saxon context) spent studying in Germany.

After defining sociolinguistic competence, the paper turns to the par-ticular instance of the pronominal address system in German. Here, an overview of previous research is included which highlights the specific areas of difficulty for the foreign language learner in acquiring these forms of address. An outline of the input opportunities presented by the study abroad context is also given. Learner and native speaker (NS) data are then contrasted with a particular focus on learners' choices of address form and on learner-specific features in this verbal behavior. Finally, the changes recorded in learners' knowledge of address register over time spent in the target speech community are detailed and discussed, also in light of current cognitive approaches to language acquisition. The study concludes with suggestions for future research.

Acquiring Sociolinguistic Competence

Sociolinguistic competence is an integral part of communicative competence, and, thus, undoubtedly a competence to be strived for by language learners (cf. Bachman, 1990; Bachman & Palmer, 1996; Canale, 1983; Canale & Swain, 1980). A component of language competence and a sub-component of pragmatic competence, sociolinguistic competence, in Bachman and Palmer's (1996: 70) model of communicative language ability, encompasses 'knowledge of the conventions that determine the appropriate use of dialects or varieties, registers, natural or idiomatic expressions, cultural references and figures of speech'. Knowledge of the address system of a language is an important part of knowledge of the appropriate register. In Bachman and Palmer's model, sociolinguistic competence concerns only knowledge. Ability is the concern of strategic competence and psychophysiological mechanisms. Strategic competence deals with the ability to assess a situation and to plan and produce an utterance verbally. This distinction between knowledge and ability is reminiscent of that made by Faerch and Kasper (1984) between declarative and procedural knowledge, where declarative knowledge is similar to the knowledge component in Bachman and Palmer's model and procedural knowledge similar to strategic competence. The degree to which speakers reveal their level of declarative knowledge depends on situational factors since stress, pressure, fatigue or complex cognitive content may lead to problems of access during communication. In such cases, speakers may produce an inappropriate utterance despite having the relevant declarative knowledge. The problem in such instances lies with speakers' procedural knowledge. Keeping the influence of procedural knowledge to a minimum in order to better access declarative sociolinguistic knowledge will, thus, be an important consideration in the methods chosen for the present study (cf. also Barron, 2003: 8–11, 85).

Forms of address in German

The address system of a language enables a speaker to refer to an interlocutor and to define the social relationship between speaker and addressee (cf. Braun *et al.*, 1986: xvii). In German, the address forms are nominal, verbal and pronominal in nature. As in many Western European languages, apart from English, two pronominal forms of address exist in German. In Brown and Gilman's (1960) terms, the 'intimate/simple' pronoun in German is *du*, the 'polite/distant' pronoun, *Sie*.[3] Table 3.1 presents an overview of the second person singular and plural personal pronouns (inflected for case).[4] Table 3.2 shows the declension of the possessive determiner for the second person singular and plural (also inflected for case) as this is also affected by the *Sie/du* differentiation (cf. Eisenberg, 1999: 170ff; Engel, 1996: 651ff).

In general, the V form (*Sie*) is employed in German where interlocutors use a title and surname to refer nominally to each other, whereas the T form (*du*) is employed among interlocutors on first name terms (cf. Weinrich, 1993: 822).[5] The transition from the *Sie* to the *du* form is an explicit procedure usually initiated by the older/more senior party (*Brüderschaft trinken*). Once offered and accepted, it is not reversed, irrespective of whether the personal relationship between those concerned changes (cf. Ammon, 1972: 80).

The pronouns of address in German only play a role in social indexing. They do *not* function on a strategic level, and *cannot*, therefore, be employed in strategic politeness to attain such goals as promoting or maintaining interpersonal relationships. In other words, the pronouns of address are obligatory signals; the speaker has no choice but to employ an appropriate form unless s/he wishes to ignore or defy the behavioral norms of the society (cf. Thomas, 1995: 152).

A choice of *Sie* in German to refer to an interlocutor generally signals a relationship characterized by formality and distance. It is the norm among adults who do not know each other well. The choice of *du*, on the other hand, denotes an intimate or informal relationship between

Table 3.1 Second person pronominal forms in German

	Nominative		*Accusative*		*Dative*	
	Singular	*Plural*	*Singular*	*Plural*	*Singular*	*Plural*
Informal	du	ihr	dich	euch	dir	euch
Formal	Sie	Sie	Sie	Sie	Ihnen	Ihnen

Table 3.2 Second person possessive determiners in German

	Nominative		Accusative		Dative		Genitive	
	Singular	*Plural*	*Singular*	*Plural*	*Singular*	*Plural*	*Singular*	*Plural*
Informal	dein (e)	deine	dein (en)/(e)	deine	deinem/deiner	deinen	deines/deiner	deiner
Formal	Ihr (e)	Ihre	Ihr (en)/(e)	Ihre	Ihrem/Ihrer	Ihren	Ihres/Ihrer	Ihrer

the interlocutors. Reciprocity of address and symmetry in the address relationship are characteristics of the address system, reflecting the fact that unlike in languages such as Japanese (cf. Besch, 1998: 117ff), for example, status in German is not of direct relevance in the choice of address form. Rather, such issues of status become a question of degree of distance. In other words, while reciprocal use of the V pronoun _Sie_ signals mutual distance and respect, reciprocal use of the T pronoun _du_ indicates mutual familiarity or intimacy. Indeed, a non-reciprocal use of address forms, where the V pronoun is used upwards and the T pronoun downwards, is found very rarely in adult language use. It occurs predominantly in communication with children, immigrant workers and the mentally ill. In other words, non-reciprocity in German mirrors an assessment by the speaker that there is a status-differential between the interlocutors, with the interlocutor of higher status employing the T form and the interlocutor of lower status the V form (cf. Ammon, 1972: 75ff; Lüger, 1993: 37ff). The T/V differentiation is, however, not as strict in the plural as in the singular since the plural T form, _ihr_, is not as intimate as its singular counterpart, _du_. Consequently, the plural T form may be employed in a group situation in which otherwise a _Sie_ form is employed. In such cases, it serves to decrease the formality of the particular situation while still maintaining mutual respect (cf. Lüger, 1993: 38).

The choice of pronoun of address is, however, not as straightforward as just described since the student revolt of 1968 popularized a system of address forms according to which the T form signaled solidarity rather than intimacy. Before this point, the solidarity system of address had only existed to a limited extent among political parties oriented to the left and within trade unions. This development led to an increased use of _du_ (cf. Morché, 1991), and to the existence of two systems of address today, the distance/intimacy system and the solidarity system. The latter system is used widely, but problematically not exclusively, in certain milieus, such as in universities, in the context of leisure activities, and in some branches of industry (cf. Amendt, 1995; Besch, 1998: 20ff; Kirsten, 1999: 254; Lüger, 1993: 43; Pastor, 1995: 3; von Au, 1996: 29f). Indeed, even to date, much uncertainty exists among native speakers in the choice of address form (cf. Besch, 1998: 24f; DAAD, 1999: 17; Glück & Koch: 1998; Zimmer, 1986: 53ff). In certain situations, this uncertainty may result in subtle negotiations regarding the choice of pronoun in interactions between strangers of similar interests and standing. If, for example, a particular interlocutor, A, chooses a familiar _du_ pronoun at the start of the interaction, and this choice is not accepted by the other party, B, then B may respond with a *Sie* pronoun to communicate the unacceptability of the *du* form.

Acquiring L2 German address forms

Mastery of the German address system is a matter of declarative and procedural knowledge. The morphosyntactic possibilities and relevant sociolinguistic rules for communication have to be learned (declarative knowledge), and control over use of these indexical forms in actual communication developed (procedural knowledge). According to Bialystok's (1991, 1993) cognitive two-dimensional information processing model proposed to explain language acquisition, the analysis and representation of L2 knowledge is only a minor task since adult L2 learners have largely completed the task of developing analytic representations of language thanks to first language (L1) knowledge. It involves such tasks as the acquisition of linguistic knowledge and the development of knowledge relating to potentially new social distinctions concerning factors such as age and sex. Rather, the primary task for learners, Bialystok argues, is to gain control over the selection of knowledge, i.e. procedural knowledge must be developed.

The present Irish learners of German have English as their L1. Consequently, mastery of pronominal indexical politeness in German represents a new task since native speakers of English, despite knowing the socio-stylistic variation, are not familiar with distinctions in pronominal reference. Address forms with an indexical politeness function in English include nominal address forms, e.g. titles, such as Mr, Mrs, Dr and Father. Age and professional status are important factors in the choice of such forms, and importantly, the use of these nominal forms in English is often non-reciprocal. In other words, in an interaction in English between a person of higher status and lower status, the person of higher status may use his/her interlocutor's first name, while the individual of lower status may well employ a title, such as Prof X, to address the participant of higher status (cf. Besch, 1998: 126f; Ervin-Tripp, 1971; Zimmer, 1986: 60ff).

Added to such difficulties is, of course, the existence of the two conflicting systems of pronominal address in German, a factor which makes the acquisition of knowledge of contextual variation especially problematic. As Besch (1998: 87) writes in this regard: *'Wenn Einheimische schon Schwierigkeiten haben, wie sollen Ausländer damit fertig werden?'* [If even the natives have difficulties, how are the foreigners to cope with it? (my translation)] (cf. also Belz & Kinginger, 2003).

The communicative effect of non-target-like address behavior by learners is difficult to judge since native speakers often show some lenience towards learners regarding politeness norms, particularly towards learners of lower linguistic competence (cf. Enomoto & Marriott, 1994: 155f). It can nevertheless be suggested that non-target-like behavior is, in general, inappropriate, particularly in the light of the partially ceremonial nature of the switch from *Sie* to *du* among native speakers, and also its irreversibility. Engaging in non-reciprocal behavior among adults – a convention described by von Au (1996: 33) as *'absolut tabu'* (absolutely taboo), will also, it is suggested, disadvantage the learner, bestowing on their interactions the flavor of an interaction between non-equals. Indeed, many of the German NS in Belz and Kinginger's (2003) study of e-mail communication between German NSs and US learners commented explicitly on the American learners' inappropriate use of these forms.

Research on the acquisition of the L2 address system in German is rather limited. There exists a cross-sectional study by Norris (2001) and a recent longitudinal study by Belz and Kinginger (2003). Norris examines the competence in pronominal address of L1 English American learners of German at different levels of proficiency (high school and university students), concentrating on issues of frequency, sociopragmatic accuracy and morphosyntactic range. The focus of Norris' study is, however, less on acquisitional issues and more on investigating the extent to which interpretations concerning pronominal address competence on the German Speaking Test, a simulated oral proficiency interview, are justified. Belz and Kinginger (2003), on the other hand, analyze how telecollaborative interaction (via e-mail) can facilitate the development of American learners' use of the T form in German over time. A certain amount of research also exists on the use and acquisition of the address system of other languages by foreign/second language learners. These findings, along with those by Norris and Belz and Kinginger, show a number of areas of difficulty for learners, as detailed in the following. They also focus on developmental issues to a limited extent.

Lower relative frequency of use of address forms

Norris (2001) found learners to use a lower frequency of pronominal address forms in tasks requiring the use of formal pronominal address forms compared to tasks demanding use of informal forms. He points out, however, that although this finding may reflect learners' tendency to avoid formal address forms, it may also be a strategic option given a higher level of face-threat in the more formal tasks. Also, DuFon (in press), in a study focusing on six learners of Indonesian during a four-month study abroad period in a homestay environment in Indonesia, found her informants to produce fewer terms of address than native speakers in naturalistic recordings involving learners and native speakers. Individual variation was, however, also noted.

As far as the relationship between proficiency and address forms is concerned, Norris reports that higher proficiency learners scored higher frequency-wise in the production of address forms across various morphosyntactic categories. However, these latter results should be viewed with caution in light of the relationship between the waffle phenomenon, a common feature of interlanguage data which has been shown to increase with increasing proficiency. In other words, more proficient learners may simply have said more than those of lower proficiency, and may therefore have produced more address forms.[6]

Lack of sociolinguistic accuracy in the use of L2 address forms

Norris (2001: 265 passim) found learners to use a low level of formal pronouns in situations demanding a formal form. However, high levels of sociolinguistic accuracy were recorded in the use of pronouns in these same situations. A high use of pronouns was, on the other hand, characteristic of situations where a familiar pronoun was needed, but levels of sociolinguistic accuracy were considerably lower in such instances. Overall, informants' ability to make sociopragmatically accurate address register selections appeared to increase with increases in global proficiency. However, individual variation in accuracy of address register also characterized the findings, particularly those of the upper proficiency levels. Sociolinguistic inaccuracy was also a feature of the e-mail data analyzed by Belz and Kinginger (2003). They recorded target-like developments in the use of the T form in German as a result of telecollaborative interaction with NSs – interaction which often included explicit instruction from the participating NSs.

The sociopragmatically appropriate use of L2 address forms appears to cause similar difficulties in other languages. Hassall (1997: 132f), for example, reporting on the acquisition of address terms in L2 requests in Indonesian, observed learners' selection of an inappropriate use of formal and intimate pronouns to be a striking feature of his role-play data. DuFon (in press) also found a similar tendency in her naturalistic data despite differences in the two studies with respect to the proportion of use of the various forms. Finally, a further study by Marriott (1995) investigated the acquisition of politeness norms of eight low-level proficiency Australian secondary school students of Japanese who spent a year in Japan. She found those learners who had employed the polite honorific style to a limited extent and with difficulty prior to their sojourn abroad overused the plain style following their year abroad.

Switching

Hassall observed learners to switch between formal and intimate pronouns in one utterance (cf. Hassall, 1997: 185), a finding also reported by Belz and Kinginger (2003: 621) and by Faerch and Kasper (1989) in a study of Danish learners' request realizations in German elicited using a discourse completion task (DCT). Faerch and Kasper (1989: 230f) explain this feature of their data with reference to morphological and sociolinguistic difficulties, the latter factor involving transfer from Danish, a language which also includes a T/V distinction, but whose distribution contrasts with that of German.

More limited grammatical functions in use of terms of address

In DuFon (in press), learners were found to use address terms in a vocative slot considerably less than native speakers. Also, the function of those vocatives realized was much more limited than in the native speaker data. This non-target-like use of vocatives continued after the learners' four-month homestay experience.

Sociolinguistic input in the study abroad context

Schmidt's noticing hypothesis (1990, 1993) is a cognitive model of L2 acquisition. It states that there is no evidence for subliminal learning in L2 acquisition. Rather, Schmidt believes that learners acquire a language by consciously noticing (whether incidentally or intentionally) and consequently understanding gaps between their interlanguage (IL) knowledge of both L2 linguistic form and sociolinguistic constraints and that of a native speaker. In other words, consciously noticing gaps between one's IL and L2 input is an important aspect of L2 acquisition.

Study abroad would appear to offer students a large amount of L2 input and also many opportunities for output, both of which would seem to provide a favorable context for the development of L2 sociolinguistic competence in the use of address forms. In reality, however, it appears that appropriate input is not guaranteed by a second language context. A basic problem with accessing appropriate input is that it is often difficult for study abroad students to establish contact with native speakers of the target L2. In third level institutions in Germany, for example, students are largely required to structure their own pace of study and choice of courses. Consequently, the university can be a rather anonymous place.[7] In addition, groups of students of the same L1, often friends, engage in study abroad. In language classes designed for study abroad students in the target speech community, these L1 groups then meet other study abroad students. As a result, learners frequently socialize with other study abroad students of the same or different L1s (cf. Boa, 1999; Maiworm *et al.*, 1993: 127; Pellegrino, 1998). On the one hand, contact with L1 speakers may play an important role in learners' adjustment to the target culture by helping to reduce possible culture shock (cf. Alptekin, 1983: 820; Brown, 1986: 35; Wilkinson, 1998a: 30ff; 1998b: 28). However, even if students speak to each other in the target language, the large amount of interlanguage talk means that the potential for development in L2 competence may not be fully exploited (cf. Porter, 1986: 215ff).

However, even with access to native speakers in the target language context, communication between a learner and these native speakers cannot be taken for granted (cf. Churchill, 2001; Rivers, 1998); and even in cases where it is given, appropriate input may not be available. Regan (1995), for example, found that the non-prestige form of negation in French was overgeneralized by Irish learners of French following a year abroad in the target speech community. Regan (1998: 72f) suggests minimal contact with users of the prestige form, such as university lecturers, to explain this development.[8] Availability of input is especially difficult in cases of non-reciprocity. Marriott (1995), for example, who found her Australian students of Japanese to increasingly overgeneralize the plain style over the year abroad, explains this by the fact that students in a homestay environment were predominantly exposed to the plain style rather than to the polite style, and also by the fact that the polite style was non-reciprocal. In other words – although students were expected to use the polite style towards superiors, such as teachers, these seniors used the plain style towards them. As a result, input and output opportunities of the polite style were limited. In addition, negative feedback was limited.

Finally, foreigner talk may also decrease the level of input of certain address forms. DuFon (in press) notes, for example, that beginners in her study were exposed to vocatives to a lesser degree than intermediate students. Also Siegal (1995b) and Iino (1996) note that native speakers of Japanese use the second person pronoun, *anata* (employed in addressing equals or subordinates), more extensively when interacting with learners than with other native speakers (cf. also Iino this volume; Schmidt & Richards, 1980: 146 on modified language input).

Method

The present study deals with learners' developing sociolinguistic competence over a year abroad, where sociolinguistic competence is operationalized as declarative knowledge of the forms of address. Specifically, the study concerns learners' knowledge of the use of pronominal address forms (including use of the second person possessive determiners) over time. It also examines the applicability of Bialystok's (1991, 1993) theory with respect to the role of declarative and procedural knowledge in the L2 acquisition of sociolinguistics.

Informants

Thirty-three Irish learners of German who spent 10 months studying in a German university/institute of technology in one of 14 different cities and towns form the learner corpus in the present analysis. Immediately prior to their year abroad, these learners ranged in age from 18 to 21 years, the average age being 19.3 years. Of the students, 78.8% were female.[9] Students were judged to be advanced adult learners of German based on the extent of their exposure to German (seven to eight years of formal instruction) and also on their subjective evaluations of their language competence.[10] Previous time spent in the target speech community ranged from zero to six months (cf. Barron, 2003, for further details of the informants). During their stay abroad, students lived in student accommodations and attended regular courses as well as courses especially designed for foreign students.

In addition, native speaker production data was elicited from 34 NSs of German at the University of Hamburg. These informants were 25.6 years on average, and 67.6% were female. Although having the advantage of being homogeneous and also comparable to the learner data, this NS data regrettably did not account for regional differences in address behavior to which students may have been exposed.

A system of code-names is employed in the present study to protect the identity of all informants. The learners are identified via the initial 'L', and the native speakers of German via the initial 'G'. The letter 'F' indicates a female informant, 'M' a male informant.

Data collection

Data were elicited three times from the learners at intervals of seven months (i.e. over a 14-month span): prior to (T1 data), during (T2 data) and towards the end (T3 data) of the year abroad, and once from the NS group. In the present study, only the T1 and T3 learner data are considered. The rather long period of seven months between data collection sessions is seen as advantageous since it is unlikely that informants were able to remember what they had written previously. As a result, potential practice effects due to possible consultation with either native speakers or of reference materials were reduced.[11]

The instrument employed was a type of production questionnaire, namely the free discourse completion task (FDCT), developed in Barron (2003) to elicit sequential aspects of offers and refusals of offers. This research instrument essentially requires respondents to imagine themselves in a series of situations and to write both sides of an open role-play or dialogue for each situation (cf. Appendix for an example).

The FDCT is a descendent of the discourse completion task (DCT), the first and most well-known questionnaire used in cross-cultural and interlanguage pragmatics. It has often been condemned from a general standpoint, and indeed, production questionnaires have been shown not to yield as rich or as much data as ethnographic methods or role-plays (cf. Beebe & Cummings, 1996; Billmyer & Varghese, 2000; Eisenstein & Bodman 1993; Johnston *et al.*, 1998; Turnbull, 2001; Yuan, 2001). However, we must keep in mind Bardovi-Harlig's (1999: 238) comment that 'We need to get away from the best-method mentality, and return to the notion of customizing the research design to fit the question'.

The FDCT offers many advantages over authentic data or role-play data for the present analysis. First, it allows for efficient elicitation of comparable data from large groups of different informants across time. It also permits the researcher to manipulate contextual variables. The primary reason for the choice of this instrument for the present study was, however, the fact that the FDCT, given its written form and the time available for contemplation, allows investigation *not* of learners' use of the address system in authentic discourse, but rather of their declarative knowledge of this system since it facilitates the collection of data 'offline', i.e. the participant is required to recall sociolinguistic information from memory and report on it rather than use it (cf. Kasper, 2000: 317). This is a crucial point since learners' underlying level of knowledge may otherwise not be reflected in the data gathered, if they are overburdened by fatigue, complex interpersonal relationships or cognitive overload as a result of difficulties which they may experience interacting in a particular 'on-line' situation where time for contemplation is at a minimum. In other words, the FDCT minimizes the effect which a lack of procedural knowledge may have on concealing sociolinguistic knowledge (cf. also Bergman & Kasper, 1993: 101; Cohen, 1997: 149). Indeed, comments from a number of informants in the retrospective interviews conducted within the larger research project (Barron, 2000, 2003) point to the difficulty of accessing knowledge in on-line communication. After completing a role-play of the offer/refusal of offer situations, one learner volunteered the following comment:

(1) LA14F, lift situation:
I kept switching between *Sie* and *du* . . . I don't do it as much () like () normally () but I did it () I noticed I did it a good bit during () the role-play

Similarly, in a retrospective interview, learner LA24F reported a similar difficulty of concealed sociolinguistic knowledge in a natural context.

(2) LA24F, lift situation:
. . . I'm used to speaking to people my own age and I always use *du*. When I meet people's parents, I automatically say *du* and I shouldn't or else half *du* and half *Sie*.

In addition, since informants play the part of a person other than themselves for one participant in the FDCT dialogue, the instrument provides information on informants' expectations of a potential interlocutor's use of the address system. In other words, it gives access to a wider understanding of the declarative system of address in the L2 than would be attainable with authentic data. As far as the NS data is concerned, the FDCT enables elicitation of stereotypical interactions in the minds of respondents and, as such, portrays the socially accepted use of address forms in a particular culture (cf. Turnbull, 2001: 49).

On the negative side, the most important limitation concerns the fact that informants interact with an imaginary interlocutor until an appropriate compromise is found. The consequences of an inappropriate choice of address form are, thus, not as serious as in real life communication. Consequently, it is possible that the degree of avoidance may be lower than in a natural setting.

Table 3.3 provides an overview of the FDCT situations and of the prompts given from the point of view of the choice of a T or V form of address. The situations represent varying constellations of social distance and social dominance. In all situations, one informant in each dialogue is a student since the informants were required to put themselves in the particular situation described. The identity of the other interlocutor, the relationship between the student and this person, and thus the appropriate choice of pronominal address form, is communicated via clues pertaining to age, degree of familiarity between both interlocutors, social status, and other variables given in the situational descriptions.

Table 3.3 Situational descriptions of FDCT items

Situation	Synopsis of situation	Sie/du clues	Address form suggested by situation
Accident	Following being knocked off his/her bike by car driven by priest, student refuses priest's offer to bring him/her to hospital.	- V form given in initiating utterance *Es tut mir wirklich leid. Geht's Ihnen gut?* (I'm really sorry. Are you [singular V form] okay?) - No first name or surname given for priest, i.e. social distance	- Distance *Sie*
Beverage	Uncle in area calls by. Niece/nephew (student) offers him refreshments. Uncle refuses.	- T form given in verbal address form in initiating utterance (... *Komm rein...* (Come in [singular T form, imperative]...) - No social distance (related)	- Intimate *du*
Lift	After guest-lecture, professor offers students who live near him a lift home. They refuse.	- No names given and age difference, i.e. social distance	- Unclear: university context: distance *Sie* or solidarity *du*
Work experience	Student offers to help new boss's son with economics. Boss refuses help.	- No names given and age difference, i.e. social distance	- Distance *Sie*
Bag	Student offers stranger of same age help carrying suitcases in airport. Stranger refuses help.	- No names given, i.e. social distance - Same age, i.e. solidarity	- Solidarity *du* or distance *Sie* possible

(continued)

Table 3.3 Continued

Situation	Synopsis of situation	Sie/du clues	Address form suggested by situation
Math	Student offers friend help in math before an exam. Friend refuses help.	- First name given, good friend, i.e. no social distance - Student interaction, same age, i.e. solidarity	- Intimate/ solidarity *du*

In a number of cases, i.e. in the accident and beverage situations, the dialog has been initiated and already includes a particular pronominal or verbal address form.

Developments in saying 'you' in L2 German

Coding of the present data involved identifying instances of a clear choice of address form in the use of the personal pronoun or the possessive determiner, an avoidance of address forms or switching between address forms. In a second step, the types of switching were analyzed to reveal learner-specific features of address behavior. In line with Blum-Kulka *et al.*, (1989: 275), misunderstood responses were treated as missing values, as were non-completed items.

Learner use of address forms over time

Table 3.4 shows the use which Irish learners and German NSs made of pronominal address forms. Here, in each data set, both interactants or only one interactant may have used a second person pronoun of address (or a second person possessive determiner). Alternatively, no pronoun of address may have been employed (coded as an avoidance strategy).[12]

All six situations elicited pronominal indexical address forms from German NSs. An avoidance strategy is only employed in the bag situation, and here only by one informant. The sub-strategy used in this case is to avoid addressing the interlocutor directly [G7F: *T'schuligung, könnte ich vielleicht beim Tragen behilflich sein?* (Excuse me, could I maybe be of help carrying those?)].

Table 3.4 Choice of pronominal address form (including second person possessive determiners)*

	Accident			Beverage			Lift			Work			Bag			Math		
	NS	T1	T3	NS	T1	T3	NS	T1	T3	NS	T1	T3	NS	T1	T3	NS	T1	T3
Sie	93.7	51.5	57.6	—	15.6	—	61.8	45.4	32.3	100.0	47.1	54.5	8.8	31.2	33.3	—	—	—
du	6.2	18.2	21.2	100.0	62.5	86.7	26.5	24.2	29.0	—	23.5	21.2	88.2	46.9	57.6	100.0	84.4	100.0
Avoidance	—	3.0	—	—	—	—	—	—	—	—	—	3.0	2.9	—	3.0	—	—	—
Switching	—	27.3	21.2	—	21.9	13.3	11.8	30.3	38.7	—	29.4	21.2	—	21.9	6.1	—	15.6	—

* All figures are expressed in percentages.

There is a large degree of harmony in the choice of pronouns among native speakers. In three of the six situations at hand, all of the German NS informants choose the same address register, all choosing *du* in the beverage and math situations, and *Sie* in the work experience situation. In addition, despite some individual variation, a large degree of agreement exists in a further two situations, i.e. in the accident and bag situations. Here, the use of *du* by the priest in the dialogues of 6.2% of informants for the accident situation is surprising as the V form is given in the initial utterance and should therefore be reciprocated. Native speakers asked to comment on this data found its use inexplicable and confusing. Variation in the bag situation, on the other hand, is thought to be a result of the uncertainty which exists among native speakers as to the appropriate system of address, i.e. the system of solidarity or distance. This uncertainty is more clearly seen in the lift situation where a significant lack of unanimity is apparent in the NS data – probably due to the student/professor constellation, where a solidarity *du* or a distance *Sie* could be appropriate.

In the learner data in T1 prior to the year abroad, as in the NS data, avoidance is infrequent (cf. Table 3.4). In the only instance in which it occurs, it follows via use of the inclusive we, an appropriate strategy for avoiding the choice of an address form in the context given [LA22F: Accident situation: *Vielleicht, sollen wir ins Krankenhaus zu fahren* (Maybe we should go to the hospital)].[13]

Such learner verbal behavior does not support findings by Norris (2001) that learners use a lower frequency of pronominal address forms in German, specifically in those tasks requiring the use of formal address forms (cf. above). Differing levels of face-threat may be the reason for this difference since Norris himself observes that this tendency of learners to avoid formal address forms may be a strategic option in more formal tasks. Alternatively, the low degree of avoidance in the present data may be a function of the elicitation instrument given the smaller degree of interaction inherent in the written FDCT in comparison with oral interaction such as in Norris (2001). In other words, learners in the present study may have been tempted to choose a second person personal pronoun or possessive determiner even when linguistically insecure about a particular choice as the consequences are not the same as in real-life interaction. Alternatively, low avoidance levels may simply point to a limited repertoire of avoidance strategies.

Unlike the German NS data, the learner data is characterized by a lack of unanimity in choice of address form. Such findings reflect those of

DuFon (in press), Hassall (1997: 132f) and Norris (2001), who find a lack of sociopragmatic accuracy in learners' use of L2 pronominal forms. However, unlike Norris' data, higher levels of accuracy in situations demanding a formal term of address are not found in the present data. Indeed, it is only in the math situation, a situation characterized by a lack of social distance, that there is unanimity among the learners in T1 that *du* is the appropriate term of address (switching aside) (84.4% *du*, 15.6% switching). This choice of pronoun reflects the German NS choice in this situation (100% *du*). The ambiguity found in the use of address forms in the lift situation in T1 also reflects German NS behavior and is proposed to be a result of the insecurity existing in the university setting as to the choice of a system of address dictated by solidarity or intimacy.

In other cases, however, where *Sie* is the clear choice for NSs, the learners use *du* to a rather large extent. In the accident situation, for example, the choice of V form should be straightforward since this form is given in the initiating utterance. Nonetheless, switching aside, over 18.2% of learners choose the T form. Also, in the work experience situation, where 100% of the German NSs choose *Sie*, 23.5% of the learners opt for a *du* form (excluding the use of *du* where switching occurs). Similarly, in the beverage and bag situations, where there is a very high level of unanimity in the NS data towards a choice of *du* (beverage: 100% *du*; bag: 88.2% *du*), the learners employ a *Sie* form to quite a large extent – 15.6% in the beverage situation and 31.2% in the bag situation – again despite the fact that the T form has already been explicitly indicated in the initiating utterance in the beverage situation.

The widespread inappropriate choice of register in the learner data is clearly not a 'playing-it-safe' strategy as often found in interlanguage data (cf. Barron, 2003; Faerch & Kasper, 1989: 245). In fact, learners overuse the T form in situations where the V form is appropriate (accident and work experience situations), rather than being careful and continuously over-using the V form. Instead, learners' non-target-like choices of address form are predominantly due, it is suggested, to a lack of sociolinguistic declarative knowledge. Specifically, learners do not appear to have mastered the principle of reciprocity, as seen in the accident and beverage situations here where the prompt given included an explicit choice of address form (this will be seen in more detail below). Also, with the possible exception of the math situation, learners do not appear adept at reading and linking the sociolinguistic constraints of the situations given with the appropriate T or V form.

Table 3.4 also shows learners' choice of register at the end of their 10-month stay. As can be seen here, avoidance levels do not undergo any change. Rather, learners continue to only use an avoidance strategy to a minimal extent. Avoidance strategies employed include not mentioning who is to be helped – e.g. in the bag situation where it is clear from the situation that it is the addressee who is to be helped [LA25M, Bag situation: *Darf ich helfen?* (May I help?)].

Developments in learners' use of *Sie* and *du* over time spent in the target speech community appear rather modest. Indeed, the only noteworthy changes that occur are those in the beverage situation. Here there is a decrease in learners' employment of the *Sie* form and an increase in their use of the *du* form, a development towards German NS use. In fact, at the end of the year, similar to the NSs, all learners not engaging in switching obey the reciprocal principle and indeed the sociolinguistic constraints of this situation, both of which dictate use of a *du* form. This development may be due to learners' greater understanding of the link between the sociolinguistic constraints of the situation and the appropriate choice of address register or of the principle of reciprocity. However, the same cannot be said of the accident situation which also explicitly investigates reciprocity. Also notable is the fact that, the overall reductions in learners' tendency to engage in switching, discussed in detail in the following, led to a more NS-like choice of pronominal address form in the bag, math and beverage situation, i.e. in the informal situations characterized by a lower degree of cognitive complexity. In other words, there is less switching in the informal situations in T3 and this leads to more target-like behavior in choice of address forms. It is to issues of switching which we now turn.

Learner-specific behavior

One of the most important differences between the German NS and the learner data has so far only been fleetingly addressed – namely the large differences in the amount of switching between the T and V forms. Switches occur in the NS data in one situation only, namely in the lift situation. These switches are of the following type only [cf. Example 3]:

(3)   G29F, lift situation:

Professor: *kann ich <u>euch</u> beide ein Stück mitnehmen.*
Du: *Nein, danke, das ist nett von <u>Ihnen</u>, aber wir möchten noch gerne einen kurzen Abstecher in eine Kneipe machen.*

Professor: *Dann wünsche ich Ihnen noch einen schönen Abend. Wir sehen uns dann morgen in der Vorlesung. Tschüß!*
Du: *Ich wünsche Ihnen auch noch einen schönen Abend, bis morgen dann. Tschüß! . . .*

Professor: Can I bring you [plural T form] both a bit of the way?
You: No thanks, that's kind of you [singular V form], but we want to go to the pub for a quick drink.
Professor: Have [V form] a nice evening so. See you tomorrow in the lecture. Bye!
You: A nice evening to you [singular V form] too. See you tomorrow. Bye! . . .

In this situation, the professor offers the students a lift using the plural T form and one of the students responds using the singular V form to address the professor. There are a number of possible interpretations for this non-reciprocal behavior. Firstly, the professor may have used a plural T form [which is not as intimate as the singular T form *du* (cf. above)] in order to lessen the formality of the situation, in harmony, it may be suggested, with a possible atmosphere at a guest lecture. The student's use of the V form in the next turn then reflects his/her assessment of the relationship with the professor, an assessment which does not contradict the professor's previous use of a plural T form. At this point, the professor switches from the plural T form he had used to a V form ('*Dann wünsche ich Ihnen noch einen schönen Abend*' [Have [plural V form] a nice evening so)]. This switch has a number of possible explanations. It could, for example, function to increase the formality of the situation, in line with the professor's mention of his lecture on the following day in the same turn [*Wir sehen uns dann morgen in der Vorlesung* (See you in the lecture tomorrow)]. A second, but more unlikely, interpretation may be that the plural T was addressed to both students, whereas the *Ihnen* in the professor's second turn may represent a singular rather than a plural V form addressed only to the person who has responded to his offer. Finally, it is also possible that the switch by the professor may represent negotiation of address form. The professor, although usually on *Sie* terms with his students, may have used the plural T form in order to change this relationship and become more familiar with the students. This is a safe method given that the plural T form is less intimate than the singular T form. The student's use of *Sie* in response may represent a rejection of this heightened solidarity or intimacy.

Consequently, this would explain why in this scenario, the professor, in his next turn, reverts to a V form.

In the learner data in T1, switches between *du* and *Sie* within one item are a prominent feature of all six offer/refusal of offer situations – supporting findings of switching in research by Hassall (1997: 185), Belz and Kinginger (2003) and Faerch and Kasper (1989). To take a closer look at the magnitude of, and types of, switching, Table 3.5 provides details of choice of address form in those interactions in which both partners employed an address form, i.e. the data in Table 3.5 is a subset of that presented in Table 3.4.

Here we see that a large number of these interactions involved a switch of some sort in T1. The type of switch identified in the German NS data above [non-reciprocal switch, plural T form (*ihr/Sie*)] is not, however, widespread. Indeed, in T1 such target-like *ihr/Sie* switches only occur in 4.5% of all interactions, or in 10.7% of all switches (total number of switches in T1 is 28). Instead, learners engage in learner-specific switching. Two particular types of such switching are identified, one which I

Table 3.5 Choice of address form as a percentage of all interactions in which both partners use an indexical address form

	Total T1 (*n* = 67)	Total T3 (*n* = 81)
Target-like use of address form		
Sie/Sie	9 (13.4%)	19 (23.4%)
du/du	30 (44.8%)	40 (49.4%)
Avoidance	— (0%)	— (0%)
Non-reciprocal switch, plural T form (*ihr*)/*Sie*	3 (4.5%)	6 (7.4%)
Total target-like	42 (62.7%)	65 (80.2%)
Non-target-like use of address form		
Non-reciprocal functional switch (social power)	8 (11.9%)	4 (4.9%)
Non-functional switch	15 (22.4%)	12 (14.8%)
Switch combination (non-reciprocal functional switch and non-functional switch)	2 (3%)	0 (0%)
Total non-target-like	25 (37.3%)	16 (19.7%)

term a 'non-functional switch', the other a 'non-reciprocal functional switch'. These types of switches are detailed below.

Non-functional switches

Non-functional switches are switches between the T and V forms of address which occur in the learner data within one dialogue without fulfilling any function. There appear to be a number of reasons for such instances of switching in the present corpus. First, highly automated pragmatic routines appear to play a role as can be seen in Example 4.

(4) LA1F, Bag situation:

Du: *Entschuldigung <u>Sie</u> bitte. Ich habe gemerkt, daß <u>du</u> zwei großen Koffer hast. Kann ich <u>dir</u> helfen?*

Junge Frau: *Nein danke. Mein Bruder ist ins Geschäft gegangen. Er kommt in nur zwei Minuten zurück. Aber danke. Das ist sehr nett von <u>Dir</u>.*

You: Excuse me please [singular V form]. I noticed that you've [singular T form] two big cases. Can I help you [singular T form]?

Girl: No thanks. My brother has gone into the shop. He'll be back in just two minutes. But thanks. That's very kind of you [singular T form]

Here, it appears that the learner intended to use a reciprocal T form since a singular T form is employed twice in the first turn, and the recipient of the offer also employs the T form. In this case, it is the learner-specific routine '*Entschuldigung Sie bitte*', based on the target form '*Entschuldigen Sie bitte*' (excuse me please), which is suggested to cause the inappropriate non-functional switch between registers within the first speaker's utterance. This learner's use of the pronominal V form in this instance is suggested to relate to input from the foreign language classroom where many role-play situations, e.g. asking directions, involve use of the pragmatic routine '*Entschuldigen Sie bitte*' in the V form.

On the other hand, morphological difficulties may also cause non-functional switching, as seen in Example 5.

(5) LA9F, work experience situation:

Du: *Entschuldigung Frau Schröder, Ich habe gerade gehört was <u>sie</u> gesagt haben. Ich studiere Wirtschaft in der Schule. Wenn <u>sie</u> es wollen ich konnte <u>dein</u> Sohn ein bißchen Hilfe geben.*

Neue Chefin: *Das ist sehr nett von <u>ihr</u>. Aber es ist nicht nötig. ...*

You: Excuse me Mrs Schröder, I just heard what you [singular V form] said. I study economics in school. If you [singular V form] want, I could give your [singular T form] son a bit of help.

New boss: That's very kind of you [singular V form]. But it's not necessary. . . .

There seems to be a clear decision here that the student should use a V form when speaking to her new boss. This is seen in the student's first turn where two V forms are employed. However, there is also a switch within this first turn, and a singular possessive determiner in the T form follows on directly from a singular pronominal V form. The T form here, *dein*, should read *Ihrem* [plural V form] according to the learner's assessment of the situation as requiring a V form of address. The presence of the T form in this instance is not due to any routine pattern which has been automated as it is grammatically incorrect (it should be *deinem* (dative) rather than *dein*); instead it is suggested to point to morphological confusion and the importance of the interplay between grammatical and sociolinguistic competence – a finding supporting previous research by Faerch and Kasper (1989: 230f) for Danish learners of German (cf. above). Indeed, similar morphological difficulties in the pronouns of address are also seen in the boss's reply [*Das ist sehr nett von ihr* (That's very kind of you [singular V form])]. Here *ihr* should, in fact, read *ihnen* (dative).

Finally, a further cause of non-functional switching in the learner data appears to be learner insecurity regarding an appropriate choice of pronominal address form. No such learner insecurity is explicitly present without doubt in the sub-set of data which includes a choice of address form by both interlocutors (i.e. data presented in Table 3.5). However, since this factor is found to be an important explanation for switching in the greater data set, it is mentioned in the present context. In Example 6 here, for instance, we have a switch from a V form to a T form in the priest's first turn.

(6)   LA26F, accident situation:

Pfarrer: *Sie sind sicher, daß du keine ernste Probleme haben?*
Du: *Ja, alles ist in Ordnung.*
Pfarrer: *Ich möchte Sie ins Krankenhaus zu fahren. . . .*
Priest: Are you [singular V form] sure that you [singular T form] don't have any serious problems?
You: Yes, everything is alright.
Priest: I would like to bring you [singular V form] to the hospital. . . .

Looking at the first utterance alone, it may seem at first sight that the choice of a V form is due to the formally similar formula *Sind Sie sicher?* (Are you sure?), a pragmatic routine in English which has been found to be often transferred into German by Irish learners of German (cf. Barron, 2003), and one may assume that the learner actually wishes the priest to employ a T form. However, such is seen not to be the case as the priest employs a V form once more in his second turn. It seems, therefore, that this particular learner's switching is due to uncertainty as to which pronominal form she should use.

Non-functional *Sie/du* switches, some of which occur within one interlocutor's turn, others which occur in one interlocutor's speech over a number of turns, are quite numerous in T1, amounting to 22.4% (plus a further 3% in combination with other switches) of all dialogs in which both parties made an explicit choice of address form (cf. Table 3.5). Of all the 28 switches present in this data set, 53.6% were non-functional (a further 7.1% included this switch in combination). As was illustrated here, they result from highly automated routine formulae, from morphological difficulties, or from learners' insecurity in the choice of *Sie/du* accompanied by a lack of avoidance strategies.

Non-reciprocal functional switches

Non-reciprocal functionally-oriented *Sie/du* switches are also found in the learner data. In T1, as many as 11.9% (plus 3% in combination with other switches) of all choices of address forms in interactions in which reciprocal behavior could potentially be observed involved such switches (cf. Table 3.5). These switches differ from the non-functional switches just discussed in that learners engage in non-reciprocal functional switching purposely in contrast to the case of non-functional switches which result from insecurities, morphological difficulties or the use of an automated routine. Example 7 serves to illustrate this type of switch.

(7)   LC6M, work experience situation:

Du: *Entschuldigen* Sie *bitte, Frau Möller. Ich habe gehört, daß* Ihr *Sohn Schwierigkeiten mit Wirtschaft hat.*

Neue Chefin: *Ja, das stimmt. Warum fragst* Du*?*

Du: *Ich habe das Fach für funf Jähre studiert. Vielleicht könnte ich etwa machen, um* Ihr *Sohn zu helfen.*

Neue Chefin: *Danke schön für* Deine *angebot, aber ich würde lieber, wenn er sich selbst etwa versucht, um die Situation zu verbessern. Er muß einfach lernen, aber er ist sehr faul*

You:	Excuse me please [singular V form], Mrs Möller. I heard that your [singular V form] son is having difficulty with economics.
New boss:	Yes, that's correct. Why do you [singular T form] ask?
You:	I've studied the subject for five years. Maybe I could do something to help your [singular V form] son.
New boss:	Thank you for your offer [singular T form], but I would prefer if he tried to improve the situation himself. He just has to study but he's very lazy.

Unlike the non-functional switches identified, non-reciprocal functional switches do not occur within one turn or within the turns of one person. Rather, each interlocutor is assigned a particular form of address and employs this consistently. Such switches only occur in the present data where one interlocutor is of a higher status than the other, and the interlocutor of lower status is the recipient of *du*, the other the recipient of *Sie*. In the particular situation in Example 7, the work experience situation, it is the boss who consistently uses the T form to the student while the student consistently employs the V form when addressing his boss. In light of the reciprocal nature of the German system of address, non-reciprocal functional switches are not possible in the German system unless one of the interlocutors is mentally deranged or a child of 14 years or less. As neither scenario is the case in the situation at hand, we can conclude that non-reciprocal functional switches are the result of a lack of declarative knowledge of the L2 system – they exhibit learner creativity with the resources of the L2 system.

It is suggested that this characteristic of the learner data is the result of negative sociolinguistic transfer from the learners' L1 since address forms with an indexical politeness function, such as titles, are often employed non-reciprocally in Irish English (cf. above). In the work experience situation in Example 7, for instance, the boss is clearly socially dominant to the student, both on the grounds of professional status and age. It is argued that the Irish learners feel the need to show respect in such situations and that they do so by employing the resources of the L2 in an L1 manner, i.e. non-reciprocally.

Switching: Development issues

At a first glance, Table 3.5 seems to suggest that learners' address behavior includes less of both types of learner-specific *Sie/du* switches with time spent in the target speech community. This is indeed the case for non-functional switches which decrease from T1 to T3. While these amounted to 22.4% (plus 3% combinations) in T1, this figure drops to 14.8% at the end of the learners' year abroad. It is noteworthy that the most significant decreases in non-functional switching were recorded in situations in which a T form was appropriate (i.e. the beverage, bag and math situations) (cf. Table 3.4).

Learners' creative use of non-reciprocal functional forms of address as a signal of social dominance is also seen to decrease over time. In Table 3.5 we see its use decreasing from 11.9% (plus 3% in combination with other switches) in T1 to 4.9% in T3. However, care must be taken in the interpretation of these results. If we look, for example, at the figures for the target-like non-reciprocal switches (plural T form), these amount to 7.4% in T3. It may have been that the learners were not aware of the differences in intimacy between use of the singular and plural T form, but rather thought it appropriate for a professor to use a plural *du* form to signal, at least in their 'learner system', his higher social status, and for the student to use a *Sie* form due to his/her lower status relative to the professor. Indeed, if this was the case, the changes in non-reciprocal functional switching are rather limited [T1: 19.4% (11.9% + 3% + 4.5%) vs. T3: 12.3% (4.9% + 7.4%)].

Finally, learners' overall knowledge and understanding of reciprocity in address behavior is seen to become more target-like over time. We see this, for example, by adding the figures for reciprocal *Sie/Sie* and reciprocal *du/du* (cf. Table 3.5) – a calculation which gives an overall increase from 58.2% in T1 (13.4% + 44.8%) to 72.8% in T3 (23.4% + 49.4%).

Assessing the Effect of the Study Abroad Context

The learners' use of the address system in German underwent some changes over their 10-month study abroad period. Such changes are seen above all in the increases in reciprocal address behavior and in the decreases in learner-specific switching between the T and V forms of address, developments which also led to an overall more target-like distribution of address forms.

Learners, for example, tended to engage in non-functional switching to a somewhat lesser extent at the end of the sojourn abroad compared to the beginning. This development points to some increase in awareness of the L2 address system even in the face of highly automated routine formula, to a higher degree of declarative knowledge and related linguistic certainty regarding the choice of address form, and/or to a higher degree of morphological competence.[14] Metalinguistic data may shed further light on whether developments in all of these factors were influential in triggering learners' development. Walsh (1994, 1995), for example, in a longitudinal study of Irish learners of German, found that a study abroad period did not necessarily lead to increases in oral grammatical competence, morpho-syntactic developments noted being dependent on individual factors. The fact that developments in non-functional switching levels were more noticeable in informal situations than in formal situations is suggested to reflect the more frequent opportunities for informal contact in the study abroad context discussed above.

Prior to the year abroad, many learners had internalized a less than target-like address system which involved non-reciprocal functional switching. This finding provides evidence that Bialystok (1993), in her cognitive model, may have neglected the full complexity of second language acquisition. According to her theory, gaining control over processing is the major challenge facing learners in L2 acquisition and the acquisition of knowledge is but a minor task. While it is not refuted that control over processing is an important component of acquisition, the present study suggests that declarative knowledge may not be as simple to acquire as assumed by Bialystok. Such findings are in line with those by Barron (2003) with reference to the development of pragmatic knowledge in a year abroad setting, and also by Hassall (1997, 2001, this volume). Whether non-reciprocal functional switching by the present learners actually decreased substantially over time is difficult to ascertain. While it appears so on the surface, a development which would point to an increase in learners' declarative knowledge of the German address system and, above all, of the principle of reciprocity, learners were also found to engage in target-like non-reciprocal switching involving a plural T – possibly with a non-target-like understanding of the use of this form. However, whether such was the case or not could not be ascertained on the basis of the present data. In other words, although learners appear to have become aware of the gap between their IL knowledge and that of the NS system due to the availability of reciprocal asymmetric input, we cannot say definitely that this was the case.

Despite these (potential) developments towards the L2 recorded in the present learners' IL address system, it cannot be denied that learners' use of the address forms retains a strong learner-like quality at the end of the study abroad period – traces of non-functional switching are still rather strong (T3: 14.8%), and non-reciprocal functional switching is either low at 4.9% in T3 or higher at 12.3%, as discussed above (cf. Table 3.5). In other words, the study abroad context did not represent a cure-all for eradicating all learner-specific features of address behavior. This would seem to be the result of insufficient appropriate input in the

L2 context, particularly in formal contexts, or the result of persisting insecurity because of the complexity of the German address system itself. However, in order to shed more light on the reasons behind these developments or lack of developments, production data must be supplemented by metalinguistic data (cf. Hassall, this volume). Only in so doing can detailed information be elicited on the input opportunities open to the foreign language learner and also on learners' awareness of sociolinguistic differences between their input and interlanguage. Finally, apart from the need for further research into learners' developing declarative knowledge, other aspects worthy of study include learners' competence in negotiating an address form in situations of uncertainty in the L2 context. Authentic data would seem to suggest itself for such research.

Notes

1. An earlier version of this paper was presented at the University of Potsdam. I would like to thank the participants for valuable comments and suggestions. Needless to say, all limitations of the paper remain the responsibility of the author.
2. Cf. Barron (2003: 58) and Coleman (1997: 13) on the recent increase in interest in study abroad research.
3. As Braun (1988: 48), however, remarks, the term 'polite form' is, of course, somewhat misleading as the use of this form in a situation which demands use of the intimate form may either be interpreted as a joke or as impolite verbal behavior.
4. The personal pronouns for the genitive case are used only to a very limited extent today (cf. Eisenberg, 1999: 170f: Engel, 1996: 651), and not at all in the present data. Consequently, they are not included in this table.
5. Recent developments, however, include the *Hamburger Sie* and the *Münchener Du*, the former of which refers to the use of the V pronoun with the interlocutor's first name, as in *'Sie Peter'*, the later which represents the use of the T pronoun + Title [*Frau/Herr* (Mrs/Mr)] + Surname (cf. von Au, 1996: 31; Lüger, 1993: 39).
6. Waffle, '...a direct consequence of learners' over-use of "external modification" or supportive moves' (Edmondson & House, 1991: 274, original emphasis), was found in a study by Blum-Kulka & Olshtain (1986) to follow a straight line with regard to proficiency. In other words, using written data, they found that linguistic constraints may prevent waffle in the early stages of language learning/acquisition but at the intermediate and advanced stage, such constraints no longer apply. However, Hassall (1997: 258 passim) in a later research project using, like Norris, oral data, argues that waffle is a feature of intermediate learners' data. Hassall observed beginners and advanced learners to approach the native speaker norm for supportive moves – suggesting a U-shaped curve of development related to linguistic proficiency. Hassall believes that the intermediate learner group's tendency to waffle may be due to a desire to differentiate themselves from beginners and also possibly to a certain lack of confidence.

7. The anonymity of German universities contrasts with other systems, such as the Irish system, in which students usually have to adhere to a rather stringent structured timetable, and consequently get to know each other quicker.

8. Cf. also Bardovi-Harlig and Hartford (1996) who examine the development of adult learners' and native speakers' pragmatic competence in the institutional context of an academic advisory meeting. They also note that, like the case of the prestige form of negation in Regan's study, appropriate input in the area of suggestions and rejections is often limited from learners' peers – i.e. from those people whose input learners value. Consequently, learners perform less than ideally in the advisory context.

9. The higher portion of females increases the external validity of the study since it reflects the large female contingent in language studies in the Department of German in University College Dublin and indeed in Modern Language Departments generally in Ireland, Northern Ireland and Germany, based on this researcher's personal experience.

10. Subjective assessments of language proficiency levels have been used extensively in year abroad studies due to their efficiency. However, caution is necessary given their subjective nature (cf. Maiworm *et al.*, 1993: 109). Nevertheless, even the use of a standardized testing procedure, such as the TOEFL (Test of English as a Foreign Language), often employed where English is the L2 under investigation, does not guarantee reliable results. Kasper (1993: 52f) notes, for example, that the proficiency of learners within the three TOEFL categories (beginning, intermediate and advanced) is possibly more variable than that between levels. The broad homogeneity of the present group of informants is aided by the fact that all informants had learnt German in the centralized Irish educational system and all had studied German in the same university department.

11. In order to further offset the possibility of this effect influencing the present data, it would have been preferable to have engaged in counterbalancing as suggested by Brown (1988: 38). Counterbalancing involves ensuring that no individual completes the same task twice – this would have meant issuing two different but comparable tests to each half of the group of 33 informants at the beginning of the study and then issuing the opposite forms to these same groups at the end of the study, thus halving the overall number of informants completing each situation. Had the researcher had access to more informants, this would have been a possible method of increasing the internal validity of the research design since when averaged, the data would have been comparative and would have enabled analysis of development over time. However, all the informants participating were needed to ensure the validity of the findings; access to an additional group of students from another university was not possible at the time. Nevertheless, as a further precaution, informants were not made aware of the focus of the study.

12. In the case of one item, the relationship between the informants was communicated via a verbal address form, i.e. via *Ach komm, das ist doch kein Problem. Wollen wir zusammen einige Übungen machen?* [Oh come on (T-form of the verb), sure that's no problem. Will we do some exercises together?] (informant G15M). This exceptional situation in the German data was also coded as a choice of *du* rather than as avoidance.

13. Data is presented as it appeared on the questionnaires. Any orthographical, syntactical or other errors are not corrected for either the NS or learner data and any emphasis used is also included. Also, both the NS and learner data, as well as being given in the original, is also translated into English for the present report. Errors present in the data are not, however, translated unless they lead to ambiguities or are of importance for the analysis.

14. It may, of course, also be argued that the developments in non-functional switching may relate to an increased control over processing. This may indeed also be so since extensive opportunities available in the target speech community to practice use of the L2 can be expected to cause informants to become more adept at retrieving and using their sociolinguistic knowledge. However, the fact that the data elicitation instrument focuses primarily on declarative knowledge should be kept in mind in this context.

Appendix

FDCT Sample item:
Du bist am Flughafen. Du siehst eine Frau in Deinem Alter mit zwei riesigen Koffern. Da Du selbst wenig Gepäck hast, bietest Du ihr Hilfe an. Sie LEHNT DEIN ANGEBOT AB.

Du:
Frau:
    :
    :
    :
    :
    :

You are in the airport. You see a girl your own age with two huge bags. As you haven't much luggage yourself, you offer to help. She REFUSES.

You:
Girl:

Part 2: Interaction and Socialization at the Host Dinner Table

Chapter 4

The Socialization of Taste during Study Abroad in Indonesia[1]

MARGARET A. DuFON

And it is probably in tastes in food that one would find the strongest and most indelible mark of infant learning, the lessons which longest withstand the distancing or collapse of the native world and most durably maintain nostalgia for it.

Bourdieu, 1984: 79

In early infancy, as we are beginning to develop the pre-linguistic behaviors that will develop into speech and language, we are also learning to appreciate the tastes of certain foods and to reject the tastes of others. During the pre-school years, as we acquire language, we are socialized further into the world of food. We learn to develop certain beliefs about and attitudes toward food in general and specific foods in particular as well as about the people who eat them. We acquire values related to food and a view of the role of food in our lives. When I speak of the *socialization of taste*, I use the term broadly to include all these things. Because taste, like one's native language, is learned so early in life, it is a fundamental part of one's personal and cultural identity (Visser, 1991). Still, although it is recognized that tastes do vary across cultural groups including national (Schlosser, 2001), ethnic (e.g. Goody, 1982; Iino, 1996; Sanjur, 1982, 1995), social class (Bourdieu, 1984; Goody, 1982), religious, gender and age (Ochs *et al.*, 1996; Visser, 1991) groups, little work has been done on how we are socialized into the world of food in our native culture and subcultures. As far as I can discern, no one has yet investigated the socialization of taste by sojourners living in another linguistic and cultural community. This chapter presents the results of what I believe to be the first study that specifically investigates the socialization of taste in a second language and culture.

This investigation builds on the pioneering work in the socialization of taste first conducted by Ochs *et al.* (1996), who compared discourse at mealtime in Caucasian American and Italian families in order to identify similarities and differences in how parents used language to socialize their young children into the world of food. They found significant cultural differences between the two groups with respect to their ways of speaking about food, which in turn reflected different values, attitudes and beliefs. Whereas American culture emphasized food as nutrition, material good and reward, Italian culture emphasized food as pleasure over all other qualities. Moreover, the Italian families attended more to the individual tastes of each family member, including the children, thus reinforcing the child's identity as an individual. In contrast, the American families' talk about food emphasized the taste preferences of children as a generic group as opposed to those of the adult group; this reinforced the identity of a child as a child rather than as a unique individual.

In a case study modeled after Ochs and her colleagues' (1996) study, Iwai (2001) contributed further to our knowledge of the socialization of taste across cultures by examining the phenomenon in a Japanese family that was socializing their young adult daughter, age 23. She found that like the Italian families in Ochs *et al.*, this Japanese family's discourse emphasized the theme of food as pleasure. More specifically, the schemata for talking about food included the relationship between food and season, different kinds of foods and their characteristics, the ingredients that make food tasty and where they come from, which shops or brands are best known for a particular kind of food, and what is the best way to eat a particular food. Furthermore, she discovered that while the adult daughter had acquired the basics of these schemata for talking about food, the mother, father and grandmother were still socializing her regarding some of the finer points of discourse about food. Thus, the socialization of taste, at least in some cultures, continues even into adulthood.

This would be especially true for adults who enter new environments where access to their traditional diet might be limited and exposure to new options abound, such as students abroad, particularly those living, eating and socializing with host families in countries quite different from their own. Given that taste preferences are developed early in childhood and are a fundamental part of one's cultural identity, any new, strange and exotic food encountered may or may not please the foreign palate. Indeed some foreign foods seem to be easily accepted while others are not.[2] Furthermore, the discourse surrounding food may also be different, causing surprise, discomfort, or even *language shock* (Agar, 1994).

In order to examine this phenomenon, I investigated the socialization of taste of study abroad language learners in Indonesia by examining the dinner table discourse of Indonesian host families and their study abroad guests. This study stands alongside other recent research on study abroad which has examined native speaker–non-native speaker interaction in homestay situations in general (DuFon, 2000a, in press; McMeekin, 2003, this volume) and in dinner table conversations in particular (Cook, this volume; Iino, 1996, this volume) in order to determine what and how study abroad learners learn about language through these interactions. Specifically, it investigates the following research questions:

- What are the thematic dimensions of taste that are prominent in dinner table discourse between native Indonesian speaker hosts and study abroad learners?
- What features of the discourse are used to convey the participants' beliefs, attitudes and values with respect to food?
- Were there any shifts in the study abroad learners' beliefs, attitudes and values with respect to food as a result of this socialization process?

Theoretical Framework

These questions are examined within a language socialization theoretical framework. *Language socialization* views language acquisition as a social process. Through interaction with competent members of the culture, a child or novice becomes a competent member of society (Ochs, 1988). This is possible because of the twofold relationship between language and socialization: *socialization to use language* and *socialization through the use of language* (Ochs & Schieffelin, 1984; Schieffelin & Ochs, 1986a, 1986b). Children or novices, such as sojourners in the host culture, are *socialized to use language* when they are taught what to say in a given context. For example, they might be instructed to compliment the food immediately upon tasting it by saying, '*Enak, Bu'* [(It's) delicious, mother]. On the other hand, children or novices are *socialized through the use of language* such that they acquire knowledge of their culture as they learn the language. The ways in which linguistic forms are used and discourse is structured carry implicit messages regarding the values, beliefs and world view of the speech community in question. For example, compliments, criticisms and warnings about the taste of food implicitly highlight the importance of food as pleasure. Who gets to perform these acts in a given context also teaches the child or novice something about his or her social identity in terms of group membership, and about his or her status and role in relationship to the interlocutor. Thus drawing on, but modifying, the ideas of the Sapir-Whorf Hypothesis (i.e. as interpreted by Mendelbaum, 1949), language socialization theorists such as Ochs (1988) believe that participation in language activities helps to construct the learner's world view as he or she acquires a language. However, it is not only the child or novice who is socialized. Language socialization theory recognizes that socialization is bi-directional. At times, the child or novice also socializes the adults or native speakers such that the latter learn to modify their behaviors, attitudes and expectations. Furthermore, language socialization is not completed in childhood, but continues throughout life as the adult enters new situations. Situations such as a promotion to a new job, entrance into a new religion, a move into an assisted living facility, or a sojourn in a foreign nation require that we be socialized into that new culture.

Method

This investigation uses data collected over a five-year period (1992–1997) during several visits to Indonesia. It combines data from my own diaries written on my acquisition of Indonesian language and culture during two stays in Indonesia as a study abroad student with data from later research, which used ethnographic methods to investigate the acquisition of linguistic politeness by study abroad learners.

Participants

My two study abroad experiences

I studied in Indonesia on two occasions: 10 weeks in an advanced-level Indonesian language program during the summer of 1992, and three semesters as a regular non-degree student at IKIP-Malang (a teacher's college) from August 1993 to December 1994. On both occasions, I lived with the same host family. My host father's father had been a government official during the Dutch colonial administration, and consequently their dining practices were Dutch-influenced. Dining with them was very similar to my own American family dining experience in that the family sat at the table together and conversed as we ate. This was not necessarily typical. In Javanese Indonesia, families do not normally eat together, and in more traditional homes, no space is set aside specifically for dining. Rather food is prepared, set on a table, and as each family member comes in, he or she fixes a plate of food and then eats it alone

(Geertz, 1961; Jay, 1969). Therefore I could not assume that the meal-time experiences I enjoyed with my host family would necessarily be experienced by other study abroad students.

In spite of the similarities between meals in my host family and those in my natural family, however, I noticed that the ways of talking about food were somewhat different than what I had experienced while growing up in the midwestern United States. I became interested in this and often commented on it in my diaries. Later, after reading *Socializing Taste* (Ochs *et al.*, 1996), I decided to pursue this topic in my own research.

My research on study abroad learners

In 1996, I returned to Indonesia to study the acquisition of linguistic politeness by study abroad learners. This particular analysis uses data from five learners who recorded dinner conversations with their host families. All the learners (four Americans, one Japanese) were 20–22-year-old college students from American universities who were participating in a semester-long study abroad program, also in Malang, Indonesia. Three of the learners – Keith, Charlene and Kyle – were native English speakers who were beginning level learners of Indonesian and had never studied abroad. The other two learners – Bruce and Tomoko – were intermediate level learners of Indonesian, having studied it previously in the United States. Both had previously studied abroad, Tomoko in the United States and Bruce in France.

Mealtime was typically the time that the learners were most likely to converse with their host families, though the frequency of eating together varied across learners. Charlene, Bruce and Kyle ate with their host families on a regular basis. Tomoko ate with her host mother less frequently. Keith almost never ate with his host family but frequently ate with his tutor's family.

My relationship to the students was that of researcher. As a researcher, I had frequent contact with them. I observed them in a range of activities and informally interviewed them. I also communicated with them through dialog journals, and in the weekly discussion group that I led. As someone with more experience with the language and culture, I willingly shared my perspective with them on issues that arose, and in this way served as an unofficial mentor to them.

In order to encourage their participation in the study from beginning to end, each participant was paid at the end. All remained in the study and fulfilled their obligations in terms of data collection.

Data collection

My diaries

I kept diaries during both study abroad experiences. The content of the two diaries is similar in that both focus on my acquisition of politeness in Indonesian, and many of the entries are concerned with dinner table discourse. Each week, I reviewed my notes for the week and identified themes and gave myself 'homework' assignments for things to pay attention to, to inquire about, or to practice. Periodically, I read all the notes from the beginning to see what patterns occurred and what changes had taken place over time.

My research on study abroad learners

A variety of data collection tools were used in order to triangulate the data collection: learner journals, audio- and videotaped interactions, and field notes.

Learner journals: The learners wrote three journal entries per week that described an incident in which they learned something about politeness in Indonesian language and culture. Thus they had to both describe the event and talk about the acquisition process. They were encouraged to write subjectively at first, putting their feelings and emotions into the narrative, and then to read what they had written, looking at the event more objectively, and to try to interpret it from another perspective. Whenever the learners tape-recorded an event, one of their journal entries for the week was to deal with the taped interaction in order to give me background information on the participants and the event, as well as some insight into how they saw the event. I photocopied and read their journals weekly, and responded to their entries both individually and collectively in group meetings (cf. Peirce, 1994). Food, eating etiquette and dinner talk were topics that often emerged in the journals and sometimes in the group discussion as well.

Transcripts of dinner table discourse: The data for this analysis were drawn primarily from a set of 17 transcripts (14 audiotaped, three videotaped) of naturalistic interactions (three to five per student) between the learners and their native speaker hosts at the dinner table. Although the learners were required to tape-record nine interactions with native speakers, I did not instruct them to record dinner table conversations, but rather let them choose the events to record. I did not want to influence the kinds of events they experienced by requiring them to record certain kinds of events nor, as mentioned above, could I assume that the learners would eat with their families. Furthermore, during the orientation given upon the students' arrival, the resident director actively discouraged some students from eating with their host families and encouraged them to eat out instead because, based on past experience, she had found that discourse at meal time often gave rise to intercultural misunderstandings. Nevertheless, these five learners recorded a total of 17 family mealtime conversations. Furthermore, at least some commented that they found meal time to be a good opportunity to socialize with the family and to practice their language. Thus these data provided the potential for insight into the socialization of taste.

Field notes: I kept three types of field notes on the participant-observations: observational, methodological and theoretical (Schatzman & Strauss, 1973). The notes contained information on my observations and conversations collected during dinner talk with native speakers and during informal interviews and the weekly discussion group with the study abroad learners; they included information about food, eating and dinner table etiquette. I periodically reviewed the notes and added methodological and theoretical notes to the observational ones.

Data analysis

The use of multiple methods provided a means of checking one source against another for consistency and variability. The journals comple-mented the transcripts in that they provided insights into the learners' perceptions and interpretations of events; the transcriptions provided evidence that either supported or failed to support their perceptions and interpretations of what took place. The field notes added my perceptions of events as I was experiencing them in the field. All of these data sources were entered into the computer using NUD*IST (Non-numerical Unstructured Data* Indexing, Searching & Theorizing) 4. The data were analyzed by coding the discourse about food, taste, and eating into various categories such that a number of themes could be identified.

Results and Discussion

Six themes were evident in the discourse about food. They included orientation to the food, food as pleasure, food as a social identity marker (particularly ethnic identity), food as gifts (but not as reward), food as a material good and food and health.

Orientation to the food

Since the learners were unfamiliar with many, perhaps even most, of the foods served in Indonesia, it was necessary to orient them to the dishes presented. The host families oriented the learners to the food by labeling it, by naming at least some of the ingredients contained in the dish and describing their function, by describing the taste of the dish, and by giving some information about how the dish was made and how it was to be eaten. Excerpt #1, a conversation between Bruce and his host mother Ibu Djumandi, illustrates some of these features.

Excerpt #1

1	**Bruce:**	*Saya senang. Apa namanya?* I like this. What's it called?	((Asks for label))
2	**Ibu Djumandi:**	*Jagung* Corn.	((Label))
3	**Bruce:**	*Jagung saja?* Just corn?	((Clarification request))
4	**Ibu Djumandi:**	*Dadar jagung.* Corn pancake	((Label))
5	**Bruce:**	*Dadar.* Pancake	((Repetition))
6	**Ibu Djumandi:**	*Dadar jagung.* Corn pancake	((Expansion))
7	**Bruce:**	*(Dadar jagung)* (Corn pancake)	((Repetition))
8	**Ibu Djumandi:**	*Ada dadar telor.* There is egg pancake.	((Ingredients))
9	**Bruce:**	*Hm*	
10	**Ibu Djumandi:**	*Tapi ini jagung- Ini ja-.* But this is corn- This is co- *Itu jagung dicampur telor* that is corn mixed with egg.	((How it is made))
11	**Bruce:**	*Oh ya dan [(.) mungkin (1) uh-* Oh yeah and [(.) maybe (1) uh-	
12	**Ibu Djumandi:**	*[bumbu?* [the seasoning? *Itu hijau?* That green thing?	((Ingredients))
13	**Bruce:**	*Ya.*	
14	**Ibu Djumandi:**	*daun.* leaf	((Label))

15	**Bruce:**	*Apa itu?*	((Asks for
		What is that?	label))
16	**Ibu Djumandi:**	*Daun bawang.*	((Label))
		Onion leaves.	
17	**Bruce:**	*Daun. Oh ya*	((Repetition))
		Leaves. Oh yeah.	
18	**Ibu Djumandi:**	*Itu untuk penyedap.*	((Function))
		That's for seasoning.	

Thus here we can see how Bruce's host mother oriented him to the food, giving him the vocabulary to identify it and talk about it as well as informing him which foods were used for seasoning, which is important if the food is to be enjoyed, and the function of the flavorful foods that add taste to the dish.[3] Bruce played an active role in the process by asking for labels, repeating and practicing them, and asking for clarification when the information was not clear to him.

The discourse also included talk of how to eat food. This included information about which foods went with others. Below Ibu Hayati indicates to Charlene how to season the food to her personal taste by showing her what to add to the food.

Excerpt #2

1	**Ibu Hayati:**	*Pakai ini ((Indicates a condiment)), enak juga.*
		If you use this, it is also tasty.
2	**Charlene:**	*Oh-ya (sedap).*
		Oh yeah (flavorful).

Discourse on how to eat also included discussion about which dishes and utensils to use or not use. Below, Keith talks to an Indonesian friend about his difficulty in eating rice dishes neatly with his fingers, the traditional Indonesian way of eating, which is still enjoyed except in formal contexts.

Excerpt #3

1	**Keith:**	*Saya- saya um- saya ada uh- waktu- um waktu sulit?*
		I- I um- I had uh- when- um when it was difficult?
		Makan dengan uh [jadi
		To eat with uh [fingers
2	**Arif:**	[*dengan jari.*
		[with fingers.

3 **Keith:**   *Mungkin dengan nasi ma- lebih- lebih sulit.*
                 Maybe with rice- ma- more- more difficult.
                 Tidak [bisa ((laughs)).
                 I can [not ((laughs)).
4 **Arif:**   [*Tidak bisa*
                     [You cannot.
5 **Keith:**   *Ya. Saya mencoba dan mencoba. Tidak bisa.*
                 Yeah. I tried and tried. I cannot.
6 **Arif:**   *Belajar kalau di- di- di- di rumah. Di dalam rumah belajar.*
                 Practice when at- at- at- at home. At home, practice.
7 **Keith:**   *((laughing)) O [ya.*
8 **Arif:**   [*ya.*
9 **Keith:**   *Biasanya nasi uh menjadi di uh baju saya.*
                 Usually the rice ends up on my shirt.

Arif considered this skill important and therefore encouraged Keith to continue trying to master the art of eating with his fingers by practicing at home, where lack of neatness is less of a problem.

Food as pleasure

The Indonesians in this study, like the Italians in Ochs *et al.*'s (1996) study and the Japanese in Iwai's (2001) study, emphasized food as pleasure. They frequently made references to taste sometimes in general terms with words such as *enak, lezat,* or *sedap* (all of which can be translated as delicious or tasty). Other times a specific taste was discussed such as *pedas* [spicy], *manis* [sweet], *asin* [salty], *asam* or *masam* [sour or acidic], *kecut* [sour], *pahit* [bitter], *gurih* [rich and oily], *sepat* [astringent] or *hambar* [bland or tasteless].

The comments on taste occurred in a variety of contexts and served several different functions. Taste labels were used to educate the learners about the taste and the label used to describe that taste. This occurred either prior to or following the actual tasting. Prior to tasting the food, when the hosts offered food, they often commented on the taste in order to encourage the guest/learner to accept the offer, or particularly when the taste was *pedas* [spicy], to warn the learner. In some cases, usually when the food was red, the learner did not wait to be warned, but instead inquired about the taste prior to eating. After tasting the food, comments on taste took the form of compliments, checks on whether the taste was good or to the liking of the recipient, and criticisms when the taste was not appealing. All of these discourse moves are necessary in order to ensure that the food is enjoyed.

To educate the learner about the taste of food

In Excerpt #4, below, Charlene's host mother, Ibu Hayati, informs her of the taste of the dish they are eating. She not only gives her the label *pahit* [bitter], but also reveals her attitude toward the taste, that is, she enjoys the bitterness.

Excerpt #4

1	**Ibu Hayati:**	Do you like this?
		(1)
2	**?:**	Ya, I like.
3	**Charlene:**	((giggles))
4	**Ibu Hayati:**	Saya suka juga. Ini Mbak, *pahit-pahit tapi enak.*
		I also enjoy it. Here, sister, it's very bitter, but delicious.

Identifying the taste and commenting on it give insight into how a particular taste is classified and experienced by the host culture, which may be different from that of the guest learner. In my own case, as a person who had not been socialized to enjoy the bitter taste, the Indonesians' enjoyment of steamed papaya leaves and other bitter foods surprised me. While I ate papaya leaves there, I did it because of their nutritional value, and not because I enjoyed their taste. The Indonesians' expressions of enjoyment of the bitter taste did not alter my ability to enjoy bitter foods such as papaya leaves; they did, however, make me aware that there are others who enjoy them, and that bitterness is not necessarily a taste to be avoided.

To encourage the guest to accept the offer of food

In Javanese Indonesian culture, the host verbally invites the guest to eat the food. These invitations often recur throughout the meal. When the host wanted to encourage the learner to try a particular food or to take more of it, he or she often commented on its good taste.

Excerpt #5

1	**Mas Joko:**	*Enak ini.*
		This is tasty.
2	**Keith:**	*Mm.*
3	**Mas Joko:**	*Silahkan tambah.*
		Please take some more.

That this kind of invitation was successful in obtaining the desired perlocutionary effect was evident from Charlene's journal (September

29, 1996), where she commented on her attempts to conform and cooperate even when her heart was not really in it: 'I even ate the snacks I really didn't want because [my host mother] insisted it was good/fresh/or hot'.

The emphasis, then, in these invitations was related to the theme of food as pleasure. The learners were encouraged to eat certain foods most often because they were *tasty*, rather than because they were *good for you* or because of *poor starving children* who were not fortunate enough to have food. In other words, through these invitations, learners were socialized into the importance of food as pleasure.

To warn the guest

The hosts did not always assume that their foreign guests would find the food tasty or to their liking. They seemed particularly concerned when offering them spicy foods. In these cases, the hosts often felt obligated to warn their guests so that they could try just a little bit first, and thus avoid the shock of a possibly unpleasant taste. Such is the case in the dialog below between Keith and his tutor, Mas Joko.

Excerpt #6

1	**Mas Joko:**	*Ini (lho Keith).*
		This one, (Keith)
2	**Keith:**	((laughs))
3	**Mas Joko:**	*Sedikit aja.*
		Just a little bit.
4	**Keith:**	[*Sedikit.*
		[A little bit.
5	**Mas Joko:**	[*Nanti pedas. Ya.* [*Coba dulu. (Try it).*
		[It'll be spicy. Yea. [Try it first.
6	**Keith:**	[*Ya* OK.

In this dialog, Mas Joko warned Keith to take just a little bit, explaining that the dish was spicy and implying that he could always take more later if he liked it. This serves to socialize the learner to the importance of pleasure in eating and of the need for the host to attend to the guest's taste preferences.

To inquire about the taste

In some cases, particularly if the food was reddish in color, the learners did not wait to be warned about spiciness, but proceeded to inquire about the taste themselves.

Excerpt #7

1	**Tomoko:**	*Apa yang pedas?*
		Which one is spicy?
2	**Mbak Wahyu:**	*O, yang pedas? Cabe. Tapi ini tidak pedas.*
		O, the spicy one? Chili pepper. But this is not spicy.
3	**Tomoko:**	*Tidak pedas?*
		It's not spicy?
4	**Mbak Wahyu:**	*Tidak. Heheh.*
		No. Un'uh

In this dialog with her tutor, Tomoko indicates that she has already been partially socialized concerning Indonesian food preferences in East Java. She was aware that some East Javanese foods are quite spicy, and did not want a dish that was too spicy for her taste, as she would not enjoy it. Her question enabled her to learn about the spiciness level of this particular food as well as the cause of its spiciness – the *cabe* or chili pepper. Furthermore, by asking for confirmation that this particular dish was not spicy, Tomoko was able to implicitly inform her host, Mbak Wahyu, of her taste preferences. Since language socialization is viewed as a bi-directional process, it is possible that Tomoko's questions served to socialize her Indonesian host into recognizing that her foreign guests might not appreciate spiciness at the same level as she does.

To compliment the food

During my first stay abroad, one of my instructors informed us that compliments on the food should be given immediately on tasting the food, not after you have finished eating the entire meal (Pak Oka, class notes, July 1992). He was socializing us to use language in a particular way. In Excerpt #8 below, we can see this behavior modeled by Mbak Tatik, a native speaker of Indonesian who had just recently joined Charlene and their host mother, Ibu Hayati, at the dinner table. She presumably had just tasted the food and commented that the food was delicious.

Excerpt #8

1	**Mbak Tatik:**	*Enak, Bu.*
		Delicious, Bu
2	**Ibu Hayati:**	*(xx?) ndak?*
		(xx) isn't it?
3	**Mbak Tatik:**	*Ya, Bu.*

This compliment served to inform the host mother that she had adjusted the seasonings so that it could be enjoyed by her boarder. Although Charlene did not participate in this segment of discourse, she was present and able to witness it. On a number of occasions, Charlene mentioned that she used the strategy of observing her host sisters, particularly at meals, as a way of learning Indonesian etiquette. In this case, the appropriate complimenting behavior in terms of both the form of the compliment (*Enak, Bu*) and its timing (immediately after tasting) were modeled for Charlene by a member of the host culture. This input implicitly instructed her concerning how and when to compliment the food and socialized her regarding the importance of food as pleasure.

To check on the taste

If a compliment is not forthcoming, the host may ask how the guest likes the food. If for any reason the food is not satisfactory, the feedback obtained will help the host adjust the seasoning next time she cooks for the guest so that the taste is to his or her liking. In Excerpt #9 below, Mbak Wahyu has just served a somewhat spicy chicken dish to Tomoko. Tomoko has just tasted the dish and Mbak Wahyu asks her about the taste.

Excerpt #9

1	**Mbak Wahyu:**	*Bagaimana?*
		How is it?
2	**Tomoko:**	*Enak*
		Delicious
3	**Mbak Wahyu:**	*Oo*
4	**Tomoko:**	*Agak (pedas)*
		A little bit (spicy)
5	**Mbak Wahyu:**	*Heheh. Heheh. (2) Pedas sedikit tapi enak?*
		Uhhuh. Uhhuh. (2) A little bit spicy, but delicious?
6	**Ibu Kost:**	*(pedas sedikit tapi enak pakai lombok itu).*
		(a little spicy but delicious with chili pepper)
		((laughter))

In this case, Tomoko found the taste delicious and a little bit spicy. Her tutor, Mbak Wahyu, reinforced Tomoko's evaluation of the dish on both counts. Mbak Wahyu's host mother also reinforced this evaluation, and expanded upon it, explaining that it was the chili pepper that gave it that delicious flavor. Thus in addition to checking on the taste here, we also see evidence of the various hosts collaborating to reinforce the learner for her ability to appropriately classify, experience and enjoy the taste as the host culture does and to orient her to the dish by explaining which ingredient accounts for its flavor.

To criticize the food

In American society, guests should never criticize the food (Visser, 1991). Even in my own home, criticism of the food was not welcome. Indonesians, on the other hand, at least among family, often criticize the food, sometimes with a directness that I found shocking. My diary entries, especially from my first stay in 1992, contain many references to the directness of their criticism. An example of this can be seen in Excerpt #10 below where I comment on the experience of my classmate, Giti, following a potluck that we had held for our host families on America's Independence Day.

Excerpt #10

Giti made Indian curry for the 4th of July party. Her *ibu* [host mother] told her it was *'kurang enak'* [not very tasty]. So much for Javanese indirectness! Giti was insulted. I don't blame her. I've noticed that Indonesians do comment on the quality of the food – at least in a family situation. They say things like, 'It's too salty/sour/oily', etc. ...The *ibu* said it needed more salt. Giti said it needed more curry powder, but the *ibu* said, 'No, just more salt'. . .

In spite of my initial language shock at hearing the direct criticisms of taste during my first summer in Indonesia, there is evidence that I was eventually socialized in the direction of criticism so that others could learn my taste preferences. I was not comfortable with it, but I was willing to attempt it. This is evident in Excerpt #11.

Excerpt #11

When I saw that [my egg was] runny I did not take it. Later [my host mother] mentioned to me that I had an egg. I answered 'masih mentah' [it's still raw].... Even though [my host father] is always very direct in his criticism of the food, I did not feel good about it. (My diary, April 8, 1994)

The reports of this kind of criticism were supported by the transcription data as well, as can be seen in Excerpt #12 below. Bruce had cooked a spaghetti dinner for a family in South Kalimantan who had befriended him during his three-week field study there. During the course of the dinner, they ask Bruce why the spaghetti is tasteless. They also criticize it for being too salty, if anything.

Excerpt #12

1	**Wawan:**	*Mengapa hambar Bruce?*	((Indirectly Criticizes
		Why is it tasteless, Bruce?	Taste))
2	**Bruce:**	*Apa?* [*Hambar?*	((Asks for clarification
		What? [Hambar?	of *hambar*))
3	**Wawan:**	[*(Hambar.*	((Confirms that it is *hambar*
		[(Tasteless.	or tasteless; reinforcing the
		Memang) hambar. Hambar.	criticism; meaning is not
		Indeed) tasteless. Tasteless.)	negotiated))
4		[*Rasanya panas (xx terlalu*	((Directly criticizes
		asin) Hambar.	the taste))
		[It's a hot taste (xx too	
		salty). Tasteless.	
5	**Ibu:**	[*(xxx panas xxx*	
		[(xxx hot xxx)	
6	**Wawan:**	*Rasanya asin mungkin (xxxx)*	((Directly criticizes the
		It tastes salty maybe (xxxx)	taste))
7	**Bruce:**	*Asin?*	((Asks clarification or
		Salty?	questions the taste as
			perceived by Wawan))
8	**Ibu:**	*(Asin, Bruce)* ((giggling	((Confirms that the taste
		noises))	is salty; does not clarify
		(Salty, Bruce)	the meaning))
9	**Wawan:**	*(Hambar, terlalu asin) ndak?*	((Reinforces criticism of taste
		(Tasteless, too salty), isn't it?	and seeks agreement))

In spite of the repeated and explicit criticisms, Bruce, was not aware of them, as is evident from his journal entry (Excerpt #13 below). He was probably unfamiliar with the word *hambar* as he seems not to have understood it. His apparent request for clarification was taken as a confirmation check and so the term was not clarified, but only repeated and he did not pursue it; meaning was not negotiated. Likewise their comments that the spaghetti was *asin*, or *salty*, did not seem to be understood by him as a criticism. This might have been because he did not understand the term *asin* or it could be that he did not classify the taste of the spaghetti in that way, so the comment '*Asin*' did not make sense to him. Although Bruce did not understand the language here, he nevertheless clearly suspected that his friends did not like the spaghetti, as is evident in his journal entry below.

Excerpt #13

This evening I went out and bought the ingredients to make spaghetti
for Wawan's family... It turned out that there was a lot more spaghetti
than I thought there would be. Everybody took a plate full, and then
proceeded to eat. It was fairly obvious that they didn't find it the
most delicious thing... I was amused since they all ate very slowly as
if they could barely get the food down. It became obvious that they
were just eating to be polite... Even though I kept telling them not to
worry if they didn't like it, they just kept insisting that they couldn't
finish because they were full (but I know the real reason). (Bruce's
journal, December 6, 1996)

Although Bruce missed the spoken criticisms and believed that the
family was reluctant to criticize his food, he was able to correctly
discern through their actions that the taste of the food was not appreciated. This message was reinforced the next day, when the family recooked
the noodles, but seasoned the dish in their own way.

Excerpt #14

Finally when everyone was eating, the *bapak* [father] came in and
insisted that I take the spaghetti home with me. I said that I was full
so they ended up only giving me half of what was left (still a lot). I
couldn't tell whether he was just insisting that I take it to eat myself,
or more so they wouldn't have to throw it away (or worse yet eat it
themselves!) The funny thing is, in the morning they brought me a
plate of spaghetti that had been fried à la Indonesian. It tasted good
despite the added grease. It was almost as if the Ibu was saying, '*Nah*
here is the Indonesian way to make spaghetti!' I appreciated the
gesture since it showed some degree of closeness. (Bruce's journal,
December 6, 1996)

In contrast to Giti (Excerpt #6), Bruce took the criticism of his cooking in
good stride. This might be due to the fact that Giti understood the direct
criticism whereas Bruce missed it and just understood the implicit criticism evident in their not eating much and then later in their recooking
the dish. It also might be that he just had a thicker skin or less ego involvement in his cooking. In any case, criticism of the food at the family
dinner table is an important part of the discourse. In cases of low social
distance, such as in the family, or in cases where a higher status
member (e.g. the host mother) speaks to a lower status member (e.g.

child, boarder, maid), criticism of poorly cooked or poorly seasoned food is necessary in order to alert the cook that adjustments need to be made in the next attempt. Only in this way can the cook strive to adjust the food so that eating it is a pleasurable experience for all.

Episodes such as these that involve labeling and commenting on the taste to inform, encourage or warn the guest, and inquiring about the taste to avoid an unpleasant experience before tasting the food, as well as checking on, complimenting, and criticizing the taste after tasting are all discourse moves that draw the learners' attention to food as a source of pleasure and the importance of getting the taste just right so that it can be enjoyed to its maximum extent. This treatment of food as pleasure and the kind of discourse surrounding it had a positive effect on the learners, causing them to change both the way in which they viewed food and the ways in which they talked about it.

Food as ethnic identity marker

Another thematic dimension prominent in the data was that of food as a social identity marker. At times a given food was associated with a particular religious identity or with a village versus urban identity, but most often with ethnic identity. This ethnic identity occurred at both the national and international levels.

At the international level, just as in Iino's (1996) study, a great deal of the conversation centered around differences between the learner's home country or other countries in which he or she had lived and Indonesia, the host country. This included talk about various aspects of food and taste, including the main food of the countries in question, internationalized foods such as sushi and pizza, the variation in taste preferences across national boundaries, the availability of important foods and seasonings (e.g. rice, chili pepper and banana), and the manner of eating foods. In Example 15, Pak Djumandi asks Bruce about the availability of sweet sticky rice in America. Bruce, who is still somewhat confused about the meaning of both *beras* (rice) and *ketan* (sweet sticky rice), mistakenly replies that rice is not available.

Excerpt #15

1   **Pak Djumandi:**   *Jadi itu- itu ketan, Bruce, aaah seperti beras.*
                          Therefore that- that is sweet sticky rice, Bruce, aaah,
                            like rice.
                          [Di Amerika ada?
                          [In America is there any?

2	**Bruce:**	[*Beras*	*tidak ada.*
		[Rice	there is none.

Questions about the availability of rice and a society's preference for eating it as compared to other staple foods frequently arose in other conversations between Indonesians and learners. Rice is the main staple food of the Javanese and an important identity marker, which separates them not only from the people of other nations, such as Americans and Europeans, whom they consider to be bread eaters, but also separates them from some of the other Indonesian cultures, such as the people of the Malukus who have traditionally eaten *sagu*, a starch from the sago palm (although rice has been becoming more popular), and the Dani of Irian Jaya or the East Timoreans,[4] for whom the *ubi*, or sweet potato, is the basic food. Rice is not only a sign of ethnic identity, but at least for some, is a sign of the ethnic superiority of those who eat rice. This became evident to me in my Javanese language class.

Excerpt #16

[The teacher] told us the Javanese are the most developed. He then said that they eat rice as compared with the people of East Timor, who eat *ubi* (tubers). Because of the Javanese influence, the East Timoreans have begun to eat rice also. The implication was that eating rice is a sign of development and culture whereas eating tubers is not. (My diary, September 6, 1994)

In addition to differences in the main food, the different regions are also famous for preferring different tastes. In Excerpt #17, Ibu Sumitro identifies a dish as a Javanese dish, which leads into a discussion of taste and ethnic identification.

Excerpt #17

1	**Ibu S:**	*Jawa. (Jawa ini).*
		Javanese. (This is Javanese).
2	**Tomoko:**	*Mhm. (so) Masakan Jawa? Masakan di dalam Jawa?*
		Mhm. (so) Javanese cooking? Cooking from within Java?
3	**Ibu S:**	*Mhm.*
4	**Tomoko:**	*Jawa Barat dan Jawa Tengah?*
		West Java and Central Java?
5	**Ibu S:**	*Mhm*

6	**Tomoko:**	*Jawa Timur?*
		East Java?
7	**Ibu S:**	*Mhm?*
8	**Tomoko:**	*Masakan tidak- tidak sama?*
		Their food isn't- isn't the same?
9	**Ibu S:**	*Ya, (tidak.)* *[(Bisa) ada beda. A-Ada (2)-*
		Yes, (it is not). [(It can be) there is a difference. Th- There
		is (2)-
10	**Tomoko:**	*[mmmmm*
11	**Ibu S:**	*Masing-masing ada apa? Spesifikasi gitu lho.*
		Each one has what? Its special characteristics in a way.
12	**Tomoko:**	*Aah.*
13	**Ibu S:**	<u>*Kalau Jawa Timur, banyak garam*</u>
		<u>In the case of East Java, lots of salt.</u>
14	**Tomoko:**	*Garam?*
		Salt?
15	**Ibu S:**	*Garam ya. Rasa asin ya?* *[Salt?*
		Salt, yeah. A salty taste, yeah? [Salt?
16	**Tomoko:**	*[m m mm.*
17	**Ibu S:**	*Mhm.*
18	**Tomoko:**	*Mm.*
19	**Ibu S:**	<u>*Jawa Tengah, rasa manis.*</u>
		<u>Central Java, a sweet taste.</u>

Ibu Sumitro indicated a particular dish as Javanese, but it was Tomoko who introduced the topic of variation in cuisine depending on location in Java. This indicates that Tomoko had already been exposed to this schema before. Ibu Sumitro confirmed that there are indeed regional differences and pointed out that the East Javanese prefer a saltier taste and identified *garam* or salt as the ingredient that gives East Javanese food its characteristic flavor. Tomoko asked for confirmation that she had understood *garam* correctly. Ibu Sumitro confirmed this and then associated the ingredient *garam* with the flavor *asin*. After Tomoko indicated her understanding, Ibu Sumitro then explained that the Central Javanese prefer a sweeter taste; this sweet taste is preferred even for foods served in the savory portion of the meal. Following the excerpt presented here, Tomoko pursued the topic, reporting that she had heard that the West Sumatrans prefer spicy food and then asking about the taste preferences of other regions such as Kalimantan and Bali. Her host mother obliged her by comparing and contrasting the tastes of these different regions.

Food in Indonesia, then, is an important marker of social identity, particularly of ethnic identity. The Indonesian hosts socialize the learners regarding this by comparing the various regions with respect to their food and taste preferences. This helps to reinforce the learners' knowledge of the rich diversity of the Indonesian people and to recognize some of the differences that might not be readily apparent to them. Additionally, the discourse socializes learners regarding the local norms regarding taste. While in my experience, the East Javanese never demanded or even expected that I (or any outsider) eat or behave exactly as they did, they were nevertheless pleased when we conformed to their local taste norms (e.g. preferring saltier rather than sweet foods, rice rather than bread). Through their discourse, they made us aware of the local norms so that we could conform and fit in if we chose to. Likewise, we, the learners, through asking for information, confirmation, and clarification actively participated in this socialization process as well.

Food as gifts

Unlike the data in the Ochs *et al.* (1996) study, the data in this study did not contain examples of food as reward, that is, food given contingent upon the performance of some other act, as was common in the socialization of American children. This is not surprising since the learners here were adults, and my experience in American society has been that when food is used as a reward to a control an adult's behavior, it is usually done to oneself rather than to another adult. Although food as reward was not evident in the data, a related theme of food as gifts, or the giving of food that was not contingent upon the performance of some other act, was prominent. *Oleh-oleh*, or gifts of food brought back from a trip, typically consist of food for which the location visited is famous (DuFon, 2003). For example, Batu is famous for its apples, Malang for its smooth-textured tempeh, and Kediri for its yellow tofu. In the example below, Mbak Wahyu has given Tomoko a cooking lesson, and they are eating the food they have cooked. Added to this is a dish of yellow tofu from Kediri, which was brought back as a food gift, *oleh-oleh*, by her host mother's younger sibling. Mbak Wahyu tells Tomoko what the food is, where it is from and how they acquired it.

Excerpt #18

1	**Wahyu:**	*Itu tahu dari Kediri.*
		This is tofu from Kediri.
2	**Tomoko:**	*Kediri?*

3 **Wahyu:**   *Heheh. Dibawakan ibu.*
               Uhhuh. It was brought for my host mother.
4 **Tomoko:**   *Oooo.*
5 **Wahyu:**   *Ya. Adiknya ibu.*
               Ya. My host mother's younger sibling.

Comments like these reinforced information the learners had been given through explicit instruction regarding the importance of bringing gifts back from trips. It also helped them to realize what were the appropriate kinds of gifts to bring back from trips (typical foods) and which foods were particular to a given location, which in turn enabled them to participate in gift-giving routines with their host families and their friends as well as to participate more fully in subsequent conversations about these same foods and practices.

Food as material good

Some discussion of food as a material good appeared in the data, though it was not as prominent as the themes of food as pleasure or food as ethnic identity marker. The talk of food as material good often centered on a food's monetary value. This included discussion of the stores, markets or *warungs* where good food could be purchased at a cheaper price. It also included a comparison of prices between the various regions of Indonesia and between Indonesia and other countries. In contrast with Ochs *et al.'s* (1996) American data, there was little discussion of the wasting of food, perhaps because not much food is wasted in Java. In my host family's household, if the higher status nuclear family members had leftovers, they were passed on to the lower status country cousins who boarded with the family and to the servants. What they did not eat traveled down the hierarchy to the garbage man and then to the stray cats that wandered in and out of the kitchen. There were a few incidents, however, when waste of food was a salient topic. One such conversation concerned Ibu Kartika's complaint about the waste of tea on guests. In Indonesia, hosts are obligated to serve their guests a beverage and the guests are obligated to drink at least a sip but that is all. Consequently, a lot of tea is wasted. The waste is particularly noticeable during those occasions when a family receives many guests, as was the case in my host family before my host parents departed on their pilgrimage to Mecca.

Excerpt #19

Ibu Kartika complained about the way they see people off to the *Haji* [pilgrimage to Mecca] here in Malang... She said that they made so much tea and the guests drank only a little. <u>So much tea was made *sia-sia* [in vain]</u>. I said that is how the Javanese like to do things. In my culture we did not like to make drinks *sia-sia* so we always asked if they would like to drink and if so, what. That way if they did not want to drink, we did not waste our time with making tea that would go to waste. But I said they don't like to do it that way here. She didn't dispute that. (My diary, April 24, 1994)

In this particular instance, I – as the learner – am trying to socialize the host by presenting an alternative course of action that would not result in so much waste. After presenting the alternative, however, I commented that, 'they don't like to do it that way here', which might be ambiguously interpreted as my acceptance of the local Javanese custom or as my criticism of it and the implicit suggestion that they ought to do it the American way. Ibu Kartika did not dispute what I said, but she also did not explicitly agree with it. This reinforced for me the value placed on hospitality toward one's guests in Indonesia. Hospitality and respect for one's guests as manifested in the serving of tea without offering them a chance to refuse (cf. DuFon, 1998) was far more important than concern with waste or the material value of the food or drink.

Food and health

The theme of food as nutrition found in Ochs *et al.'s* (1996) American data was far less prominent in these Indonesian data. There was in fact only one reference to specific nutrients (i.e. the vitamins in bananas) in the entire corpus. However, there were references to the connection between food and health. For example, both the learners and the Indonesians talked about the relationship between the quantity of food consumed and body weight. Both also referred to the low nutritional value of some foods such as candy, coffee and alcoholic beverages. Both groups talked about the ability of food to make one sick. However, the learners' journal entries reflected that they were more concerned about eating food that was unhygienic, too old or contained germs, probably because they were more vulnerable to these conditions than the Indonesians were. Nevertheless, for reasons of politeness, they were likely to avoid telling their hosts of this concern.

The Indonesians, on the other hand, sometimes talked about specific foods that they believe cause or contribute to certain diseases or conditions; for example, eating too much pineapple causes hemorrhoids, eating the Ambonese banana can interfere with a woman's reproductive abilities, and eating fried foods and seasonal fruits and drinking iced beverages aggravate a cough. This kind of talk socialized the learners regarding Indonesian folk beliefs concerning food and bodily conditions. In some cases, the learners rejected these beliefs. For example, when Kyle was alerted to the fact that drinking iced beverages aggravates coughing, his retort indicated that he was socialized in his native culture to believe the opposite – that drinking iced beverages soothes a cough.

Excerpt #20

1	**Ibu:**	*Mas Kyle [batuk jangan minum es.*
		Mas Kyle, [(if you) cough, don't drink ice.
2	**Kyle:**	*[ya?*
		[yeah?
		Minum es? Mengapa?
		Drink ice? Why (not)?

.
.
.

3	**Ibu:**	*Batuk.*
		Cough.
4	**Kyle:**	*Batuk?*
5	**Pak Budi:**	*O tidak- tidak boleh.*
		Oh, it's not- not good.
6	**Kyle:**	Oh OK.

.
.
.

7	**Kyle:**	*Mengapa-, mengapa ini um tidak bagus untuk- untuk?*
		Why, why isn't it good to- to?
8	**Pak Budi:**	*Kalau flu? Pi- uh pilek, batuk, minum es?*
		If you have the flu? Ru- uh runny nose, cough, drink ice?
9	**Kyle:**	Mhm.
10	**Pak Budi:**	*Makan es? Tidak bisa sembuh.*
		Eat ice? (You) cannot get well.

.
.
.

11	**Kyle:**	*Ya ketika saya menjadi sakit di uh rumah saya di Amerika?*
		Yeah, if I get sick at uh my home in America?
12	**Pak Budi:**	*Ah*
13	**Kyle:**	*Ibu saya selalu mem- memberi [es untuk saya.*
		My mother always gi- gives [me ice.
14	**Pak Budi:**	[*Ooooh*

At the point where this conversation ended, both participants had put forth their views on the relationship between ice and coughs, each trying to socialize the other. Neither appears to have accepted the folk beliefs of the other, but each is at least aware of another point of view. In my own case, although I did not record it in my journal or field notes, I came to shift my beliefs regarding the relationship between coughs and ice, fried foods and seasonal fruits. My own hypothesis testing following the presentation of these beliefs indicated that they were accurate; that is, all those foods aggravated my cough and I became healthy faster by avoiding them. The process of socialization makes the novice aware that another view exists and perhaps causes them to question their own belief system. It does not necessarily bring immediate change but can plant a seed that might eventually germinate and cause a shift in point of view.

Conclusions

Through their dinner table conversations, the study abroad students were socialized into the world of food in East Java by their Indonesian hosts; to some extent, the American students also socialized their Indonesian hosts. Six different thematic dimensions of taste were prominent in the discourse: orientation to the food, food as pleasure, food as a social identity marker, food as gifts, food as a material good, and food and health, with the first three being the most prominent. Each of the themes and how they were realized in the discourse is summarized below.

The first prominent theme was orientation to the food. It was realized through a variety of means including labeling the foods, naming at least some of the ingredients in a dish and describing their function, describing the taste of the dish, and giving some information about how the dish was made and how it was to be eaten. The study abroad learners played an active role in this process by asking for labels, repeating and practicing them, and asking for clarification when needed. This theme is most likely a widespread, possibly universal, theme that emerges when novices who are unfamiliar with the foods participate in the meal. It is possible, however, that the precise ways in which novices are oriented to the food through language varies across cultures. This chapter presents evidence concerning how orientation to the food is accomplished in Javanese Indonesian culture, and invites comparison with other cultural-linguistic groups.

The primacy of food as pleasure corresponds with both Ochs *et al.'s* (1996) Italian families and Iwai's (2001) Japanese family, and contrasts with Ochs *et al.'s* American families, who emphasized other themes more than food as pleasure. A number of discourse moves were utilized in order to implicitly send the message of the importance of food as pleasure. These included labeling the taste of food to educate the learners about the taste, commenting on the good taste when offering food to encourage the learners to taste it, warning the learners (or in the learners' case, inquiring) about spicy food so that they would not be unpleasantly surprised by the taste, complimenting the food immediately after tasting it, checking on whether the taste was good or to the liking of the taster, and criticizing when the taste was not appealing. All of these discourse moves are necessary in order to ensure that the food is enjoyed.

The relationship between taste and identity in this study corresponds to some degree with the findings of Ochs *et al.* (1996). In their study, however, food marked individual identities in the Italian case and age group identity (child vs. adult) in the American case. In the study presented here, which involved intergroup contact at the table, the importance of food as a national or regional ethnic identity marker was particularly salient. This was accomplished through questions about the foods and food preferences of the learners' cultures, and through statements that compared the peoples of the various countries and regions with respect to their food and taste preferences. This corresponds with Iino's (1996) study, which compared study abroad learners with their host families, and found that certain foods served as ethnic identity markers, and one's ability to enjoy them reinforced that identity.

The Ochs *et al.* (1996) study dealt with the socialization of children whereas this study dealt with the socialization of adults. Therefore, it is not surprising that the theme of food as reward, as found in the dinner talk of American families, was not salient here as adults would be less likely to control other adults with food rewards. However, the theme of food as gifts was salient. The learners' diaries often mentioned concern with what kind of *oleh-oleh* or gifts they should bring back from a certain place. During the dinner table talk, Indonesian hosts pointed out which foods had been given as gifts, where they had come from, and who had given them. This helped to demonstrate to the learners not only the importance of bringing gifts back from their excursions, but also which kinds of gifts to bring back.

While the theme of food as material good appeared occasionally, it differed from Ochs *et al.'s* (1996) American data in that food waste was not too much of a concern in Indonesia and was rarely discussed. This probably stems in part from the fact that little food is wasted. However, even when the topic did surface, other concerns such as hospitality and showing respect for the guest emerged as more important.

In contrast with Ochs *et al.'s* (1996) findings, the nutritional value of food was rarely discussed. However, the theme of food and health was sometimes present. During these conversations, the Indonesians presented their beliefs about the effects of various foods on one's health. These beliefs often conflicted with the study abroad learners' beliefs, and they in turn sometimes tried to socialize their hosts by presenting their contrasting beliefs. At other times, they shifted their beliefs to conform with those of the Indonesians.

In language acquisition, certain features of a second language are easy to acquire while others are difficult; these difficulties are due in part to the fact that they conflict with strongly ingrained first language patterns. Likewise in taste, certain preferences have been acquired that may make some preferences of the target culture difficult for the learner to acquire. Consequently, it may be more difficult to socialize the tastes of a non-native adult learner than it is to socialize the tastes of a native child learner. As with adult second language acquisition, socialization may be only partial. The evidence here indicates that the Indonesians were only partially successful in socializing their study abroad learners into their world of food. In some cases the learners resisted the Indonesians' attempts at socialization, and even tried to socialize their hosts. Yet there was some success not only in introducing the study abroad learners to new foods or in changing their eating behavior but also in changing the way in which they viewed food, as is evident from Kyle's comment below.

> My eating behavior has changed. Now I eat a lot in the morning, plus my eating etiquette has changed. Things that taste good taste really good. I kind of look at the food differently, with more respect. (Kyle's journal, Week 5, October, 1996)

Pedagogical Implications for Teaching Study Abroad Learners

To date, only a few studies have been conducted on the socialization of taste. These studies indicate that the dinner table is a site of socialization that offers many opportunities for learning *through the use of language* about a culture's values, beliefs, attitudes and view of food, and for learning *to use language* in certain ways in order to talk about food. Mealtime is the time that the learners in this study reported conversing with their host families a lot. Outside of mealtimes, there was typically less verbal interaction. Therefore mealtime was an important time for conversational practice for them. Additionally it is clear that sharing meals with Indonesian families and friends was an important means of socialization. During the meal, the learners were acquiring information about food and taste, how Indonesians view food, how they treat it, how they experience it and how they use it to identify themselves as united to or separate from others. Therefore, in order to get the greatest benefit out of the study abroad experience, it is crucial that study abroad learners be placed in a homestay situation in which they eat with their host families on a consistent basis.

Secondly, certain themes such as food as pleasure are widespread, perhaps universal, across cultures. However, the value placed on any one theme varies cross-culturally. Furthermore, the discourse that reflects and promotes that value also varies cross-culturally, and can result in language shock in intercultural interactions. Such was the case with the criticism of food in this study, at least for some of the study abroad learners. Consequently, prior to going abroad as well as during their stay in the host country, it would be beneficial to provide some explicit instruction regarding the taste preferences, beliefs, attitudes, and values with respect to food in the host country, and to educate learners concerning how language use supports these values, attitudes, and beliefs. For example, warning learners that they may very well receive criticism if they choose to cook for their Indonesian hosts could reduce language shock should this happen. Increasing their understanding by explaining the reasons behind the criticism (the importance of food as pleasure) and encouraging them to accept the criticism as constructive so that they can adapt their cooking to better fit the tastes of their Indonesian hosts could also lessen the likelihood of a negative affective response.

Thirdly, prior to going abroad, it would be useful to raise the learners' awareness (e.g. Rose, 1994) of their own taste preferences and to determine to what extent these are particular to them as an individual, to their family, to the various subcultures (ethnic, religious, regional) of which they are a member, and to their nationality. Learners might begin by reading *Socializing Taste* (Ochs *et al.*, 1996). They could then be assigned to observe the ways in which they and their family or friends talk about food as they eat, either by taking notes or by tape-recording and partially transcribing their meal time discussions. The individual experiences could then be compared and contrasted in class discussions. To the extent that diversity exists within the classroom, learners would become aware of the factors that influence taste preferences and the discourse on taste. Some comparison of other cultures' taste preferences and ways of talking about food could also be accomplished through various observation assignments (e.g. in supermarkets or restaurants that cater to different subcultural groups), or through the use of selected video clips or book excerpts [e.g. Amy Tan's (1989) *The Joy Luck Club*], where different foods, tastes, ways of eating, and ways of talking about food are evident and could be compared to the learners' culture.

Additionally, it is important to remember that many nations, like Indonesia, are ethnically and culturally diverse. There is not one Indonesian taste; rather taste preferences vary from region to region as well as from individual to individual. Providing some introduction to the taste preferences of at least some of the ethnic groups in the host country will help learners to appreciate the discussion of taste differences that often emerges in mealtime discourse in their host country, and to deepen their awareness of the diversity that exists within the country. Providing them with information on some of the stereotypes that the host culture has about the tastes of the learners' home cultures will help prepare them for some of the questions and comments they might receive regarding their individual or cultural eating patterns. Discussing possible ways of responding to these questions and comments could prove useful later when the learner is actually abroad.

Ochs and Schieffelin (1984) tell us that socialization is a lifelong process. For learners of Indonesian as a second language, this is indeed good news. They can return to Indonesia many times and each time continue to enjoy eating as they learn about the Indonesian values, beliefs, and world view associated with it. They can continue to experience food as pleasure and develop their appreciation for the many tastes of Indonesia.

Notes

1. The trips to Indonesia during which I collected my data were partially supported by a Bilingual Education Fellowship and grants from The East–West Center in Honolulu, Hawai'i, the Consortium on the Teaching of Indonesian, (COTI), Foreign Language and Area Studies (FLAS), and the College of Arts and Sciences at the University of Hawai'i-Manoa.
2. Iino (1996) distinguishes between culturally restricted foods such as *nattoo*, which are strongly associated with a Japanese identity, and internationalized foods such as teriyaki and tempura, which have more universal appeal and consequently do not have the same insider identity marking potential.
3. Visser (1991: 97) indicates that in ancient Greece and Rome, guests were also oriented to the food in a similar manner either through the use of menus or an explanation from the host or a specially instructed slave. The orientation consisted of indicating the different dishes to the guests, sometimes explaining what their ingredients were and how the dish had been prepared. The provenance, the freshness, and the age of the food and wines were also included.
4. East Timor was still part of Indonesia at the time the data were collected.

Chapter 5

Joint Construction of Folk Beliefs by JFL Learners and Japanese Host Families[1]

HARUKO MINEGISHI COOK

Introduction

From the perspective of language as a semiotic tool, this chapter examines the collaborative telling of folk beliefs in dinnertime conversations between learners of Japanese as a foreign language (henceforth JFL learner) and their host families. By 'language as a semiotic tool', I mean that language is not a symbolic object to describe the world but is a resource that can change the self and the environment (cf. Leontyev, 1981; Luria, 1976; Vygotsky, 1978, 1986; Wertsch, 1985). Language is a socially organized phenomenon, and meaning is not solely a property of linguistic form but is situated and negotiated in social interaction. It is also 'a medium for collaboratively constructing and evaluating ideas and recasting "facts" as interpretations' (Ochs *et al.*, 1992: 39).

Everyday storytelling is universal and socially and cognitively multi-functional. It is a fundamental means of construction of social identity (Bruner, 1990; Ochs & Capps, 1996; Schiffrin, 1996; Scollon & Scollon, 1981), language socialization of a novice (Bamberg, 1987; Blum-Kulka, 1997; Heath, 1983; Minami, 2002; Ochs & Taylor, 1994, 1995), and theory building (Blum-Kulka & Snow, 1992; Ochs *et al.*, 1989; Ochs *et al.*, 1992). Storytelling is a means of expressing events in our daily lives. A story is always told from a point of view (Labov, 1972a), and we express who we are by telling stories from our own point of view. Furthermore, the activity of storytelling is a way of transforming ourselves by revealing our assumptions and gaining insights on multiple perspectives (Schiffrin, 1996). By telling stories, we become aware of our hidden assumptions and of different views of a narrated event. Telling is also a collaborative activity between or among participants (Duranti & Brenneis, 1986; Goodwin, 1979; Jacoby & Ochs, 1995). Participants co-construct a sentence, stance, emotion or ideology in the telling. In this sense, the activity of collaborative telling interactionally aligns participants.

Everyday storytelling has been investigated in the context of family dinnertime talk, for cross-culturally, it is a social context where story-telling routinely occurs with the same family members (Blum-Kulka, 1997; Heath, 1983; Ochs *et al.*, 1989, 1992; Ochs & Taylor, 1994). Family din-nertime is bracketed by the beginning and ending of the meal, and is a time when family members spontaneously share stories. Family storytell-ing is a speech event in which children learn how to express who they are in a culturally appropriate manner (Blum-Kulka, 1997), and it is a locus for developing children's perspective-taking, metacognition, analytical/ critical thinking and theory reconstruction (Ochs *et al.*, 1992). Ochs and her associates propose that the activity of storytelling is an act of collaborative building of a theory. By participating in the joint activity of storytelling, children are given opportunities to acquire the skills to see events from perspectives different from their own, and thus learn that there are multiple versions of a so-called fact.

Storytelling provides a chance for problem solving. A problem is typi-cally told jointly by multiple members of the family, and thus told from different points of view. Seen from a different perspective, an event initially depicted as a problem can be resolved in the course of the telling. For this reason, Ochs *et al.* (1989) refer to family dinnertime as 'an opportunity space':

... a somewhat unique time period for many families wherein there is some assurance of a relatively captive audience for sounding things out. Dinnertime is thus an opportunity space – a temporal, spatial and social moment which provides for the possibility of joint activity among family members. (Ochs *et al.*, 1989: 238)

Since dinnertime talk is a routine activity with the same family members, it has a great impact on not only children's but also adult family members' cognitive and social development. It is an 'opportunity space' in which the family members can present, challenge, and reinterpret versions of 'fact' as well as co-construct shared perspectives, emotions and stances. It is in this space where family members jointly create, change and recreate their reality and social identities.

Ochs *et al.* (1992) propose that stories are theories because they satisfy the two conditions necessary for a theory. A theory offers explanations, and the explanations offered are challengeable. Everyday stories are theories, for they explain how a problematic event of a protagonist happened or will happen and can be challenged because they are merely one version of a fact. Since everyday stories are typically composed of events that the teller experienced, heard about or expects to happen, they have a temporal dimension. In contrast, folk beliefs concerning food, social customs and language often lack this temporal dimension, but they qualify as theories in that they provide explanations of generalizations. Since there are other possible explanations of the phenomenon in question and exceptions to the generalization are always found, folk beliefs are challengeable. For example, the folk belief that no foreigners can eat *nattoo* (fermented soybeans) because it is uniquely Japanese gives an explanation to the generalization that foreigners cannot eat *nattoo*. One can challenge it by offering a different explanation to the generalization as well as by providing an exception to it. In particular, when members of other cultural groups are present, folk beliefs are more likely to be challenged because members of other cultural groups are more likely to see things from different perspectives.

While there have been many studies looking at dinnertime talk in family settings, the phenomenon has not been extensively investigated between foreign language learners and their host families (although see DuFon, 2000a, this volume; Iino, 1996, this volume; Wilkinson, 1995, 2002). Family dinnertime talk involving a foreign language learner differs from that among immediate family members in some respects. One of the differences is that while immediate family members share the same cultural background, the host family and foreign language learner do not. When people from different cultural backgrounds gather, it is human nature to discuss and compare the differences and similarities in their cultural backgrounds and practices. While immediate family members tend to focus on topics of personal accounts in dinnertime talk (Blum-Kulka, 1997; Ochs *et al.*, 1989, 1992), the host family and visiting language learner often talk about different practices in their respective cultures (DuFon 2000a, this volume; Iino, 1996). What do comparisons between different cultural practices at dinnertime cognitively and socially entail? Are different versions of folk beliefs accepted or challenged? Do they help the participants understand different perspectives? The present study examines dinnertime talk between JFL learners and their host families. The goals of this study are to investigate (1) who initiates the telling of folk beliefs and how the initial telling develops during dinnertime, and (2) how the activity of telling folk beliefs provides opportunities to develop the participants' metacognitive awareness of each others' cultural practices.

Previous Studies on Dinnertime Talk between JFL Learners and their Host Families and Theories on the Japanese

To date, micro-analytic studies of dinnertime talk between foreign language learners and their host families have been scarce (although see DuFon, 2000a, this volume; Iino, 1996, this volume; Wilkinson, 1995, 2002). In particular, to the best of my knowledge, there are only two studies on dinnertime talk between JFL learners and their host families, those of McMeekin (2003, this volume) and Iino (1996, this volume). McMeekin (2003, this volume), based on conversation data collected from JFL learners in classrooms and homestay families in Sapporo, Japan, compared communication strategies used in negotiation in the two different settings. She found that JFL learners engage in more negotiations with the host family than they do in the classroom, and thus they receive more comprehensible input of the target language from the host family. McMeekin illustrates that through negotiations with host family members, the learners not only receive comprehensible input but also information on customs and practices of Japanese society. Iino (1996) investigated video- and tape-recorded dinnertable conversations of 30 pairs of American JFL learners and their host families who lived in Kyoto, Japan. He found that the Japanese host families use a different set of norms in speaking to their guests than they use when addressing native Japanese. In addition, the host family members talk about topics such as the uniqueness of Japanese culture. He reports that comparison of the cultures of Japan and the United States was the most common topic in his study. In sum, he points out that the different set of norms used by the Japanese host families symbolically positions JFL learners as outsiders of Japanese society, and that this behavioral pattern parallels the ideology of *nihonjinron*, or theories on the Japanese.

Nihonjinron (theories on the Japanese) is an ideology that states that the Japanese are unique and different from the rest of the world, in particular the western world. According to Yoshino (1992), this ideology restores and reinforces the national identity of Japanese by creating a division between things Japanese and the western world. It explains Japanese behavior and characteristics in terms of uniqueness and difference and creates a sharp dichotomy between Japanese and westerners.[2] *Nihonjinron* permeates folk beliefs about Japanese and westerners, stereotyped accounts without scientific evidence. Some examples of this line of thinking are that certain food items are so uniquely Japanese that no foreigner can eat them. Japanese culture is so different that no foreigner can understand and appreciate it. The Japanese language is so difficult that no foreigner can master it (cf. Miller, 1982). Some folk beliefs even posit physical differences as an explanation of cultural difference. For example, the Japanese traditional vegetarian diet is attributed to the longer length of the Japanese intestine, which is said to be suitable for digesting vegetables and grains. *Nihonjinron* permeates not only the daily life of Japanese but also scientific fields. For example, one of the most popular books published in the 1970s was written by a Japanese physician named Tsunoda (1978), who on the basis of scientific experiments argued that the Japanese brain is different from that of westerners, because Japanese process vowels and consonants in the opposite hemisphere of the brain. More recently, psychologists Markus and Kitayama (1991) argue that while American culture values an independent self, Japanese culture emphasizes the interdependence of self. Japanese are, thus, more group-oriented. There are a number of publications on intercultural communication, sociolinguistics and sociology as well, which attempt to make the point of how different Japanese are from westerners by using simple dichotomous variables (see Miller, 1995b). Since the collapse of the bubble economy in Japan around 1990, the Japanese have lost some of their confidence in their cultural superiority over the West and hence have become less enthusiastic in promoting *nihonjinron* (Sugimoto, 1997). Nonetheless, the ideology of *nihonjinron* is still alive and pervasive in contemporary Japanese society. It creates a sharp dichotomy between Japanese and foreigners (in particular westerners) emphasizing the uniqueness of the Japanese people, culture and language.

Iino (1996) suggests that the use of different speaking norms by Japanese host families and a unique choice of topics in conversations with JFL learners can be partly attributed to *nihonjinron*. For example, in his data, one of the manifestations of *nihonjinron* is that the Japanese believe that certain Japanese food items such as *nattoo* (fermented soybeans) are so unique that foreigners cannot eat them. He reports that the behavior of the Japanese host families ranges from extreme praise such as *yuushuu na gaijin* 'excellent foreigner' to the withholding of a food item from the student when their American student eats uniquely Japanese food. He claims that comments such as *yuushuu na gaijin* 'excellent foreigner' deviate from the native Japanese speaking norm, for no Japanese utters such a phrase to another Japanese when he or she eats uniquely Japanese food, for example. He shows that the choice of a topic such as *nattoo* (fermented soybeans) is in line with other discursive practices of the Japanese host families such as code-switching to foreigner talk, which separate the Japanese from the non-Japanese. Iino's study indicates that by the use of a different speaking and interpreting norm from the one used in native Japanese conversation, the Japanese families create the 'other' in interactions with American students both in the content and the manner of their talk.

However, Iino's study (1996) does not directly address the question of how the JFL learners respond to host families' comments on cultural stereotypes. Dinnertime talk involving a JFL learner is potentially an 'opportunity space' in which the participants exchange different perspectives on their folk beliefs and possibly change them. In order to see how a topic unfolds and what happens in this process, we need to raise the following questions: Who initiates a topic on folk beliefs on culture and stereotypes? Once a topic is initiated, is it accepted or challenged? Who challenges it? As the result of the challenge, do the participants shift their perspectives on the topic? When the topic is not challenged, what happens? What is accomplished by the telling of such folk beliefs? The present study builds on Iino's observations and investigates how the dynamic process of co-telling writes and rewrites versions of the participants' folk theories about the Japanese and exchange students' home cultures.

Method

The data come from 22 video- and audio-taped dinner table conversations of eight JFL learners and their Japanese host families, who reside in the Tokyo area. The data used in this study are a part of a larger study involving nine JFL learners and their host families.[3]

Participants

The eight learners consisted of four female and four male learners, whose Japanese proficiency level ranges from approximately novice to advanced on the OPI (Oral Proficiency Interview) scale.[4] Since the purpose of the study was neither to measure the learner's proficiency level nor their improvement, assessment of the learners' Japanese proficiency level was not an essential component of the study. Therefore, no proficiency test of Japanese was given to the learners. The OPI level given in Table 5.1 is a subjective assessment based on the conversational data that I collected. As for the nationality of the learners, Julie was Korean, and Alice and Mary were British. The rest of the learners were American. The learners were all college students, who studied Japanese as a foreign language at university prior to coming to Japan. They were enrolled in a year-in-Japan program for foreign students at a

Table 5.1 JFL learners

Name*	Japanese proficiency level (OPI scale)	Japanese language learning experiences prior to arriving in Japan	Length of stay in Japan
Alice	Novice	2 years in university	4 months
Tom	Novice	5 semesters in university	4 months
Rick	Intermediate/low	3 years in university	4 months
Julie	Intermediate	2 years in high school 2 semesters in university 3 months in a language institute	4 months
Greg	Intermediate	4 years in university	4 months
Skip	Advanced/low	2 years in university	9 months (+2 months)
Ellen	Advanced	6 years in high school 2 years in university mother is native Japanese	8 months (+3 years)
Mary	Advanced	1 year in university mother is native Japanese	12 months

*All the learners' names are pseudonyms.

Japanese university in the Tokyo area, studying the Japanese language as well as subjects related to Japan. During their stay in Japan, which was typically nine or ten months, they lived with a Japanese host family. At the time of data collection, Mary and had lived in Japan with the host family for 12 months, Skip for nine months, and Ellen for eight months. Both Mary and Ellen had a mother who was a native Japanese speaker. Ellen had also lived in Japan for three years between the ages of six and nine. Skip had lived in Japan two months before during summer. The rest of the learners had lived in Japan with their host family for four months at the time of the data collection.

The host families were typical middle-class Japanese families in the Tokyo area, who spoke standard Tokyo Japanese. Table 5.2 shows who

Table 5.2 Host families

Host family	Members who participated in dinnertime talk	Reason for hosting a learner
Alice's family	Host mother Host brothers (ages 10 and 7) Host sister (age 5)	Interest in foreign culture Wanted foreigners to understand Japan
Tom's family	Host mother and father Host sister (age 19)	Interest in international exchange
Rick's family	Host mother and father Host brother (age 24) Host sister (age 30)	Be able to get to know a foreigner Good for the family members
Julie's family	Host mother	Learned from a former professor of the husband
Greg's family	Host mother	Wanted to learn about foreign culture
Skip's family	Host mother Host sister (college age)	The daughter lived in a foreign country and stayed with a host family
Ellen's family	Host mother and father	The daughter wanted to learn English
Mary's family	Host mother and father Host brother (college age)	The daughter lived in a foreign country and stayed with a host family

in the host family participated in the dinnertime talk with the learner. Participants in the dinnertime conversation were either the host parents or the host mother and host siblings, in all cases except for Skip and Julie. Only the host mother and the learner were present at the dinner in the host families of Skip and Julie. The host siblings were college age or older except for Alice's host family, which had three small children. All the families had past experiences of hosting a foreign student. Their reason for hosting a foreign student was mostly due to an interest in foreign culture. Skip and Mary's families volunteered to be a host family because they wanted to reciprocate the kindness their daughters had received from their host families when they studied abroad. The host families spent about one to three hours a day with the learners at home. All but Tom's host family said in the questionnaire that the learners and the host family members spoke with each other in Japanese more than 90% of the time. Only Tom's host family reported that they spoke in Japanese with Tom more than 60% of the time. Their self-reports seem to correctly reflect their practice, for almost all conversations in the data were carried out in Japanese. Only Tom and his host family sometimes switched to English, for his host father seemed to want to use English. For the most part, code-switching to English was rare.

Data collection and analysis

In order to record the conversations, the researcher asked the learners to place a video camera on a tripod and a small audio-cassette recorder on the dinner table. Dinnertime conversations were recorded three times (three different evenings) by each learner, with one exception. Skip recorded the conversation only once for 90 minutes. The learners and the host families were asked to turn off the TV during dinner.[5] The length of the dinnertime conversations ranged from 30 to 90 minutes, averaging 52 minutes. The researcher was not present at the dinner in order to keep the conversation as natural as possible [what Iino (this volume) calls the 'remote observation method']. After the recordings were made, to find out more about the background of the learners and host families, separate questionnaires were given to the learners and their host families. The entire corpus of conversations was transcribed and subject to microanalysis. Folk beliefs were first identified, then categorized according to topic. Each token of a folk belief was then examined and categorized according to who initiated the topic, whether the folk belief was accepted or challenged; and when it was challenged, who challenged it.

Telling of Folk Beliefs

In what ways are folk beliefs expressed in the dinnertime conversation between the host family and the JFL learner? To investigate this question, I tabulated instances of explicitly mentioned topics of folk beliefs on culture. By topics of folk beliefs on culture, I mean topics that assert or compare the generalization or stereotype of some aspects of culture, that of the Japanese hosts or that of the learners. In the present corpus of 22 dinnertime conversations, I found a total of 52 instances in which participants explicitly expressed folk beliefs about culture. This means that at each dinnertime conversation, on the average, at least two such instances of folk beliefs were discussed. These 52 instances fell into seven topic categories. Table 5.3 shows the topics of folk belief that appeared in the present data.[6]

Table 5.3 shows that cultural comparisons and/or stereotypical comments were made most frequently in relation to topics of food and eating habits, social customs, and language. Topics of food and eating habits were most frequently discussed (42.3%), perhaps because the conversations took place at the dinner table. As we shall see in the examples that follow, Japanese hosts often referred to the uniqueness of Japanese food (see also Iino, 1996), a practice that is consistent with *nihonjinron*. The participants compared the social customs in Japan and those in the learner's home countries ranging from what people do on Valentine's Day to what barbers do in the barbershop. The topic of language included comparisons of Japanese and English as well as comments on Japanese as a difficult language.[7] As we will see in the discussion that follows, culture-related topics served as a resource through which the Japanese host families expressed the folk belief of the uniqueness of the Japanese or that of the superiority/inferiority of the Japanese. The host families frequently mentioned that certain food items and certain social customs are found only in Japan. The belief that the Japanese are superior or inferior to westerners was expressed as a comparison. For example, Japanese food is more delicious than American food, or Japanese graves are gloomier than their American counterparts.

Telling is a dynamic process in that it makes the participants aware of their assumptions, and recasts 'facts' as interpretations. To see this

Table 5.3 Topics of folk belief on culture

Topics	Raw number	Percentage
Food and eating habits	22	42.3%
Social customs	16	30.7%
Language	6	11.5%
Business/price	3	5.8%
Biological/psychological trait	2	3.9%
Japanese traditional art	2	3.9%
Gender role	1	1.9%
Total	52	100%

process, we will investigate how the topics that assert or compare cultural stereotypes were initiated, developed and evaluated in the course of conversation. The data were tabulated according to the following three categories: (1) Who initiates a topic on folk belief, a Japanese host family member or the JFL learner? (2) Once initiated, is it accepted or challenged? (3) Who challenges it? Table 5.4 shows the patterns that emerged.

Table 5.4 indicates that half of the time (48.1% + 1.9% = 50%) the topic of folk belief was unchallenged, and half of the time (40.4% + 9.6% = 50%), it was challenged. Challenges came mostly from the learner (40.4%) but sometimes from another member of the host family (9.6%).[8]

When the topic was not challenged, the expressed view was jointly cast as a fact, whereas when it was challenged, often a different perspective was collaboratively constructed. Except for one instance, all the topics of folk belief were initiated by the Japanese host family members, which suggests that, compared with the JFL learners, the Japanese host families did not hesitate to make stereotypical judgments about their own culture nor about those of others. Due to the sociopolitical climate of western societies, American and British students in particular were perhaps more cautious in making stereotypical judgments of other cultures (Condor, 2000; Tusting *et al.*, 2002; van Dijk 1992). However, a close examination of the conversation data reveals that the learners were often co-tellers jointly constructing folk beliefs with host family members. Since the number of challengeable topics that occurred in dinnertime conversations differed from family to family, and the number of learners in the study was rather small, I did not tabulate the correlations between frequencies of challenges and the learners' proficiency level. However, even novice learners challenged a folk belief that was initiated by a host family member. For example, novice learners with a four-month stay in Japan, such as Alice, sometimes challenged host family members. Excerpt #1 illustrates Alice's challenge to her host mother's

Table 5.4 Initiator and challenger of topics of folk beliefs

Challenger	Initiator	
	Host family member	*JFL learner*
No challenger	25 (48.1%)	1 (1.9%)
JFL learner	21 (40.4%)	—
Host family member	5 (9.6%)	0 (0%)

tacit assumption that Japanese food is strange to foreigners. As a result, the host mother changes her mind.

Excerpt #1 Alice (012402)

1 **HM:**   *kitto ne Arisu no tomodachi nee (.) saisho ni ne kita hi no*
            bangohan wa hutsuu no Igirisu ryoori ga ii n ja nai
            Maybe your friend on the evening of her arrival, English
            food would be good, wouldn't it?

2 **A:**   *un*
            um

3 **HM:**   *daijoobu?*
            Would that be OK?

4 **A:**   *Igirisu ryoori?*
            English food?

5 **HM:**   *tsukaretenai? tsukareteru toki ni sa sushi da no Japanese da no*
            tsukareru. Daijoobu?
            Won't she be tired? When she is tired, eating sushi and
            Japanese food would be tiresome. Would those (sushi and
            Japanese food) be OK?

6 **A:**   *nan demo ii.*
            Anything would be fine.

7 **HM:**   *nan demo ii.*
            Anything would be fine.

8 **A:**   *un*
            yeah

9 **HM:**   *jaa sushi demo?*
            Well, then how about sushi?

Here Alice's English friend is coming from England to visit her in Tokyo soon, so the host mother is wondering what to cook for dinner on the day the friend arrives. In line 1, she suggests that English food would be good and gives the reason why in line 5. She says that Alice's friend will be tired when she arrives from England, and might find it tiresome to eat Japanese food. The tacit assumption is that Japanese food is so different from English food that it is strange to English people. The host mother's proposal to cook English food for Alice's friend may be taken as a kind consideration. In line 6, Alice refutes her host mother's position that her British friend would prefer English food when she is tired. In line 7, the host mother accepts Alice's position by repeating what she just said. It may be that Alice's response in line 6 is made out of politeness (i.e. the host mother does not have to go to extra trouble to cook English food). In any case, the host mother's offer is not readily accepted. The fact that in line 9 the host mother offers to prepare *sushi* (Japanese food made of rice seasoned with vinegar topped with raw fish) indicates that she has changed her assumption that eating Japanese food is tiresome for a foreigner. Here the host mother in the collaborative telling with the novice learner Alice constructs a new perspective on Japanese food.

We tend to think that lower-level proficiency learners are incapable of performing various social acts using the target language. Examples such as Excerpt #1, however, suggest that such an assumption is incorrect. In the present study, the two novice-level learners who had been in Japan for four months were capable of challenging and/or aligning with the Japanese host family members when they engaged in the discussion of cultural folk beliefs in Japanese.

Collaborative Construction of Folk Belief

In this section, I will qualitatively examine what happens when the topic is challenged and unchallenged. By 'challenge', I mean both total and partial disagreements.

Challenges to folk beliefs

While both the JFL learners and the host family members challenge folk beliefs, the former do so far more frequently than the latter. The learners challenge by presenting a perspective from their own culture, typically providing a counterexample by stating that the challenger is an exception to the stated case, or asserting the 'universal point of view'. By 'universal point of view', I mean the point of view that claims that all human beings are in essence the same regardless of cultural differences. This is a position diametrically opposed to *nihonjinron*. Challenges create an 'opportunity space' (Ochs *et al.*, 1989) where both parties, but in particular the host family members, potentially become aware that what they have believed to be true may not be true, or what they have held to be true unconsciously becomes conscious knowledge.

A different perspective from another culture

Excerpt #2 illustrates how the learner's perspective changes the host mother's personal perspective on a Japanese traditional custom. In this segment, the host mother is explaining to Julie the Japanese custom of cherry blossom viewing.

Excerpt # 2 Julie (012502)

1	**HM:**	*saku no wa sangatsu no owari gurai sakura ga un saku no wa ne* It's about the end of March when cherry blossoms bloom.
2	**J:**	*gakki hajimaru toki* when the semester starts
3	**HM:**	*un soo da ne un* Yeah, that's right, yeah.
4	**J:**	*to dooji watashi tachi asobi ni [iku* ((laugh)) At the same time, we go play.
5	**HM:**	[*un* uh huh
6	**HM:**	*minna osake o motte iku **no*** Everyone takes sake.
7	**J:**	*UN?* what?
8	**HM:**	*un* uh huh
9	**J:**	*kooen no naka ni?* inside the park?
10	**HM:**	*un tabun ne ano waseda no mukai gawa no a- kokusaibu no mukai gawa no ano moo chotto saki iku to sakura ga kirei na tokoro ga aru **no***. Probably uh the opposite side of Waseda, the opposite side of the International Center, uh if you go further, there is a place where the cherry blossoms are pretty.
11	**J:**	*hai hai* yes, yes
12	**HM:**	*soko ni [minna iku **no*** Everyone goes there.
13	**J:**	[*WAA* Wow!
14	**HM:**	[*un* uh huh
15	**J:**	[*OSAKE:?* sake?
16	**HM:**	*un* uh huh
17	**J:**	*niawanai awanai* They don't go together. They don't go together
18	**HM:**	*awanai?* They don't go together?

19 J: *funiki ga*
            An atmosphere (is not)
20 HM: *un*
            yeah
21 J: *nande ka hon toka*
            Why not books?
22 HM: [*uun chigau **no** nihonjin wa*
            Un uh different, the Japanese are.
23 J: [(   ) ((laugh))
24 HM: *sakura no shita de obentoo to*
            under cherry blossoms, we have lunch boxes and
25 J: *un*
            uh huh
26 HM: *sore kara*
            and then
27 J: *obentoo wa au*
            A lunch box will match.
28 HM: *obentoo wa daijobu?*
            Is a lunch box all right?
29 J: *un*
            yeah
30 HM: *sore to osake*
            and *sake*
31 J: *huun osake?*
            uh *sake?*
32 HM: *un*
            uh huh
33 J: *uun*
            nn
34 HM: *na **no** ((laugh))*
            that's the case.
35 J: (   )
36 HM: *un*
            uh huh
37 J: *kirei na hana no shita ni*
            Under beautiful cherry blossoms
38 HM: *un*
            uh huh
39 J: *hanaki no shita ni hon o yonde*
            Under cherry blossoms read a book

40   **HM:**   *un aa [sono hoo ga romantikku da na*
             nn uh that would be more romantic.
41   **J:**   [((laugh))
42   **HM:**   *un*
             Yeah.

In this segment, when the host mother explains this Japanese custom, the learner Julie offers the challenge that cherry blossoms and *sake* (Japanese rice wine) do not go together. In line 6, the host mother explains that everyone takes *sake* to cherry blossom viewing. In line 7, Julie produces a repair initiator in a loud voice, which suggests that she cannot believe that people take *sake* to the park to see cherry blossoms. In line 8, the host mother confirms what she said in line 6, and Julie asks again if people really take *sake* to the park (line 9). The host mother does not respond to this question and goes on to explain more about the location of flower-viewing. Then, Julie says OSAKE:? with a prolonged vowel [e] uttered with a rising intonation in a loud voice (line 15), which also suggests Julie's disbelief that the Japanese drink *sake* while viewing cherry blossoms. In line 17, Julie challenges the Japanese custom of drinking *sake* while viewing cherry blossoms. She mentions that *sake* does not match the atmosphere of flower viewing. She asks why people don't bring books instead of *sake* (line 21). In line 22, the host mother justifies the Japanese custom of drinking *sake* while viewing cherry blossoms by saying *chigau no Nihonjin wa* 'different, the Japanese are'. She attempts to justify the Japanese custom by appealing to *nihonjinron* (theories on the Japanese), but her attempt is not successful. Her justification neither convinces Julie nor resolves the conflicting views between the two. The host mother continues to tell Julie about the Japanese custom of bringing lunch boxes and *sake* to cherry blossom viewing. Julie is not yet convinced by the host mother's explanation. In line 34, the host mother concludes her explanation with *na no* 'the case is'. Then, Julie repeats her idea of reading a book under cherry blossoms (lines 37 and 39). In line 40, the host mother finally agrees with Julie that reading a book would be more romantic than drinking *sake*.

Note that in presenting the custom of cherry blossom viewing, the host mother constantly uses the final particle *no* as seen in lines 6, 10, 12, 22 and 34 [e.g. minna osake o motte iku **no**; sakura ga kirei na tokoro ga aru **no**; soko ni minna iku **no**; uun chigau **no** Nihonjin wa; (sore to osake) na **no**], but does not in line 40, which suggests that she finally agreed with Julie's view at the personal level. The final particle *no* is a nominalizer, which makes the sentence a nominal sentence.

It indexes a group 'voice' (Bakhtin, 1981/1935) rather than the speaker's individual voice (Cook, 1990a, 1990b). In other words, it indexes that the proposition is the generally accepted view of the group.[9] Since a fact is a generally accepted view by a group, the proposition with the particle *no* is taken as a fact (Aoki, 1986). When the proposition expresses social customs or norms, the particle *no* may index the speaker as a spokesperson of society who is presenting the socially accepted view. For this reason, the particle *no* is a tool for persuading others without confronting them with a personal opinion. In this sense, the host mother presents the custom of cherry blossom viewing from the generally accepted view in Japanese society rather than her personal opinion. After being confronted with Julie's challenge and proposal, the host mother says:

40 **HM:** *sono hoo*   *ga*   *romantikku*   *da*   *na*
       that   SUB   romantic   COP   FP
       That would be more romantic.

This utterance ends with the copula *da* followed by a sentence-final particle *na*. The particle *na* is an informal variant of the particle *ne*. When the speaker is a female, the particle *na* often indexes that the speaker is addressing herself (cf. Uyeno, 1971). Thus, here the host mother is telling herself that reading a book is more romantic than drinking *sake*. Since the sentence-final particle *no* does not occur in this utterance, the utterance indexes that the speaker is speaking in her personal voice. The shift from utterances with *no* in lines 6, 10, 12, 22 and 34 to an utterance without *no* in line 40 suggests that the host mother keeps her personal view apart from the general view of Japanese society. In presenting the Japanese custom of cherry blossom viewing, she was speaking in the voice of a spokesperson of Japanese society but when she realizes that Julie's idea is more romantic, she speaks in her own personal voice. In line 40, she is in agreement with Julie at the personal level. Thus, Julie's challenge presented the host mother with an alternative activity to do while cherry blossom viewing.

In Excerpt #3, the host sister's position is challenged by the learner Skip. In this host family, the host sister believes that Japanese food is delicious but American food is not. In lines 1 and 2 she expresses the view that American food does not taste good based on her own experiences in the United States. Thus, her utterance in line 4 is interpreted in the frame of a comparison of America versus Japan.

Excerpt #3 Skip (061001)

1 **HS:** *datte, watashi amerika de oishii mono tabete nai n da mon.*
            But, I did not eat anything delicious in America.
2 **S:**   *tabeteru yo.*
            You ate (something delicious.)
3 **HS:** *tabete nai yo. Oishiku nakatta mon datte.*
            I did not. Food did not taste good.
((A few minutes later.))
4 **HS:** *nihon no- nihon no ryoori sugoi oishiku nai?*
            Isn't the Japanese- Japanese cuisine very delicious?
5 **S:**   *oishii*
            It's delicious.
6 **HS:** *oishii deshoo.*
            It's delicious, isn't it?
7 **S:**   *oishii oishii tama ni hen dakedo, daitai oishii.*
            It's delicious, delicious, but sometimes it's strange. But
             mostly delicious.
8 **HM:** [(((laugh))
9 **HS:** [(((laugh))
10 **HM:** *sorezore chicchai toki kara no aji ga aru mon ne.*
            Each of us has a taste we are used to from childhood.
11 **S:**   *un*
            uh huh

Skip first agrees with the host sister, but in line 7 he challenges the host sister's sweeping generalization that Japanese food is delicious, but American food is not. He does so by adding the modifier *tama ni* 'sometimes' to soften the face-threatening act of challenge. In line 10, the host mother finally says that we all prefer food that we are used to from childhood, which justifies Skip's challenge to the host sister. In line 11 Skip produces a token of acknowledgment and the host sister does not counter-challenge her mother. At this point, the taste of Japanese food is no longer absolute but is relative to one's own cultural tradition or background. Skip's challenge to the host sister's stereotype provides an opportunity for the host mother to share her view.

A counterexample as an exception

The JFL learners may give a counterexample in order to challenge the stereotypical view expressed by a host family member. Rather than directly give a counterexample, to be polite, they often present it as an exception to the rule. Such exceptions can be drawn from the learner's own personal practice or observations. In Excerpt #4, the host mother and brother display their folk belief that Americans live on beef. The learner Rick challenges this folk belief by stating that his family in the United States eats more chicken than beef.

<u>Excerpt #4 Rick (011702)</u>

1 **HB:**   *Amerikajin nante sa (.) mi- nani? Amerika de kyoogyuubyoo ga*
           mikkatara sa (.) minna taihen da yo ne
           Americans al- uh If mad cow disease were found in America
           all (Americans) would be in big trouble.

2 **R:**   [*un?*
           Uh?

3 **HB:**   [*Amerikajin minna kyoogyuubyoo jan.*
           All Americans would contract mad cow disease.

4 **HM:**   ((laugh))

5 **R:**   ((laugh))

6 **HM:**   *niku no- niku no nai seikatsu ja nai mon ne?*
           meat- there they cannot live without meat.

7 **R:**   *un*
           uh huh

8 **HM:**   *niku no seikatsu da mon nee.*
           They live on meat, don't they?

9 **R:**   *un*
           uh huh

10 **HB:**   *nihon wa niku ga nakute mo seikatsu ga dekiru kedo sa*
           In Japan we can live without meat.

11 **R:**   *un*
           uh huh

12 **HB:**   *Amerikajin wa tabun seikatsu dekinai*
           Probably Americans cannot live without it.

13 **R:**   *un ha: dekinai* ((laugh)) (1.5)
           Uh huh uh:: cannot

14 **HB:**   *taihen da to omou=*
           It would be difficult, I think.

15 **HM:**   =*buta yori gyuu wa taberu no ne?*
           You eat beef rather than pork, don't you?

16 **R:**   *un*
           uh huh

17 **HM:** *gyuuniku no ne? suteeki toka ooi desho?*
            I guess you eat a lot of beefsteak?
18 **R:**   *un* (5.0) *demo gyuu yori tori niku taberu*
            uh   but we eat more chicken than beef.
19 **HM:** *a- soo=*
            Is that so?
20 **R:**   *=to omou (.) un*
            I think (.) uh huh
21 **HM:** [*un*
            mhmm
22 **R:**   [*boku no kazoku wa*
            my family
23 **HM:** *un*
            uh huh
24 **HB:** *kenkoo dakara desho?*
            because it's healthy?
25 **R:**   *un uun? (.) un*
            uh huh? (.) yeah.
26 **HB:** *dakara abura ga sukunai*
            So it's less greasy.
27 **HM:** *aa sokka* (2.0) *ie de tsukuru toki wa okaasan*
            Oh yeah. (2.0) When your mother cooks at home
28 **R:**   *un aa tsukau?*
            Yeah, uh she uses it.
29 **HM:** *un* (.)
            mhmm
30 **R:**   *ano-*
            well-
31 **HM:** *toriniku o tsukau*
            She uses chicken.

Here in lines 1 and 3, while talking about mad cow disease, the host brother makes an assertion that if mad cow disease were found in America, all Americans would contract it, which presupposes that all Americans eat beef. In lines 6 and 8, the host mother explicitly expresses this presupposition. Then in lines 10 and 12, the host brother makes a stereotypical comparison between Japan and United States regarding meat eating. In line 13, Rick does not challenge the host brother's stereotypical generalization at this time but produces an acknowledgment token. But when the host mother comments that Americans eat more beef than pork in lines 15 and 17, Rick offers as a counterexample his personal account that his family eats more chicken, in lines 18, 20 and 22. Both the host brother and mother display an acknowledgement of Rick's statement. The host brother does so by giving an explanation why and the host mother, by repetition. In so doing, the host family members acknowledge that there are exceptions to the generalization. Thus, the stereotype initially presented is no longer valid.

Universal point of view

Challenges may take the form of an assertion of the universal point of view, which claims that the nature of all human beings is basically the same. In the present data, there are three such cases. In all three cases, one host family member has the universal point of view and challenges another who believes that the Japanese are different from the rest of the world. The presence of the JFL learner at the dinner table triggers differences in opinion among the Japanese host family members. In Excerpt #5, the host mother's folk belief, which presupposes *nihonjinron* is challenged by the host father's universal point of view.

Excerpt #5 Mary (012802)

1 **HM:** =*obaachan wa?*
Your grandma?
2 **M:** *a obaachan wa iru=*
Uh my grandma is still alive.
3 **HM:** =*a- genki na no?=*
Uh is she healthy?
4 **M:** =*mada genki genki. Chotto atama ga boketeru mitai dakedo @saikin wa@*
She is still healthy healthy but seems to be a little forgetful recently.
5 **M:** [*huun·*
Uh huh
6 **HF:** [((laugh))
7 **HM:** =*arutsuhaimaa na no kashira=*
I wonder if she has Alzheimer's.
8 **M:** =*e?=*
What?
9 **HM:** =*arutsuhaimaa na no kashira ne=*
I wonder if she has Alzheimer's.
10 **M:** =*iya sonna n ja nai kedo [yappari toshi totteru n ja nai*
No, it's not that but after all she is old, I guess.

11 **HM:**   [*un*
                                                mhmm
12 **M:**   =[*moo nankai mo onaji koto* [*yuu no onaji kaiwa de*=
            She says the same thing many times in the same
            conversation.
13 **HM:**   [*un*   [*hu:n*
            uh huh   oh
14 **HM:**   =*un un ja soo yuu no wa are ne yappa nihonjin mo igirisujin mo*
            issho na no ne=
            uh uh well in that regard the Japanese and the British are the
            same, aren't they?
15 **HF:**   =*issho da yo ningen da mon*=
            We are the same since we are human beings.
16 **HM:**   =((laugh))=
17 **HF:**   =*n*((laugh))=
            yeah.
18 **HM:**   =*hu:n*=
            uh huh.

In Excerpt #5, the host mother asks Mary about her grandmother who lives
in England. She says that her grandmother has become forgetful because
of her age. Then in line 14, the host mother states that both Japanese and
English people are the same in that regard. The way she says it is contrastive. The propositional content of line 14 is reproduced for explanation:

14 *soo yuu no **wa** are ne yappa nihonjin mo igirisujin mo issho*
    such Nom Top that FP also Japanese too English too same
    na no ne
    COP FP FP
    'well in that regard the Japanese and the British are the same, aren't
    they?

The antecedent of *soo iu no* 'in that regard' is forgetfulness in this context.
The topic marker *wa* in *soo iu no wa* 'as for that regard' marks a sentential
topic. When an element is selected as a topic, it implicitly contrasts with
another element that is not selected (Cook, 1993; Kuno, 1973). Thus, the
particle *wa* can mark a contrast. Therefore, the host mother's utterance
can imply that in one aspect, the Japanese and British are the same but
in other aspects, they are not. The host father in line 15 expresses his
view that all human beings are made equally.

15 **HF:**   *issho*   *da*   **yo**   *ningen da*   *mon*
            same   COP   FP   human COP   FP
            We are the same *yo*.   We are human beings.

Here the host father's utterance with the sentence-final particle *yo* demonstrates his understanding of the contrastive interpretation of the host mother's utterance (i.e. in one aspect, the Japanese and British are the same but in other aspects, they are not). The sentence-final particle *yo* is a pragmatic assertion marker (Cook, 1991). It is often used when the speaker asserts something new or different from what the speaker assumes the hearer knows or believes (Maynard, 1997). The host father's assertion of the sameness of the Japanese and British challenges the host mother's perspective of *nihonjinron*. He then adds the reason (*ningen da mon* 'we are human beings'), which expresses the universal point of view.

A refusal of a challenge

An opportunity to jointly construct a different view can be missed when the initial teller of a folk belief flatly refuses the challenge. This happened only once in the present data when a child challenged the mother's stereotypical comment about the Japanese. This is illustrated in Excerpt #6. Here the host mother is telling Alice that all Japanese love cream puffs.

Excerpt #6 Alice (012402)

1 **HM:**   *nihonjin wa shuukuriimu daisuki [minna daisui*
            Japanese love cream puffs   everybody loves them
2 **A:**   [*u::n*
                                               mhmm
3 **HM:**   *ojiichan mo obaachan mo kodomo mo.*
            Grandpa, grandma and children (all love them).
4 **HB:**   *Koochan kirai.*
            I do not like them.
5 **HM:**   *nihonjin ja nai yo.*
            You are not Japanese
  A: ((laugh))

In line 3, she emphasizes the comment she made in line 1 by elaborating who all the Japanese are. Then in line 4, the 10-year-old host brother challenges his mother by saying that he does not like cream puffs, which invalidates the host mother's statement because the host brother is obviously Japanese. At this point, instead of accommodating his assertion and repairing her prior statement, she justifies her stereotype by claiming that her son does not fit her category. Perhaps because challenged by her own young son, the host mother needed to save her face in the presence of the JFL learner.[10]

In sum, an example like Excerpt #6 is very rare in the present data. In fact, this is the only instance in which a challenger is made to be wrong. This is perhaps because the challenger is a young child, it is easier for his mother to flatly reject him. Most challenges and their reactions in my data are expressed in a more polite manner, and help the participants collaboratively construct a new perspective.

Collaborative construction of a fact

Not all folk beliefs are challenged. In the present data, as shown in Table 5.2, about half of the time, folk beliefs and stereotypes are unchallenged. However, this does not necessarily mean that a Japanese host family member is the teller of a folk belief and the learner is a passive recipient of this folk belief. Rather both parties often collaboratively construct the initial teller's proposition about a folk belief as a fact. The learner participates as a co-teller to align him/herself to the initial teller's view or co-construct a proposition. In Excerpt #7 the learner Rick is a co-teller aligning himself to the host mother's view. Just prior to this segment, the participants were talking about the Japanese version of the proverb, 'When in Rome, do as the Romans do'. After a short pause, the host mother brings up the topic of the Japanese food *nattoo* (fermented soybeans) and comments that Rick is unusual in that he likes it. This statement presupposes that foreigners do not like *nattoo* and that since Rick is a foreigner, it is unusual for him to like it.

<u>Excerpt #7 Rick (011602)</u>

1	**HM:**	*demo nattoo ga suki na n te ne?*
		But that you like *nattoo*
2	**R:**	*un*
		uh huh
3	**HM:**	*mezurashii ne?* ((laugh))
		is unusual, isn't it?
4	**R:**	°*henna gaijin*°
		a strange foreigner
5	**HS:**	*henna gaijin*
		a strange foreigner
6	**R:**	((laugh))
7	**HM:**	*henna gaijin* ((laugh))
		a strange foreigner

Although the host mother omits *gaijin ni shite wa* 'for a foreigner' in line 3, her utterance is understood that liking *nattoo* is unusual for a foreigner due to the presupposition implicit to the context. Also since it is said right after they talked about the proverb, 'When in Rome, do as the Romans do', the host mother's utterance even implies that when it comes to *nattoo*, no foreigner can follow the proverb, which makes Rick even more unusual for a foreigner. In line 4, Rick whispers that he is a strange foreigner, the idiomatic expression often used to describe foreigners who can behave like Japanese. His whispering indicates that he is playing the role of an 'animator' (Goffman, 1981). In other words, Rick is speaking for the host mother and sister in their words, but not in his own. In lines 5 and 7, both the host sister and mother align themselves with Rick by repeating *henna gaijin* 'a strange foreigner'. Thus, all three participants orient to each other's viewpoint and interactionally co-construct the fact that Rick is a strange foreigner (*henna gaijin*).

In another instance (Excerpt #8), the host family members and the learner co-construct an utterance. Here the topic of conversation is food that is considered uniquely Japanese. The host father says that *nori* (a type of seaweed used for *sushi*) is found in South Korea, by which he implies that *nori* is not unique to Japan. Then the host mother, the learner Tom and the host father in this order co-construct a proposition over three turns (lines 6–8), stating 'but (line 6) *nattoo* and/or *furikake* (powdered dried fish and seaweed) (line 7) exist only in Japan (line 8)'.

Excerpt #8 Tom (013102)

1 **HF:** *no- nori wa aru no ne nori wa kankoku ni mo aru shi nori*
           no- *nori* there is *nori*   also in South Korea, there is *nori*
2 **T:**   *kankoo?*
            Koree?
3 **HF:** *kankoku=*
            South Korea
4 **T:**   *=kan[koku kankoku*
            South Korea South Korea
5 **HF:**   *[kankoku ni mo aru.*
                 It's also in South Korea.
                 (1.0)
6 **HM:** *demo=*
            but
7 **T:**   *=nn nattoo (.) furikake ((laugh))*
            uh *nattoo*   *furikake*
            (4.0)

8	**HF:**	*koryaa moo nihon shika nai* ((laugh))
		They exist only in Japan.
9		*rukkusu: ne (.) sutorenji ((laugh))*
		looks (.) strange.
10	**T:**	((holding the *nattoo* package and reading the brand name of
		nattoo.))
		Shooitsu (.)nattoo=
		Shooitsu nattoo'
11	**HF:**	*=soo [da ne*
		That's right.
12	**T:**	[*((laugh))*
13	**HF:**	*sore wa minna ano (.) nn taberarenai ne (.) hotondo no hito wa*
		That nobody uh (.) can eat, (.) most people
14	**HM:**	*nn=*
		uh huh
15	**HF:**	*=ano gaikokujin wa=*
		uh foreigners
16	**T:**	((looking at the food on the table))
		=( ) nattoo to: (.) nani?=
		( ) *nattoo* and (.) what?
16	**HM:**	*=naga negi negi*
		green onion, onion

In line 9, the host father elaborates on the proposition co-constructed over the three previous turns by saying that *nattoo* looks strange. He code-switched and said it in English with a heavy Japanese accent. In line 13, he makes his point that nobody can eat *nattoo*. Given the topic of uniquely Japanese food, what he meant by saying *minna* 'nobody (with the negative predicate)' is *no foreigners*. His self-repairs first to *hotondo no hito* 'most people' and secondly to *gaikokujin* 'foreigners' display his realization that the same *nihonjinron* assumption may not be shared by the learner Tom. Thus he narrows down the category of people who cannot eat *nattoo* from *minna* 'everyone' to *gaikokujin* 'foreigners'. Tom does not challenge the host father's view but rather actively participates in co-construction of the folk belief. In this way, the learners sometimes take the role of an active co-teller to jointly construct a Japanese folk belief.

Dinnertime Talk as 'An Opportunity Space'

Dinnertime talk between a JFL learner and his host family is 'an opportunity space' in various senses of the word. Folk beliefs based on *nihonjinron* (theories on the Japanese) are still pervasive in Japanese society. However, when another version of the story is presented to the Japanese host family members, they may reconsider an alternative story. In this sense, dinnertime talk between a JFL learner and his host family provides an opportunity for the Japanese host families to re-examine their own cultural assumptions and become aware of different perspectives. In so doing, they discover what they have believed to be true may not be true and learn a new version of the reality. For example, in Excerpt #2, the host mother finally realizes that reading a book under cherry blossoms is another way of enjoying cherry blossoms, which she perhaps never considered before Julie proposed it. This realization implies that drinking sake is not the only way to enjoy cherry blossoms. In Excerpt #4, the host mother and brother, who believed that all Americans are beef lovers, learn from Rick that not all Americans prefer beef.

Folk beliefs appear in talk both as a form of utterance and the 'frame' of the utterance (Goffman, 1974; Tannen, 1993). The daily presence of the JFL learners at the dinner table provides an opportunity for the Japanese host family members to make implicit cultural assumptions and categoriz-ations that frame an explicit utterance. For example, in Excerpt #8 above, in line 13 the host father says, *sore wa minna ano (.) nn taberarenai ne (.) hotondo no hito wa* 'that all uh (.) cannot eat it (.) most people'. He used the words, *minna* 'everyone' and *hotondo no hito* 'most people'. Given that the 'frame' that surrounds this utterance is that foreigners cannot eat *nattoo*, the words *minna* 'everyone' and *hito* 'people' entail the category of people who cannot eat *nattoo*, and thus the words *minna* and *hito* imply foreigners. In fact, he repairs the words, *minna* 'everyone' and *hito* 'people' to *gaikokujin* 'foreigners' immediately. Perhaps these repairs are a recipient design on the part of the host father, and also evi-dence that he realizes that the JFL learner Tom may not share the same frame and thus would not interpret his utterance the same way as native speakers of Japanese. The fact that the host father made these repairs suggests that an unconscious cultural assumption is made to become conscious in the presence of the JFL learner. A member of the host family sometimes points out that the expressed idea or its assump-tion is not correct. In Excerpt #5 above, when she learns that the learner's grandmother in England forgets things, the host mother states *ja soo yuu no wa are ne yappa nihonjin mo igirisujin mo issho na no ne* 'in that regard the Japanese and the British are same'. This statement is remarkable if the speaker's assumption has been that the Japanese and the British are phys-ically and/or psychologically different in general. The host father's utter-ance in his subsequent turn makes such an assumption explicit by pointing out that since we are human beings we are the same. There are numerous similar examples in the present data. Thus the JFL learner's presence at dinnertime talk is a good opportunity for the Japanese host family members to consciously examine their folk beliefs and cultural assumptions, which often unconsciously underlie their daily conversations.

For JFL learners, dinnertime talk provides an opportunity to reconsider their own stereotypes about other cultures. In the present data, JFL learners rarely initiate stereotypical comments on the Japanese or any other culture. For example, one of the typical stereotypes of the Japanese often mentioned by Americans is that the Japanese are indirect and polite. Perhaps by living in Japan, they have learned that not all Japanese interactions are indirect and not all Japanese behave politely. Still, participation in the talk on cultural stereotypes and generalizations is a good chance for them to reflect on their own cultural stereotypes about other cultures.

Dinnertime talk is an opportunity space for the participants to co-construct shared perspectives and emotions. Rather than engaging in the potentially face-threatening act of challenging their hosts' stereotypical generalizations, learners can take the position of participating in the co-telling. In so doing, learners downplay their 'othered' position. In these cases, the propositional content of their utterance implies separateness or difference of the Japanese from the rest of the world, but since co-telling indexes a shared perspective, emotion, and stance among others, the discursive practice of the activity of co-telling with the host family brings the JFL learner and the host family closer together. For example, in Excerpt #7, Rick's being a *henna gaijin* 'a strange foreigner' is symbolically a whispered position, in which he is an animator. His whispered position becomes a source of joint telling and laughter in which he too takes up the position of one perpetuating the *nihonjinron* (theories on the Japanese).

As we have seen above, part of being Japanese is constituted by participation in the discourse of *nihonjinron*, in particular in conversations with foreigners. Dinnertime talk provides an opportunity for the learners to be socialized into the discourse of *nihonjinron*. By 'socialized into the discourse of *nihonjinron*', I do not mean that learners come to truly believe in Japanese folk beliefs. What I mean is that they can participate in the telling of a folk belief and jointly construct a shared perspective and emotion with the Japanese host family. For example, both Rick's whispering of *henna gaijin* 'a strange foreigner' in Excerpt #7 and Tom's co-construction of the uniqueness of *furikake* and *nattoo* with his host parents in Excerpt #8 suggest their considerable socialization into the discourse of the *nihonjinron* around food items. Both Rick and Tom have spent only four months living in Tokyo with the host family. Their Japanese proficiency levels are relatively low (Rick's level is intermediate-low, and Tom's level is novice). Since the topic of so-called 'uniquely Japanese food' such as *nattoo* is frequently discussed in dinnertime conversation between the learner and the host family (e.g. Iino, 1996), after only four months of living in Japan with the Japanese host family, Rick and Tom have been socialized into the discourse of *nihonjinron*. Julie's length of stay in Japan is also four months, and her Japanese proficiency level is intermediate, a little higher than Rick's. However she is still learning about drinking sake under cherry blossom trees. She is not aligning with the host mother's perspective on cherry blossom viewing. The extent of learners' socialization into the discourse of *nihonjinron* seems to have more to do with how frequently they are exposed to such discourse and maybe their personality differences rather than with the length of stay and the language proficiency level. This would be an interesting inquiry for future research.

In sum, dinnertime talk between JFL learners and their Japanese host families provide an opportunity space both in terms of the content of talk and discursive practice. Since folk beliefs are ideology deeply rooted in society, the participants in host family dinnertime conversations may not change their folk beliefs overnight. However, dinnertime conversation takes place regularly over the duration of the learner's stay with the host family, which is typically nine months in an academic year program. Therefore, it is an excellent opportunity for both parties to reexamine their own cultural assumptions and learn to see things from different perspectives.

Summary and Conclusion

This chapter has demonstrated that co-telling is a dynamic process, which provides an opportunity for transforming one's stereotypical folk beliefs, rather than a static environment for perpetuating them. In dinnertime talk between JFL learners and their Japanese host families, folk beliefs and stereotypes are frequently discussed. The findings are that such topics are almost always initiated by a Japanese host family member, and that half of the time, topics of folk belief are challenged. Challenges are made more frequently by the learners. The learners challenge the beliefs because they come from different cultural backgrounds and thus have different perspectives.[11] For example, contrary to the

Japanese perception, drinking sake and flower viewing do not go together from Julie's perspective. Also the learner's observations do not match the generalization that the host family makes. For example, Rick does not agree with his host family's belief that all Americans eat beef. Skip does not agree with his host sister's assertion that all Japanese food tastes good. The learners do not challenge beliefs in a confrontational manner. They even state their challenges in the form of exceptional cases. Unchallenged folk beliefs are often collaboratively constructed by the host family member(s) and the learner in the discourse. In this way, both parties are aligned in stances with respect to the folk belief in question. The activity of co-telling brings the host family member(s) and the learner closer, bridging the gap between 'us' and 'other' as well as socializing the learner into the discourse of Japanese folk beliefs.

In this process, the host family members, as well as the learner, have an opportunity to become aware of their hidden assumptions and different views of the narrated events and ideas. Both parties become aware that what they have believed to be true about Japanese culture and about the learner's culture may not be true. Ochs (1996) proposes that socialization is in part a process of learning an interpretation convention different from one's own. In this sense, what I have illustrated in this chapter is a socialization process for both parties. The learners and host families are both socialized into a discourse in which events are viewed using an interpretation convention that differs from their own. Ochs (1991) mentions that socialization is a lifelong process, and further suggests that lifelong socialization is the link between the micro-world of daily interaction and the macro-social order:

> A species-wide characteristic of human beings is that they may experience socialization across the lifespan. Indeed, societal change may be related to the possibility of lifelong socialization, as each instance of socialization is an opportunity space not only for continuity of tradition but also for transformation in the expected social order and in what counts as knowledge and competence. (Ochs, 1991: 143)

In this light, daily dinnertime talk between the JFL learner and the host family is part of the socialization process for both parties, which in the long run may have an impact on cultural belief systems at the societal level in both Japan and the learners' home country.

Notes

1. This research was supported by the Japan Studies Endowment Special Project Awards and NFLRC (National Foreign Language Resource Center). I am

grateful to all the JFL learners, the host family members who participated in the study, and the Japanese institutions which made it possible for me to collect data. My thanks also to Takako Araki, Misato Sugawara and Ritsuko Narita who assisted me in the transcription of the data as well as Yumiko Enyo who helped me in assessing the learners' Japanese proficiency level. A shorter version of this article was presented at the American Association for Applied Linguisitcs Annual Meeting, March 2003, Arlington, Virginia, at the Second Language Studies' brownbag talk, November 2003, University of Hawai'i at Manoa, and at the San Diego State University Linguistics Department, March 1, 2004.

2. See Kubota (1999), Sugimoto (1997) and Yoshino (1992) for further discussions on *nihonjinron*.
3. At the time of writing the draft of this article, the data collection from the ninth learner was not complete.
4. Yumiko Enyo, who was trained to be an OPI evaluator, assisted me in evaluating the learners' Japanese proficiency level.
5. Although the learners and the host families were asked to turn off the TV during the dinner, a few host families did not turn off the TV.
6. Instances when the participants discussed how certain words in one language are translated into the other were not included in the tabulation of this category.
7. Often the participants asked how to say something either in Japanese or in English. However, I did not include these inquiries in the tabulation.
8. Only Alice's host family had small children. In the data, only once a child (age 10) challenged a folk belief.
9. The group members vary depending upon the context. The group could consist of the speaker and the addressee, the speaker, the addressee and a third party or the speaker and society in general.
10. Children are socialized through the use of language (Schieffelin & Ochs, 1986b). A mother's statement such as the one in line 5 conveys a message to children that to be Japanese, they are expected to fit into certain patterns of behavior which the Japanese society imposes on its members. In my data, only Alice's host family has young children. Therefore, not many examples of cultural generalizations directed toward young children are found in the data. But for small children, it is a great opportunity to have a JFL learner in the house. These children are exposed to more frequent discussions on cultural folk beliefs and their challenges than the average Japanese child. It would be interesting to investigate the socialization process of children who are members of host family households.
11. One of the reviewers suggested that the JFL learners challenge beliefs as an attempt at alignment with the host family, for a challenge is a rejection of the 'othered' position.

Chapter 6

Norms of Interaction in a Japanese Homestay Setting: Toward a Two-Way Flow of Linguistic and Cultural Resources

MASAKAZU IINO

Introduction

It is often claimed that 'the only way that students ever acquire functional language ability, at least at advanced levels, is during study abroad' (Miller & Ginsberg, 1995: 393). Indeed the intuitively positive effect of study abroad on second language acquisition has attracted the attention of scholars involved in language education (e.g. Barron, 2003; Brecht & Davidson, 1992; Churchill, 2003c; DeKeyser, 1986, 1990; DuFon, 1998, 2000a, 2000b, 2003; Freed, 1990b, 1995b; Ginsberg et al., 1992; Makino, 1995; Pellegrino, 1998; Siegal, 1995a, 1995b, 1996; Spada, 1985, 1986; Wilkinson, 1995, 1998b, 2002; Yamamoto, 1995), particularly because of the social interactions that occur outside the classroom. Recently, researchers have conducted various types of research to investigate exactly what, in these outside-of-the-classroom situations, the participants are experiencing (e.g. Cook, this volume; Churchill, 2003c; DuFon, 1998, 2000a, 2000b, 2003, this volume; Hassall, this volume; Iino, 1993, 1996; Knight & Schmidt-Rinehart, 2002; McMeekin, this volume; Siegal, 1995a, 1995b, 1996; Wilkinson, 1995, 1998b, 2002).[1]

One type of contact situation in study abroad contexts – the homestay – can be examined from a variety of disciplines such as language education, cultural anthropology and group dynamics. Homestays are not artificially created experimental settings, nor naturally emerging random groups. They are arranged under various assumptions and expectations for both host and guest members. This study draws on data from my previous study (Iino, 1996), an ethnographic study that investigated linguistic and cultural learning in natural settings during a homestay program. This study is also one of the few that includes an examination of non-standard Japanese codes (e.g. foreigner talk, regional dialects) that non-native speakers routinely encounter. Participants' role and identity confusion will be illustrated through examining small group dynamics and the language use that occurs in these contexts.

Norms of Interaction in Homestay Settings

This study is situated in the theoretical framework of microethnography of social interaction (also called ethnographic microanalysis, Erickson, 1996), which originates in interactional sociolinguistics (e.g. Gumperz & Hymes, 1964, 1972; Hymes, 1974; Saville-Troike, 1996). Through closely examining videotaped interactions, the goal of such studies attempts to interpret 'real time processes in face-to-face encounters' (Gumperz, 1982: vii) and to understand the situational framing in which participants are not only following cultural norms but also are actively constructing local environments. Microethnographic studies emphasize the locally created dynamics of interactional norms, while 'the more usual kinds of sociolinguistics' (Erickson, 1996: 294) tend to emphasize the static relationship between language use and certain social attributes such as class, gender, and ethnicity (e.g. Labov, 1972; Trudgill, 1974). This does not mean that the local performance is not constrained by broader cultural patterns or societal norms in microethnographic approaches. Rather, it attempts to examine the fluidity of interactions which could not have been seen without relying on videotaping technology, and thus were academically neglected in the past. In this study, how norms of interaction – the notion of 'appropriate' language use including both verbal and non-verbal behaviors – are perceived and negotiated in homestay situations is investigated.

Language use and identity in homestay setting

Knowing how to communicate appropriately and effectively in a particular speech community, or sociolinguistic competence, is a part of 'communicative competence', a term introduced by Hymes in 1972. Although 'appropriateness' has been a core concept in sociolinguistic theories since that time, issues concerning who sets the rules of appropriateness and who judges the deviations from the set rules are not at all settled. This is particularly true in contact situations such as those involving second language learners. Other more complex issues involve role expectation and the identity of the non-native speaker. For example, different expectations of appropriateness in contact situations may result in modified language use which can lead to different norms than those seen in native situations (Iino, 1996). Furthermore, language use is fluid, and shifts according to context. Ogulnick (1998: 139), in her autoethnography about her language learning experiences in Japan, expressed the idea that 'in every linguistic situation there is a complex interplay between gender and other social structures such as class, race, culture, age, sexuality and nationality, and one's language constantly shifts according to shifting power relationships in different contexts'. Also recognizing the important role that power relationships play in language acquisition, particularly in linguistically diverse societies where code choice is an identity marker, Siegal (1996) noted that language learning involves far more than simply acquiring a target language variety; it also entails understanding the social significance of using a par-ticular code, which requires that the learner discern the power structures within the social hierarchy and the language varieties associated with them. Once this is accomplished, learners can present their identities by 'choosing a code that matches their (desired) identity in a given situation' (Siegal, 1996: 358). In some cases, learners might actively resist conform-ing to native norms, particularly if doing so conflicts with the identity that they wish to present (DuFon, 2004). In Japanese society, where 'foreigner (or "other") identity' (Siegal, 1996: 377) is a salient concept, code-switch-ing from native situational norms to contact specific norms, which include foreigner talk and dialectical code-switching, is a practice observed in homestay contexts that reflects the identities of the participants (Iino, 1996). In this way, the notion of broad cultural norms for appropriate language use is called into question.

Regarding the notion of language and culture, Cook (this volume) illustrates how folk beliefs about language and culture are collabora-tively constructed and challenged during host family-guest learner inter-actions. She states that 'In this process, the host family members, as well as the learner, have an opportunity to become aware of their hidden assumptions and different views of the narrated events and ideas. Both parties become aware that what they have believed to be true about Japanese culture and about the learner's culture may not be true' (p. 149). Assumptions are thus negotiated, 'continually checked against experience and revised' (Tannen & Wallat, 1993: 61). In the following section, some important underlying assumptions in the homestay setting are examined.

Assumptions affecting the homestay experience

The first assumption that both host and guest participants may have for a homestay program may be the 'fantasy' that the host family experience is an excellent environment for the American guest students to learn authentic Japanese language and culture. The reasoning is that Japanese hosts have rich resources to teach American exchange students and American students are deficient in Japanese language skills and cultural knowledge. This assumption can be called the 'working group assumption' as defined by Bion (1975). The 'working' goal of the group is to facilitate for the Japanese hosts, and to learn Japanese for the American students. Illustrative of this dynamic in Spanish speaking contexts, Knight and Schmidt-Rinehart (2002), based on their interviews with host families, see the host families' facilitating roles in three major ways: linguistically, culturally and psychologically. The majority of the host families 'see their "job" extending beyond the basic charge of providing shelter and food; they play the roles of teacher, tutor, and counselor' (p. 198). Pointing out that students may not be taking 'full advantage of this rich linguistic and cultural haven' (p. 198), Knight and Schmidt-Rinehart suggest that the students, the home institution, and the in-country program should make an overt effort to integrate a homestay component into their academic program and to make better use of the homestay's potential resources. Concurring that students do not take full advantage of the study abroad context, Miller and Ginsberg's (1995) investigation of a study abroad program in Russia found that their American learners' narrowly defined 'folklinguistic' theories of language acquisition (e.g. focusing more on words and syntax rather than communicative aspects of language) delimiting their learning opportunities. They suggested the need to articulate both in-class and out-of-class experiences to support the evident comparative advantages of study abroad.

The second assumption can be called the 'basic assumption' (Bion, 1975) which governs and binds the group behavior as the 'norms' of the group. Although various norms within this basic assumption are largely unconscious, two of the most salient basic assumptions are discussed here. First, since the participants are 'in the same boat' (Slater, 1966: 152), i.e. in a situation where they cannot separate in the middle of the program except for unavoidable reasons, their norm of interaction is usually characterized in terms of avoiding confrontation, 'saving each other's face' (Goffman, 1959: 244), or being nice throughout the life of the group. The important agenda of the homestay program is to provide food and accommodation for the students. Although the rights and obligations set in the homestay situation are not necessarily clear (e.g. students pay a small honorarium in many programs, but this is not considered to be a fee such as is paid to a hotel), the basic assumption is that the host families are hosting the students as good-will volunteers. The students as care receivers, therefore, must be 'nice' to the hosts for receiving these services. The other basic assumption is that the American guests are 'different' from the Japanese hosts, not only linguistically, but in other aspects such as ways of thinking and behaving. This 'difference' of membership derives from the *'group-as-a-whole* [phenomenon, which] assumes that individuals are human vessels that reflect and express the group's gestalt' (Wells, 1985: 114). That is, individual American guests cannot be free from their membership as Americans when interacting with non-American people. This is because when the guests speak, they speak not only for themselves but also 'via the unconscious for the group. Moreover, what may be understood as individual initiative and behavior in a social setting may well be the distribution and expression of the "group's force" that has "canalized" individual action' (Wells, 1985: 124).

As we shall see in this study, there are in fact different characteristics ascribed at birth – e.g. race, nationality, religion – between the Japanese hosts and the American guests. It seems though that the overemphasis on these differences in the Japanese media and scholastic works – Japanologies (cf. Cook, this volume; Iino, 1996; Yoshino, 1992) – has a strong effect on reinforcing the 'group-as-a-whole' phenomenon which influences the norms of the group.

The third assumption may be the mortality of the group. What differentiates short-term homestay experiences from 'natural' families is the salient knowledge of their mortality. Homestay families are born knowing they must die (cf. Slater, 1966: 12). This short lifespan as a group may have a distinct effect on the relationship between Japanese hosts and American students. What cannot be tolerated if the relationship continues, say, for 50 years, may be tolerated if it is only for two months.

Major Research Questions

The purpose of this study is to empirically investigate what the underlying norms of interaction are in a homestay setting in Japan. The fundamental research questions to be addressed are:

(1) What roles are participants expected to play within the host family environment? To what extent do they conform to or resist these roles?

(2)   What are the underlying norms of interaction in the homestay setting
      in Japan? How does this affect language use?

The Study

Setting

The setting for the study was an eight-week intensive summer (1992,
1993 and 1994) program in Kyoto, Japan that offered English-speaking
American students an opportunity to learn Japanese not only in the classroom but also in the homestay setting.

Method

The study employed video recordings of naturally occurring interactions, collected by what I call the *remote observation method* (i.e. video
recording without the researcher's presence, cf. Ochs *et al.*, 1989).
Drawing on previous analytical interest in table talk (Blum-Kulka, 1997;
Cook, this volume; DuFon, this volume; Erickson, 1990; Ochs *et al.*,
1989; Shultz *et al.*, 1982; Theophano, 1982), dinner table episodes of 30
Japanese families and American students were videotaped and repeatedly analyzed for what the participants do and say in real time as they
interact.

Both formal and informal interviews with the American students, the
Japanese families and the program co-ordinators were also conducted
throughout the program. Other sources of data collected included questionnaires regarding their reflections on the homestay experiences, the
application forms of both students and host families, records of the meetings held for the host families before and after the program, journals
written by students and evaluations from both students and families.

Participants

Japanese host families

The host families typically consisted of two to five members. Most host
fathers were company or government employees or business owners,
though some were professionals (e.g. doctor, lawyer, college professor)
or had other occupations. About half of the heads of families were in
their fifties though some were as young as 30 and others were in their
sixties. Host family members who spent the most time with students
were the host mothers because the host mothers were most frequently
at home. Moreover, many of the students reported that they talked
most with their host mothers due to linguistic reasons such as clear

pronunciation and adjusted vocabulary. Most of the host families reported that they usually spoke Kyoto dialect to each other at home.

The self-reports of English proficiency for the most proficient member of the household shows that in more than half of the families someone spoke and understood English fairly well. Since English is a required subject in most Japanese junior high and high schools, we can assume that almost all of the host family members had formally studied English before. Most of the host families also had experience hosting foreign students at least once before this program, and had sent at least one family member abroad before the program. Some of them had lived in the United States for more than a year (up to two years) to study.

In sum, the Japanese host families were established middle to upper-middle class members of society exposed to foreign people and culture through hosting foreign students or through visiting foreign countries prior to the program. This suggests, as I will discuss later, that both Japanese hosts and American students have the potential to exchange language resources; thus the contact situation in the host families held the potential for being a two-way bilingual situation. The English proficiency of the Japanese participants can be an important factor which affects communication strategies because the use of English for facilitation (e.g. translating and explaining the meaning in English) is an important aspect of code-switching.

American guest students

Most of the students were undergraduate students whose age ranged from 19 to 22. The majority of the students were Caucasian (Anglo, non-Hispanic) and about one-third were of Asian descent. About 40% of the students were male and about 60% were female. Most of the students had two or three years of formal instruction at prestigious institutions in the United States, and some of them had started studying Japanese in high school. The levels of Japanese proficiency of the American students were intermediate to advanced-high if measured by the ACTFL scale. For most of the students, this program was their initial visit to Japan.

Findings

Role expectation and conformity in language use

Short-term, small group interactions

The first anxious moment in the homestay program may have been when the Japanese hosts and the American students met for the first time. In a large meeting room, Japanese hosts waited for students coming from the Osaka International Airport. When the students entered the room, both hosts and students tried to find their matched partner from a distance, based on the picture which had been sent out to each side about two weeks before the program. 'He must be John', 'They must be Tanaka-san', 'He doesn't look like the one in the picture' – the room was filled with expectation and anxiety. After the program administrator called the matched names of hosts and students, they proceeded to the middle of the room and bowed to each other and shook each other's hands. '*Hajimemashite, douzo yoroshiku* (Nice to meet you)', – the first Japanese utterance for some of the students produced to a native speaker in Japan. Soon after, the room was filled with lots of laughter and it seemed that the initial anxiety level was lowered after the participants found that they could communicate after all. One Japanese host father with a big smile said to all in the room, '*Konna beppin san yattara zutto uchi ni ite hoshii wa* (She is so good-looking, I wish she could stay at our home forever)'. Every one laughed. '*Anoko kawairashii ne* (she looks cute)', '*anoko nihongo jozu ne* (his Japanese is good)', – comparison and competition was already beginning among the hosts. Outside the building, the newly introduced partners headed for the hosts' cars, some to Mercedes or Lexus, and some to small Japanese cars, carrying huge suitcases filled with Japanese dictionaries and grammar books. Their homestay experiences started in a joyful mood.

'*Kore kara no ni kagetu kan amerika jin no gakusei o jibun no musuko musume to shite nakayoku yatte itadakitai to omoimasu* (please regard the American students as your son or daughter for the next two months, and get along with them)'. This was a passage from the speech made by the director of the program in the opening ceremony. However, even though hosts and students started their interaction based on the assumption that they would stay in host families as a new family member – as a son or a daughter – the relationship between them cannot be as easily formulated as the director of the program implied. How to treat each other, and therefore, how to interact with each other became one of the crucial issues that the participants later expressed in the interviews. In short, a question concerning the relationship between the hosts and the students remained.

Meaning, in general, can be formulated out of each interaction differently across different relationships of speakers. For example, what language teachers regard as 'negative transfer' may not always result in pragmatic failure (Tannen, 1985). Some pragmatic errors can be viewed as charming and cute in a particular situation. What matters for judging appropriateness of speech in pragmatics is the environment in which the utterance is made. It is, therefore, important to pay attention to what the relationship is between the host families and the guest students from the point of view of group dynamics, and how it is different from other situations such as business meetings or classroom interactions.

Role and identity confusion

Both Japanese hosts and American students played certain predictable roles consciously or unconsciously during the two months. The addition of a foreign guest in a Japanese family inevitably influenced the way of life of the host family, affecting their base norms. One host family told me, '*gakusei ga kaetta ato mata shisso na tabemono ni modottan desu yo* (after the student left, we came back to our simple menu again)', which illustrates that both Japanese families and American students lived an 'unusual' or at least a 'different' life from their daily lives before and after the program. Some students were told to call their host parents '*otoosan* (dad)' and '*okaasan* (mom)' which would probably never happen if the guest student had been a Japanese person. It is not an easy task to measure the distance or the intimacy level between the participants in the homestay situation. In the homestay situation, roles that participants play vary from family to family. This makes it difficult to prescribe and generalize what is an appropriate speech act in such environments.

The difficulty in selecting interactional norms may derive from how participants want to present themselves in relation to the situation. This confusion is not necessarily specific to the homestay situation. However, in an institutional setting such as in a company or in a school, it would probably be more formulaic, allowing interactants to decode socially defined variables (e.g. status variables such as boss–subordinate, professor–student) which would influence the participants' behavior, including the choice of the level of speech. It may be true that such formulaic speech is 'more' applicable in institutional settings. Also, in institutional settings, speakers have role models whom they can emulate. For example, a newly appointed young man in a company is expected to speak like his colleague and to use honorifics when speaking with customers. However, in a homestay setting, the students have no role models. Even if they have a host sister or brother, the students' role is not identical to that of the host sister or brother.

Some of the MBA (Master of Business Administration) students who had lived in Japan for several years mentioned that the most difficult challenge they faced while in Japan was how to identify themselves and how to select a role to play in Japanese society. This confusion directly questions if and how far non-Japanese in Japan are expected or allowed to assimilate with native Japanese. Speaking fluent Japanese may not always be sufficient nor even appropriate in some situations. In fact, 'speaking like a native' can at times be inappropriate. One participant, who was a graduate student in an MBA program and who had lived in Japan for five years said:

> I still don't know if I should speak Japanese or English when I meet a Japanese person. I think I speak better Japanese than their English, but I sometimes feel it inappropriate for me to speak in Japanese.

Another student who also worked in a Japanese company for two years said:

> I played the role of *gaijin* in most situations. I understand Japanese, but if I speak Japanese, I feel I lose control over the situation. So, even when my Japanese business partner speaks poor English, I choose to speak English.

It seems to me that there are many more factors than 'speaking like a native' to be considered when we discuss 'communicative competence' for non-native speakers communicating with Japanese in Japanese.

In addition to the issue above of language choice, many American students said that they felt much more freedom and control of the content of the conversation, and that as long as they acted like a *gaijin*, their behavior (e.g. language errors, topic choice, manners) was tolerated. This appears to be a strategy whereby the care-receiver surrenders power to the care-providers. This strategy can be observed between children and parents, female and male, students and teachers (cf. Heller, 1988). What is common among these relationships is that there exists at least one distinct power differentiation in them which cannot be challenged. If we look at the language proficiency of native and non-native speakers of a language, the 'nativeness' cannot be easily challenged by non-natives.

In order to portray the expected non-threatening *gaijin* figure, one student said he actually played the role of a clown by pretending to be as ignorant as possible about the Japanese language and Japanese culture. He went on:

> If I speak good Japanese, I thought they would not think me *kawaii* (amiable) and expect me to use all the keigo rules and manners. I don't know much about keigo and I have no intention to be like a Japanese businessman. I didn't feel it necessary to master the

Japanese language unless you really want to live there for the rest of your life, and I don't want to do that.

In his case, speaking like a native Japanese was not his goal. As the above MBA student said, it was his tactic to surrender. By playing a *gaijin* role, a foreigner may be able to avoid responsibility for complying with the social norms which would otherwise be expected in native situations.

Toward a two-way flow of linguistic and cultural resources

As seen above, confusion regarding the role that each participant was expected to play became a crucial issue in the program. In viewing the issue of the foreigners' role in the host culture, two approaches are proposed here: the cultural deficiency approach (pet model) and the two-way enrichment approach. These two approaches are often discussed as 'orientations' in the language planning field (e.g. Ruiz, 1984) when viewing the power structure between dominant language speakers and minority language speakers in a society. I use these terms to refer to how people perceive linguistic and cultural differences in contact situations.

In the deficiency view, the basic role of the students is as care-receivers, whereas the hosts are care-providers. Considering the high cost of housing and food in Japan, economic reasons seem to play an important role in shaping their relationship as illustrated by comments from the two participants below:

I cannot afford to rent an apartment in Japan, and it's difficult to find one for such a short term and for a foreigner.

I checked the *weekly mansion* (a studio apartment rented on a weekly basis), and the rent was about $1400 a month. I just cannot afford it. $600 for the host family honorarium is a good deal.

The homestay family is also expected to be responsible for protecting the guest student in a new environment and this was important for some participants:

My mother allowed me to go to Japan as long as I stay with a Japanese family who takes care of me. She doesn't want me to stay in an apartment.

Care-receivers are constructed as being deficient and needing a place to stay, food, and a lot of assistance in the foreign environment.

In some cases, the students had to go through a rather stressful initiation period with their host families. For example, they had to know how and when they should use the bath and shower, whether they could open the refrigerator, and how to use the telephone. Care-receivers know that they cannot offend care-providers in the interests of maintaining a more comfortable environment. The host's way of life becomes the 'base norm', and the guest students are expected to follow that base norm. This suggests that the students are usually placed in a relatively powerless position in the host family situation. Particularly in this homestay program where the Japanese hosts are goodwill volunteers, the rights and obligations matrix between the hosts and the students is asymmetric.

As many of the students felt the effects of the deficiency view, they complained that they were treated like babies and dolls in the family. These students did not readily accept the role of *gaijin* guest. Some students commented:

> They showed me how to do the tea ceremony, how to do calligraphy, and how to do flower arrangements every night after dinner, which made me crazy. I didn't have time to study. I've already done those kind of things and I'm not really interested in them. I'm here to study Japanese which I can use for business in the future.

> I was a pet in the home. As long as I appreciated whatever they did, everyone was happy even though I didn't speak well.

The relationship between the hosts and the students tends to be, as described in the above 'pet' metaphor used by the student, that the students are highly dependent on the hosts. This power relationship derives from the fact that visitors are deficient in the norms of the host culture. People tend to treat others based on the perceived power relationship – who can set what kind of norms in the particular situation. This cultural deficiency theory in contact situations (cf. Neustpuny, 1985) is based on the assumption that host members have the target/base cultural norms, and that visitors are learning to reach as close as possible to those targets. In a traditional educational environment, obedient students are considered to be good learners. They obey what teachers tell them to do and say, without questioning or challenging. Teachers, in return, give rewards (sometimes real cookies) to learners. Language classrooms are not an exception. Researchers' descriptions of speech become prescriptions, and teachers try to teach these rigid rules to learners. 'Being a good pet in the host family is the best tactic', said one student participant. He said he played the role of a pet (one-way care receiver) with which host members were pleased. The assumption that learners and visitors are deficient in the host culture's norms has been taken for granted in traditional language education. This view always looks at host members as ideal speakers of the language, and learners as deficient participants in the host culture (i.e. hosts can provide resources for learning, and learners can only receive those resources from the hosts).

However, not everyone can be a pet. Being a pet requires the existence of a pet and a care-provider. One actor alone cannot be a pet, it requires that care-providers perceive themselves as being needed by the pet, and thereby provide unlimited care. The above example of the MBA student's tactics of being a pet or a *gaijin* was made possible because the Japanese people he interacted with acknowledged his pet role, whether it originated in sympathy, love, despair or indifference. Had he not been an American, a blond, blue-eyed, elite student, he might have encountered a different reaction, a possibility that has also been raised by Norton and Toohey (2001) who note that issues of race, the body and attractiveness might affect the learners' access and reception in the community. As one of the program co-ordinators commented, 'a pet without a certificate of pedigree' would possibly experience a rather different treatment in Japanese society.

While the cultural deficiency model appears to have been applied by many of the participants, it does not seem to paint the whole picture of what is actually happening in the host families, as seen in the data elicited in the interviews. Another way to view the role relationship in contact situations is as a 'two-way' exchange, although these two approaches need to be viewed as a continuum. In this approach, the power relationship is not necessarily fixed and one-way, but dynamic and two-way. In this 'two-way' approach, the students are not the only one-way care and information receiver. Dinner table conversations reveal rich evidence that a two-way cultural exchange takes place continuously. In a similar setting, Cook's study (this volume) elaborated this point, focusing on the process of challenging and modifying folk beliefs by both the students and the hosts.

The following conversation shows an example of a two-way cultural exchange where the American student, Steve, is teaching his host mother (HM) how to pronounce 'herb' in American English. The host mother learns that the 'h' in 'herb' is silent at the same time that Steve learns the name of the herb.

Excerpt 1

1 **Steve:**   *sore nan desu ka*
            what is that?

2 **HM:** *kore shiso, anata ga tabete iru no wa kore to kore o mikkusu shita desho, kore wa shiso*
this, shiso, what you are eating is the mixture of this and this, this is shiso
3 **Steve:** *shiso*
4 **HM:** *a kind of habu, habu*
5 **Steve:** herb?
6 **HM:** *haabu*
7 **Steve:** herb, herb
8 **HM:** *haabu*
9 **Steve:** *eich*
'H'
10 **HM:** *wa hatsuon shinai*
you don't pronounce the 'H'!
11 **HS:** *shinai no*
no?
12 **HM:** *honto, ah, so*
really, I see
13 **HF:** *habu kyandi kato omotta, herb candy nan da*
I thought 'habu' candy, but should be 'herb' candy, I see
14 **HM:** *ah, so, iya, tekkiri habu kato, nihongo de habu*
ah, right. I had no doubt about the pronunciation 'habu', in Japanese. It is 'habu'

While the example above shows a successful case of two-way cultural exchange, unfortunately not all contact situations can be characterized as such. There are hostile and power-struggle contact situations as we see in various political and business negotiations or anti-immigration movements. What conditions make a two-way cultural exchange approach possible? Based on the characteristics of the homestay situations, it may be possible to build some hypotheses for the conditions of a two-way cultural exchange.

First, if the consequence of the interaction can possibly cause a change in the power relationship, it is more difficult for the two-way cultural exchange to take place. The nature of the interaction needs to be non-competitive. Second, if there are fewer time and energy constraints in the situation, more two-way cultural exchanges will take place. Third, if both parties are interested in the other culture, particularly in the language, it is easier for the two-way cultural exchange to take place. This was particularly the case in the homestay program, where the primary objective expressed by the students for participating in it was to improve their Japanese. They had a folk belief that staying with a Japanese family was the best way to learn Japanese language and culture as shown below:

I think staying with a Japanese family is the best way to improve my Japanese and to understand Japanese people.

I need to be forced to speak Japanese in an authentic and natural environment.

I didn't want to stay in a dorm, because if we have other Americans there, we will definitely speak English. I didn't want to speak English in Japan.

At the same time, some of the Japanese hosts had expectations of receiving language (English) and cultural resources from the guest students as found in the questionnaires and interviews. They also considered the homestay experience to be a learning experience for themselves:

We have high school children, so we hope that having an American student in our family will stimulate and motivate our children to learn more about English.

My son is going to the U.S. next summer to study English, so all our family agreed to accept an American student.

I stayed with an American family in California before, and had a great time. So I feel I want to return such a feeling to Americans.

As was observed in the interviews, it seems that some participants, particularly the guest students, were not explicitly aware of the fact that the guest students were also a rich source of multicultural experience for the host families. Thus, it is suggested that the participants be explicitly informed that homestay situations are potentially capable of providing rich linguistic and cultural resources for both the host family members and the guest students. Dinner tables in host families are in fact negotiation tables where members of two different cultures may become aware of differences, start negotiating, and modify their own culturally bound perceptions.

Underlying norms of interaction in homestay settings in Japan

Negotiatiatons of appropriateness of language use

As seen above, study abroad programs, including homestay experiences, are often believed to offer a rich environment where the students are exposed to authentic and target-like language use and receive meaningful feedback from native 'teachers' on their grammatical and sociolinguistic appropriateness. However, the following data show that the Japanese hosts tend to have a different set of rules of speaking which are applied to non-native speakers of Japanese. The way they react to the Japanese language spoken by the American students shows a manifestation of their unconscious language attitudes, particularly in interaction with non-advanced learners shown in the data. The following example, in which a host mother is discussing the sociolinguistic mistakes made by another learner, illustrates that errors are perceived as *cute* and to be tolerated.

Excerpt 2

1	**Bryan:**	*shitsurei ja nai*
		isn't that insulting?
2	**HM:**	*demo kawairashii janai*
		but, I think she sounded cute
3	**Bryan:**	*a, sou desu ka*
		ah, is that right?
4	**HM:**	*shitsureitte iu yori kawaikatta yo*
		it was more cute than insulting

In many cases, grammatical errors and cases of sociolinguistic inappropriateness that the students made were not corrected. It seems that most negotiations took place regarding the meaning of vocabulary words while grammatical errors (e.g. *kekkon shita mae ni* ⟨the student's ungrammatical utterance⟩–>*kekkon suru mae ni* <grammatical form, before I get married>, *umi kara tooi da kara* –>*tooi kara*, <since it's far from the sea>) were largely tolerated as long as the meaning was clear.

In addition, very good Japanese was an object of wonderment and laughter. This was evident in a gift-giving incident in which an American female student gave a gift to her host family.[2] Gift-giving, an important part of Japanese culture, has been identified as problematic even for native Japanese (Noguchi, 1998). In the particular incident recounted here, the American female student used a formulaic expression, '*tsumaranai mono desu kedo douzo* (this is a useless thing, but please accept it)', when she gave a gift to her hosts. In a questionnaire, the host mother recalled that event as follows:

When she first arrived at our home and gave us a gift from the U.S., I was very surprised to hear her (the student) saying '*tsumaranai mono desu kedo douzo* (this is a useless thing, but please accept)'. I thought there is no such custom in American's mentality as '*tsumaranai mono*', so I felt she was forced to say such phrases. (Translated by the researcher)

She had learned the expression in a language class in the United States. However, the entire family started laughing and was surprised to hear that Japanese expression which is generally only used by grown-ups in particularly formal settings. In Japanese culture, even college students are generally regarded as not yet having reached full adulthood, as they have not yet become _shakaijin_ or full-fledged members of society. This kind of wonderment reaction can be observed when a child uses appropriate greeting phrases (e.g. good morning, thank you) to an adult. Although age plays an important role in the choice of appropriate language use, what triggered laughter in this situation had more to do with the mismatch of expectations in the use of a highly culturally-bound expression. In other words, these formulaic expressions are more consciously learned as rules of speaking, a part of native culture. Hence, once such expressions are produced by non-native speakers, they become a marked use of the language, possibly signaling a crossing of the ethnolinguistic boundary (cf. Miller, R.A., 1977, 1982; Miller, L. 1995a). This case illustrates the Japanese hosts' folk belief about their value system that humbleness expressed by phrases such as _tsumaranai mono_ are unique to Japanese, and that it is unnatural and over-accommodating if used by non-native speakers.

In some cases, the host families' beliefs about appropriate Japanese language for non-native speakers were manifested as they challenged classroom instruction. For example, one host mother criticized the Japanese class for teaching too much difficult Japanese such as _kango_ (Chinese compound words), and told her guest student that many Japanese people do not understand these difficult words. It seems that the host mother's intention was to please the student and to be nice to her; her statement may manifest her belief that it is not necessary and may be impossible for non-native speakers to learn Chinese character-based Japanese literacy, which she herself felt was difficult.

Accommodation in language use

Illustrating how group norms were negotiated, the host families, mostly unconsciously, code-switched their linguistic codes (daily Kyoto dialect) when they addressed the American students. Most of the host families reported that they usually spoke Kyoto dialect to each other at home. However, those who were shown the video recorded data of their own dinner table conversations with the American guests were surprised to find that the variety of Japanese used was distinctively different from what they would normally use among native Japanese speakers.

It appears that they believe that Kyoto dialect is not a correct form of Japanese to be taught to non-native learners, or that they assume that non-native learners would not understand Kyoto dialect. Similarly, in other contexts, it has been reported that NSs, for whom the foreigner-non-foreigner role differences are salient, tend to use the standard speech style if they consider that to be the expected variety for NNSs (Harder, 1980; Janicki, 1986; Katz, 1981). This type of speech adjustment functions as an identity marker emphasizing the role relationship between the interlocutors. As hosts to an American guest, the families in this study perceive the appropriate speech variety to be Tokyo dialect, as half of the host families reported in the questionnaire (Iino, 1996). Their presentation of the Japanese language is hyper-normalized so that it fits the correct image of standard Japanese as they believe it should be heard by foreigners. What they believe to be correct Japanese is not necessarily the authentic Tokyo dialect. In fact, it tends to be neither Kyoto dialect nor Tokyo dialect, but instead, FT (foreigner talk).

In the following example, when one host grandfather used Kyoto dialect with the American guest, he was corrected by the host sister (HS) and his dialect was translated into Tokyo dialect by the host mother (HM). The grandfather (GF), who is not familiar with Tokyo dialect, could not switch his Kyoto dialect as other younger members of the family did. He keeps using Kyoto dialect to everyone during the conversation, including the guest student, Donna. However, every time Kyoto dialect was used by the grandfather, it was translated or corrected by other family members.

Excerpt 3

1 **GF:**   *kotoshi no gion san wa doyoubi ya na*
           this year's Gion festival is on Saturday, right? ((Kyoto dialect))

2 **HM:**   *sugoi hito yaro na*
           I bet there will be a lot of people ((Kyoto dialect))

3 **HM:**   *shichi gatsu no sanju ichi nichi, saigo no nichiyobi ni wa kyoto de*
               atagosan to yuu yama ni noborun desu, atago san to yu namae no
               yama, kaji ni awanai to iwarete imasu, nijikan kurai ka na
               July 31st, the last Sunday, people climb a mountain called
               Atago, a mountain called Atago, if you climb, it is said
               that you won't have a fire, I guess it takes about two hours
4 **GF:**   *shindoi*
               tough ((Kyoto dialect))
5 **Donna:**   *shindoi?*
               tough? ((Kyoto dialect))
6 **HM:**   *taihen*
               tiring ((Tokyo dialect))
7 **GF:**   *ban yade*
               in the evening ((Kyoto dialect))
8 **HS:**   *ban ja wakarahen, yoru*
               she doesn't understand *ban*, it should be *yoru*
9 **GF:**   *yoru*
               night

The Kyoto dialect word *shindoi* (line 4) was immediately substituted with
the corresponding Tokyo standard word, *taihen* (line 6) by the HM. Also,
the word *ban* (line 7) was corrected and substituted with a more commonly used word, *yoru* (line 8) by the HS: '*ban ja wakarahen, yoru*' (she
doesn't understand *ban* (evening), it should be *yoru*). The GF repeated
yoru, accepting the HS's correction (line 9). These follow-up repair acts
indicate the adjustments of the code by other bidialectal members of the
family. This is one example of such collaborative acts among the interlocutors. A simple hypothesis is that elderly people and young children
are not exposed to Tokyo dialect in their daily speech domains. Except
in the few cases of elderly people and children, almost all the other speakers of Kyoto dialect code-switched into Tokyo standard dialect when they
addressed the American guest students.

Language is inherently norm-bounded; grammatically, cognitively
(e.g. overly long sentences cannot be understood) and socially (Higa,
1976). Every individual has a scheme of appropriacy conditioned by
society (i.e. what one perceives others would think is normative).
However, many Japanologists have over-emphasized how homogeneous
Japan is, and tend to overlook the existence of the marginal diversity
which resides within it (Noguchi & Fotos, 2001). Japanese language
education is not an exception. Educators have been interested in

making materials which are based on the idealized standard. They have
not tolerated the *ozomashiki nihongo* (fearful Japanese) (Umesao, 1986) produced by foreigners. At the same time, they have not paid attention to the
actual language use such as FT or dialect produced by the native speakers.
Learners of Japanese as a second language do not usually have an opportunity to be exposed to varieties of Japanese other than the Tokyo dialect
while they are outside Japan, and believe that all Japanese people speak
more or less the same language since the nation is so homogeneous. It
seems that the over-emphasis in the past on the homogeneity of the Japanese people, society and language by many Japanologists and Japanese
educators has painted a misleading picture and sometimes has negatively
influenced learners' attitudes toward the culture that they experience in
the local setting.[3]

The Japanese hosts' *overaccommodation* ('making more adjustments
than are necessary or appropriate to the interaction', Zuengler,
1991: 239) might have been perceived by the American guest students
as being condescending or controlling (Coupland *et al.*, 1988: 32;
Ogulnick, 1998), even though the hosts in fact had positive intentions.
Indeed, it has been reported that NSs tend to control interactions with
NNSs (e.g. Long, 1981b; Scarcella, 1983b). Researchers such as Ellis
(1985), Snow *et al.* (1981) and Valdman (1981) have all pointed out such
a possibility of miscommunication as a negative aspect of FT use. In the
same vein, Beebe and Giles (1984) have argued that FT use also can be
perceived by NNSs as signifying their lower status in relation to NSs.
In addition, FT use also signifies the guest student's status as being
gaijin (foreigner), hence marking the distance between the two groups.
In any event, the participants in contact situations need to be aware of
the potential for miscommunication deriving from the modification of
language use.

Assuming that only one language, *the ideal Japanese*, is spoken during
dinner table conversations with Japanese host families is rather misleading and inaccurate. It is naive to conclude that the participating host
families and students speak native-like Japanese in these situations
simply because the students are there to learn *authentic* Japanese.
Language use in these situations is indeed dynamic and colorful. Multiple
languages and simplified usages were observed, which were unlike the
model Japanese dialogues found in language textbooks. The way the
Japanese hosts present Japanese language and culture, and the way
they react to the American students' language use and behavior were
different from those of their native situations. Thus, the hosts' reaction
to the American students' language use suggests that what is regarded

as appropriate in a native situation is not necessarily so for situations involving foreigners, and what is inappropriate for natives can be accepted in these contact situations.

Multiple role and identity issues in contact situations were raised as seen above. Non-native speakers are not always expected by native speakers to speak and behave like a native, and at the same time non-native speakers themselves may not wish to speak and behave like a native (cf. Hassall, 2004 for similar findings in pragmatic problems for non-native speakers of Indonesian). It seems that this kind of mismatch of role expectations held by native speakers and non-native speakers can cause misunderstandings. For example, if the American students expect the Japanese hosts to speak as they do in native situations and want them to correct linguistic mistakes, those students may be disappointed by the hosts' modified speech. Or, if the American students behave like a native Japanese, then the Japanese hosts may feel that the student is a *henna* (strange) *gaijin*.

Implications and Conclusions

In this chapter, participant role expectations in the host family environment and the underlying norms of interaction were examined with particular attention to their language use. Both Japanese hosts and American students experienced role confusions and sometimes identity conflicts as expressed in the interviews and in their language use. Dynamic use of varieties of Japanese and modified interactions were also observed. Japanese hosts and American guests need to be more consciously aware that the homestay experience can provide a meaningful opportunity for language and cultural exchange from both sides, since participants in this type of program typically have strong motives to learn from each other. As evidenced by Cook (in this volume), who investigated such an 'opportunity space' (Ochs *et al.*, 1989) focusing on how participants challenge folk beliefs, participants were thus negotiating and creating a new local environment.

Based on these findings, learners of Japanese need to be informed of the fact that they may encounter such linguistic diversity as well as modified norms of interactions in contact situations. Both NSs and NNSs need to be aware that the unconscious language use in contact situations tends to be deviant from that of native situations, and is largely motivated by the positive basic assumption (*being nice*) in homestay situations. Fortunately, learners in the homestay program in most cases were treated as welcomed guests, and therefore received little negative judgement for their inappropriate language use. Learners need to remember that *being nice* is not the only situational basic assumption, but other negative basic assumptions such as *being competitive* or *being distant* exist. The existing social and personal positive or negative prejudice and people's attitudes toward the language have little to do with efforts that learners or teachers make.

However, the paradox is that these NS practices in interacting with learners more or less shape the communicability of the learners' deviant language use. These practices are influenced by ethnicity, nationality, gender, age, attractiveness or personality, which, in turn, shape the holistic interpersonal relationship. They go beyond the scope of accuracy and appropriateness of language use. It is impossible to surgically remove from actual language use these social and interpersonal factors which may be beyond the learners' and even the native speakers' control, but it is still necessary to inform learners of existing unavoidable issues such as foreigner talk and the perceived power difference in dialect use, and to raise awareness on both sides. It should be emphasized that not all the necessary cultural aspects of language use can be teachable, because the dynamics of situations often override the normalized ideal culture. Study abroad experiences should provide rich opportunities to foreground the issue in a more salient way.

Notes

1. Although the 'myths of study-abroad "magic"' (Wilkinson, 1998b: 33) are believed among learners and educators, Rivers' study (1998) showed that the homestay is a negative predictor for speaking gain, has no apparent effect on listening, and is a positive predictor for reading gain. He quantitatively compared the linguistic gain of students in the homestay environment and their dormitory placements. This counter-intuitive result implies, according to Rivers, that students may benefit from training in the management of linguistic input.
2. DuFon (2003) obtained similar findings for learners studying abroad in Indonesia.
3. Many students were complaining that they had difficulty in understanding their conversations with host families because of Kyoto dialect, saying that the local dialect is a '*warui kotoba* (bad language)'. One student commented that the host members had to use '*henna kotoba* (strange Japanese)' because they cannot speak the standard dialect. In another case, one student said, 'I'm lucky. My host family speaks standard Japanese because they are educated'. This phenomenon was observed particularly among the advanced learners, such as those who had resided and worked in Tokyo for several years and had confidence in communicating in Tokyo dialect. Their attitude toward Kyoto dialect was very negative. This led the students to further look down on speakers that use a non-standard dialect of Japanese, and to appreciate

less the value of the local culture. Later on, those same students commented, 'Kyoto dialect is the worst language – *Kyoto ben wa saitei no kotoba desu*', 'We don't need to study Kyoto dialect to conduct business in Tokyo', 'Kyoto is so backward in contemporary Japan'. Another student said, '*karera mo waruin desu yo. jibun tachi demo kyoto ben tsuuji nai to omotteiru desho* (People in Kyoto are to blame, because they also think that Kyoto-ben is not intelligible to out-siders)'. In this way, it did not take long before the American guest students formed negative views toward the regional dialect, and the Japanese hosts were apologetic to the American guests about their use of Kyoto dialect. Thus, the participants tended to form or maintain a view that the local dialect is an impediment to learning correct Japanese.

Part 3: From Home to School in the Study Abroad Environment

Chapter 7

Negotiation in a Japanese Study Abroad Setting

ABIGAIL McMEEKIN

Introduction

In NS–NNS interactions, interlocutors are frequently faced with problems in communication that stem from the learner's imperfect command of the target language. These problems often must be negotiated in order to achieve a satisfactory level of understanding. In a study abroad setting in particular, where many opportunities exist to interact with native speakers, negotiation is not only a part of successful communication but also plays an important role in facilitating SLA. This is because negotiation is thought to maximize three conditions necessary for SLA: (a) exposure to comprehensible input, (b) opportunities for output modification, and (c) focus on form. Accordingly, this study focuses on five second language learners of Japanese and compares their negotiations with native speakers in the Japanese study abroad classroom and host family setting. The findings show how the differences in negotiation in these two contexts either promote or fail to promote these three conditions and how this ultimately affects students' opportunities for SLA.

Review of Study Abroad Literature

In the last two decades there has been considerable research on study abroad and its effect on SLA (see esp. Freed, 1995a, 1998; Collentine & Freed, 2004 for reviews; Coleman, 1998 for a review of European research on study abroad). As a result, we know that language acquisition in a study abroad setting depends on a myriad of factors, one of the most important being the context in which learning occurs. As Freed (1995a, 1998) points out, there is a general assumption that formal language learning paired with immersion in a natural speech community provides the best environment for language learning. However, while study abroad research has examined many aspects of formal classroom and/or informal out-of-class contact and its possible effect on SLA, the findings are essentially mixed. Some studies suggest that the informal, non-classroom contact often typical of study abroad may not benefit students as much as previously thought (Day, 1985; DeKeyser, 1991; Enomoto & Marriott, 1994; Freed, 1990b; Iino, 1996; Marriott, 1995; Segalowitz & Freed, 2004; Spada, 1986). These studies have found that a variety of factors (see Huebner, 1998 for a review of different factors) such as the learner's proficiency level along with the type of out-of-class interaction students participate in (L1 vs. L2 use, interactive vs. non-interactive and so on) (Freed, 1990b; Freed *et al.*, 2004; Spada, 1986); the quality and type of target language input students are exposed to (Hashimoto, 1993; Iino, 1996, this volume; Marriott, 1995; Segalowitz & Freed, 2004); their gender-related roles and experiences in the target community (Polanyi, 1995; Talburt & Stewart, 1999; Twombly, 1995); feedback on errors from NSs (DuFon, 2000b; Siegal, 1995b); learners' attitudes and motivation (see Coleman, 1998 for a review); learners' intercultural sensitivity (Wilkinson, 1998b); and learners' perceptions of target language norms (Siegal, 1995a, 1995b) affect how out-of-class contact benefits students. In contrast, other studies suggest that informal, out-of-class contact is beneficial to students and may result in increased fluency (Freed *et al.*, 2004; Laudet, 1993; Walsh, 1994); gains in oral proficiency (Coleman, 1996; Martin, 1980); gains in syntactic complexity (Lennon, 1990; Walsh, 1994); increased acquisition of vocabulary and/or increased semantic density of words used to convey ideas (Collentine, 2004; Lennon, 1990; Milton & Meara, 1995); gains in the Oral Proficiency Interview and listening comprehension (Huebner, 1995a); acquisition of certain pragmatic features (DuFon, 2000b); opportunities to challenge stereotypes (Cook, this volume); and better conditions for second language acquisition (McMeekin, 2003; Parr, 1988).

Despite the abundance of research on different aspects of formal classroom or informal, out-of-class contact in a study abroad setting, many questions remain as to what specific types of interactions students participate in in both contexts, and how this affects SLA. It is this question that the present study attempts to answer. By focusing on NS–NNS interactions and comparing the negotiations that occur as a result of comprehension difficulties in both the host family setting and the study abroad classroom, this study provides insight into the quality of target language input that students are exposed to in each context and how this ultimately affects opportunities for SLA. While not specifically about negotiation, a few studies have examined students' use of communication strategies (similar to negotiation moves) to overcome communication breakdowns (DeKeyser, 1991; Lafford, 1995, 2004). However, their focus differs greatly from that of the present chapter. DeKeyser (1991) used interviews and picture reconstruction to compare the differences in communication strategy use between students who had studied abroad and those who had stayed home and found that there were no significant differences in communication strategy use between the two sets of students. Lafford (1995, 2004) used the oral proficiency interview to compare communication strategy use between study abroad and stay-at-home students. Lafford (1995) found that her study abroad subjects displayed a broader repertoire of communication strategies and this may have improved their overall communicative competence. Lafford's (2004) second study found that students who studied abroad used fewer L1-based communication strategies and fewer communication strategies overall compared to those who stayed at home. She suggested that this may have been due to contextual expectations of informal, out-of-class interactions with NSs that discouraged students from focusing on the gaps in their interlanguage and encouraged them to get their meaning across clearly and efficiently regardless of their linguistic deficiencies. Still, findings from these three studies reveal little about the actual communication problems students face in study abroad, how these problems are solved jointly by the NS and NNS, and how this affects SLA. By specifically comparing NS–NNS negotiations of communication breakdowns in unelicted interactions in the study abroad classroom and the host family context, the present study focuses on how students and their native speaker interlocutors engage in negotiation to deal with actual communication problems, and how the process of negotiation itself affects students' opportunities for SLA.

Review of Negotiation Literature

Negotiation researchers not only believe that interaction in general facilitates SLA, but that negotiation as a specific type of interaction optimizes conditions in such a way as to maximize the possibilities for language acquisition (Foster, 1998; Gass & Varonis, 1985; Long, 1981a,

1983, 1985a, 1985b, 1996; Pica, 1987, 1991, 1993, 1994; Pica *et al.*, 1986, 1987, 1989, 1991, 1993; Porter, 1986; Varonis & Gass, 1982, 1985a, 1985b). By 'negotiation', what is meant is:

> . . . the modification and restructuring of interaction that occurs when learners and their interlocutors anticipate, perceive, or experience difficulties in message comprehensibility. (Pica, 1994: 494)

Research has shown that the modification and restructuring involved in negotiation (a) make input comprehensible for the learner (Gass & Varonis, 1994; Loschky, 1989, 1994; Pica, 1992; Pica *et al.*, 1986, 1987), (b) provide opportunities for learners to actively modify their output (Pica, 1987; Pica *et al.*, 1989, 1991; Silver, 1999), and (c) focus learners' attention on form by providing learners with positive and negative evidence (Gass & Varonis, 1989; Long, 1996; Pica, 1987, 1994, 1996; Pica *et al.*, 1986, 1987, 1989).

Classroom studies and negotiation

Over the years, research has often focused on how negotiation maximizes the three conditions mentioned above. However, very few studies (Brock *et al.*, 1986; Chun *et al.*, 1982; Long, 1996; Pica, 1987; Varonis & Gass, 1985a) have looked at negotiation in informal, non-classroom contexts. The majority of negotiation studies use classroom data obtained from a variety of elicitation methods ranging from very controlled (picture reconstruction, story retellings) to less controlled (interview, role play).

Studies that have looked at how negotiation maximizes opportunities for comprehensible input in the classroom have shown that negotiation facilitates learner comprehension considerably more than exposure to pre-modified input (Gass & Varonis, 1994; Loschky, 1989, 1994; Pica, 1992; Pica *et al.*, 1986, 1987). This is because in negotiation students have the opportunity to request clarification (e.g. 'What do you mean?', 'Huh?') of utterances they do not understand, and the clarifications that result are often reformulated versions of the original utterance (e.g. the use of a different word, form or example) that aid in comprehension. Negotiation is such a powerful agent in comprehension that even when exposure to negotiation is only indirect (peripheral), studies show that students still benefit from it (Pica, 1992; Pica *et al.*, 1986, 1987). Although not a negotiation study, Ohta (2001) noted similar findings when she found that students who only peripherally participated in interactions between the teacher and other classmates were sometimes able to use the feedback gleaned from that interaction correctly later on in the class, indicating that they had indeed noticed and benefited from it.

Factors found to affect the frequency or amount of negotiation in the classroom are often another focus of negotiation research. In general, studies have noted that significantly more negotiation work occurs in tasks with a two-way required exchange of information than in one-way tasks (Crookes & Rulon, 1988; Doughty & Pica, 1986; Foster, 1998; Long, 1981a, 1989, 1990; Pica, 1987; Pica & Doughty, 1988); in tasks involving pair or small group work rather than teacher-fronted interaction (Foster, 1998; Pica & Doughty, 1988); in tasks which generate student interest in the topic being discussed (Foster, 1998); in tasks involving unfamiliar topics (Gass & Varonis, 1984; Pica, 1992; Plough & Gass, 1993) and in tasks that require students to produce more output (Shortreed, 1993). Although the mention of non-task related factors is rare in the data, Rulon and McCreary (1986) and Pica (1987) cite students' concerns for face as one of the factors that reduced negotiation in the classroom, mainly because students did not want to embarrass themselves by asking the teacher for clarification or confirmation when they didn't understand something.

That negotiation facilitates learner modification of output has also been shown in several classroom studies. These studies found that when given feedback on the comprehensibility of their messages, learners often modify their original message in an attempt to make it more comprehensible (Pica, 1987; Pica *et al.*, 1989, 1991). There are a few studies that suggest that learner production of modified output actually promotes SLA (Ohta, 2001; Silver, 1999). Ohta (2001) noted that peer interaction (NNS–NNS) increased accuracy partly because learners were able to catch each other's errors, provide immediate feedback and subsequently correct their own errors by modifying their output. Similarly, Silver (1999) found that among three treatment conditions, only the negotiation condition in which students were pushed to modify their output resulted in both immediate and sustained positive effects in second language learning.

Factors affecting the quantity of learner modification of output are similar to those that affect comprehensible input. For example, findings show that lower proficiency learners exhibited less learner modification of output because they had fewer linguistic resources to do so and NSs were generally reluctant to ask for clarification because of the learner's low proficiency level (Pica & Doughty, 1988; Shortreed, 1993). In contrast, advanced learners were more likely to modify their output perhaps because they had the linguistic resources to do so (Holliday, 1988; Pica, 1987). In general, tasks requiring an information exchange (Pica *et al.*, 1989) and those that involved pair work rather than teacher-fronted work (Pica & Doughty, 1985; Rulon & McCreary, 1986) were found to increase learner modification of output. Another important finding was that regardless of the task, learners were more likely to modify their utterances in response to NSs' open signals (i.e. requests for clarification – 'What?', 'Huh?') as opposed to closed signals (i.e. reformulations, requests for confirmation – 'You mean xxx?') (Lyster & Ranta, 1997; Pica, 1992, 1996; Pica *et al.*, 1989, 1991).

Though the relationship between negotiation and focus on form has always been depicted as an indirect one, Pica (1994) argues that, 'a perspective on negotiation as directly influencing the learning of L2 structures and forms fits well with negotiation data' (p. 508). She points out that during negotiation learners' attention is drawn to L2 form through both positive evidence and negative evidence. Studies show that positive evidence is abundant in negotiation when interlocutors provide comprehensible input by repeating, segmenting, manipulating, and moving words and forms, as well as by providing descriptors, examples and explanations (Pica, 1994, 1996; Pica *et al.*, 1986, 1989, 1991). These modifications often serve to draw learners' attention to the linguistic features of words, forms, and to the relationships between form and meaning. As for negative evidence (feedback), Long (1996) maintains there are two types: direct evidence such as 'grammatical explanations or overt error correction' and indirect evidence such as 'failure to understand, incidental error correction in a response, communication breakdowns, confirmation checks...' (p. 413). Both types of negative evidence prompt students to notice the gaps in their interlanguage and modify their utterances to make them more target-like. Thus, what is suggested is that focus on form arrives out of participation in interaction that provides opportunities for exposure to comprehensible input and modification of output.

There are only a handful of studies that provide some empirical support for a positive relationship between negotiation of form and second language learning. One such study is Donato (1994), who found that negotiation of form helped NNS dyads not only solve form problems correctly in a planning task, but that a majority of those forms were used correctly one week later in the actual task. Swain and Lapkin's (1995) study showed similar results in that learners who jointly negotiated linguistic problems in a communicative task later gave correct solutions on a test according to whether they solved the problem during the previous negotiation. Another study by Nobuyoshi and Ellis (1993) indirectly indicated that learners who were pushed to modify their output showed immediate improved performance as well as greater accuracy over time.

Although few in number, these studies suggest that negotiation results in increased control over forms.

Non-classroom studies and negotiation

As mentioned above, studies that have focused on non-classroom interaction and negotiation are limited in number (Brock _et al._, 1986; Chun _et al._, 1982; Pica, 1987; Varonis & Gass, 1985a). Some studies suggest that non-classroom interaction results in fewer negotiations because learners want to save face by not asking for clarification and admitting their inadequate command of the L2 (Varonis & Gass, 1985a) or because difficult topics, which may result in more negotiation, can and are often avoided or dropped because they are problematic (Long, 1983). Richardson's (1997) work on foreigner talk in a semi-informal non-classroom context and Iino's (1996) dissertation on foreigner talk in Japanese host family interactions revealed similar findings. They found that because of concerns for the NNS's face, NSs were less likely to call attention to NNSs' language deficiencies and this resulted in fewer opportunities for negotiation. Another reason cited for fewer negotiations in informal conversation is that the focus on communication (as opposed to accuracy) results in less feedback from the NS about the accuracy of the NNS's message (Chun _et al._, 1982). Perhaps for this same reason (focus on communication) learners were found to make very few output modifications in response to NS feedback in informal conversation (Brock _et al._, 1986). However, while most studies found that informal conversation did not facilitate negotiation and/or modification of output, Long and Sato (1983) found that there was more negotiation and therefore more comprehensible input available to students in the non-classroom setting as opposed to the classroom setting. In general, however, these findings suggest that negotiation in informal, non-classroom settings is unlikely to facilitate the conditions necessary for SLA. Nevertheless, further research is needed to substantiate such a claim. Accordingly, the present study attempts to answer the following questions:

(1) What are the differences between NS–NNS negotiation in the study abroad classroom and the host family setting in terms of:
   (a) The frequency of negotiation
   (b) Comprehensible input
   (c) Learner production of modified output
   (d) Focus on form
(2) How do these differences affect opportunities for SLA?

The Study

Setting and participants

The purpose of this study was to examine the negotiations between five second language learners of Japanese and their NS interlocutors in the Japanese study abroad classroom and host family setting. The data were collected during a study abroad program in Japan during the summer of 1999. The program offered beginning- to advanced-level instruction for a period of eight weeks in the summer. It included not only formal classroom instruction in Japanese, but also a host family program in which students lived with Japanese families for the duration of their stay.

The participants in this study included five female native speakers of English studying Japanese, their Japanese teachers, and their host family members (Table 7.1 below). The five students were given the following fictional names: Susan, Amy, Jamie, Mandy and Lisa. Susan was in the intermediate level class, Amy, Jamie, and Mandy were in the same high-intermediate class, and Lisa was in the low-advanced class.

Because three of the five subjects were in the same class (see Table 7.1), only three Japanese teachers participated in the study. All three teachers were native speakers of Japanese but were also fluent in English and had been teaching Japanese for several years in the United States. There were also five Japanese host families. Except for Jamie's host family members, who were fairly new to the program, the other host families had considerable experience with non-native speakers of Japanese. They were used to talking with foreign students and were familiar with the types of cultural and linguistic problems that occurred in conversations with them.

The data

The main data come from video- and audiotaped interactions between the students and their NS interlocutors (instructors and host family members) that occurred in the classroom and host family setting. Because the focus was on NS–NNS interactions, student–student interactions in the classroom were not analyzed unless the interaction was a multi-party one that involved the instructor as a main participant. Video- and audiotaping was conducted according to suggestions based on Duranti (1997) and Iino (1998). I influenced the interaction as little as possible by leaving the room during the video taping, called 'remote

Table 7.1 Participant information

Students		Host family members	Instructors
*Name	**Class level		
(1) Susan=	Intermediate	(1) Susan's Family: Mother, Grandmother	(1) *Instructor Hoshino: (female) Susan's intermediate teacher
(2) Amy=	High Intermediate	(2) Amy's Family: Mother, Father	(2) *Instructor Endo: (male) Jamie, Amy and Mandy's high intermediate teacher
(3) Jamie=	High Intermediate	(3) Jamie's Family: Mother	
(4) Mandy=	High Intermediate	(4) Mandy's Family: Mother, Father	
(5) Lisa=	Low Advanced	(5) Lisa's Family: Mother, Father	(3) *Instructor Yoshimura: (female) Lisa's low advanced teacher

*All names have been changed
**Based on a placement examination or reading/writing/listening/and speaking ability.
Note: Approx. age of students is 18–20 years old.

observation' (Iino, 1998). The participants were told to talk the way they normally would if the camera and tape recorder were not there.

The data used in this analysis were taken from a larger corpus of video- and audiotaped material. From each of the five host families and each of the three classrooms, three 50-minute recordings were taken from the larger set of data, one from the beginning of the study abroad program, one from the middle, and one from the end. Thus the total amount of data used in this analysis consists of nine 50-minute long (7.5 hours) video and audio recordings from the classroom and 15 50-minute long (12.5 hours) recordings from the host family setting. For hypothesis testing and triangulating purposes supplemental data were also obtained through informal interviews with the teachers and host family members, and from students' weekly journal entries in English about how the recording sessions went. Weekly audio-taped group discussions with the students were also conducted in order to discuss the recording sessions.

Data analysis

Both quantitative and qualitative analyses were used to determine to what extent negotiations in both the classroom and host family setting provided the three essential conditions for second language acquisition. For the most part, Pica's (1996) analytical framework was followed. For the quantitative portion, the number of negotiations was determined based on the number of times either the student or the NS displayed 'difficulties' in either production or comprehension. The amount of comprehensible input provided in negotiations was determined by calculating the number of times NSs responded to students' requests for clarification by clarifying their own utterances. Similarly, the amount of student modified output was determined by counting the number of times students modified their output in response to NSs' requests for confirmation or clarification.

Lastly, the extent to which negotiations promoted focus on form was determined qualitatively, based on (a) whether NSs made comprehensible input available to students in the form of reformulations, repetitions, examples and/or explanations that provided them with salient, quality input that drew their attention to form-meaning relationships, and (b) whether the student modified their output, indicating that they had noticed and incorporated NS feedback.

Quantitative Results

Negotiation frequency

The analysis revealed that students engaged in more negotiations in the host family setting than they did in the classroom. In fact, on average, students engaged in 4.2 more negotiations per 50 minutes in the host family than they did in the classroom setting (Table 7.2).

Table 7.2 Negotiation frequency in classroom and host family setting

	Total # of negotiations	*Ave. # of negotiations/50 min.*	*Percentage (#) of peripheral negotiations*
Host family	286	19	0 (0)
Classroom	133	14.8	61.65 (82)

An important feature of classroom negotiation was that the majority of them were peripheral, between the instructor and other students, meaning the subjects did not directly participate in the negotiation, but were indirect observers. This is important to note because research has shown that peripheral participation in negotiation is most likely just as beneficial to students' language acquisition as direct participation (Ohta, 2001; Pica, 1992; Pica *et al.*, 1986, 1987).

Comprehensible input

The second research question deals with the differences between NS–NNS negotiation in the study abroad classroom and the host family setting in terms of promoting comprehensible input. Thought to be one of the necessary components for SLA, comprehensible input in negotiation was evidenced when NSs modified their speech in response to requests for clarification from the student. Table 7.3 below indicates the number of times a student requested clarification and the number and percentage of these times that NSs clarified their utterance to make it more comprehensible.

As shown in the table, in response to students' requests for clarification, host family members modified their utterances more than twice as much as instructors in the classroom did. This suggests that host family members provided students with more comprehensible input than instructors did in the classroom.

Table 7.3 NS clarification in the host family and the study abroad classroom

Setting	Number of student requests for clarification	Number of NS clarifications	Percentage of NS clarifications
Host family	88	72	81.8
Classroom	43	16	37.2

Modified output

In negotiation, student production of modified output was evident in two ways. The first was when a student responded to a NS request for clarification ('What?', 'Huh?' and so on) by modifying their original utterance. The second was when students responded to NS requests for confirmation ('Do you mean xxx?', 'Oh, you <u>went</u> to the store?' and so on) by subsequently modifying their output to incorporate the feedback modeled in the confirmation request.

Table 7.4 Student modification of output in the host family and study abroad classroom

Setting	NS requests clarification	Student modification of output	NS requests confirmation	Student modification of output
Host family	67	45 (67.1%)	223	71 (31.4%)
Classroom	53	43 (81.1%)	46	17 (36.9%)

Table 7.4 shows the number and percentage of times NSs requested clarification or confirmation of students' unclear utterances, as well as the number of times students modified their utterances in response. The analysis suggests that students in the classroom made more attempts to make their utterances comprehensible, accurate or acceptable than they did in the host family setting for both requests for clarification (81.1% vs. 67.1%) and requests for confirmation (36.9% vs. 31.4%) – a difference of 14 percentage points and 5.5 percentage points respectively. The analysis also shows that in both settings students modified their output more in response to NS requests for clarification than to requests for confirmation. This is consistent with the negotiation literature, where studies have shown that there is a difference in how students respond to these two signal types (Pica, 1992).

Qualitative Results

The qualitative results are divided into three sections. The first section discusses the factors that may have had an effect on the frequency of negotiation in both settings. The second describes and discusses the different aspects of comprehensible input in the host family and the classroom setting and how that input meets the need for focus on form in terms of positive evidence. The third section examines student modification of output in both settings and how the act of NS feedback as well as modifying one's utterance meet the need for focus on form.

Factors affecting frequency of negotiations

Differences in the interaction may explain why so much more negotiation occurred in the host family setting as compared to the classroom. For example, unfamiliar topics that included talking about abstract and culturally based entities were commonplace in the host family. Such topics often forced students to compensate for their lack of knowledge in the L2 by using negotiation. There is also some indication that because the participation structure in the host family was more symmetrical, students were able to openly exchange ideas and information with their host family members and to choose topics that interested them – they were therefore encouraged to participate more actively in conversations. As a result, students may have been more motivated to overcome comprehension difficulties because they were more invested in the topic.

In contrast, classroom interactions and topics seemed to be carefully controlled by the instructor, making interactions asymmetrical and reducing the chance that difficult or unfamiliar topics might occur. English was also used frequently as a resource to clear up comprehension or production problems, which meant that negotiation was often unnecessary.

Comprehensible input and focus on form

Host family setting

The analysis showed that in most cases family members went to great lengths to explain things to students, often providing several repetitions, reformulations, explanations and examples to help the student understand what was being said. This was perhaps a reflection of the host family members' role of caregiver in which they felt responsible for making the conversation smooth, and for maintaining a high level of comprehension for the student. Host family members used different strategies to make their utterances more comprehensible, including rephrasing (i.e. moving or changing a word or phrase), circumlocution, or repetition, where they often made some words more salient than others. These adjustments not only played an important role in helping the students understand their utterances, but also in providing students with positive evidence and drawing their attention to form. For example, the following excerpt is representative of the types of negotiations that occurred in the host family. Here, one of the students, Mandy (Ma), negotiates the meaning of a word with her Host Father (F) and Mother (M).

Excerpt 1

Comprehensible Input – Host Family

1 **F:**   *mandy utsutte ru kana*
            I wonder if Mandy is being filmed
2 **Ma:**   *nani?*
            what?
3 **F:**   *utsutte ru kana?*
            Is she being filmed?

4 **Ma:** *utsu-?*
film-? **(request for clarification)**
5 **F:** *kore [kore bideo kamera ni utsutte imasu [ka* ((points to camera))
this [this are you being filmed by the camera **(clarification)**
6 **M:** [*utsutte ru wa* [*kochigawa kara yoku utsutte iru*
[it's filming [it's filming well from this side
7 **Ma:** *utsutsu wakarimasen donna imi desu ka*
I don't understand *utsutsu* what does it mean?
(request for clarification)
8 **F:** *utsuru*
it's *utsuru* **(clarification)**
9 **M:** *bideo ni utsuru utsuru*
to be filmed filmed by a camera **(clarification)**
10 **Ma:** *oh to like like toru? [utsuru?=*
oh to like like to film? To film?= **(request for confirmation/ clarification)**
11 **M:** [*un =un bideo de=*
[yes =yes by video= **(confirmation)**
12 **F:** =*denki ga tsuite ru kara* ((points to camera))
=because the light is on ((points to camera)) **(clarification)**
13 **M:** *totte iru deshoo* ((points to camera))
it's filming right? ((points to camera)) **(clarification)**
14 **Ma:** *hai*
yes
15 **M:** *sore ga un ano: utsuru tte*
that is um well called *utsuru* **(clarification)**
16 **Ma:** *ah hai*
ah yes

The above excerpt illustrates the lengths that host family members went to in order to make their utterances comprehensible. In this particular instance, Mandy requests clarification of the word in question, *utsutte iru* (to be filming – intransitive) in line 4. In the negotiation that follows, what is revealed to Mandy is not only the meaning of the word, but also positive evidence of its structural and semantic properties including how it is used in a sentence and how it is conjugated, as well as what words it may share similar meanings with. In terms of positive evidence and focus on forms, Mandy is exposed to a variety of different forms of the verb such as the informal forms, *utsutte ru* (to be filming – intransitive) and *utsuru* (to film – intransitive), and the formal form, *utsutte imasu* (filming – intransitive). In addition, she is given information about sentence structure and about how the subject (video camera) fits into the sentence and what particle it takes, *ni* (by – instrumental). On the semantic level, Mandy is shown that the words *toru* and *utsuru* can be used similarly to refer to the same type of action. As Pica (1994) points out, these types of modifications are important sources of comprehensible input in terms of positive evidence because they not only make the meaning of lexical items accessible to the student, but they also provide opportunities to draw students' attention to form, which heightens their awareness of the discrepancies between their own interlanguage system and that of the target language.

Study abroad classroom

In contrast to the host family setting, instructors in the classroom clarified their utterances less than half of the time in response to requests for clarification from students (see Table 7.3 above). This is probably because rather than clarifying their own utterances, instructors often opened up the floor for other students to clarify the utterance. This practice is common in classrooms and is influenced by the teacher's traditional role and the focus on learning. However, although student clarifications provided some form of comprehensible input, they often failed to provide the type of information that is thought to facilitate SLA such as highlighting features and forms of the L2. This was primarily because most students did not have a full command of the L2 and this undoubtedly affected their ability to provide clarifications that maximize the type of input most conducive to SLA. Moreover, English was often used to clarify utterances and this affected the quality of input provided to students. Excerpt 2 (below), however, illustrates a typical classroom negotiation where the instructor clarifies the meaning of a word during a definition formulating activity. Here, Student 5 (S5) asks for clarification of the word *juutai* (traffic jam), which has just been brought up as a new vocabulary word. In response, Instructor Hoshino (H) provides clarification.

Excerpt 2

Comprehensible Input – Study Abroad Classroom

1 **S5:** *uh um uh eego de is it just to wait in a crowd*
          uh um uh in English is it just to wait in a crowd?
                                        (request for clarification)

2 **H:**   *ah juutai no koto desu ne*
       you are talking about traffic jam right?   **(request for confirmation)**

3 **S5:** *uh huh*
       uh huh   **(confirmation)**

4 **H:**   *juutai wa kuruma dake desu ne*
       traffic jams are only cars.   **(clarification)**

5 **S5:** *ah*
       ah

6 **H:**   *kuruma ga komu to juutai desu hai S2 san* ((calling on another student))
       when cars are crowded together that's a traffic jam, yes S2 ((calling on another student))   **(clarification)**

This negotiation is similar to those in the host family setting in that the clarification provides positive evidence in terms of the meaning and the semantic features of *juutai* (traffic jam), specifically that it involves cars and that it occurs when cars are crowded together. Moreover, by offering a circumlocution (line 6), the student is provided with input on how to formulate a simple definition of a word in Japanese, *kuruma ga komu to juutai desu* (when cars are crowded together that's a traffic jam). Note, however, in line 1 how the student uses English to ask for clarification of the word in question. Both instructors and students in the classroom used English more often than host family members did, mainly because it was a resource that was available to them and it was a fast and easy way to clear up comprehension difficulties. This often resulted in fewer negotiations as well as less target language input in negotiations that did occur.

Although the above negotiation is similar to what one might see in the host family setting, there were a lot of classroom negotiations where instructors used prompts and display questions to push the students to solve their own comprehension problems, or opened up the floor for other students to clarify or solve the problem. This indicated that instructors were not just willing to give students the answer, but expected them to be active problem solvers, reflecting the focus on learning in the classroom.

Modification of output and focus on form

Host family setting

Students did not modify their utterances as much in the host family setting as they did in the classroom. How frequently students modified their utterances had a lot to do with how host family members responded to their unclear utterances. Rather than simply ask for clarification, host family members were more likely to attempt to understand a student's unclear utterance, and then offer a reformulated version of what the student had said in the form of a request for confirmation ('Do you mean xxxx?'). Consequently, as in Pica's study (1992), students were less likely to modify their output in response to requests for confirmation as compared to requests for clarification. Sometimes, even when host family members started out requesting clarification of a student's utterance, they often ended up requesting confirmation after they had formulated a good idea of what the student was trying to say. To illustrate, in Excerpt 3 (below) Mandy (Ma) is talking to her host mother (M) about not having received any letters from home yet.

Excerpt 3

Student Modification of Output – Host Family

1 **Ma:**   *watashi wa mada tegami o moraimasen deshita*
              I didn't receive the letter yet
2 **M:**   *dare kara? ah! ichido mo tegami ah mada moratte inai?*
              from who? ah! You haven't received a letter ah even once
              yet?   **(request for clarification,**
                                                             request for confirmation)

3 **Ma:**   *hai mada moratte inai*
              yes I haven't received one yet   **(confirmation, modification**
                                                             of output)

In line 1, Mandy fails to use the correct form of the verb *morau* (to receive) and this causes momentary confusion as to the meaning of her utterance. The host mother initially asks for clarification (line 2) perhaps because she cannot guess what Mandy is trying to say, but she then immediately understands and offers a corrected version as a request for confirmation (also line 2). At this point, because the host mother understands, there is no need for her to model the correct version in the L2 and ask Mandy to confirm it. However, she does exactly that. Then Mandy repeats the corrected verb form, essentially modifying her original utterance. Thus, if lack of comprehension is why negotiation is triggered in the first place, why then does the mother insist on offering Mandy the corrected version of her original utterance and request confirmation of it even after it is clear she understands Mandy's utterance? It is possible that the host mother requests confirmation to make sure that she has accurately deciphered what

Mandy is talking about. While this in part may explain the host mother's action, there is perhaps another explanation, namely, that the host mother's model of the correct L2 version is an indirect correction or a corrective recast of Mandy's error, as when mothers recast their children's utterances to make them more accurate or comprehensible. The host mother's feedback simultaneously provides important input by making it obvious that there is a problem with Mandy's utterance and by providing the correct version. Mandy's modification of the original utterance (line 3) shows that Mandy noticed the difference between the form she used in her original utterance and the L2 model her host mother provided.

Although in the above excerpt, Mandy modified her output following a request for confirmation, students were more likely to modify their utterances in response to a NS request for clarification. Consider the following excerpt that shows Mandy's host mother (M) using requests for clarification to understand Mandy's (Ma) unclear utterance. Here Mandy is trying to explain about taking a placement test, but does not know the phrase in Japanese so she foreignizes the word to make it sound like Japanese.

Excerpt 4

Student Modification of Output – Host Family

1 **Ma:**   *demo watashi puresument tesuto o torima- u- ukemashita*
             but I took t- took the placement test
2 **M:**   *un? nani testo?*
             what? what test?   **(request for clarification)**
3 **Ma:**   *pureesumento tesuto [anoo wakarimashita? wakarimasu ka=*
             placement test um did you understand? do you understand?=
4 **M:**   [un
             =u:n chotto wakarimasen donna tesuto?
                                 [yes
             =u:m I don't understand. what kind of test?
                                                                 (request for clarification)
5 **Ma:**   *ano: do- samaa shiken wa donna reberu no kurasu ni ireru no*
               shiken desu
             um do- the summer test is a test for which class level to put
               you in   **(modification of output)**
6 **M:**   *ah kurasu wake shiken?*
             ah a placement test?   **(request for confirmation)**
7 **Ma:**   *hai*
             yes
8 **M:**   *un un*
             yes yes

```
 9   Ma:   hai
            yes
10   M:    u::n
            h::m
11   Ma:   kurasu ni wakeru?    [no shiken?=
            a test to divide you [into classes?=   (modification of output)
12   M:                          [un   =un
                                 [yes  =yes
```

Mandy's host mother is unable to understand the type of test Mandy is talking about. Therefore, rather than providing the phrase in question and then seeking confirmation of it, which seemed to be the preferred choice for NSs in the host family setting, the host mother asks for clarification and Mandy is prompted to make her utterance more understandable by modifying it (line 5). As Varonis and Gass (1985b) note, when the speaker's utterance is uninterpretable or marginally interpretable and the listener has little or no confidence in their interpretation, they are more likely to give an overt indication of incomplete understanding such as 'what?' or 'huh?'. On the other hand, when the listener is able to interpret the remark and has relative confidence that the interpretation is correct but wants to make sure, they request confirmation. Thus, because Mandy's clarification (lines 3 and 5) gives the host mother enough information for her to decipher the type of test, she provides the word/phrase, then requests confirmation of it (line 6). In response to this feedback, Mandy modifies her original utterance to make it more target-like, although not perfectly correct (line 11).

One wonders why host family members preferred to decipher students' unclear utterances and then request confirmation of them rather than ask for clarification. There are a few plausible explanations for this. A NS has two choices when confronted with a student's unclear utterance, to request confirmation or request clarification. Requests for confirmation are perhaps more efficient in terms of time and energy when dealing with a breakdown in communication. This view is supported by Poulisse (1997), who maintains that participants often choose to use certain strategies because they adhere to universal principles of communication, especially to the Principles of Economy and Clarity (Leech, 1983). Attempting to decipher what the student is saying, then offering a model of it in the L2 and having the student confirm it is more efficient than having the student try to clarify his or her own utterance especially when the student may not have the linguistic resources to do so. Moreover, in terms of the Principle of Clarity, the model that the NS offers the student to confirm is undoubtedly the clearest and most intelligible version of what the student is trying to say. Thus, in terms of clarity and economy, when the NS does all the work, the breakdown is less likely to be disruptive and the immediate, salient feedback from the NS provides excellent input for the student. Another reason NSs may prefer requests for confirmation over requests for clarification is because it may be less face-threatening to the student to offer them a version of the utterance to confirm rather than challenge their linguistic ability by forcing him or her to clarify the utterance.

However, while requests for confirmation may be used for the sake of smooth communication, students were less likely to modify their utterances in response to requests for confirmation. This may be because in host family conversations where the main focus was on communication, students had a tendency to use NSs' modeled feedback for immediate communicative purposes and therefore often did not attempt to repeat or incorporate the feedback simply because doing so may have disrupted the flow of the conversation. Moreover, if students were at a lower proficiency level, they may have been unable to incorporate feedback due to their inadequate linguistic resources. This may have been the case especially if the student's original utterance had several errors in it and the subsequent feedback was too difficult for the student to be able to incorporate it into his or her next utterance (Richardson, 1997).

Study abroad classroom

Table 7.4 indicates that students modified their output more in the classroom than they did in the host family setting. The high number of student modifications in response to instructors' requests for clarification seems to reflect the goals and expectations of the classroom. Lyster and Ranta (1997) point out that corrective feedback and learner uptake in the classroom almost constitute an adjacency pair, where teachers are expected to provide feedback on students' utterances, and students are expected to incorporate the feedback into their interlanguage by modifying their output. For example, the following excerpt illustrates a negotiation in the classroom between Amy (A) and Instructor Endo (E), who is asking the students to describe their recent field trip to a small town.

Excerpt 5

Student Modification of Output – Study Abroad Classroom

1   **A:**   *takusan kaimono ga arimasen*
            there's not a lot of shopping

2	E:	*kaimono ga arimasen?*	
		there's no shopping	(request for clarification)
3	A:	*takusan arimasen*	
		not a lot	(modification of output)
4	E:	*kaimono shopping?*	
		shopping shopping?	(request for confirmation)
5	A:	*hai*	
		yes	(confirmation)
6	E:	*you can't?*	
		you can't?	(request for clarification)
7	A:	*uh hai dekiru dekimasen*	
		uh yes can can't	(modification of output)
8	E:	*ah kaimono ga dekimasen u::n*	
		ah you can't do shopping h::m	

Amy triggers the negotiation in line 1 by saying, *takusan kaimono ga arimasen* (there's not a lot of shopping), which Instructor Endo (E) sees as an inaccurate utterance. Therefore, he repeats Amy's utterance with a question intonation, essentially prompting Amy to modify her utterance to make it more accurate. However, instead of modifying her utterance she repeats her mistake again. Thus, in line 4, Instructor Endo requests confirmation from Amy that she is talking about shopping. Amy then confirms this, however, it is clear at this point that she does not recognize that Instructor Endo is requesting clarification because her utterance is unacceptable. In line 6, he attempts to prompt her to use the correct form by code-switching into English and requesting clarification. Amy finally understands that she is supposed to modify her utterance and she does so by producing the form, *dekimasen* (can't). This indicates that Amy has noticed the gap between her interlanguage and the target-like form and modified her output accordingly. Amy does not, however, incorporate the form into her original utterance. This is probably why Instructor Endo gives a model of the corrected version of the utterance at the end of the negotiation.

At first, it is not clear whether Instructor Endo requests clarification because he does not understand Amy's utterance or because he finds it inaccurate. In fact, he seems to be trying to keep a tone of free conversation and this is perhaps why Amy does not recognize the fact that something is wrong with her original utterance. It is only at the point where Instructor Endo code-switches into English in an attempt to get Amy to reconsider her initial utterance that we see that perhaps he has understood her original utterance but wants her to modify it to make it more accurate. Lyster and Ranta (1997) have labeled this as the 'didactic function' of negotiation, 'the provision of corrective feedback that encourages self-repair involving accuracy and precision and not merely comprehensibility' (p. 42). Instructors commonly integrated this type of negotiation of form into their activities, often acting as if there was a comprehension problem even when there was little or no evidence of a communication breakdown.

Still, there are instances of genuine negotiation in the classroom, which Lyster and Ranta (1997) call, 'the conversational function of negotiation' (p. 42), when comprehension problems are real rather than perceived. These types of negotiation were most numerous in the host family where communication is the goal, but also sometimes occurred in classroom interactions. When they did occur in the classroom, it was usually during tangential talk, which was most common in Instructor Endo's class. This type of talk is generally less structured and unexpected, so unfamiliar topics can come up that cause comprehension problems that need to be negotiated. Consider for example, the following negotiation between Instructor Endo (E) and a couple of students, S7 and S2, who are trying to explain about a type of boat that does 'dock tours' in California.

Excerpt 6

Student Modification of Output – Study Abroad Classroom

1 **S2:** *boat desu ga*
            it's a boat but.   **(modification of output)**
2 **E:**   *booto?*
            a boat?   **(request for confirmation)**
3 **S7:** *bus slash boat*
            bus slash boat   **(modification of output)**
4 **E:**   *a:h dokku ga mieru basu?*
            a:h a bus where you can see docks?   **(request for confirmation)**
5 **S7:** *hai basu*
            yes bus   **(confirmation)**
6 **S2:** *boat desu booto demo tire ga arimasu*
            It's a boat boat but it has tires   **(modification of output)**
7 **S7:** *umi to- ni hairu*
            it goes in the ocean   **(modification of output)**
8 **S2:** *umi no ue ni arukemasu*
            It can walk on the ocean   **(modification of output)**

9 E: *eh!? ja dooro o hashitte umi ni mo hairu?*
       what!? so it rides on the road and also goes into the ocean?
                                               (request for confirmation)
10 S7: *hai hai*
        yeah yeah   **(confirmation)**
11 E: *a soo ja sekkaku rosu ni ittara ne* [((laugh))
        oh, well then if I ever go all the way to Los Angeles (I'll have to
        go on it)
12 S7: [((laugh))
        [((laugh))

A close look at what transpires indicates that this was probably a 'conversational negotiation' where the requests for confirmation were motivated by real comprehension problems (Lyster & Ranta, 1997). This is perhaps why this negotiation seems to resemble those in the host family setting. For example, rather than requesting clarification until the students are able to fully modify their utterances, Instructor Endo attempts to decipher the utterances and then provide target-like models in the L2 for the students to confirm (lines 2, 4 and 9). These requests for confirmation encourage the students to modify their output in lines 6, 7 and 8. What is interesting is that Students 7 and 2 alternate modifying their description of the boat from *boat desu booto demo tire ga arimasu* (Its a boat boat but has tires), to *umi to- ni hairu* (it goes in the ocean), to *umi no ue ni arukemasu* (it can walk on the ocean). These modifications not only show that students actively test out hypotheses about form and meaning, but also suggest that students may use each other's utterances to build a subsequently more complex utterance. Moreover, Instructor Endo's L2 model of how the sentence should be expressed gives the students immediate feedback on the differences between their interlanguage forms and the target-like version. One caveat however, is that the students used a lot of English (lines 1, 3 and 6). Thus, the quality of some of their modified output may not be as conducive to SLA because they were able to rely on English and were not forced to find ways to make their utterances closer to the target-like version. However, the use of English to clarify one's utterance is perhaps inevitable in the classroom where time constraints often restrict teachers and students from engaging in lengthy and difficult negotiations.

Summary and Implications for SLA

This study compared negotiations between students and their native speaker interlocutors in two study abroad settings, the classroom and

the host family. Findings showed that students engaged in more negotiations in the host family than in the classroom partly because conversations in the host family were characterized by a wider variety of topics,
fewer opportunities to use English, and symmetric interaction. Moreover,
because students were more motivated to actively contribute to the
conversations, they were able to openly exchange ideas and information
in the L2 and choose topics that they were interested in.

As for the amount of negotiation students participated in and its
effect on SLA, it has often been argued that what is important in negotiation studies is not necessarily the amount of negotiation that students
engage in, but the quality of that negotiation in terms of how it promotes the conditions for comprehensible input, modified output and
focus on form. While this may be true, it seems reasonable to assert
that the amount of negotiation students engage in ultimately affects
the extent to which these three conditions are present. Therefore,
because students participated in more negotiation in the host family
than they did in the classroom setting, students may have had more
opportunities to improve their command of the target language. The
fact that so many of the negotiations in the classroom were peripheral
does not necessarily add to the gap between the host family and classroom setting in terms of opportunities for SLA. In fact, studies show that
students who participate peripherally in classroom interactions still
benefit from what goes on in those interactions (Ohta, 2001; Pica,
1992; Pica *et al.*, 1986, 1987).

In terms of comprehensible input, the analysis revealed that host
family members were more than twice as likely to clarify their utterances
in response to students' requests as instructors were. In fact, host family
members went to great lengths to make their utterances comprehensible
to students. In doing so they provided students with rich positive L2
input and focus on form through circumlocutions, repetitions, explanations and examples. They did this perhaps because they felt it was
their role as caretaker to do so. In the classroom however, because instructors often responded to student requests for clarification by opening the
floor for other students to provide clarification, the input may not have
been as beneficial with regard to native-like input or focus on form.
However, when the instructors themselves offered clarifications, the
input provided was similar to that which was provided in the host
family setting, but it did not contain as much repetition or as many
examples perhaps due to time constraints. What this suggests in terms
of SLA is that students were provided with more comprehensible input
and therefore more positive evidence of target-like forms in the host

family than they were in the classroom, which is important for SLA (Long, 1996; Pica, 1996).

On the other hand, students modified their output significantly more (81.1% vs. 67.1%) in the classroom than in the host family setting. This was more than likely due to the difference in the way the NSs responded to students' unclear utterances which was in turn based on the expectations associated with each context. Because the focus in host family interaction was on communication, NSs often requested confirmation to solve comprehension problems. This proved to be more efficient in terms of time and effort put into solving the problem and was perhaps less face threatening for the students. Efficiency also explains why students did not clarify their utterances as often in the host family setting, precisely because it would have taken more time and effort and been more disruptive to the conversational flow to do so. Batstone (2002) also points out that in communicative contexts learners may not be as inclined to focus on form as they would be in a learning context; therefore we can expect a reduction in the number of times students modify their utterances to make them more grammatically acceptable. In the classroom, however, the focus on learning meant teachers used requests for clarification to push students to modify their output and notice differences in form even when there was not necessarily a comprehension problem (didactic negotiation – Lyster & Ranta, 1997). Thus, students in the classroom modified their output more, perhaps because they were expected to attend to form and improve their linguistic skills as a normal part of classroom interaction.

The difference in how NSs responded to students' unclear utterances, and whether students modified their utterances as a result of NS feedback, has important implications for SLA. First of all, Pica (1996) suggests that NS responses to students' unclear utterances (i.e. requests for clarification and confirmation) provide students with negative feedback that pushes them to notice the gap between their interlanguage and the L2. In particular, requests for clarification draw students' attention to form and push students to manipulate their interlanguage to make their utterances not only more comprehensible, but also more linguistically accurate. The negative feedback provided in requests for confirmation is much more indirect and therefore may not be as perceptible to students as requests for clarification. Nevertheless, requests for confirmation provide positive evidence in the form of a target-like model of the students' original utterance and therefore reveal important and timely information about lexical and structural features of the L2 (Long, 1996). Although the link between requests for confirmation and

SLA appears weak, some studies show that even when students did not exhibit immediate uptake of feedback given in recasts in the form of repetition or modification of output, there was evidence that the students had noticed the information and that it had an effect on their interlanguage over a period of time (Doughty & Varela, 1998; Mackey & Philip, 1998; Ohta, 2001; Philip, 1999). This suggests that although students did not modify their output in the host family setting as much, they probably noticed the reformulated input that their host family members provided through requests for confirmation and it is likely to have had a positive effect on their SLA.

In conclusion, although host family negotiations seem to provide more comprehensible input and the classroom more opportunities for student modification of output, the analysis suggests that focus on form is a strong part of negotiation in both settings. Thus, it appears that a combination of in- and out-of-class interaction with native speakers in a study abroad environment provides students with maximum opportunities for exposure to comprehensible input, modification of output and focus on form. However, study abroad research would benefit considerably from future studies involving more participants that focus not only on opportunities for NS–NNS negotiation in a variety of study abroad contexts, but also on how negotiation affects interlanguage development over time.

Chapter 8
Variability in the Study Abroad Classroom and Learner Competence

ETON CHURCHILL

Introduction

In a 1995 review, Huebner observed that lacking in the research on study abroad was any close investigation of classroom dynamics and their affect on foreign language attainment (Huebner, 1995b: 199). Indeed, there were very few papers on the host classroom at the time of Huebner's review, and only a handful of subsequent articles have emerged since. Studies on learner attitudes towards instruction have been conducted in the Russian context (Brecht & Robinson, 1995), in European settings (Carlson et al., 1990; Kauffman et al., 1992) and on Japanese learners in North America (Shaw et al., 1994; Woodman, 1999). Meanwhile, other studies have investigated language acquisition and learning strategies in the home classroom and host environment (Hisama, 1995; Huebner, 1995a; Iwakiri, 1993) and opportunities for language acquisition resulting from differences in NS–NNS negotiation in the host classroom and host home (McMeekin, this volume). These studies have illustrated that there is a 'wide range of student opinions on the formal instruction component of the study abroad program' (Brecht & Robinson, 1995: 320), and that '[t]he overseas experience also seems to result in a much wider variety of performances and behaviors among students than does study at home' (Huebner, 1995a: 191). However, as effects of classroom instruction have largely been studied indirectly through measures of proficiency, attitudes towards instruction and reports of learning strategies; the politically, socially and culturally situated practices of the study abroad classroom have remained largely unexamined.

Whereas most of the studies cited above have relied on learner reports and surveys on their attitudes toward classroom instruction, more recent studies have begun including data collected in class. In the European context, Wilkinson (2002) found that classroom discourse norms affected out-of-class speech practices. Also, Talburt and Stewart (1999) used data from a culture and civilization class to argue that gender and race are subjects that learners must learn to confront while overseas. In addition, McMeekin (2003, this volume) has examined classroom discourse in the Japanese context. These studies have begun to open the door into the study abroad classroom, but more are needed.

Noting the impracticality of any wide-scale quantitative study of the effect of classroom experiences in the study abroad context, Brecht and Robinson (1995) suggest that 'more insight into the value of formal instruction in this rich environment' could be attained through the use of ethnographic methods 'in which the research design consists of participant and non-participant observations, interviews, and self-reports'. They lament however, that 'to date ... we are unaware of any such in-depth investigations of the study abroad experience' (pp. 317–318). While some studies have used qualitative methods to examine the out-of-class experiences of learners working and studying abroad (cf. Cook, this volume; DuFon, 1998; Hassall, this volume; Iino, 1996; Ogulnick, 1998; Siegal, 1995b; 1996), the dynamics of host classrooms have yet to be investigated. The following account of participant classroom experiences is a much needed effort to begin filling this gap.

Conceptual Framework

In design and theoretical approach, this qualitative investigation into the study abroad classroom experiences of Japanese high school learners of English is influenced by the work of Bonny Norton Peirce (Peirce, 1994, 1995; Norton 2000) and a variety of other researchers interested in the complex relationships between identity, positionality, language acquisition and the politically, socially and culturally negotiated dynamics of the environments in which learners find and place themselves (e.g. McKay & Wong, 1996; Ogulnick, 1998; Siegal, 1995b, 1996; Toohey, 1998; Watson-Gegeo & Gegeo, 1992; Willet, 1995). As Watson-Gegeo (2001) stated, '[p]eople learn language(s) in social, cultural and political contexts that constrain the linguistic forms they hear and use and also mark the social significance of these forms in various ways' (p. 21). When language learners travel overseas, they enter a learning environment that has been constructed by a variety of locally negotiated social, cultural and political dimensions that affect their place in the host classroom and the degree to which they can participate. These local dynamics arise within macro-level deliberations between administrators and faculty during pre-program planning. The current study is an initial attempt to investigate how dynamics at both the micro and macro level shape student opportunities to engage meaningfully and productively in the host classroom. As a rubric to discuss the micro-level dynamics of specific classrooms, I shall draw on Gee's (2003) learning principles to highlight features of classes that promoted student involvement. While Gee developed these principles in his discussion of how video games facilitate learning and literacy development, he also argues that the principles are 'equally relevant to ... learning in content areas' (p. 49). I believe that the data and discussion that follows help support Gee's assertion.

Participants and Research Sites

The data for this study were collected in the context of a larger study (Churchill, 2003b) conducted in the fall of 1999 on a one-month study-abroad program in Belleville (a pseudonym). In accordance with practices established over the 10 years of the exchange program, second-year high school students from an intensive language program in Japan spent three weeks in one of four host schools, attending mainstream classes and staying with host families affiliated with the schools. The last week of the program was spent traveling and sight-seeing. For a variety of reasons largely related to differences in academic calendars, the exchange began in the middle of October and lasted through the first week of November. Illustrative of the occasional negotiations between host and home institutions, coordinators at Kansai High (the home school) had attempted to extend the length of the host experience in Belleville to one month or longer. However, host coordinators and administrators felt that three weeks was the longest time that could be made available due to the demands of the local school calendar, difficulty in finding host families and the additional demands that the program placed on teachers.

Negotiations between the host schools and Kansai High over the length of the program point to the busy calendars at the host schools and commensurate demands placed on faculty. Three of the host schools (Middle School, St Martin's and Belleville Country Day) are private prep schools with 40–60 teachers for 315–600 students. While the teacher–student ratio at these schools is rather favorable when compared to many other teaching environments, the strong academic orientation of the schools coupled with seasonal coaching assignments, dorm duty, and advising duties places considerable constraints on faculty time and energy available for additional projects and programs. While faculty at Belleville High, a large suburban public high school of 1000 students, do not have the same responsibilities as faculty working at the host private schools, their class size is considerably larger (30–35 students) and they often teach more class hours per week. None of the faculty received any additional compensation for taking Japanese students into their classes. Furthermore, indicative of the degree of commitment to the program, it was not uncommon for faculty to act as host families in some cases. As with many short-term exchange programs, beyond announcements at faculty meetings and internal memos, there was no orientation for faculty on incorporating exchange students into mainstream classes.

Many of the teachers (coordinators and classroom teachers) on both sides of the exchange had several years of experience with the program. However, this was the first experience for some of the classroom teachers. Meanwhile, other teachers were taking on new roles within the program in 1999. As a case in point, my first experience in preparing students for the program was in 1992. In 1994, I accompanied students to the United States and acted as a chaperone for the first time. In subsequent years, my role in this exchange was rather limited as I taught students in other classes and was only occasionally involved in preparing students for their time abroad. Then, I became extensively involved in preparations for the 1999 exchange and acted as lead chaperone. In a like manner, the degree of other teachers' involvement in the exchange changed from year to year.

The participants in the 1999 iteration of the exchange were 35 female and four male Japanese second-year high school students. With few exceptions, this was the first time that these students had traveled to an English-speaking country. Prior to their departure for the United States, they had had three years of English language instruction at the junior high level and a year and a half of intensive instruction (12–14 hours a week) by native speakers of English in an EAP content-based program at Kansai High. While the participants came to the program with similar language learning experiences, as with most intact classes, within the group there were noticeable skill-based (e.g. writing, speaking) and affective differences among the students. A single proficiency measure cannot do justice to the within-group differences and individual variation among 39 high school EFL learners, so perhaps the reader will note with care the characterization of the participants as high-beginner to low-intermediate speakers of English (based on the ACTFL Oral Proficiency Interview).

In the six weeks prior to their departure, instruction focused on orienting the participants to Belleville, its environs and host schools. The pre-departure syllabus was based on previous practices and adjusted according to feedback from evaluations from students and host families. A largely notional-functional based speaking class attempted to provide participants with aural and oral skills to assist them in their time overseas. In writing class, the participants wrote letters to their prospective host families and were trained to observe and take notes on their learning experiences. These observations, some of which are reported here, were recorded in journals they kept while overseas. In reading and listening classes, students were introduced to the host schools and to course offerings. With the help of three chaperones, in addition to informal discussions with students who had gone to Belleville, the students made their class selections from lists of available classes. They were encouraged to take courses in foreign language, Freshman English (or an ESL class where available), art, music, lower-level math and beginning science; and discouraged – with few exceptions – from taking courses with heavy reading loads (e.g. the social sciences). Their course preferences were sent to the host schools to allow coordinators to generate class schedules for the students prior to their arrival. Accompanying the course preferences, descriptions of individual students were included to help facilitate host family placement.

Method

The data for this study were collected through a variety of ethnographic methods including participant journals on their classroom experiences, classroom observations, and informal interviews (Bernard, 1994) with participants and teachers. As mentioned in the previous section, the students were trained to take notes on their classroom and out-of-class experiences (see Churchill & Vivathanachai, 2000 for a description of how the journal observations were presented to the participants). In this way, this study was influenced methodologically by the work of Bonny Norton Peirce (Peirce, 1994; 1995; Norton 2000) and by Roberts and her colleagues (cf. Roberts *et al.*, 2001). During training sessions in Japan, a few students recorded notes in Japanese and then wrote their commentary in English. However, student observations were progressively made in English. With very few exceptions, their observations were recorded in English while they were in Belleville. Thus, the data from student journals presented in this paper are identical to what the students wrote – they have not been translated or corrected.

During their three-week stay, the students were instructed to make two formal classroom observations in which they drew a floor plan of the classroom, recorded the positions of the students and teachers, and took notes on classroom interaction during a 20-minute period. Following their classroom observation, the students summarized their notes and then composed a brief commentary on what they observed. As many students were paired in classes together, their field notes on specific classes could be triangulated.

In addition, throughout our stay in Belleville, I communicated on a regular basis (every two to three days) with chaperones from Kansai assigned to the other schools, and made visits to the four schools. During these visits and discussions with fellow chaperones, I took notes on student classroom experiences. I also heard directly from the students about their concerns and successes. As much of my time was spent at St Martin's, I met informally with several classroom teachers and they kept me apprised of the progress of individual students. I also had regular meetings with the participants and heard about their classroom experiences. I have supplemented these reports with classroom observations at St Martin's and select recorded interviews with students. Although much of my time was spent at St Martin's, I was familiar with the other institutions and the experience of previous study abroad students from Kansai High. In a previous iteration of the program, I spent the majority of my time at Belleville Country Day and made visits to the other schools. Furthermore, upon our return to Kansai High, several class hours were devoted to an evaluation of the exchange during which time participants further elaborated on their classroom experiences.

My position as a chaperone for the participants coupled with the emphasis on student observations, supported my interest in portraying the study abroad classroom experience from the students' perspective. I believe this has been an under-represented viewpoint in the literature on study abroad and also one that could constructively inform future programs. However, by foregrounding the students' experiences, I have admittedly deemphasized the voices of administrators and opinions of classroom teachers in Belleville. This paper should be read accordingly.

In the discussion that follows, I will begin by describing two initial classroom experiences that will illustrate how macro factors can influence classroom dynamics. Then, I will turn to three exemplary learning experiences and attempt to extract classroom practices and learning principles (Gee, 2003) that contributed to positive evaluations by the participants. I will contrast these positive experiences with classroom practices and structural factors that tended to alienate participants. I will then conclude with recommendations for future study abroad programs and argue that perceived variability in learner competence in the study abroad classroom is largely constructed through the interaction of program factors and local classroom dynamics.

Orientation and the First Days of Classes

Because of differences in school schedules, I was able to accompany the participants during their initial orientation at Belleville High and St Martin's. While there was considerable variation in how the first day was experienced by the participants at each of the four schools, by contrasting St Martin's and Belleville High I hope to demonstrate how the first encounter at the schools shaped subsequent classroom experiences.

Being welcomed into the community at St Martin's

Mr Wade, a senior physics teacher with nine years of experience with the Kansai–Belleville exchange, organized the initial contact at St Martin's, a small boarding school where time and space (e.g. weekly chapels, school meetings) are set aside for the explicit purpose of fostering a sense of community. As we shall see below, Mr Wade made effective use of the resources available to him to integrate the participants into the school.

When I walked in the front door at St Martin's, one of the first things to catch my eye was a small bulletin board on an easel across from the receptionist's desk. At the top, a red and white sign read 'Introducing the students from Kansai School'. Below pictures of the nine Kansai students placed around the edges of the bulletin board, the student's names were written followed by a brief description of each student. In this way, the participants attending St Martin's were being introduced to the community even before their arrival. In Wenger's (1998) terms, *brokers* (pp. 108–109) at St Martin's and Kansai High had worked together to create an artifact to facilitate the *boundary encounter* (p. 112) by introducing the Kansai students to the school.

As I was looking at the participants' pictures, a few St Martin's students, campus friends assigned to guide the Kansai student's through their first day, arrived from the dining room and introduced themselves. They were carrying copies of the Kansai students' class schedules which had been created based on participant class preferences sent to St Martin's in early September. One student approached Kazuko and Nori and said, 'You must be Kazuko', 'You're Nori, right? My name is Susan ... Let's take a look at your schedule and see which class you have first'. As the introductions finished, the Kansai students took out copies of the schedules and consulted with their peers.

Thus, upon arrival the participants were getting a chance to meet peers and receive class schedules that largely coincided with their anticipated experience at St Martin's. The class schedule was a document created with the help of brokers (teachers and the academic dean) at both schools. As such, the schedules were a reification, the 'making into a thing' (Wenger, 1998: 58), of the participants' evolving negotiation with and understanding of their host school.

By providing both the Kansai students and the campus friends with schedules, Mr Wade gave the students a shared task to negotiate through-out the day, and an artifact containing information upon which to base their interaction. As Wenger notes, through the process of reification, people create objects that are 'points of focus around which the nego-tiation of meaning is organized' (p. 58). The participants at St Martin's would use their schedules to continue the process of making meaning out of their American school experience. As campus friends guided the Kansai students through their first day, they helped map out their day based on the coded information on their schedules (colors for class periods, numbers for classrooms and initials for teachers' names). The schedules also identified the participants as students – not visitors – who should be attending a given class at a given time in a given place. If confused, they could ask anybody in the school to help them find, for example, their physics class during orange period in Room 5. Thus, the brokers not only provided the participants with a tool to make meaning out of their experience, but also helped create an identity for the partici-pants in a vocabulary that was universally understood in the school. Before we accompany Kazuko and her friends from Kansai into their physics, math and English classes, let us first turn to the reception at Belleville High.

Initial days at Belleville High

In contrast to the welcoming at St Martin's, the reception at Belleville High was far less personal and inclusive. This was reflected in the use of resources sent from Kansai High. I did not ask what became of the par-ticipant photos and descriptions sent to Belleville High, but they were not posted in the school in the same manner that they had been at St Martin's. As for the participants' class schedules, Mr Ripley, the principal at Belleville High, explained upon our arrival that the participants' class schedules had not yet been made. In the meantime, Mr Ripley suggested that the participants follow a Belleville student to their classes for the first few days. This practice was historically consistent with previous iterations of the exchange at Belleville High and a source of tension between organizers at Kansai High, who were eager to have students get into classes of their own, and the administration at Belleville High.

There are two points worth mentioning here regarding the limited use of resources (e.g. student descriptions, photos and class preferences) at Belleville High. First, because the Belleville campus friends welcoming the Kansai students had no background information on their guests, the greetings were comparatively stiff. Secondly, as the participants were not provided with their own class schedule, it was considerably more difficult for their peers and teachers to make meaning out of their presence. Moreover, the participants themselves could not easily establish where they belonged in the school. The Kansai students were clearly marked as temporary visitors accompanying Belleville High students to classes in a labyrinth of concrete halls. In many cases, their presence in classes was inconsequential at best, and perhaps intrusive at worst.

To illustrate this point, let us look at Nanae's first classroom experience. Following a tour of the school conducted by Mr Ripley, the participants were paired up with their guides and went to the second period class. Coming to Belleville High six weeks into the semester, Nanae not only entered a classroom setting in which local practices and routines had already been established, but she and her guide Alice arrived five minutes late. To appreciate the experience from Nanae's perspective, listen to her describe her first class at Belleville.

> The teacher is standing at the front and talking about today's class. Students are sitting like a circle. I am sitting at the front next to Alice. Students are talking to each other and eating something like candy, chocolate, etc. One student share some textbooks for each student. Students are checking own homework. Students are answering in order. After that, teacher said do the questions in the textbook. But students are talking. I also talking. Amy said to me, 'Can you show me the dictionary?' I said 'Sure'. Also, the other side girl said so. Teacher is saying, 'You shouldn't speak, you should be writing'. Now, we are quiet. Everybody is writing journal. I don't know what I should do, so I'm writing about class. Everybody is writing ... (Nanae, Journal 1B.2)

While a few students tried to talk with Nanae, their attempts were cut short by the teacher's desire to proceed. In a class where two conflicting needs – that of the students to get to know a new member and that of the teacher to conduct his lesson as planned, the teacher's desire to maintain order prevailed. Like the bilingual students in Toohey's (1998) study of classroom practices, Nanae's attempts 'to interact with more capable, English-speaking peers were curtailed' (p. 79) and she was excluded 'from just those conversations in which [she] legitimately might peripherally participate with child experts' (p. 81). Confused and shut off from her supportive peer, Nanae did her best to imitate the behavior of the other students in the class.

Meanwhile, the sharing of resources – in this case Nanae's electronic dictionary – subverted the teacher's classroom practices. Alice's English teacher was attempting to go about his lesson and lead a large classroom of students while handling the commotion generated by the unexpected presence of a visitor. Given his educational objectives, the way in which he responded to Nanae's unsanctioned interaction is to be expected. The point here is not to question the teacher's response, but rather to highlight the school-wide reception given Nanae. This and the subsequent introduction she received to her first class in conjunction with the limited – if any – forewarning that Alice's English teacher was provided all conspired to shape Nanae's initial classroom experience in non-trivial ways. The overall effect was that Nanae was denied access to classroom activities, practices, identities and affiliations that might have helped her in subsequent classes. While other examples from the initial days at Belleville High are not quite as dramatic, the overall picture is not one of integration into classroom practices. However, when students eventually received their class schedules on the fourth day, things began to improve for them and their teachers. Having illustrated how perfunctory orientation at the host school can influence class dynamics, let us return to the first classes at St Martin's for an example of a more typical classroom experience.

A More Typical Class

On the second day at St Martin's, I observed Kazuko and Miya's first physics class. At the beginning of class, Mr Wade introduced Kazuko and Miya to the class and taught his 10 students how to say good morning in Japanese. After Kazuko and Miya found seats in the third row of long veneer tables, Mr Wade returned a set of quizzes to the ninth-grade students who filled up the first two rows and part of the third row next to Kazuko and Miya. After announcing when the next extra-help sessions were scheduled, Mr Wade began his lesson on motion by drawing a graph with velocity and time axes on the board, labeled v and t. He paused for a moment to look over his class of students and then reminded a few that they should be taking notes. A boy sitting next to Miya put away his history homework and took out a notebook. As Mr Wade began to go over a few time–distance problems writing $d = v^*t$ on the board, Kazuko pulled out her electronic dictionary to look up a few words. Checking her dictionary with the words on the whiteboard, she talked briefly with Miya. Of the comments I could hear, Kazuko said to Miya, '*Ahh*, "t" *da!*' ('Oh, it's "*t*"'). Excited at having figured out the meaning of the formula, Kazuko and Miya smiled and nodded to each other. Kazuko then began to take a few notes, looking intermittently at the board as Mr Wade continued his explanation. Thirty minutes into class, Mr Wade came to Miya and Kazuko and gave them a copy of the quiz he had returned at the beginning of class. Kazuko picked up the paper and started working on one of the problems, and Miya joined her. At the end of class, Mr Wade went through a calculation on the velocity of a ball as Kazuko took notes. As class ended, Mr Wade wrote the homework assignment on the board and collected the students' recent assignment. When I asked Miya about the class later in the day, she said that it was not that difficult because she had done some of this material in junior high school.

This description is fairly characteristic of many of the participant classroom experiences. Coming into class in the middle of the term, Kazuko and Miya were left up to their own devices to make meaning out of the class. Like Nanae in Alice's English class, they were faced with the task of decoding content in a flow of discourse that had started at the beginning of the academic year. Fortunately, for Kazuko and Miya, their previous experience with physics and with the universal symbols indicating time, distance and velocity greatly facilitated their task. It also helped that they were able to confirm their evolving understanding with each other. Because of their background knowledge, they could basically follow the class and get something out of it. As Shaw *et al.* (1994) found in their study of Asian learners in Boston, previous subject knowledge 'help[ed] support an on-going positive sense of self . . . in an English-speaking setting that more typically taxes their abilities as learners' (p. 39). Their understanding of the subject material helped. But perhaps equally important was the way in which preparation for their initial participation in class had been previously arranged between the host and home institutions, and how the teacher welcomed the students into his class.

'By Teachers, Classes will Change'

After I observe some classes, I thought each class has specific things. By teachers, classes will change a little. (Risa, Journal 2B.3)

In [different] instructional approaches, students learn the subject
matter; however, in each, they learn a different relation to the subject
matter and to the community in which the information is regarded
as important, through their varying participation in the process of
learning. (Rogoff, 1994: 211)

The participants frequently discussed differences in their individual
teachers. Following her observations of Spanish class and Music
History class at St Martin's, Risa noted how differences in classroom
styles influenced the 'varying participation [of students] in the process
of learning' mentioned by Rogoff. In Risa's Spanish class, the teacher
and students were 'friendly' and laughed a lot because the teacher was
'fun and interesting'. In Music History class, the 'students are very
quiet', 'serious' and 'don't laugh much'. In Risa's view, while there
were many similarities between the two classes (devoted teachers and
focused students), the differences between these two classes and all of
her classes at St Martin's could be attributed to the various styles of the
teachers.

Based on my observations and on those of the participants, there was
indeed a great deal of variety in the way that classes were conducted.
Some of the differences are probably related to the individual school
cultures (e.g. private vs. public, day vs. boarding), pre-program preparation, student-teacher ratios, and subject matter. However, other
factors such as interaction patterns suggested by the spatial arrangement
of furniture, teachers' understanding of their roles, the amount of time
sanctioned for student interaction and the adjustments made by teachers
and students in response to the newcomers shaped the class ecology in
important ways. Modifications to classroom organization and interaction,
or the relative lack thereof, influenced in non-trivial ways the learning
opportunities offered to the participants.

To illustrate this point, let us first turn our attention to three examples
of positive learning experiences. The first is in Kazuko and Natsumi's
English class at St Martin's. We will then visit Natsumi in her math
class and the third example will come from a French class at Middle
School. In each of these cases, I shall attempt to relate the specific cases
to generalizable learning principles based on the work of Gee (2003).

Kazuko never mentioned her physics class in her journal, but she wrote
about her English class twice. Also describing the same English class in
her journal, Natsumi drew a large oval table with the teacher seated at
the head and Kazuko and Natsumi on either side of her. A large box in
the middle of the table is labeled, 'English Dictionary'. Commenting on

the oval table and the seating arrangement in the class, she wrote, 'Students sit around the desk. Teacher sit too. It is good to have class because it can make good environment to learn. They can look each other's faces. Their distance is very near . . .' (Natsumi, Journal 1B.2). She noted how the students were asking many questions and seemed to be having fun. Natsumi could not understand the short story they were discussing in her first class. However, following her second English class she said, 'I had English class yesterday and it was difficult. But I had English class today and it was little understand'. Concurring with Natsumi, Kazuko reported in an informal discussion on classes 'Ah . . . English class . . . we can participate'. When I asked how she was participating, she said that she had been called on by the teacher to read aloud in class. While Kazuko and Natsumi had difficulty in understanding the discussion of the short stories, Mrs Dimple soon found a way to use their lack of understanding to modify her classroom discourse.

Six days after their first English class, Kazuko wrote about Mrs Dimple's class in very positive terms, saying that she enjoyed being able to study with the other students in the class.

Today, October 25th, at the 5th period, I participated in Freshman English (teacher is Mrs Dimple) class with Natsumi. We already took this class for about 5 times. I like this class the best in St Martin's, because I can enjoy class with St Martin's students, although I couldn't understand all of they said. But I can say that we could participate . . . First, the class started. Mrs Dimple came to the class and talked about today's schedule, about 5 minutes. Her English is very fast that I can't catch it sometimes. Then she asked everyone, 'Can anyone tell the outline of this?' to let us understand the story. Soon, David who is very kind (he try to help us everytime!) raised his hand, 'Oh, yes! I can tell them!' Then he started to explain to us, so we could understand general contents. Then, Mrs Dimple started to discuss more detail of the story. At that time, almost all students gave a lot of opinion, so everytime we can have lively discussions. I think it's very nice because all students participating in the class, and we can study all together. Soon, the student's opinions became too many, so the class became annoying as we can't catch Mrs Dimple's voice. So, she said, 'Wait! Wait! My talk is not finish yet!' in a loud voice. After she said, again started students' opinions. After the discussion, Mrs Dimple told about homework and next class's contents. This time, also I understand the class, and I really think that I want to take a lesson like this in Japan. (Kazuko, Journal 1B.2)

Rather than leave the Kansai students to their own devices, Mrs Dimple benefitted from their presence by having David summarize the story for the entire class. While checking the St Martin's students' comprehension, she was constructing an interaction for Kazuko and Natsumi that was closer to their level. In effect, Mrs Dimple was allowing for some 'communicative accommodation' (Schieffelin & Ochs, 1986b: 174) to take place such that the discussion was within their 'regime of competence' (Gee, 2003: 71). She then added to David's description, thus helping the entire class build a collective understanding that was then further developed in the lively discussion that ensued. The way that she restructured her class dynamics made a space for Kazuko and Natsumi and significantly affected their view of the learning experience and their opportunities to interact. While Kazuko and Natsumi did not understand everything that was being said, they were getting a general idea of the topic by scaffolding off David's interpretation, Mrs Dimple's elaboration and the class discussion. Perhaps more importantly, they were also getting the message that their presence in the class was being accounted for as class dynamics were restructured to involve them in a literacy event. In contrast to Nanae, who was inadvertently excluded from the discourse of her English class, Kazuko and Natsumi were explicitly included by the teaching strategies used by Mrs Dimple.

In Rogoff's (1994) terms, Mrs Dimple's class was being conducted according to a 'community-of-learners model' (p. 212). In such pedagogical models, 'organization changes from dyadic relations between teachers responsible for filling students up with knowledge and students who are supposed to be willing receptacles to complex group relations among class members who learn to take responsibility for their own learning and the group's functioning' (Rogoff, 1994: 214). Unlike Alice's English class at Belleville High, Mrs Dimple's English class was far from being didactic and even at times verged on being chaotic.

To add a further analytical level, we may draw on Gee's (2003) framework of principles incorporated into the design of facilitative learning environments. Several of Gee's 36 learning principles (pp. 207–212) appear to have been highlighted in Mrs Dimple's class, but for our current discussion it may be helpful to focus specifically on the interaction between the insider principle, the 'regime of competence' principle, and active/critical learning principles in Natsumi's description of her class. By asking David to summarize the story, Mrs Dimple emphasized his position as an insider and producer of knowledge. Simultaneously, as Mrs Dimple's use of the insider principle allowed David to take on a virtual teaching identity in the class, Natsumi and Kazuko were allowed 'to operate within, but at the outer edge of [their] resources', or within their regime of competence, such that the class was 'challenging but not undoable' (p. 209). Finally, as exemplified by this interaction and Natsumi's description of the 'lively discussion' in which everyone participated, allowing the students to 'study together', their learning became truly active. Furthermore, Natsumi's observation that the students expressed 'a lot of opinions' suggests that they were probably being critical in their discussion of the story. The interaction of these principles helped make this a compelling learning environment for Natsumi and Kazuko despite the obvious challenges of discussing short stories in a mainstream freshman English class.

Natsumi was fortunate enough to have another class in which several of Gee's (2003) learning principles promoted her participation in constructive ways. On Natsumi's third day at St Martin's, I observed her algebra class. Spread throughout a classroom with wall-to-wall blackboards, there were about 15 chairs with writing desks attached to the right arm. The teachers' desk was pushed into a corner of the room. At the beginning of the class, Mr Peters gave the nine ninth-grade students a quiz and Natsumi worked on the quiz as well. As they were writing, he came over to Natsumi and took a handful of change out of his pocket and asked Natsumi if she knew the word for each coin. Puzzled, Natsumi correctly identified each coin and then answered how many nickels were in a quarter. Mr Peters then looked at Natsumi's quiz and helped her with a few more vocabulary words. About seven minutes into class, he collected the student quizzes but let Natsumi keep hers so she could continue working with it after class. He then had the students write the solutions to their homework problems on the board, assigning one problem to two students. Going from one problem to the next, Mr Peters talked through each solution step by step. When there was a mistake, he asked the class to help make corrections. As he went through each problem, Natsumi took notes.

At one point, a student in the class announced that she was having a difficult time setting up the equations based on the word problems, so Mr Peters spent several minutes going over a word problem involving a quantity of money made of dimes and nickels in which 'the number of dimes is four less than three times the number of nickels'. First he outlined the best way of setting up the problem (letting x be the number of nickels, and expressing the number of dimes in terms of x, the # of dimes $= 3x - 4$). Then he challenged the class to see if they could express the nickels in terms of the number of dimes. After some extensive interaction between Mr Peters and the students, they solved the problem both ways. He then announced that problem number 9 was particularly difficult, and asked for a volunteer to present the problem to the class. A well-dressed blond girl raised her hand and Mr Peters asked her to go over her solution. She wrote on the board explaining each of her steps as she modeled her presentation on Mr Peters' earlier discussion of the homework. With five minutes left in the class, Mr Peters then asked all but four students to go to the board and write their names where they stood. He then wrote Natusmi's name on the board and said, 'Natsumi, I have a spot here for you ... This is your spot. You stand here and I'm going to have you do some problems'.

As we can see, Mr Peters exercised some of the same principles we saw operative in Natsumi's English class. Namely, students were being positioned as producers (not just consumers) of knowledge – following Gee's (2003) insider principle, and they were being afforded opportunities to play with new identities (identity principle) as evidenced by the blond girl presenting/teaching her solution to the class and Natsumi's being given a place at a board with the other students. Furthermore, the learning was active and critical and all students, including Natsumi, were being afforded opportunities to practice together (practice principle).

At first, Natsumi was rather surprised to be called to the board, but she did so when Mr Peters asked her once again. Saying that he wanted to check the students' comprehension, he wrote the following on the board $-10 - 20 - (-25) = ?$ As he wrote, he read the equation and all the students copied the equation. Rereading the equation more slowly, he then helped Natsumi as she copied the equation. After she had solved the problem, he checked the other students' work and confirmed that Natsumi had come to a similar conclusion. He repeated the process with another equation involving subtraction and multiplication. He then turned to several equations involving exponents, beginning with X^2 moving to X^5 and finally $(X^5)^2 = X?$, saying that the class had not done this before. Getting the correct answer from the students, he asked them to explain why they added exponents in some cases and multipled them in others. Throughout the class, he focused on correct answers and encouraged students to make corrections based on the work of their peers. Thus, Natsumi was confirming her answers with others at the same time that the St Martin's students modeled their answers on her work.

Again drawing from Gee's (2003) framework, we can see not only that the learning was active, but that the construction of meaning (in this case, solutions to math problems) was distributed among the students (Gee's dispersed principle). Moreover, Mr Peters, a 20-year veteran math teacher, assisted Natsumi in setting up problems which helped her operate within her level of competence. Once he had confirmed that she was processing the English vocabulary of mathematics, he let her write equations on her own. Notably all these math problems did not require Natsumi to transfer a word problem into a mathematical equation, a task that might tax Natsumi's listening skills. Playing on Natsumi's strength as an experienced learner of algebra, Mr Peters set her up for success in the eyes of her classmates while also letting them learn from her. In this way, Mr Peters positioned Natsumi not only as a participant, but as a competent peer who could contribute to the learning of her classmates (the insider principle). By highlighting the successes of each individual student and lowering the consequences of mistakes (the psychosocial moratorium principle), Mr Peters provided 'intrinsic rewards' 'for learners at all levels of skill' thus exercising Gee's achievement principle (Gee, 2003: 208) and increasing the learners' degree of investment in, or commitment to, his class and each other (committed learning and affinity group principles).

A third example of the Kansai students learning together with their host peers occurred at Middle School in Kumiko's French class. Four Kansai students attended Mr Stanley's French class, and they all commented positively on the experience. On the first day that the Kansai students attended his class, Mr Stanley reorganized the class seating arrangement so that individual Kansai students were paired up with students from Middle School. Furthermore, Mr Stanley had everyone's name written on the board so that the students could get to know each other. As one student noted, 'He wrote everyone's name at the beginning, so I could memorize their name easily' (Taka's Journal, Oct. 19th). This was important for participants like Taka who found it 'difficult to memorize the names of Middle School students' (Taka's Journal, October 25th). The participants' journals not only refer to their classmates by name in their descriptions; but they also contain mention of meeting these students throughout the day at Middle School and of having short exchanges, sometimes in French and sometimes in English. In this way, Mr Stanley's French class fostered a community of peers that the participants could interact with throughout the day. Gee (2003) refers to such associations of learners as an 'affinity group that is bonded together through shared endeavors, goals, and practices' (p. 212) in learning environments where active and dispersed learning is facilitated through supportive networks.

Mr Stanley also modified his lessons so that the four Kansai students could teach their peers numbers in Japanese while they all learned to count in French. Concerning this experience, Kumiko wrote 'I teach some Japanese words for Dan and Hunter. They were interested in Japan. I'm very glad' (Kumiko, Journal 1B.2). Mr Stanley also had the students stand up together and move their bodies in a Total Physical Response type activity. 'After that, we practiced name of time in French like a dance. For example, Mr Stanley said "3 o'clock" (in French) and we made watch with our leg. It was very interesting for me' (Kumiko, Journal 1B.2). Thus, the ways in which Mr Stanley restructured the seating arrangement in his class, his positioning of the participants as both teachers and learners, and the ways in which class activities were conducted allowed the students to learn and laugh together. Applying Gee's (2003) framework to the dynamics in Mr Stanley's French class, we can see that the active learning principle, the insider principle and identity principles are being exercised as the Japanese learners of English were encouraged to take on identities of teachers of Japanese and learners of French as they interacted with their peers.

Factors Negatively Affecting Student Participation

Unfortunately, such positive learning experiences were not enjoyed by all the learners. There were many instances where they felt alienated even as they were being immersed in the host schools. In several of the participant journals, they reported that a given class was not interesting because 'the teacher doesn't pay me attention' (Hiroyuki, Journal Oct. 20th) or because 'I couldn't join in [the classes]' (Tamaki, Journal November, 1st). In a pattern observed at all four schools, students who felt particularly removed from a specific class stopped going to the class altogether towards the end of the program. Suggestive that this is not an unusual pattern in exchange contexts, a similar trend of students opting out of classes in which they felt excluded from the classroom discourse was reported by Shaw and his colleagues in their study of Asian students attending school in the Boston area (Shaw *et al.*, 1994: 34). Similarly, Brecht and Robinson (1995) found that a lack of interest and follow through by some Russian teachers in an exchange program for American students led to 'negative reactions to language classes' (p. 333). In the following discussion, rather than describing individual cases, I will touch on program-wide factors, teacher variables, classroom structures and influences related to class content and practices that played a role in negatively influencing the experiences of the participants.

At the program level, we have already observed how student integration into the host school can be both positively and negatively shaped by pre-program planning. In instances − such as that of

Nanae's first class – where students are not efficiently placed in classes at the outset of the program, teachers caught off guard may be unclear about the students' status in their class. Moreover, the integration of language learners into host classroom communities may be postponed until their course schedule is established. In comparatively short-term programs, this constitutes a loss of precious time.

Another program-level practice that can distract from learner involvement are cultural outings and school events. Two commonly incorporated components of exchange programs are sight-seeing tours for the visiting students and cultural presentations by the students at the host schools. When these activities are conducted during the school day, visiting students are pulled out of classes. While there may be other benefits to such activities (e.g. a break from classes, intercultural understanding), they can disrupt student involvement in their new classroom communities. While the number of outings and extra-curricular events scheduled during classes in the Belleville–Kansai exchange have been reduced over the years, in the 1999 iteration there were still at least two events over the course of three weeks at each school that required students to be removed from classes. In cases where student involvement in classroom practices was progressing smoothly, these extra-curricular activities probably affected student participation only slightly. However, in cases where students were already feeling isolated due to program-wide factors and local classroom dynamics, it is unlikely that these activities made any positive contribution to their integration into classes.

At the host schools themselves, teacher experience, teaching style and teacher familiarity with the Kansai–Belleville exchange played a role in shaping student integration. As previously mentioned, there was no specific orientation given to the faculty, and individual teachers had varying degrees of exposure to students in the program. Experienced teachers who had students from Kansai in their classes in previous iterations of the exchange, such as Mr Peters and Mr Stanley, proved to be comparatively adept at integrating the Japanese students into their mainstream class. Similarly, teachers such as Mrs Dimple who had several years of experience and who already conducted their classes in a community-of-learners model, were equally successful in fostering a positive learning experience. In contrast, teachers with less experience and little previous contact with the students from Kansai were more at a loss as to how to incorporate the newcomers into their class activities. Furthermore, when a teacher-centered approach was taken, the participants developed an indifferent attitude towards the class at best. At worst, feeling isolated and ignored, they began questioning the value of further investing their time and energy. As found by Toohey (1998) and McKay and Wong (1996), many of the unfavorable consequences of teacher-centeredness can be intensified for English language learners new to the American classroom. In this way, teacher-related variables such as overall experience, previous contact with similar learners and amount of sanctioned student-to-student discussion interacted to affect the participants' learning experiences in non-trivial ways.

While individual teaching approaches appeared to have influenced the degree of sanctioned interaction between the participants and their American peers which in turn contributed to their affective response to specific classes, it is worth noting that these teaching practices took place within the physical architecture of individual classrooms. As Natsumi noted, the large oval table in Mrs Dimple's English class allowed all of the students to be near each other and to see each other's faces, which facilitated communication and helped create a 'good environment to learn'. Similarly, Natsumi's math class was in a small room with blackboards on all four walls, allowing the students to see each other's work and affording Mr Peters the opportunity to be supportive of Natsumi, while using his interaction with her to teach other students. In contrast, the orientation of furniture and learning technology in other classrooms discouraged participant interaction with their American peers. For example, Ichiko, a student who responded positively to Mr Stanley's French class, wrote that she did not like her computer class 'because I couldn't communicate with students because they have their own computer and they are working on it' (Ichiko, Journal October, 21st). By the second week of classes, following a missed day in the school infirmary, Ichiko stopped going to the computer class altogether. In other classes, a large number of desks or large desks that were difficult to rearrange, coupled with a single blackboard at the front of the room, favored a teacher-centered approach. This limited the activation of several of the learning principles discussed earlier, thus contributing to the isolation of newcomers.

Another factor mitigating participant involvement was the organization of participant activity during class evaluations (e.g. quizzes). This was particularly true of classes in the first week of the program for which the Japanese learners could not have prepared even if they had wanted to. Echoing the dynamics in Nanae's first class, Ichiko wrote of a class on her second day during which the 'students did a test, so we couldn't join so much' (Ichiko, Journal, Oct. 20th). While some teachers, such as Natsumi's math teacher, seized on the opportunity presented by the in-class evaluations to work directly with the participants, this was more the exception than the rule. In fact, several participants reported that they were instructed to go to the library when the rest of the class was being evaluated. This practice either tended to leave the participants alone within the host school or afforded them the opportunity to congregate with their friends from Kansai, two positions that promised considerably less input than active participation in their mainstream classes.

In the discussion of factors that negatively affected the participants' classroom experience, it is noteworthy that *the difficulty of a particular subject in and of itself did not lead to an unfavorable evaluation* or absenteeism by the participants. As we have seen, some students were more or less successfully integrated into mainstream freshman English classes while others such as Nanae were comparatively isolated. Similarly, students in some French and math classes were able to participate, learn some content and actually help teach something to their American peers, while students taking identical subjects in other class settings felt significantly separated from the classroom community. For the Japanese learners, their mainstream courses were certainly challenging, but it was only when this challenging content was combined with some of the distancing classroom structures and practices outlined above that they felt frustrated, negatively evaluated their experiences and sometimes withdrew themselves from class (either as instructed to do so by their teachers or of their own volition). Conversely, course subjects – such as art – that were consistently evaluated favorably by the participants may have been easier to handle in terms of content, but these classes also engendered interactional patterns that were facilitative of many of Gee's (2003) principles of learning. In other words, the semiotic domain of individual classes was not the sole determinant of successful involvement.

Conclusion

This chapter constitutes a preliminary attempt to investigate the local dynamics of mainstream classrooms as these ecologies respond to the incorporation of exchange students. The portrait that emerges is one of a great deal of variation – within the same program, sometimes within the same host institution, between similar content courses, and even between different courses taken by the same student. While this variation could be observed through the contrastive discussion of individual classes, the variation was not generated by local classroom interaction alone. By examining both macro-level and local dynamics, we can begin to learn from successful cases to help improve future programs. Furthermore, the variation reported here has implications for future research and – at a theoretical level – encourages one to consider what constitutes learner competency.

In some respects, the findings are not that astonishing in that they coincide with those reported in numerous studies on the classroom learning experiences of immigrant students in the United States (e.g. Benesch, 2001; McKay & Wong, 1996; Statzner, 1994; Toohey, 1998; Willet, 1995) and those on learner attitude towards formal instruction in the host context (e.g. Brecht & Robinson, 1995; Shaw _et al._, 1994). The myriad of learner experiences presented in this chapter can best be summarized in the words of Willett (1995), found in her ethnographic study of immigrant children in a first grade class. Willett states that '[t]he sociocultural ecology of the community, school, and classroom shaped the kinds of micro-interactions that occurred and thus the nature of their language learning' (p. 473), 'identity, social relations, and communicative competence' (p. 488). Willett's claim is echoed in the words of many researchers conducting situated studies on language learning (e.g. McKay & Wong, 1996: 604; Norton & Toohey, 2001: 314; Siegal, 1996: 374; Watson-Gegeo, 2001: 21), on learning disorders (McDermott, 1993: 295) and Alzheimer's (Hamilton, 1994: 165 and 172), and in the area of situated cognition (e.g. Lemke, 1997: 41; St. Julien, 1997: 263–264; Walkerdine, 1997: 63–64).

As noted in the comparison of the reception at Belleville High School and St Martin's, at least some of the initial classroom experiences were influenced by the degree to which brokers in the program successfully oriented the participants and classroom teachers to each other. In particular, the collaborative construction of classroom schedules and student descriptions, which helped reify the participants' projected experience into artifacts easily identifiable within the host community, expedited participant integration into the microcosms of specific classrooms. In instances where administrators did not make efficient use of available resources, there was a greater likelihood that exchange students had initial experiences such as that of Nanae. Furthermore, in the absence of time and resources devoted to teacher orientations, considerable variation could be attributed to teacher experience with the program. Finally, this study points to how program-wide scheduling of cultural excursions and cultural presentations can have an adverse affect on local dynamics between host classrooms and exchange students.

The implications for future programs are that pre-departure coordination between host and home institutions is integral to the successful involvement of exchange students; that a pre-program teacher orientation is preferable where possible, and that it is important to consider the implications for the host classroom when scheduling extra-curricular events.

In instances where teacher orientation is not administratively feasible, teachers new to a program could be encouraged to work closely with those who have been successful in integrating students into their classes. In their discussion with more experienced peers, these teachers might be encouraged to take a self-reflective look at the learning principles that they promote in their classes.

When a newcomer comes to class, there may be nothing easier than to have the student take an available seat and to continue teaching as one always has. In the absence of teacher orientation and clearly stated program objectives, this is also a response that time-pressed teachers devoted to their work – yet unfamiliar with the exchange program in question – might take. However, depending on the existing classroom practices (e.g. degree of teacher-centered instruction) and the commensurate learning principles being actively promoted, a business-as-usual approach may not be one that is most conducive to exchange student integration, the creation of supportive networks of native speakers, and – indeed – ultimate language learning. Rather, the participants in this study had the most positive experiences in classrooms where a change in the local ecology, resulting from their presence, was proactively acknowledged and integrated with ongoing facilitative learning principles.

As we saw in our discussion of the three cases of Natsumi's English class, her math class and Mr Stanley's French class, it is also in these instances that learning principles advocated by Gee (2003) were most salient. These classes engendered dispersed, active – and sometimes critical – learning that invited participants to experience new identities as they operated within their respective regimes of competence, sometimes when their classmates were positioned as teachers – or producers of knowledge – in accordance with the insider principle. In some very unique cases, they were even encouraged to teach (as in Mr Stanley's French class) or positioned such that their activity (such as Natsumi's work at the blackboard in Mr Peters' class) helped teach their native speaking peers. While such interactive dynamics may not be easily constructed in every content class, the regime of competence principle coupled with positive reinforcement (achievement principle) and the lowering of consequences for risk taking (psychosocial moratorium principle) found in many classes helped promote participant involvement. Moreover, in some cases, the sanctioned in-class interaction played a role in creating affinity groups (such as the students in Mr Stanley's French class) that allowed the participants to develop networks of native speakers outside of class. In contrast, teacher-centered classes and, in many instances, written activities in which students were expected to work on their own (e.g. quizzes), discouraged student interaction, cut off opportunities for interaction with native speakers and sometimes even led to the most extreme form of distancing from the classroom community. In this way, the diverse classroom experiences reported here and elsewhere (Churchill, 2003b) point to some of the sources of variation while also suggesting that the learning principles advocated by Gee contributed to the more positive instances of participant involvement in mainstream classes.

In terms of implications for further research, this study confirms a trend of wide variation reported in study abroad experiences and begins to uncover some of the sources of the 'wider variety of performances' found in study abroad contexts as compared to study at home (Huebner, 1995a). Taking first the classroom context in and of itself, as has been noted elsewhere (e.g. McKay & Wong, 1996), classroom politics and dynamics generated by local practices within existing structural constraints and the learning principles that they favor, or inhibit, tend to be all the more accentuated for the ESL learner. As we have witnessed, the consequences of macro-level decisions by administrators on the local classroom dynamics are potentially even more acute for short-term study abroad learners. Moreover, as classrooms can be important environments in which affinity groups can be fostered, the classroom dynamics – if positively constructed – can play an integral role in nurturing the study abroad student's networks of native speakers. The greater the variation in host classroom experiences, the greater the variation one might expect in interaction with target language peers outside of class. For study abroad students whose time is limited, one might expect to find more variation than for students who are immersed for a longer period. Thus, for researchers interested in documenting gains in proficiency resulting from study abroad as compared with study at home, the challenge entails not only measuring pre- and post-program proficiency levels, but also documenting how the program wide integration of participants into the host school affects local classroom dynamics, and the degree to which classroom interaction further promotes opportunities for language practice and acquisition beyond the classroom walls.

In terms of theory, the variety of participant experiences in the classrooms of Belleville illustrate that, depending on how they were incorporated into the class, the participants were being constructed as more or less competent. Natsumi was positioned as an expert on exponents in her math class and as a competent, but novice learner, in her English class. Meanwhile, Nanae and many of her peers were constructed as being far less competent in identical subject areas. In each class, variable degrees of competency were being strongly suggested to each learner even as they were afforded varying degrees of freedom to renegotiate perceptions of their linguistic abilities and understanding of the subject matter. The point is that their competencies were 'situationally contigent' (St. Julien, 1997: 264). As St. Julien notes,

> The project of bringing context, knowledge, and schooling into productive contact with competence has yielded to a reframing in which context and knowledge are brought together in the situation and the competence a person exhibits is a complex, socially constructed result of cognition that spans the formerly separated categories. (p. 264)

An understanding of language learner competence from such a constructivist perspective has important implications for decisions made by the host classroom teacher, administrator and researcher alike.

Part 4: The Influence of Individual and Program Variables on SLA Abroad

Chapter 9

Study Abroad Social Networks, Motivation and Attitudes: Implications for Second Language Acquisition

CHRISTINA ISABELLI-GARCÍA

Introduction

In order to study the development of a learner's oral communication skills and accuracy while abroad, extra-linguistic factors that may influence the acquisition process must also be considered. Studies that examine learners' attitude, motivation and behavior in the host environment and link these factors directly to linguistic development can show that learners may not magically become fluent speakers simply by being surrounded by the target language. One aspect of the host environment is the informal relationships contracted by the individual learner, which have been referred to as 'social networks', a term coined by Milroy (1987a). Analysis of these social networks can be used to account for linguistic development and variation between speakers at the level of the individual, and external tools – such as diaries – can document if motivation and attitude influence the establishment of social networks.

Research has shown that immersion in the target culture is of great value to learners' second language acquisition (SLA), especially in improving oral production ability (Brecht et al., 1993; Collentine, 2004; Freed, 1990a, 1990b; Freed et al., 2004; Isabelli-García, 2003; Kaplan, 1989; Lennon, 1990; Liskin-Gasparro & Urdaneta, 1995; Milleret, 1990; Polanyi, 1995; Segalowitz & Freed, 2004). Studies have also shown that the amount of contact with native speakers is an important factor in the acquisition of sociolinguistic and sociocultural knowledge (Lafford, 1995; Lapkin et al., 1995; Marriott, 1995; Regan, 1995; Siegal, 1995a).

There are, however, inconsistencies in study abroad (SA) research since claims are made based on different acquisition aspects, and distinct amounts of time spent abroad and the type of interaction between learners and native speakers is frequently not specified. Research on study abroad, similar to many studies in SLA, does not account for sociolinguistic dimensions and prevents insight into the nature of learners' language (Firth & Wagner 1997).

This investigation aims to fill this gap by examining the effect of extra-linguistic influences. Specifically, this study asks: What individual extra-linguistic factors (such as motivation, contact with the host culture outside of the classroom and attitudes towards the host culture) can be related to the development of oral communication skills and accuracy? The findings of this study will add to the current literature on what is known about how interaction with the context affects motivation (Syed, 2001; Nikolov, 2001; Ushioda, 2001) and vice versa. Moreover, this study provides evidence of a four-way connection between motivation, significant target language interaction with native speakers in social networks, cultural adjustment, and SLA during the SA experience.

Literature Review

This study explores how differences in motivation and attitude can affect social interaction in the host culture and culminate in minimally extended social networks with native speakers. When learners are in a context where interaction occurs with a more expert speaker, they notice new or correct structures in the expert speaker's language or feedback (Donato, 1994). Building on the framework of Gass and Varonis (1994), in which attention allows learners to notice a mismatch or discrepancy between what they know about the language and what native speakers produce, Donato adds the notion of 'scaffolding' to describe the process by which learners develop their interlanguage through interaction. Additional restructuring outside the classroom acquisition context occurs through a process of destabilization, in which an increase in error rate in one area may reflect an increase in complexity or accuracy in another, followed by overgeneralization of a newly acquired structure (Lightbown, 1985). When additional syntactic patterns become available to learners, restructuring or destabilization occurs. This destabilization is at the base of language change.

On the surface, SA offers learners plenty of opportunities for interaction, to notice the gap and to engage in scaffolding. In the 30 years following Schumann's (1976) claim that the environment in which the learners interact, the opportunities to use the language, and learners' motivational and attitudinal patterns all seem to positively influence their successful rate of acquisition, investigations have agreed (Brecht *et al.*, 1993; Kaplan, 1989; Milleret, 1990; Polanyi, 1995) and disagreed (DeKeyser, 1991; Freed, 1990a; Higgs & Clifford, 1982; Krashen & Seliger, 1976; Schmidt, 1983; Segalowitz & Freed, 2004; Spada, 1985, 1986). However, there is considerable variation in the language learning experiences of SA students. Some variation may be attributable to motivational factors and the learners' interaction with the context that, in turn, affects investment.

Attitudinal factors may also cause variation since attitudes towards the target language and community influence one's second language (L2) learning behavior (Gardner & Lambert, 1972). Studies of motivation in SLA have identified various kinds of motivation orientations: integrative (Gardner, 1985; Gardner & Lambert, 1959); instrumental (Gardner & Lambert, 1959; Gardner & MacIntyre, 1991); resultative (Hermann, 1980; Savignon, 1972; Strong, 1984); and intrinsic and extrinsic (Dörnyei, 2001). Categorization of learner motivation is not black and white, but rather motivation represents a continuum of orientations (see Dörnyei, 2001 for more detailed analyses on motivation).

Integrative motivation embraces socio-cultural, socio-educational, and socio-psychological issues like belonging in a group, receiving affection, and identifying with the foreign language community. Instrumental orientation, on the other hand, deals with the utilitarian use of the language for personal gain, like finding a job or furthering a career. Resultative motivation arises when learners who experience success or failure in learning become more or less motivated to learn. That is, motivation may cause L2 achievement; however, it is also possible that motivation is a result of learning. Learners who have intrinsic motivation may not hold distinct attitudes, positive or negative, towards the target-language group. This motivation involves the arousal and maintenance of curiosity and can fluctuate as a result of such factors as learners' particular interests. On the other hand, extrinsic motivation involves performing a behavior to receive some extrinsic reward or to avoid punishment (Dörnyei, 2001).

Such conceptions of motivation do not capture the complex relationship between relations of power, identity, and language learning (Peirce, 1995). Rather, if the learners have some sort of 'investment' to learn a second language, they do so with the understanding that they will acquire a wider range of symbolic and material resources. The concept of investment envisions the language learner as having a complex social identity and multiple desires. Learners are not only conveying information but also creating and maintaining their identities. Therefore an investment in the target language is also an investment in their social identity, which is constantly changing and shifting. The notion of motivation used in this investigation to describe the four learners draws on both Peirce's notion of investment and the various types of motivation described above. A more complex understanding of motivation is needed and an important question remains: how does the environment in which the learners interact create, foster, and maintain motivation?

For learners entering SA contexts, interaction with the context is most likely mediated by their various stages of acculturation. In order to accomplish the act of integrating into a new surrounding, Bennett (1986) poses the acculturation model, which states that one must pass through a state of ethnocentrism in order to reach a state of ethnorelativism or acculturation. This progress from ethnocentrism to ethnorelativism occurs through a sequence of six states.

The first three states fall under the principle of ethnocentrism: the learner (a) denies the existence of cultural differences, which includes isolation and separation stages; (b) recognizes the reality of cultural differences but makes an effort to preserve hegemony of one culture over another; (c) and minimizes cultural differences in an effort to deal with the recognition that it is not tenable to preserve the superiority of one culture over another. The last three states fall in the category of ethnorelativism, the learner: (d) acknowledges the possibility of differences among cultures in adapting to the environment; (e) adapts to the host culture, and a sense of understanding and pluralism arise; and (f) accepts differences between cultures and enters a state in which these differences become essential to identity (p. 27).

The theory of ethnolingual relativity is built on the work of Bennett (1986). The central idea is that openness to contrasting cultural and linguistic patterns of other peoples and a refusal to be limited by one's own cultural and linguistic experiences can facilitate L2 learning. Social attitude may be linked to ethnolingual relativity as learners without an open perspective may be less motivated to learn a new language since it would seem less relevant to them (Citron, 1995).

One promising way to look dynamically at motivation and acculturation is through the use of social networks (Blom & Gumperz, 1972; Milroy, 1987a) documented by student diaries. Social networks are likely to correlate closely with how the learners envision themselves in the host culture. One cannot expect that learners will be motivated to learn the target language and integrate themselves into the host culture if they find themselves in a state where segregation of the two cultures is still an integral part of their cultural outlook. Thus, drawing from theories of social networks developed in first language communities, I am applying the framework of social networks to learners in a SA context in this study. The learners that will interact mostly within their L1-speaking territory (in this case L1 English-speaking learners) are those who form closed, or dense, multiplex networks with other members of their L1 group and do not interact with the host culture. Their contacts will mostly be with one another, making their role relationships multiplex, as can be seen in Figure 9.1.

Each person X is viewed as a focus from which lines radiate to points (persons with whom X is in contact). In this dense network structure of English-speaking members, interaction will normally be in English; such interaction is, naturally, not conducive to acquiring the target language. The learners who participate in this type of network structure curb their opportunities to interact with native speakers. They accordingly limit chances to notice new or correct structures in the native speakers' language or feedback, which restricts the new information that can scaffold onto their already developing interlanguage.

SA learners who have open personal networks, moving outside the first language (L1) English-speaking territory of their fellow SA acquaintances, will establish contacts in the host culture, presumably with native speakers. Even when the learner is housed with a family and seems to have easier access to a new social network, relationships with the new members still have to be built since interaction does not always take place with the host family (Knight & Schmidt-Rinehart, 2002; Rivers, 1998; Wilkinson, 1997, 1998a, 1998b, 2000).

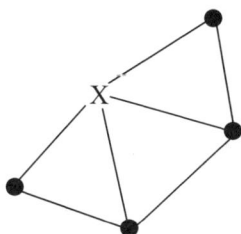

Figure 9.1 High density, closed personal network structure. (X is the focal point of the network) (Milroy, 1987a: 20)

In this low density, open uniplex network, learner X associates with local people (points) in a single capacity (see Figure 9.2). In other words, the individual interacts with others as just a colleague or employee, rather than in multiple capacities such as friends may do. This open personal network characterizes the network of a typical SA learner who maintains contact with several native speakers. Within these conversations on a simple topic, over time, the learner can become an expert at talking about, for example, only school topics. The learner is infrequently exposed to topic variety that comes up in multiplex interactions where arguments and supporting of opinions occur.

Although this uniplex network is the only type that a learner can expect to establish when new to the country, this situation changes when the learner's social network extends to a more multiplex structure. Within a multiplex network, the interactions with native-speaker members help the learners' interlanguage reach a close approximation of the L2 faster. Learners in a multiplex network are required to speak to each member in various capacities. In this manner, the interactions will then likely include a wider range of topics that allow the learner to practice varying aspects of the L2 with more frequency. This provides opportunities to notice gaps (Gass, 1997; Gass & Varonis, 1994; Schmidt, 1993; Schmidt & Frota, 1986) and engage in the scaffolding (Donato, 1994; Lantolf & Appel, 1994) that promotes restructuring of the interlanguage. Learners in extended networks with native speakers will acquire a set of linguistic norms that are enforced by exchange with those native-speaker contacts. Campbell (1996) hinted at this in her self-study when she made a conscious effort to access the social group in order to acquire language while socializing with the members of the group.

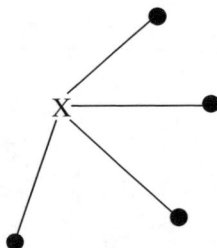

Figure 9.2 Low density, open personal network structure. (X is the focal point of the network) (Milroy, 1987a: 20)

'Network zones' are important to understanding the role that social networks play in successful interaction. The persons who are directly linked to X belong to his [or her] *first order* network zone (Milroy, 1987a). Each of these people may be in contact with others whom X does not know, but with whom X could come into contact via the first order zone. These more distantly connected persons form X's '*second order* zone' (p. 46) (Figure 9.3).

Messages that pass along these network links are seen as transactions, governed by the principle that the value gained by an individual in a transaction is equal to or greater than the cost. These transactions may consist of greetings, civilities, jokes, information or assistance, and when they flow in both directions between links, they are considered 'exchanges'. When learner X participates in a social network in which native-speaker Y (friend of a friend) is part of a second order zone that is closed, then his or her chances of observing and participating in prolonged interaction will then be considerably increased.

There have been few studies on SA that have integrated Bennett's model of acculturation to help account for changes in learner attitude and motivation that might influence the learners' desire to interact with native speakers. Another area that has yet to be brought to the area of SA is a more complex notion of motivation that includes resultative motivation and investment. Without studies that focus on the interdependency of language acquisition, interaction, attitude and this complex notion of motivation, L2 researchers will not understand the effect that the learners' perseverance to maintain social interaction has on their own language acquisition process. Moreover, due to the growing

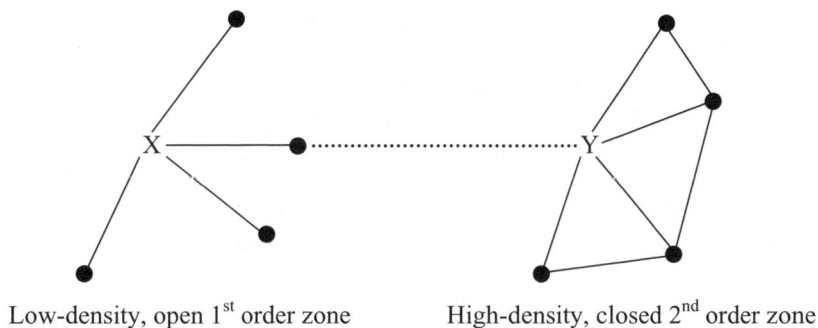

Low-density, open 1st order zone   High-density, closed 2nd order zone

Figure 9.3 Low density network showing first and second order zones (Milroy, 1987a: 48)

participation of learners in SA programs, there is a need for data that can empirically show parents, teachers, and learners the kinds of linguistic development that can be expected from spending a semester abroad and the factors that may influence this development.

Participants

The participants for this study were selected from a group of SA students who were part of a consortium of three large U.S. public universities in Buenos Aires, Argentina. Prospective participants agreed to fill out a questionnaire from which students were selected on the basis of certain criteria outlined by Huebner (1995a), namely: (a) a willingness to participate in the project; (b) a pre-program oral proficiency interview level of Intermediate, according to the ACTFL Proficiency Guidelines (1986); (c) background factors such as foreign language and cultural background (i.e. those who had traveled extensively or had studied or spoke any language other than English were disqualified); (d) motivation to learn Spanish; and (e) realistic expectations of program outcome.

The participants were Caucasian, ranging in age from 19 to 21 years old. Three males and one female served as the informants for this study. They were from diverse regions of the United States and were eager to volunteer as participants in this study.

One student lived with a host family and three lived in student apartments with one to three roommates from different parts of the world. Those who did have English-speaking roommates had a rule to communicate with each other only in Spanish. At the time of the fieldwork, two informants taught conversational English in small language schools as a source of income. The language learning environment for the participants can be characterized as dual: a weak classroom and a strong natural environment. At the sponsoring university abroad, the subjects attended a language class for a total of two hours a week that was for all international students and was taught exclusively in Spanish. There was no textbook, but rather a pamphlet of 'homemade' creative activities, reading excerpts, and grammar paradigms. There was no homework assigned or exams administered. The participants took regular curricular courses with local students in fields such as Agriculture, Economics, International Business, and Politics from the sponsoring private university or from two other universities in the city. The participants' lives outside the classroom varied from being active with native speakers to being limited to activities with other English-speakers.

Data Collection and Analysis

This study uses both a quantitative and qualitative methodology. Analyses were performed on the four types of data: pre- and post-program oral proficiency interviews; informal interviews; diary entries for motivation/attitude orientation; and social network contact logs.

Simulated Oral Proficiency Interview and Informal Interviews

The quantitative measurements were derived from a pre- and post-test Simulated Oral Proficiency Interview (SOPI) and five informal interviews. The sole purpose of the SOPI was to have quantitative data on pre- and post-program proficiency. In addition to the SOPI, the investigator developed an informal interview to elicit data for various oral language skills. The prompt questions were designed to persuade the participants to narrate personal experiences, express and support opinions, relate past activities, and share future plans. All interviews were conducted exclusively in Spanish. These 15-minute recorded interviews were conducted once a month, for a total of five times over the course of the study.

Trained SOPI raters scored the SOPIs to determine the pre- and post-program oral proficiency ratings of the four student participants. The SOPIs were double-rated for reliability and, if a discrepancy was found between the two ratings, a third rater was used. Following a modified version of the ACTFL Guidelines (1986), the SOPIs were rated according to the criteria described for only four levels: Intermediate Low; Intermediate Mid; Intermediate High; and Advanced[1] (for a description of the levels see Byrnes and Canale, 1987: 16).

The learners' informal interviews were transcribed and analyzed for: (a) tense selection of present versus past; (b) imperfect versus preterite aspect selection; (c) person-number (subject-verb) agreement; and (d) gender-number agreement. The focus was limited to these syntactic elements since any considerable number of errors in (a) and (b) could hinder comprehensibility. Errors in (c) and (d) were targeted because accuracy in agreement is an element that shows improvement over time in language learners. These syntactic elements were also focused on since the SOPI guidelines list confusion of aspect and tense selection and agreement errors as markers of distinct oral proficiency levels. A more detailed version of the classification of linguistic accuracy and results for each participant can be found in Isabelli-García (2004).

Diary entries and network contact logs

Another especially important aspect for assessing SA proficiency development are tasks that help identify the environments, activities, and sociocultural views that lend themselves to more or less successful language acquisition. One means by which learners can record their thoughts, achievements, strategies, and impressions of the culture is through diaries (Bacon, 1995; Oxford & Crookall, 1989). To this end, the participants were given notebooks in which they kept weekly diary entries. The entries were written in English so that no subject material would be avoided due to limited linguistic capabilities in Spanish. The students were instructed to make comments on their perception of their language progress, and relay positive or negative events that had occurred within that week.

The learners' social attitudes were measured and operationalized based on culture-specific comments from their diaries and informal interviews that included: (a) comparisons stating that one culture or system was better or worse; (b) descriptions of Argentines' personalities, actions or way of life; (c) feelings about a particular situation or event; and (d) new perspectives on the host country, people or experience. Any comments in these categories are significant since they offer a window into the learners' opinion-formation process.

By making comparisons, the learner is compelled to make evaluative comments. For example, the tendency to make more comparisons by stating that the U.S. culture exceeds that of Argentina in some aspect may be an indicator of a negative social attitude toward the host culture. If that attitude is constantly reported, then a conclusion about the learner's overall social attitude is made. For this study, the learners' culture-specific comments found in their diary entries were tallied and evaluated. If the total number of positive comments was greater than the negative comments, the learner was characterized as possessing a positive social attitude toward the host culture. If the opposite tendency prevailed, the learner was considered to have a negative social attitude. If the number of positive and negative comments were equal, then the learner was characterized as possessing a neutral social attitude, which did not occur with any of the learners in this study.

The learners' motivational orientation (intrinsic, instrumental or integrative) was obtained by two means. One method was based on comments in the initial, pre-program questionnaire that consisted of: (a) personal opinions based on their language learning experience as a whole, and (b) explanations for taking certain actions. The second approach was by translating the learners' positive or negative attitude to a high or low motivational orientation, respectively. This manner of determining the learners' motivation is more reliable than implementing the usual self-report medium.

The participants were each given seven daily log sheets to fill out and a short page of instructions to help them recognize the personal networks in which they interacted. These log sheets were filled out at three different times during their stay abroad and returned to the investigator during the first, eighth and fifteenth week.

After interviewing the participants and collecting the network logs and weekly diary entries, the learners' social networks were identified. The social network concept is used here as an illustrative device for describing social relations abroad from which one can learn how the learner participants envision and incorporate themselves in the host culture. These networks show how the learners position themselves in their new environment and, more importantly, they show the extended network of acquaintances, possibly predicting advancement in SLA.

Results and Discussion

Table 9.1 shows the ratings each participant received on the SOPI given prior to and following the SA experience: All learners but one showed improvement in their pre- and post-SOPI. Stan, Tom and Sam showed a difference of one level between interviews and Jennifer remained at the same proficiency level as when she started.

The qualitative data were used to describe the learners' social networks, their attitudes, and their orientations towards learning. The social networks of four participants' in the host country along with excerpts and analyses of their diary entries are presented here. Extralinguistic features such as instances of positive or negative motivation and attitude are examined.

Table 9.1 Simulated Oral Proficiency Interview ratings

	Pre-program SOPI	*Post-program SOPI*
Stan	Intermediate High	Advanced
Tom	Intermediate Mid	Intermediate High
Sam	Intermediate Mid	Intermediate High
*Jennifer	Intermediate Mid	Intermediate Mid

*Learner stayed at same proficiency level.

Stan's attitudes and social network

Stan's overall disposition during the SA program was positive, as was noted in his weekly diary entries. Stan had a positive attitude towards his experiences in Buenos Aires and had high motivation to study Spanish and understand the new culture. He was continually eager to experience not only the 'real, big-city' life of Buenos Aires but also the very distinct culture of interior Argentina. His eagerness to learn more about the culture correlated with his high motivation to learn Spanish.

As evidenced from Excerpt (1), he wanted to go beyond just learning the language to get the full meaning of what it meant to be Argentine.

(1) This past weekend I went to Cordoba. [...] I spent two days in a friend of a friend's home, which was really nice. [...] It was good to spend a weekend with a family. I think I have a better idea of Argentina, of course more trips are necessary to improve the idea even more.

Stan's goal of understanding Argentina is reflected in his investment in learning the target language.

Stan lived in a university apartment with two Americans and one Mexican and, according to his Network Contact Log, spoke more Spanish than English in his social activities with his roommates and other acquaintances. During his first week he tended to socialize with his American friends because of the small number of Argentines in his social network, as can be seen in Table 9.2 and Figure 9.4, but Spanish was his language of choice.

Table 9.2 Stan's (X) first and second order zone social networks with Argentines

Month	SOPI rating	1st order zone uniplex members	2nd order zone multiplex members	Total social network members
1	IH	1		1
3		3	3	5
5	A	3	5	7

SOPI = Simulated Oral Proficiency Interview; IH = Intermediate High; A = Advanced.

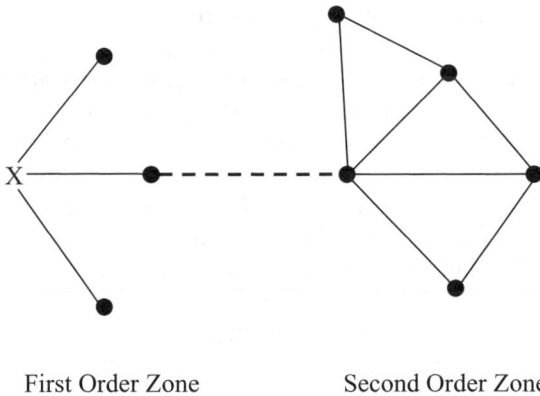

First Order Zone   Second Order Zone

Figure 9.4 Stan's (X) first and second order zone social networks with Argentines.

Although he remained in the circle of friends with the roommates and several other American students, Stan stayed in contact with a friend of a friend who lived in Cordoba, a city about 10 hours from Buenos Aires. By the third month, he had become closer to this friend. As tallied from his self-reported Network Contact Logs at this time, Stan's social network consisted of five Argentine friends; three were members of his first order zone, uniplex social network and three were members of his second order zone, multiplex social network (one member being the conduit between the two networks). He entered into the second order zone through the friend of a friend who then introduced Stan to his two friends, and included him in activities with them.

By the fifth month, Stan had already taken two trips to Cordoba and consequently, his second order zone social network increased to five people due to the friends he made during those visits. These friends also came to visit him in Buenos Aires and all were planning a trip to Chile in the following months. According to his Network Contact Log, when he was socializing with both Americans and Argentines (mostly in Spanish) it was not uncommon for him to argue a point with a friend or to tell a story.

As measured from his diaries and informal interviews, Stan's positive attitude and high motivation were factors in the maintenance and development of his social networks from that of a first order zone to that of the preferred second order zone. By the last month, the latter consisted of friends in Buenos Aires and close friends from Mendoza and Cordoba.

Stan's second order zone social network, his positive attitude, and high motivation correlate with changes seen in his linguistic accuracy from the beginning of the program. The high linguistic accuracy during his first month (91%) gave Stan, who wanted to learn the real side of Argentina, the self-confidence to initiate and sustain different topics and use a range of speech functions from early on in the program. I assume that these social situations may have allowed Stan to participate in interactions in which he was able to detect discrepancies between his language and that of the target language, possibly giving him the opportunity to restructure his L2 knowledge. Accordingly, the more frequently that Stan participated in these social interactions, the more restructuring may have occurred, leading to development in his linguistic accuracy over time. By the fifth month, his average linguistic accuracy had risen to 94.2%.

Stan's ability to reach the later stages of ethnorelativism and to minimize cultural differences (Bennett, 1986) reflected the positive attitude that he maintained throughout the SA program. I posit that this attitude and extended social network was the basis for why Stan showed development in linguistic accuracy, moving from Intermediate High to Advanced by the end of the program.

Tom's attitudes and social network

During his first four weeks in Argentina, Tom lived with an Argentine host family in an affluent part of Buenos Aires. They included him in family meals and social outings. When the semester started, Tom moved into student housing with a French student and they spoke Spanish when addressing each other. In his first-month diary entries, Tom tended to make neutral comments about his observations, such as the lack of importance of punctuality in Latin American countries. An account of Tom's social network activity during his five months can be seen in Table 9.3 and Figure 9.5.

During Tom's first month, the members of his uniplex first order zone represent his host family members and three SA administrators. These associations were uniplex since his role with them was as a guest with his family and as a new SA student. During the third month, Tom was no longer living with his host family, and his contact with them decreased significantly. Instead, his social network during the third month consisted of five Argentines whom he had met at the church where he volunteered, and four other Argentine acquaintances with whom he had gone out several times. By the fifth month, Tom frequently had lunch with the group of five volunteers and began spending time with one Argentine

Table 9.3 Tom's first and second order zone social networks with Argentines

Month	SOPI rating	1st order zone uniplex members	2nd order zone multiplex members	Total social network members
1	IM	7		7
3		9		9
5	IH	9	(1) in progress	9

SOPI = Simulated Oral Proficiency Interview; IM = Intermediate Mid; IH = Intermediate High.

girl, Romina, having lunch with her and talking to her on the phone. Romina represents the beginning of a social network extension from first order zone members, with whom he associated in a uniplex manner, to a second order zone. Romina alone cannot be considered part of a second order zone social network; only when Romina includes Tom in her circle of friends and frequent interactions with those members occur can the social network be considered multiplex.

It appears that Tom's social network of fellow volunteer workers began out of the necessity to gain academic credit at his home university. Although the need to earn credit initially motivated him to integrate himself into a new social circle, this motivation became more complex during the program. He gained and maintained friendships with

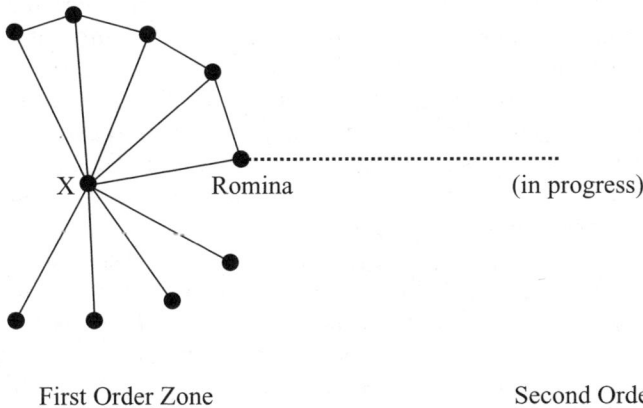

First Order Zone   Second Order Zone

Figure 9.5 Tom's (X) first and second order zone social networks with Argentines.

people from another ethnolinguistic group he wanted to know better and with whom he wanted to communicate. In other words, Tom made an investment in learning the target language; to make and maintain Argentine friendships.

By the fifth month, Tom had adapted to the Argentine social and academic system, demonstrated by his successful library research and also by his social network of Argentine volunteers. Although it may be the case that Tom adapted to the Argentine lifestyle, he indicates his belief in Excerpt (2), taken from his fifth month diary entry, that the U.S. culture dominates over the Argentine culture.

(2)   One major problem I see for this country is whether or not the people will have the training and knowledge to advance as they want. I think major changes need to be made to give the people greater access to the needed learning materials [...]. I am being critical but it is only because I think there is a lot of room for improvement.

This excerpt was written after Tom relayed the difficulty he experienced in obtaining articles in the library and getting simple tasks accomplished, which he stated was an impediment to the advancement of the Argentine people. Although Tom did not stop at the stage of anomie and did not give up trying to learn the language, he still showed a hegemonic attitude toward the Argentine culture by condescendingly wondering if the people of Buenos Aires would have the training and knowledge to advance. This excerpt shows that one can adapt to the culture without liking everything. Tom separated those things he did not like about the Argentine culture from his experience in learning about the culture.

The enduring presence of these observations and comments is not necessarily hegemonic but the critical/patronizing evaluations of those observations are. But this was not an obstacle to Tom's acculturation, which may be an important step in the establishment of social networks. This acculturation was illustrated by the fact that Tom's social network grew to include a group of nine Argentines, the majority of whom were participants in his volunteer program.

Despite his continuing hegemonic attitude toward Argentina, Tom's social network of Argentines, his measured positive attitude towards the host culture, and his high motivation to learn the language affected his L2 development. Tom showed development in linguistic accuracy (90% during the first month to 96.2% during the last month) and stopped struggling to create appropriate forms as he was doing during his first two months abroad. An example from the first two months can be seen in Excerpt (3).

(3)   Sí, nosotros fuimos, despúes de ir al cine, un otro bar cuando no **hay much-**, cuando no **había, no había** mucha gente yo, yo llamé otros **amigos** y **me, me dijo, me dijeron** que hay mucha gente en su departamento y, y van al boliche todos juntos.

*Yes, we went, after going to the movies, another bar when **there isn't** a lot, when **there weren't, there weren't** a lot of people I, I called **other friends** and **he, he told me, they told me** that there are a lot of people at their apartment and, and that they are all going to the dance club together.*

By the end of the stay abroad, Tom was able to produce more advanced speech functions, such as telling a detailed narrative and description and supporting his opinions.[2] Accordingly, his oral proficiency rating increased one level from Intermediate Mid to Intermediate High.

Sam's attitudes and social network

Sam lived in an apartment with three other exchange students, two Americans and a Mexican, with whom he reported speaking both Spanish and English. During his first week in Buenos Aires, his diary entry made reference only to his perceived progress in the acquisition of the language and to some difficulties he had in understanding Argentine colloquialisms. By the fifth week, his diary entry consisted of a lengthy discussion of his experience with corruption in Buenos Aires and various situations in which corruption occurs:

(4)   Corruption here is quite rampant [. . .]. Somebody told me that the police had to take cuts from whores, black market people to even be able to operate. And Menem calls this a First World country [. . .]. Argentines seem to think that they are the shit of South America for some reason. I read an article in a newspaper here that made some statement about the fact that God was Argentine. Whatever.

His reference to the fact that the former President of Argentina, Carlos Saúl Menem, called Argentina a First World country is, in fact, sarcastic. He questions how Argentina could belong to the First World when there is corruption and bribery taking place in a range of occupations, from the police force to ordinary businesses. One can only assume that he is comparing this activity to what he believes does not occur in the United States, a 'First World' country. Sam reinforces his perception of the hegemony of the United States over Argentina through derogatory remarks about cultural differences. In his view, the American society is morally superior to that of the Argentines.

By the end of the SA program, the low opinion that Sam had for male Argentines, who in his opinion were 'full of annoying prides', was quite evident. Sam was disgusted by the disregard that Argentine men seemed to show toward women. Throughout the duration of the program, it was shown through his diary entries that Sam regarded Argentine men as corrupt, foolish, and disrespectful towards women. These entries outnumbered his positive remarks about the host culture, which translated into a low motivation to learn the language. This perception may explain why his social network of Argentine acquaintances was limited to three to four people (two men and two women) throughout his SA experience, which is shown in Table 9.4 and Figure 9.6.

Those who were part of Sam's first order zone network during his first month were the two program organizers and his Spanish grammar teacher in Buenos Aires. By the third month, his social network included one program organizer and three Argentines whom he frequently went out with in large groups of SA students; his network decreased to the program organizer and two Argentines by his fifth month. He showed no indication of extending this first order zone uniplex relationship to a multiplex one with any of the members. Sam's lack of investment in learning the target language, his negative attitude toward the host culture, and low motivation hindered him from building significant social networks with Argentines.

He tended to socialize with other SA learners in English and, according to his Network Contact Log, he did speak in Spanish but usually in large groups of people. Although large group conversations can provide much exposure to listening to Spanish, they probably did not allow Sam the opportunity to practice various speech functions such as giving a supported opinion or a detailed description and narration, all of which need substantial floor time to accomplish. Surprisingly, Sam's

Table 9.4 Sam's first and second order zone social networks with Argentines

Month	SOPI rating	1st order zone uniplex members	2nd order zone multiplex members	Total social network members
1	IM	3		3
3		4		4
5	IH	3		3

SOPI = Simulated Oral Proficiency Interview; IM = Intermediate Mid; IH = Intermediate High.

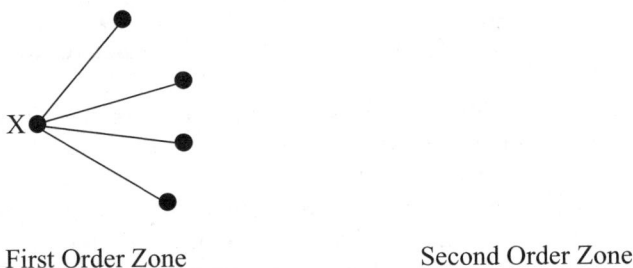

First Order Zone   Second Order Zone

Figure 9.6 Sam's (X) first and second order zone social networks with Argentines.

average linguistic accuracy in Spanish improved, from 93% to 98.8%, but this was not attributed to his social networks. Although his linguistic accuracy improved, he did not show any development in producing more advanced speech acts such as supporting an opinion or giving a detailed narration, as did Stan and Tom. He produced accurate grammar in his brief responses (13.4 average words per response, lowest of all learners in this study) and avoided elaboration wherever possible linguistic difficulties could arise. Sam's interviews were characterized by his focus on the production of accurate grammar and functions lacking in content and detail.

Sam's pre- and post-program SOPI scores were Intermediate Mid and Intermediate High, respectively. Considering Sam's few opportunities to practice Spanish with native speakers, his preference for using English in social situations as the semester progressed, his negative attitude towards the people of the host culture, and low motivation, how can his proficiency development be explained? In offering a possible reason for Sam's jump in proficiency levels, we must look at an element from Sam's profile: he read many Argentine newspapers. Although Sam may not have participated actively (speaking vs. listening) in many conversational interactions with Argentines, his exposure to written text may have enabled him to develop certain aspects in his speech, such as semi-organization and connectedness, use of appropriate vocabulary and accuracy of grammar. It did not, however, enable his development of advanced discourse skills.

Jennifer's attitudes and social network

Jennifer showed motivation in her pre-program questionnaire to be part of the SA program. Her pre-program expectation was to become competent in the language. She was an instrumentally motivated learner as revealed in her desire to incorporate Spanish in her future career in agriculture.

During her first month, Jennifer maintained a very positive attitude in her diary entries, in which she discusses the members of her social network at the time. Jennifer's diary entries focus on practices that do not happen in the Unites States, but seem to indicate her belief that they should exist: relaxation in the classroom, camaraderie with the instructor, and gentlemanly behavior of 18-year-old men toward women. These descriptions were tallied as positive attitudes toward the host culture but a negative attitude can be seen in some diary entries. For example, in Excerpt (5), she posits the advantage of the U.S. culture over that of Argentina:

(5)   When I am running in the park alone, the men playing soccer often stop and look and yell things at me. That would never happen in the U.S. I think it stems from arrogance because they think that all women want to impress them.

Excerpt (5) evidences a gendered experience, similar to that of other women who study abroad (cf. Polanyi, 1995; Talburt & Stewart, 1999; Twombly, 1995). Since (5) was one of two mentions of a gendered experience in Jennifer's diary and interviews [see Excerpt (6)], it can be concluded that her experience abroad was influenced by these events. Although initially experiencing the euphoria of being in a new country, Jennifer showed signs of the second stage of ethnocentrism during the first month in that she recognized the reality of cultural differences but at times preserved the hegemony of her culture over the target culture. She peaked into the second stage of ethnocentrism but because she preserved her hegemonic feelings towards the host culture, which is characteristic of belonging to the first stage, it can be concluded that Jennifer did not advance past the first of six stages. This illustrates how complex attitudes can be for individuals even at a specific moment in time.

Jennifer's initial signs of positive attitude disappeared within the initial week of her stay abroad. Jennifer experienced an unpleasant first month because she was living with a single woman who treated Jennifer like a tenant in a very small apartment. She gave her a key and had little or no contact with her. This tenant-like situation corroborates conclusions of other researchers on the lack of interaction that can take place in a host family (Knight & Schmidt-Rinehart, 2002; Rivers, 1998; Wilkinson, 1998a, 1998b) and underscores the positive impact that a good relationship with a host family can offer (DuFon, this volume; Law, 2003; McMeekin, this volume). After rejecting another family comprised of only a husband and wife, she finally decided to live with a four-member family that included two children. The extensive moving around that Jennifer did from host family to host family could have made it considerably more difficult to move from a uniplex level to a richer social network. Each time she moved, she was almost back at square one working on the uniplex level. Her social network during the first month, which can be seen in Table 9.5, consisted of her host family (four members) and three Argentine classmates with whom she spoke Spanish.

Following these initial weeks in Argentina, Jennifer's social network of Argentines decreased to include only her host family and her American friend and remained this way throughout the duration of her stay abroad. With her host family, she usually had breakfast or a cup of coffee during the day. More importantly, she often played with the children or watched TV with them in Spanish. She also socialized on a regular basis with English-speaking people, going out or having dinner with them. In her diary entries, Jennifer indicated in her third week diary entry that her small social network with Argentines had influenced her progress in acquiring the target language. She was frustrated trying to speak Spanish and noted that it was difficult to speak when the majority of the people with whom she had talked to spoke English.

A week later, during her fourth week abroad, Jennifer also began to be critical of the Argentines' mannerisms and lifestyles. In Excerpt (6), Jennifer comments on the political incorrectness of pointing out and directly commenting on one's physical appearance, especially concerning the topic of weight.

Table 9.5 Jennifer's (X) first and second order zone social networks with Argentines

Month	SOPI rating	1st order zone uniplex members	2nd order zone multiplex members	Total social network members
1	IM	7		7
3		4		4
5	IM	4		4

SOPI = Simulated Oral Proficiency Interview; IM = Intermediate Mid.

(6)   I have noticed that Argentine men are not at all shy about telling a girl she is fat. Several times I have been walking on the street or with friends and someone has pointed out the fact that I am not stick thin. I can't imagine being an Argentine woman and putting up with that [...].

Excerpt (6) reveals that Jennifer felt isolated and separated from the new Argentine culture, evidencing the effect that the 'ugly' *piropos* (catcalling) had on her (cf. Twombly, 1995). She even mentioned during her fourth informal interview that she felt that she did not have a part in the Argentine culture and was fed up with trying to 'find a place'. Jennifer's feeling of isolation feeds her negative attitude toward assimilating to the culture, which is translated into her low motivation to learn the language. This is also evidenced by the fact that halfway through the semester, her social network of Argentine friends consisted of only her host family. A possible explanation for Jennifer's feelings is that the manner in which native speakers treated her may have led her to feel inadequate as a member of a social group, which potentially may have prevented her from making further efforts to participate (Pellegrino, 1998). However, according to student perspective studies, feelings of inadequacy may also arise in light of difficulties learners have using their L2 to achieve communicative goals (Pellegrino, 1998).

According to her Network Contact Log, by the fourth week she was spending the majority of her time with an American friend, going to movies, exercising and traveling together. Although she reported that she spoke more Spanish than English in social situations, she participated in fewer activities and not only spoke less Spanish than during her first weeks abroad, but less English as well (see Figure 9.7). A possible explanation for Jennifer's self-report data is that it was easier for her to remember instances when she spoke Spanish and therefore tally it. When she was in Spanish social situations, she was with the children of the household or other Argentine staff or faculty of the SA program, in which the social interaction was not consequential. That is, interaction with these people may have not have involved extended discourse but was tallied as a social interaction nonetheless. The sense of isolation that Jennifer felt from the Argentine community overcame her. Many cultural things bothered her and instead of minimizing the cultural differences to adapt to the environment she maximized her time with what she was familiar with, American friendships and the English language. These American friendships served an important function: they provided the confirmation of native identity necessary to enable her to face the

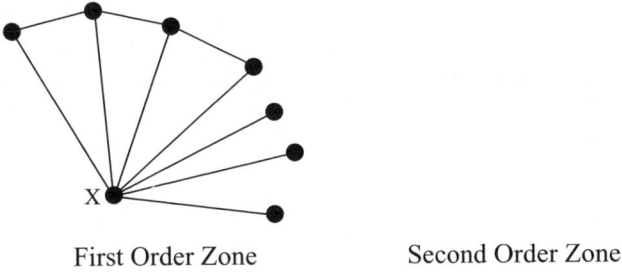

First Order Zone   Second Order Zone

Figure 9.7 Jennifer's (X) first and second order zone social networks with Argentines.

potentially threatening situations of linguistic and cultural difference (Wilkinson, 1998a).

The establishment of social networks in a new environment, however, cannot be accomplished without advancement of the learner's cultural awareness and, the SA participant must reach a state of ethnorelativism before this occurs (Bennett, 1986). Jennifer stagnated in the first of six stages towards reaching this state of ethnorelativism, never gaining cultural awareness and finally giving up altogether on making Argentine friends.

Although Jennifer had a positive degree of development in linguistic accuracy (82.2% to 91.8%), there was no progress in her overall oral proficiency; she scored at the Intermediate Mid on both pre- and post tests, which was illustrated in the extreme brevity and limited quantity of her speech. Jennifer also relied solely on the use of the present tense regardless of the form needed, which may be partially explained by the fact that she did not have the opportunity to practice narrating in the past in Spanish; most of the time she did not talk to adults but rather to children. Past research may explain Jennifer's experience in her homestay interactions that may have consisted largely of short formulaic exchanges, such as greetings and simple requests (Frank, 1997; Wilkinson, 1998a). This resulted in a greater ability to communicate without necessarily holding the floor for a long time (Segalowitz & Freed, 2004).

I do not know enough to say what caused Jennifer's failure to acquire the past tense or if a single factor played a part in her lack of development in oral proficiency. One reason could have been that Jennifer did not seek opportunities with native speakers in which she could practice more advanced conversational strategies such as discussing topics of current public or personal interest. This fact corroborates the importance of a broader network in order to be exposed to more varied language models (Campbell, 1996). In addition, the negative attitude that Jennifer had toward the host culture and her low motivation to learn the language hindered her from including more Argentines in her social network; she lacked any investment to learn the target language.

Conclusions

Overall, this study has illustrated that the type of motivation the learners had in learning the target language, the attitude they maintained toward the host culture, and the strength of their social networks were all connected. This helps explain the variation that may exist among individual learners' processes in SLA. One could posit that variation could be caused by the fact that some of the learners in the program were lazy or not intelligent (Cholakian, 1992; DeKeyser, 1991) whereas others refute this notion (Pellegrino, 1998; Wilkinson, 1997). We must keep in mind, however, that the students that participated in this SA program go through a rather rigorous selection process based on instructor recommendation letters and grade point average.

What was shown was that some learners' (Sam's and Jennifer's) diary excerpts started out on a neutral or positive note but, during the five months, changed to a negative attitude. On the other hand, other learners' attitudes remained neutral or positive throughout the process with fluctuations of negativity depending on the circumstances (Stan and Tom). All learners invariably felt frustrated at one point or another during the program, but it is interesting to note how these situations were dealt with depending on the individual learner. An analysis of the diary entries and Network Contact Logs provided an inside look at the learners' thoughts and opinions toward the new host cultural experiences. These measurement tools indicated that the positive or negative aspects of their thoughts and opinions played a role in their desire and drive to build a new social network (Stan and Tom). The study thus confirms the claim that motivation is not a fixed personality trait but must be understood with reference to social relations of power that create the possibilities for language learners to speak and that learners' social identities are complex, multiple and subject to change (Peirce, 1995). Also, it confirms that changes in motivation among students occur as a result of interactions or lack thereof (Wilkinson, 2002), as happened with Jennifer.

Why is it that Stan showed development in his linguistic and oral communication skills whereas Jennifer did not progress after the mid-point of the semester? Of course, these two participants represent the extremes in this study but, nonetheless, these questions are reasonable to ask. It was shown that the learners with high motivation (Stan and Tom), as opposed to low motivation (Jennifer and Sam) developed more extensive social networks with Argentines. Stan and Tom developed connections into a second order zone social network, allowing for more practice in functions of a more advanced level. What was also shown is that the motivational orientation (integrative, instrumental, resultative, extrinsic or intrinsic) of three of the learners changed to another type during the stay abroad, depending on the ability of the learner to interact in social networks. For example, Stan, who was integratively motivated at the start of the program, had no trouble maintaining his motivation due to his success in interacting in a social network, with no fluctuation in motivational orientation. Jennifer, Sam and Tom, who began the program with an instrumental motivation, which associates a desire for learning the L2 with a recognition of the more practical merits of learning the target language, all experienced different fluctuations in their motivational orientation. Jennifer, who failed to create a social network and reported negative experiences, may have exhibited a resultative low motivation and negative attitude toward the host culture. The case was similar to that of Sam, who from the onset had a negative attitude resulting from his perception of corruption and annoying behaviors of the members the host culture. Tom, who had success in creating a social network, changed from an instrumental motivation to an integrative and intrinsic motivation throughout the rest of his stay abroad.

The data show that the learners' continued motivation was influenced by their success, or lack thereof, in incorporating themselves into social networks. As stated earlier, I posit that the interaction with native speakers that took place in the social networks fostered opportunities for negotiation (see McMeekin, this volume), attention to gaps in feedback, and restructuring in the interlanguage. In other words, there is a conduit between motivation and language acquisition in the SA context, which is interaction in social networks.

The learners in this study went abroad with the intention of gaining a rewarding experience. Once there, all the learners invariably went through all or some of Bennett's (1986) six stages of acculturation. Throughout the program, however, all but Jennifer showed progression, some more than others, toward a state of ethnorelativism (or acculturation) in which the learners acknowledged the possibility of differences between the two cultures. The difference in learner progress through these states of cultural awareness is linked to their experiences, motivation, personalities and abilities to handle difficult new situations. The

learners, Sam and Jennifer, who remained at the state in which they preserved the hegemony of their culture over the new host culture maintained a negative attitude toward the host culture. This attitude
invariably influenced with whom they chose to interact, most likely an
American. The maintenance of social networks with native speakers of
the host culture may be more difficult if the learner does not wish to or
know how to foster a new social relationship. The negligence of or care
for social relationships by the learner is caused by many factors, but in
the SA context, the learner's cultural awareness or acculturation plays
an important role.

From the data in this study we have also learned that students are
sometimes rebuffed by a new group of acquaintances. Some learners
give up while others persevere, trying and trying again, learning strategies to align themselves with people of a different culture in order to
be more easily accepted into a social network of friends. The data show
that the learners who incorporated themselves into social networks
were the ones who aligned themselves to the new culture through volun-
teering at a local church, traveling long distances to visit with friends of
friends, and becoming tolerant of cultural annoyances. Being in the SA
environment for an extended period of time allowed the learners opportunities to create, foster, and maintain motivation and social networks
with the target-culture. This experience allowed the learners to recognize,
minimize and finally accept cultural differences, which resulted in an
impetus for learning, providing the learners the chance to work their
way to understanding and to interaction.

Significance of the Study

While there were learners who tried to incorporate themselves into
new social networks, there were others who did not. The learners in
this study that showed an 'investment' in learning the L2 and had high
motivation were those that had more extended networks, which correlated with gains in linguistic accuracy. Although missed opportunities
for interaction and less development in language could be due to the
fact that some institutional and environmental factors may increase
distance between students and the host culture (Churchill, this volume;
Wilkinson, 1998a), other research, including the present, have shown
additional possibilities.

The data from this study show that the unwillingness to interact and
create social networks with the speakers of the host culture stemmed
from motivational and attitudinal deficits maintained by the learner.

This claim has also been shown in previous research (Citron, 1995; Gardner, 1985; Gardner & Lambert, 1959; Yashima *et al.*, 2004). Hassall (this volume) makes similar conclusions that motivation is the key to understanding learners' behavior abroad and that those who reject opportunities for interaction lack a sufficiently strong motivation to learn the language.

Milroy (1987b) instructed field workers that the way to collect reliable conversational data was through their incorporation into second order zone social networks. Integration into social networks also proved to be valuable in this study for the learners' development of linguistic and oral communication skills since multiplex relationships facilitated participation in more extended conversations. Interacting within these social situations allowed the learner to practice certain L2 linguistic aspects in a more thorough manner, speaking on topics and in functions beyond everyday speech.

Social networks with native speakers allow the SA learner expanded opportunities for interaction. The input that the learner is exposed to in such interactions at first is often beyond their comprehension, leading the learners to negotiate for meaning (see McMeekin, this volume) by asking clarification questions. Through this interaction the learners may also notice gaps in their production by comparing it to what their native counterpart is saying, as was similarly noted by Gass and Varonis (1994). Not only do the learners notice gaps and improve linguistic accuracy but they also may apply more advanced communicative skills to their developing interlanguage through scaffolding strategies (Donato, 1994; Lantolf & Appel, 1994).

In this study, the learners who maintained extended social networks and who practiced linguistic elements not otherwise allowed them, are evidence that informal, out-of-class contact can greatly enhance acquisition.

The conclusions of this study, therefore, not only present more data among the contradictory evidence that informal, out-of-class contact may or may not enhance acquisition (Freed, 1995a), but also have made considerable inroads into illustrating the complex relationship between motivation, acculturation and the development of social networks that ultimately provide opportunities for exposure to the target language and extended interactions that may be the driving force behind language acquisition in the SA context. Through an examination of four cases and building on previous work on study abroad, we have furthered our understanding as to some of the sources of differential development of the social networks necessary to enhancing language learning.

In terms of implications for programs, it is important that SA organizations carefully place students in host families and develop tutoring programs (Campbell, 1996; Law, 2003) and be realistic about the goals that they may promise to the learners to recruit them. It is also important to inform the programs of the other elements that need to be fostered during a stay abroad. For one, programs could benefit from ways to successfully create social networks, such as: including a required volunteer program while abroad (Twombly, 1995); incorporating as part of the curriculum internships with local businesses or universities; or, including independent projects that require the L2 learner to interview various native speakers on distinct topics throughout their stay abroad.

Notes

1. The other ACTFL proficiency levels outlined by Byrnes and Canale (1987) – Novice Low, Novice Mid, Novice High, Advanced Plus, and Superior – were not applicable to the learners in this study.
2. See Isabelli-García (2003) for a more elaborate discussion on speech functions.

Chapter 10
Language Learning Strategies in the Study Abroad Context

REBECCA ADAMS

Introduction

Study abroad is one of the most praised, if least understood, institutions in modern higher education. Freed (1995a) explains that there has been an assumption held by students, teachers, parents and administrators that students who study abroad learn language better than those who study in the classroom or those who are immersed in the second language without receiving formal instruction. On the basis of this assumption, a large and ever increasing number of American undergraduate and post-graduate students are enrolling in semester and year abroad programs. This assumption, however, has never been convincingly supported by empirical research. Miller and Ginsberg (1995) characterize learner and facilitator beliefs about the benefits of study abroad and language learning in the study abroad context as 'folklinguistic', noting that they often do not correlate and sometimes even contradict current understanding of language acquisition. Collentine and Freed (2004) note that such beliefs concerning the benefits of study abroad may still exist because the institution itself has not been sufficiently studied. Up to the mid-1990s, according to Freed (1995a), only 8% of researchers had conducted systematic pre- and post-testing of study abroad program participants. While interest in the role of context in language acquisition has increased in recent years, many empirical questions about the nature of language learning in study abroad remain unaddressed (Collentine & Freed, 2004).

Study abroad has been shown to impact learners psychologically, culturally and linguistically. In terms of psychological impact, study abroad experiences enhance motivation and confidence (Bachner & Zeutschel,

1994; Bicknese,1974). Study abroad can also cultivate a positive view of the host culture (Svanes, 1987), and lessen the impact of culture shock (Kitao, 1993). Linguistically, study abroad has most often been implicated in the learning of oral communication proficiency (Brecht *et al.*, 1991; Huebner, 1995a; Ikeguchi, 1996; Segalowitz & Freed, 2004). In Ikeguchi's study, learner's self-rating of their oral communication proficiency gains closely matched that of their teachers. This suggests not only that study abroad facilitates the learning of oral communication, but that self-assessment may be an accurate means of measuring this language learning. Segalowitz and Freed (2004) found that study abroad learners made greater oral proficiency gains than learners who remained at home. Subcomponents of oral communication have also been shown to be influenced by study abroad. Fluency is one sub-area of oral communication that has been extensively studied in study abroad students. Study abroad has been implicated in increasing speaking rates (Moehle & Raupach, 1983), the use of formulatic expressions (Lafford, 1995; Raupach, 1983), and the use of lexical fillers (Freed, 1995c). Freed *et al.* (2004) also found that learners who studied both in study abroad and in immersion contexts increased their fluency compared to learners in traditional programs. Study abroad has also been implicated in the development of narrative abilities and the production of more lexically dense language (Collentine, 2004).

Empirical research of study abroad has linked successful language learning in study abroad to individual factors including pre-study abroad proficiency (Armstrong, 1986; Brecht *et al.*, 1991, 1995; Freed, 1995c; Ginsberg, 1992; Lapkin *et al.*, 1995; Stansfield, 1975). Such studies have generally found that beginning learners are most likely to make noticeable progress during study abroad (Brecht *et al.*, 1991; Freed, 1995c; Lapkin *et al.*, 1995; Stansfield, 1975). However, more proficient learners have also demonstrated learning in study abroad (Lennon, 1990). Additional individual factors, including strategy use, might also mediate the effectiveness of study abroad for language learning.

Language learning strategies

Language learning strategies have been defined as 'operations used by learners to aid the acquisition, storage, and retrieval of information' (Oxford & Nyikos, 1989), or as 'techniques, approaches, or deliberate actions that students take in order to facilitate the learning and recall of both linguistic and content area information' (Chamot, 1987: 71). They can be seen as the tools that learners consciously employ in the cognitive process of acquiring a new language. Language learning strategies can be automatic or learned (Oxford, 1990) and are seen as integral to the process of learning a language. Research indicates that all language learners employ strategies; they differ, however, in the number, type, and frequency of strategies used (Bialystok, 1987; Kuntz, 1999; Naiman *et al.*, 1978; O'Malley & Chamot, 1990; Oxford, 1990; Oxford & Nyikos, 1989; Tamada, 1996; Watanabe, 1990). An early conclusion of language learning strategy research is that students who employ a larger range of strategies more consistently are better language learners (Oxford, 1990). As Oxford and Nyikos (1989) explain, 'Better language learners generally use strategies appropriate to their own stage of learning, personality, age, purpose for learning that language, and type of language. Good language learners use a variety of learning strategies' (p. 291).

Language learning strategy use has been measured empirically using several different methods, ranging from verbal reports (e.g. Anderson, 1991) to the use of strategic inventories (e.g. Oxford & Nyikos, 1989; Paige *et al.*, 2004). Perhaps the best known instrument is Oxford's (1990) *Strategic Inventory for Language Learning* (SILL). The SILL is composed of 80 statements about the use of different strategies. Respondents are asked to mark if the statement is never true of them, generally not true of them, somewhat true of them, generally true of them, or always true of them. In this way, the SILL gathers information both on students' repertoire of strategies and on the frequency of their use of each strategy. The SILL divides strategies into 'direct strategies' which apply directly to the linguistic task, and 'indirect strategies' which help the learner to manage the language learning process as a whole. The direct strategies are grouped into three groups: memory strategies (Factor A), cognitive strategies (Factor B), and compensation strategies (Factor C). These are strategies that learners use to remember new information, process information, and maintain communication even if they do not have sufficient proficiency for the situation they are in. The indirect strategies are also grouped into three groups: metacognitive strategies (Factor D), affective strategies (Factor E), and communication strategies (Factor F). Learners use these strategies to organize the learning experience, to cultivate a positive belief system about language learning, and to learn in a communicative setting. As with all strategy use, the appropriateness of the strategies listed on the SILL is related both to the characteristics of the learner and the characteristics of the learning context (Bialystok, 1987; O'Malley & Chamot, 1990; Naiman *et al.*, 1978).

Language learning strategies and study abroad

Qualitative research has indicated that the study abroad experience may influence the way that learners approach language learning (Calvin, 1999; Campbell, 1996; Trosset, 1986; Warden *et al.*, 1995). Learners in these studies often changed their use of strategies to create and make use of language learning opportunities. For example, in Campbell's (1996) study, she adjusted her use of socially-based strategies to gain entrance to the second language community. Quantitative research has also indicated that study abroad can influence the use of language learning strategies. Lafford (1995) found that the survival strategy use of study abroad students was similar to that of non-study abroad students, but noted that, in her population of Spanish learners, study abroad learners used more fillers and connectors as well as more attention getting strategies than the non-study abroad control group. Like Huebner's (1995a) Japanese learners, her subjects who had been in a study abroad program used more words than non-study abroad students in a role-play testing situation. In a further study, she found that study abroad learners significantly decreased their reliance on L1 strategies (Lafford, 2004). This research indicates that study abroad may have a significant effect on learners' use of second language strategies.

Empirical research has also connected the study abroad experience with a wider range of learning strategies. In Watanabe's (1990) study on the effects of college entrance exams in Japan on language learning strategy use, over 300 Japanese students of English at two different universities in Japan completed the SILL in order to determine if students who entered college by taking an entrance examination used more or fewer learning strategies than those who entered college on recommendation. Although study abroad was not his focus, Watanabe included residence abroad as one of his study variables. He found that students who had spent three months or more in English-speaking countries generally used more communication strategies than students who had not, regardless of other factors.

In a more controlled study, Tamada (1996) administered the SILL to 24 Japanese students of English studying together in an intensive university preparation course in Great Britain. Although the course the students were involved in lasted less than two months, Tamada was able to demonstrate that students significantly increased their use of both metacognitive and communication strategies. Data acquisition involved using a modified SILL and examining strategy preferences before and after study abroad. There were also changes in cognitive, social and compensation strategies, which indicates that study abroad could have wider reaching effects than those found in Watanabe (1990). When asked why they believed that their learning strategy preference had changed, students indicated that the need to communicate with native speakers, coupled with the pressure of not falling behind their group, motivated them to increase their use of language learning strategies. This indicates that the experience of studying abroad, which exposes students to authentic communication, can influence students to increase their use of at least certain language learning strategies.

While the findings of Watanabe (1990) and Tamada (1996) are suggestive, it cannot be assumed without further study that they apply to students from other cultures who study abroad. One of Watanabe's principle findings was that students' use of strategies was strongly influenced by their experiences in the Japanese educational system. Tamada's students also indicated that the change in their strategy use was at least partially attributable to adjusting to a radically different learning environment. Because educational systems differ cross-culturally, it is possible that the effect of study abroad on language learning strategy use will differ by culture as well. It is important to extend research on the relationship between study abroad and language learning strategy use to multiple cultural contexts.

Kuntz (1999) examined the use of language learning strategies among adult American students. Her students of Arabic were studying in two different programs, one in Yemen and one in Morocco, where the teachers were either native speakers of Arabic or native English speakers who were Arabic experts. She used a questionnaire that asked students and teachers to rate the importance of using various strategies in order to determine whether study abroad students and their teachers held similar beliefs about language learning and strategy use. She found that, while students in the two programs held similar beliefs concerning strategy use, they differed greatly from their teachers. She further found that conflicting beliefs about strategy use and effectiveness affected the way that strategies were taught. For example, students and teachers differed significantly in their estimation of the importance of using compensation strategies. The students rated them as much more important than teachers did. Kuntz found that, accordingly, compensation strategies tended to be left out of the curriculum. She suggested that student and teacher understanding of strategies is important to curriculum development.

While all of these studies yielded interesting and suggestive findings about the relationship between study abroad and language learning strategy use, much remains to be learned. As discussed above, it is unknown whether or not the findings of Tamada (1996) and Watanabe (1990) apply to other language learning contexts. While Kuntz's (1999) research broadened the context of learning, her study did not investigate the effect of study abroad on the use of language learning strategies. Additionally, none of these studies investigated the effects of individual and program characteristics on language learning strategies.

A current on-going study (Paige *et al.*, 2004) investigates the impact of strategies training on culture and language learning in study abroad. Based on the principles of strategies-based language instruction (for more detail, see Cohen & Weaver, 1998), this long-term qualitative and quantitative research seeks to determine whether explicit strategy instruction impacts learners' use of strategies in study abroad, and whether this in turn affects learning measured through speech acts. This research has uncovered interesting differences in the application of strategies training, indicating that the study abroad context may influence the conscious adoption of strategies. While very interesting, these findings address the effectiveness of strategy instruction in the study abroad context, not the direct effect of study abroad on the use of strategies. Further research on the impact of study abroad on language learning strategy use can clarify the role of study abroad in helping students become better language learners.

Research questions

As was explained above, a fuller characterization of language learning strategy use in study abroad may enhance our understanding of language development. In order to evaluate the effect of study abroad on language learning strategy use, this study is focused on the following questions:

(1) Does the study abroad experience impact participants' use of language learning strategies?
    (a) Do different program characteristics moderate the impact of study abroad on language learning strategy use?
    (b) Do individual characteristics moderate the impact of study abroad on language learning strategy use?
(2) Does the acquisition of language learning strategies influence students' self-reported gains in second language proficiency?

Method

Design

This study follows a pre-test/treatment/post-test design. The independent variables examined are the treatment (study abroad), program variables, personal variables and effects of changes in language learning strategy use on proficiency. The dependent variables are the students' scores on pre- and post-program administrations of the SILL.

Participants

All participants were native speakers of American English and all came from an American educational background. As Bedell and Oxford (1996) pointed out, the use of learning strategies is often strongly tied to ethno-linguistic background and educational experience. According to their findings, the participants in this study – all students at the same university – should have had fairly similar patterns of learning strategy use prior to study abroad.

Students were enrolled in two- or four-month programs in the Dominican Republic, France, Brazil, Spain and Austria. The programs were quite similar: in all programs, learners participated in a pre-study abroad orientation program, were housed with native speakers, participated in group travel, and attended group classes taught in the target language with other members of the study abroad program. Their classes were taught either by university faculty that accompanied the students, or by language instructors from local universities. Differences between these programs are summarized in Table 10.1.

Table 10.1 Program characteristics

Program	Language	Number in program/ research participants	Length in months	Native speaker instructors
Dominican Republic	Spanish	42/18	4	Yes
France (Winter)	French	13/8	4	No
Brazil	Portuguese	12/10	2	No
Spain	Spanish	61/30	2	No
France (Spring)	French	24/14	2	Yes
Austria	German	11/6	2	No

Instruments

Two instruments were used in this study: the Strategic Inventory for Language Learning (SILL) and a two-part questionnaire on demographics and language use. The SILL, which was described earlier, has been rigorously tested for reliability and validity (Oxford, 1986; Oxford & Burry-Stock, 1995; Watanabe, 1990), and has been found to have 'internal consistency reliability around the 90s, strong predicative validity with relation to performance, and concurrent validity as evidenced through correlations with language performance, learning style, and setting characteristics' (Bedell & Oxford, 1996: 49).

The two-part questionnaire (see Appendices A and B) was developed by the researcher. The purpose of the first, pre-program section was to gather demographic data and data on the students' previous language learning experience. The purpose of the second, post-program section was to gather data on the students' experiences in their study abroad programs.

The data collected using the questionnaires were used to assign students to the nominal groups (such as proficiency groups) that were used in the analysis of the data according to program variables and personal variables. The post-program questionnaire also asked the students to rate their own improvement in several different areas of second language proficiency. Students were instructed to rate their improvement in listening, speaking, reading, writing, vocabulary, pronunciation, grammar and overall language proficiency using a four-point scale. These data were gathered to determine whether students who experienced greater language proficiency gains also experienced increases in their language learning strategy use. Together, the parts of the questionnaire asked the students about their language learning, their previous experiences abroad, and their use of the target language during their time spent overseas.

Data collection

Participants completed the instruments during their pre-program study orientation classes and during the last week of study abroad. Of the 163 total students enrolled in these study abroad programs, 132 were present when the pre-program instruments were completed. Of these 132 students, 86 students, or 65% of the original sample, also completed both post-program instruments and were therefore included in the data analysis.[1]

Data analysis

The students' pre- and post-study abroad SILL scores were compared to determine if there was any statistically significant difference between pre- and post-program strategy use and, if so, in which strategy types these differences occurred. The data on all the study abroad students were compared using MANOVA to see if there was any change in strategy use during study abroad programs among students attributable to any of the program variables or personal variables, and to see if students who experienced language proficiency gains also experienced changes in language learning strategies. When significant differences were uncovered, post-hoc analyses (including univariate F-tests of groups differences and post-hoc Buonferroni analysis) were used to determine where the differences lay. Since many factors were analyzed, the following section presents only a brief overview of the important findings. For the sake of brevity, rather than reproducing all the MANOVA tables for each factor, only those that uncovered significant differences will be included.[2]

Results and Discussion

Program variables

Program variables are those that characterize the program rather than the individual learner. They include length (two or four months) of program, study abroad language, time spent on tourism-oriented group travel, language use (LU) during group travel, LU in classes, type of residence, LU in the residence and overall LU. The data on program variables were gathered on both the pre- and post-program questionnaires. The program variables are displayed in Table 10.2.

The only significant difference among the program variables was the amount of time learners spent in tourist related travel as a group. If learners went on day or weekend trips out of town, they were required to travel with other learners from the study abroad group as a safety precaution. The descriptive statistics on the effect of days of travel on language learning strategy use are displayed in Table 10.3. These data were analyzed as discussed above. The results of the analysis for the effect of days of tourism on the use of language learning strategies is presented in Table 10.4.

The amount of time students spent traveling with their study abroad group significantly affected the change in their use of communication strategies. While all students increased their use of communication strategies, students who participated in group travel for less than 20 days experienced a significant increase in their use of communication strategies, but students who traveled for more than 20 days did not. Based on these data, it seems that limiting group travel during study abroad

Table 10.2 Program characteristics

Characteristics	Groups	N	Characteristics	Groups	N
Length of program	4-month	19	LU in class	<50%	11
	2-month	67		> 51%	75
American roommate	Yes	66	LU at home	1–2 hrs.	21
	No	20		2–4 hrs.	27
				>4 hrs.	26
Days of tourism	<20	57	LU in tourism	<25%	33
	>20	29		26–50%	31
				>51%	22
Language	French	22	LU total	<25%	66
	Spanish	48		26–50%	20
	German	6		>51%	30
	Portuguese	10			

promotes the use of communication strategies. Likely, this is because group travel isolates students from native speakers, diminishing opportunities to participate in authentic communicative exchanges. Since the amount of time that students used the target language during group travel did not have a significant effect on the use of communication strategies, it cannot be assumed that merely encouraging students to use the target language would limit this effect. It seems that speaking to other English speakers, either in English or in the study abroad language, does not foster acquisition of communication strategies as much as speaking to native speakers.

None of the other program variables significantly affected a change in the students' use of language learning strategies. That program variables would have so little effect on strategies like cognitive and compensation strategies came as a surprise. If study abroad were really challenging the students to communicate in new situations, it seems likely that they would use more cognitive strategies to process the language learning that they experienced. The lack of increase in the use of cognitive strategies indicates that the study abroad programs investigated here are not challenging the students appreciably more than they are challenged in the classroom.[3]

Table 10.3 Tourism and language learning strategies

Strategy type		<20		>20	
		Pre	Post	Pre	Post
Memory	Mean	50.8	44.3	48.8	45.1
	S.D.	4.3	5.5	4.1	5.2
Cognitive	Mean	85.2	91.7	82.9	91.5
	S.D.	7.9	7.7	7.5	7.3
Compensation	Mean	31.9	31.6	30.9	31.6
	S.D.	2.7	3.0	2.6	2.8
Metacognitive	Mean	52.4	49.5	50.5	51.1
	S.D.	6.3	6.1	5.9	5.8
Affective	Mean	13.9	20.7	14.1	21.5
	S.D.	3.0	3.5	2.8	3.3
Communication	Mean	23.6	30.4	31.5	35.2
	S.D.	3.8	4.6	3.1	3.7
Total	Mean	239.8	259.3	264.5	275.4
	S.D.	24.8	28.6	19.8	21.6
Total	Mean	248.8	270.2	258.1	271.5
	S.D.	19.0	21.8	21.3	24.6

Table 10.4 MANOVA: Days of tourism and language learning strategies

Variable	Value	F	DF	P
Memory	0.95765	0.755	2, 69	0.557
Cognitive	0.94097	1.066	2, 69	0.376
Compensation	0.90760	1.714	2, 69	0.150
Metacognitive	0.96045	0.703	2, 69	0.591
Affective	0.98439	0.273	2, 69	0.895
Communication	0.78744	4.379	2, 69	**0.002**
Total strategy	0.95046	0.888	2, 69	0.473

Additionally, it seems intuitive that students who spoke the study abroad language most in their homes, classes and on group travel would have to increase their use of various compensation strategies. On the other hand, it is possible that students most dedicated to using the study abroad language appreciably increased their proficiency, such that at the end of the experience they did not need to rely on compensation strategies as much. Students who did not seek as many communicative experiences would simply not have as many opportunities to increase their compensation strategy use. While this is a possibility, it is unlikely that a two- or four-month experience abroad could impact the students' proficiency profoundly enough to do away with the need for compensation strategies. Another possibility, also discussed above, is that these study abroad programs did not challenge the students to communicate in enough new and difficult situations so as to cause them to employ additional compensation strategies.

In all, differences in study abroad programs had very little effect on the students' acquisition of language learning strategies. It should be remembered, however, that all of the programs involved in this study were university group programs. If other types of study abroad programs, such as academic exchanges or intensive language programs, had been examined, perhaps differences in the programs could cause more significant differences in students' use of language learning strategies. It is possible that, while no single characteristic of university group programs can affect language learning strategy use significantly, the difference between participation in an academic exchange and participation in a university group program could significantly affect strategy use.

Personal and background variables

Personal and background variables are the differences that students bring with them to the study abroad experience, independent of the experience itself. Information on personal and background variables was collected on the pre-program questionnaires. The variables examined in this section include: gender, proficiency level (based on pre-study abroad class placement), previous experience abroad, and previous strategy instruction. The personal characteristics are summarized in Table 10.5. Analysis of the data indicated that proficiency levels and previous experience abroad had no significant effect on the use of language learning strategies during study abroad. The remaining variables are discussed below.

Table 10.5 Personal characteristics

Variable	Gender		Proficiency level				Previous experience abroad			Previous strategy instruction	
	Male	Female	100	200	300+		<1 month	1-3 months	>3 months	Yes	No
Group											
N	73	13	4	32	50		65	8	13	13	73

Gender

The descriptive statistics regarding the use of language learning strategies by male and female students before and after study abroad are presented in Table 10.6. As above, these data were submitted to MANOVA to determine whether males and females used language learning strategies differently in study abroad. Where significant differences were found, the data were submitted to post-hoc Buonferroni analysis. The results of the MANOVA are presented in Table 10.7.

Gender was a significant variable in use of cognitive and affective strategies. Unlike the effect of days of travel, discussed above, the differences in the use of cognitive strategies originated at the beginning of the study and persisted throughout, with males consistently using more cognitive strategies than females. However, males and females experienced similar gains in the use of cognitive strategies during study abroad. Differences between males and females in language learning strategies are well documented (see Chamot, 1987; Oxford, 1990; Oxford & Nyikos, 1989). It would be very surprising to find no differences at all

Table 10.6 Gender and learning strategies

Strategy type		Female		Male	
		Pre	Post	Pre	Post
Memory	Mean	44.3	38.0	45.6	40.3
	S.D.	1.9	2.4	2.6	3.2
Cognitive	Mean	82.5	84.9	92.6	94.8
	S.D.	3.5	3.7	4.7	4.9
Compensation	Mean	29.7	29.4	27.3	29.2
	S.D.	1.3	1.3	1.7	1.8
Metacognitive	Mean	50.7	45.6	58.4	51.4
	S.D.	2.9	3.0	3.9	4.0
Affective	Mean	16.2	17.7	22.6	21.4
	S.D.	1.3	1.6	1.8	2.2
Communication	Mean	31.5	31.5	34.8	31.1
	S.D.	1.5	1.8	2.1	2.3
Total	Mean	252.4	248.0	278.0	271.4
	S.D.	9.0	10.6	12.0	14.2

Table 10.7 MANOVA: Gender and learning strategies

Variable	Value	F	DF	P
Memory	0.99239	0.284	2, 74	0.754
Cognitive	0.92091	3.178	2, 74	**0.047**
Compensation	0.96863	1.198	2, 74	0.308
Metacognitive	0.94622	2.103	2, 74	0.129
Affective	0.84626	6.722	2, 74	**0.002**
Communication	0.95747	1.643	2, 74	0.200
Total strategy	0.93298	2.658	2, 74	0.077

between men and women on any part of the SILL. These data make it clear, however, that study abroad is equally effective for men and women in terms of acquiring cognitive language learning strategies.

Gender also played a significant role in the use of affective strategies. At the beginning of the study, females used significantly fewer affective strategies than male students. However, while females significantly increased their use of affective strategies during study abroad, males' use of affective strategies remained constant. By the end of the study, however, the gap between males and females in the use of affective strategies was no longer statistically significant. Thus, while females tended to significantly increase their use of affective strategies during study abroad, the experience did not foster use of affective strategies for males. These differences could indicate that study abroad may be more effective for females than for males in terms of fostering a positive view of themselves as language learners and helping them to be better able to manage the emotional demands of the language learning experience. However, the substantial imbalance in the number of male and female participants renders these findings somewhat speculative, and they should be interpreted with caution.

Previous strategy instruction

Table 10.8 summarizes the descriptive statistics associated with the strategy use by learners according to their previous exposure to strategy instruction. As above, MANOVA were used to determine whether previous strategy instruction impacted learners' use of language learning strategies. The MANOVA results are presented in Table 10.9.

Previous strategy instruction had a significant effect on the students' acquisition of memory strategies. On the pre-program questionnaires, most of the students who indicated that they had received previous

Table 10.8 Previous strategy instruction and learning strategies

Strategy type		Yes		No	
		Pre	*Post*	*Pre*	*Post*
Memory	Mean	48.1	41.0	41.7	37.4
	S.D.	2.6	3.3	1.7	2.2
Cognitive	Mean	89.8	92.3	85.2	87.5
	S.D.	4.8	5.0	3.2	3.3
Compensation	Mean	29.2	30.8	27.7	27.8
	S.D.	1.7	1.8	1.1	1.2
Metacognitive	Mean	57.5	49.2	51.6	47.8
	S.D.	4.0	4.1	2.7	2.7
Affective	Mean	20.6	20.4	18.2	18.7
	S.D.	1.8	2.2	1.2	1.5
Communication	Mean	34.4	32.1	31.9	30.5
	S.D.	2.1	2.4	1.4	1.6
Total	Mean	278.3	268.9	252.2	250.5
	S.D.	12.2	14.4	8.1	9.6

strategy instruction explained that the instruction had been in learning mnemonic devices to help them to remember vocabulary or grammar rules. Students who had received strategy instruction indicated on the pre-program SILL that they used significantly more memory strategies

Table 10.9 MANOVA: Previous strategy instruction and learning strategies

Variable	Value	F	DF	P
Memory	0.90535	3.868	2, 74	**0.025**
Cognitive	0.97812	0.828	2, 74	0.441
Compensation	0.95151	1.885	2, 74	0.159
Metacognitive	0.95736	1.648	2, 74	0.199
Affective	0.97098	1.106	2, 74	0.336
Communication	0.97549	0.930	2, 74	0.399
Total strategy	0.92508	2.997	2, 74	0.056

than students who had not received strategy instruction. However, the learners who had received strategy instruction also significantly reduced their use of memory strategies by the end of study abroad, while students who had not received prior strategy instruction maintained their level of memory strategy use. By the end of the program, there was no longer a significant difference among learners in their use of memory strategies. This may be related to the nature of the strategy instruction. Perhaps the mnemonic strategies they had learned before were not applicable in the more communicative study abroad context. It is also possible that the lack of strategy instruction on study abroad allowed them to forget the strategies that they had been taught. As with the analysis on gender-related differences, the results related to previous strategy instruction merit caution. There was also a substantial imbalance in the number of learners who had and had not received strategy training previously. Among learners who had participated in strategy learning, it is likely that instruction type, duration, and intensity differed. These findings, while suggestive, do not provide a full picture of the effect of previous strategy training.

Overall, personal and background variables had very little significant effect on the development of language learning strategies. Possibly, no one learner type was pre-disposed to gain better language learning habits from study abroad than any other learner type. With the exception of the female learners' tendency to gain affective strategies, it seems that all the learners in this study were essentially equally impacted by the study abroad experience.

Self-reported language gains and language learning strategy use

After answering questions on personal, background and program variables on pre- and post-program surveys, the students who participated in study abroad were asked to rate their improvement in several different language areas. They were asked to choose whether their proficiency had improved 'not at all', 'slightly', 'moderately' or 'very much' in listening comprehension, reading comprehension, speaking, writing, pronunciation, grammar, vocabulary and overall proficiency. These data were also analyzed to determine if students' self-ratings of proficiency change were related to the changes in their SILL scores for each factor and the total. The self-reported language gains are summarized in Table 10.10.

The use of various learning strategies was related to perceived gains in listening, writing, pronunciation, grammar and overall proficiency. These

Table 10.10 Self-reported language learning

Language learning gains	Listening	Reading	Speaking	Writing	Pronunciation	Grammar	Vocabulary	Overall proficiency
Not at all		1				3		1
Slightly	4	10	5	24	17	18	8	4
Moderately	17	41	39	38	32	41	36	38
Very much.	64	33	41	23	36	23	41	42

Cells of *n* < 5 were removed from the analysis.

will be discussed in detail below. The reporting of results here, as above, will be limited to those areas of language learning that related significantly to the use of learning strategies.

Listening

Table 10.11 displays the descriptive statistics for the use of strategies by learners who perceived that their listening comprehension had improved 'slightly', 'moderately' and 'very much'. These data were submitted to a MANOVA to determine whether self-reported improvement in listening comprehension was related to increased use of language learning strategies. The results of the MANOVA are summarized in Table 10.12 below.

Where significant differences were found, post-hoc _t_-tests were performed using the Buonferroni adjustment to determine where the groups differed. For memory strategies, post-hoc analysis revealed that students who indicated that they had improved only slightly in listening comprehension significantly decreased their use of memory strategies. Students who indicated that their listening comprehension had improved

Table 10.11 Listening comprehension and learning strategies

Strategy type		Slightly		Moderately		Very much	
		Pre	_Post_	_Pre_	_Post_	_Pre_	_Post_
Memory	Mean	49.9	40.2	38.4	42.3	38.7	39.2
	S.D.	4.5	6.2	3.3	4.5	2.8	3.8
Cognitive	Mean	83.9	79.8	69.9	77.9	69.0	76.5
	S.D.	8.7	9.3	6.4	6.8	5.3	5.7
Compensation	Mean	29.9	23.7	30.7	30.1	31.5	29.8
	S.D.	3.1	3.5	2.3	2.6	1.9	2.2
Metacognitive	Mean	55.2	41.2	42.7	54.6	42.6	47.9
	S.D.	6.8	7.4	5.0	5.4	4.2	4.6
Affective	Mean	23.6	18.2	17.4	21.1	14.5	19.3
	S.D.	3.4	3.6	2.5	2.6	2.1	2.2
Communication	Mean	30.27	23.7	28.6	31.2	29.8	30.3
	S.D.	3.7	4.2	2.7	3.0	2.3	2.6
Total	Mean	272.2	242.5	225.7	255.6	225.5	240.9
	S.D.	21.3	26.9	15.6	19.6	13.1	16.5

Table 10.12 MANOVA: Listening and strategies

Variable	Value	F	DF	P
Memory	0.81318	3.486	4, 128	**0.010**
Cognitive	0.94123	0.984	4, 128	0.419
Compensation	0.93365	1.118	4, 128	0.351
Metacognitive	0.71347	5.885	4, 128	**0.001**
Affective	0.81487	3.449	4, 128	**0.010**
Communication	0.91531	1.448	4, 128	0.222
Total strategy	0.83840	2.948	4, 128	**0.023**

moderately or very much increased their use of memory strategies, although this difference was not significant. Because memory strategies include strategies such as using sounds or sound-and-image combinations to remember new words or phrases, it is not surprising that an increase in these skills would be accompanied by an increase in listening comprehension skills.

Turning to metacognitive strategies, students who indicated that they had increased their listening comprehension 'moderately' or 'very much' also had significantly increased their use of metacognitive strategies. Metacognitive strategies include such actions as deciding to pay attention, focusing on details, and focusing on meaning. All of these should foster improvement in listening comprehension. Interestingly, students who indicated that they only 'slightly' improved their listening comprehension used significantly fewer metacognitive strategies after study abroad than before. This decrease in metacognitive strategy use is very likely linked to their marginal improvement in listening comprehension. Together, these findings seem to indicate that learners who increase their use of metacognitive strategies will likely experience greater gains in listening comprehension as well.

As was seen with memory strategies (Factor A) and metacognitive strategies (Factor D), students who rated their listening comprehension improvement as 'moderate' or 'very much' also significantly increased their use of affective strategies. Students who rated their listening comprehension improvement as 'slight' also significantly decreased their use of affective strategies even though they used the most affective strategies at the beginning of the study. Affective strategies include lowering anxiety and carefully taking risks in language learning, both of which should allow students to focus on aural input. It is therefore not surprising that an increase in listening comprehension be associated with increased use of these strategies.

As has been consistently seen with listening comprehension and other SILL factors, students who increased their listening comprehension 'moderately' or 'very much' also significantly increased their use of language learning strategies overall. Students who only improved their listening comprehension 'slightly' significantly decreased their use of language learning strategies overall. Increases in the use of strategies in study abroad seem to be overall linked to increased listening comprehension proficiency.

Writing

Table 10.13 summarizes the use of language learning strategies before and after study abroad according to students' perceived gains in writing ability during study abroad. As above, these data were submitted to a MANOVA to determine whether learners who perceived different

Table 10.13 Writing ability and learning strategies

Strategy type		Slightly		Moderately		Very much	
		Pre	Post	Pre	Post	Pre	Post
Memory	Mean	39.9	36.4	41.7	41.2	45.3	44.3
	S.D.	2.9	4.0	3.0	4.1	3.4	4.7
Cognitive	Mean	73.7	75.9	72.2	78.2	76.9	80.2
	S.D.	5.7	6.1	5.8	6.1	6.6	7.0
Compensation	Mean	31.2	28.7	29.7	26.7	31.3	28.2
	S.D.	2.0	2.3	2.0	2.3	2.3	2.7
Metacognitive	Mean	43.6	44.0	46.9	47.9	49.0	51.7
	S.D.	4.5	4.8	4.5	4.9	5.2	5.6
Affective	Mean	17.3	16.9	17.5	18.4	20.8	23.3
	S.D.	2.2	2.4	2.3	2.4	2.6	2.7
Communication	Mean	28.5	27.7	29.0	26.9	31.2	30.5
	S.D.	2.4	2.7	2.4	2.7	2.8	3.1
Total	Mean	231.8	232.8	236.4	244.2	255.3	262.0
	S.D.	13.9	17.5	14.1	17.8	16.1	20.3

levels of improvement in their writing ability during study abroad also had similar changes in their use of language learning strategies. The results of the MANOVA are summarized in Table 10.14.

As can be seen, changes in strategy use for memory and affective strategies were also related to perceived improvement in L2 writing. As above, Buonferroni analysis was used to determine the source of the differences. This analysis indicated that a similar relationship exists for L2 writing and memory strategies as with listening comprehension. All students tended to decrease in their use of memory skills; however, students who improved their writing proficiency very much or moderately did not experience a significant decrease in their use of memory strategies. On the other hand, students who improved their writing proficiency only slightly experienced a significant decrease in the use of memory strategies. Thus, the students who better retained their pre-program levels of memory strategies were better able to improve their writing ability during study abroad. Putting words into context to remember them and note-taking are examples of memory strategies that would also help students to increase their writing skills. It is likely that by retaining and using strategies such as these in study abroad, students were able to improve their writing ability.

The relationship between L2 writing and affective strategies is similar. There were no initial significant differences between the groups in terms of their affective strategy use, but by the end of study abroad, the students who indicated that their writing proficiency had improved 'very much' also had significantly increased their use of affective strategies. Students who experienced only 'slightly' or 'moderately' improved writing ability did not significantly change their use of affective strategies.

Table 10.14 MANOVA: Writing ability and learning strategies

Variable	Value	F	DF	P
Memory	0.86129	2.481	4, 128	**0.047**
Cognitive	0.96050	0.651	4, 128	0.627
Compensation	0.95102	0.814	4, 128	0.519
Metacognitive	0.92586	1.257	4, 128	0.291
Affective	0.79572	3.873	4, 128	**0.005**
Communication	0.91933	1.375	4, 128	0.246
Total strategy	0.89195	1.883	4, 128	0.117

Similar to listening comprehension, being able to take risks and lowering anxiety, along with similar affective strategies, should help students to improve their writing fluency.

Pronunciation

Table 10.15 summarizes the descriptive statistics associated with perceived improvement in L2 pronunciation during study abroad. As with the previous analyses, these data were submitted to a MANOVA to determine whether learners' perceived gains in pronunciation were related to the changes in their use of language learning strategies during study abroad. The results of this analysis are displayed in Table 10.16.

As can be seen in Table 10.16, only the use of memory strategies was related to gains in pronunciation. There was a significant decrease in the use of memory strategies for students who rated their improvement as 'slightly' or 'moderately'; however, there was no significant difference in the use of memory strategies for students who gave themselves self-ratings of 'very much' for improvement in pronunciation. As with

Table 10.15 Pronunciation and learning strategies

Strategy type		Slightly		Moderately		Very much	
		Pre	Post	Pre	Post	Pre	Post
Memory	Mean	39.1	37.4	45.6	42.2	42.2	42.4
	S.D.	3.2	4.3	3.1	4.2	3.3	4.6
Cognitive	Mean	71.4	74.2	75.7	77.2	75.7	82.9
	S.D.	6.1	6.5	5.9	6.3	6.4	6.9
Compensation	Mean	29.2	27.8	31.7	27.2	31.2	28.3
	S.D.	2.1	2.5	2.1	2.4	2.3	2.6
Metacognitive	Mean	43.9	43.0	49.1	50.6	46.5	50.1
	S.D.	4.8	5.2	4.7	5.1	5.1	5.5
Affective	Mean	16.5	16.6	18.9	20.7	20.1	21.4
	S.D.	2.4	2.5	2.3	2.5	2.5	2.7
Communication	Mean	29.4	26.0	30.1	28.7	29.3	30.4
	S.D.	2.6	2.9	2.5	2.8	2.7	3.1
Total	Mean	228.2	230.7	249.0	250.0	246.1	258.3
	S.D.	15.0	18.9	14.5	18.3	15.8	20.0

Table 10.16 MANOVA: Pronunciation and learning strategies

Variable	Value	F	DF	P
Memory	0.84800	2.750	4, 128	**0.031**
Cognitive	0.92973	1.187	4, 128	0.320
Compensation	0.94149	0.979	4, 128	0.421
Metacognitive	0.92474	1.277	4, 128	0.283
Affective	0.90816	1.579	4, 128	0.184
Communication	0.92780	1.222	4, 128	0.305
Total strategy	0.92239	1.319	4, 128	0.266

listening comprehension, many memory strategies involve the recognition of sound patterns and the association of sound and images to increase memory. Paying attention to sounds in this way could help students to improve their own pronunciation as they practice using the language in the host country. While this is certainly not all that is involved in the improvement of pronunciation, these strategies could possibly help the students to make their pronunciation more native-like.

Grammar

Table 10.17 displays the means and standard deviations for the strategy use before and after study abroad by learners according to their perceived improvement in their L2 grammar. Table 10.18 summarizes the MANOVA results.

As can be seen from Table 10.18, perceived improvement in grammar was related only to compensation strategies. Compensation strategies are those that help speakers to communicate even when their linguistic competence does not meet the communicative demands of the situation. Thus, a focus on increasing the use of compensation strategies should not encourage students to focus on improving their grammar. Indeed, students who rated themselves as having minimal improvement in grammatical proficiency used the most compensation strategies throughout the study. While all groups decreased in their use of compensation strategies, those who rated themselves as having improved 'very much' or 'moderately' in their grammar usage significantly decreased their use of compensation strategies, while those who did not perceive improvement in their grammar usage did not significantly decrease their use of compensation strategies. This perhaps indicates that the students who felt that they

Table 10.17 Grammar and learning strategies

Strategy type		Slightly		Moderately		Very much	
		Pre	Post	Pre	Post	Pre	Post
Memory	Mean	45.3	42.0	44.1	43.1	41.6	38.4
	S.D.	3.2	4.4	3.3	4.4	3.2	4.3
Cognitive	Mean	73.9	73.7	76.9	79.1	71.9	79.6
	S.D.	6.2	6.6	6.3	6.7	6.1	6.5
Compensation	Mean	29.3	24.7	32.0	27.6	28.4	27.6
	S.D.	2.2	2.5	2.2	2.5	2.1	2.4
Metacognitive	Mean	46.0	45.9	50.8	48.3	46.3	45.8
	S.D.	4.9	5.3	4.9	5.3	4.8	5.2
Affective	Mean	19.3	20.3	21.1	20.4	19.4	16.7
	S.D.	2.5	2.6	2.5	2.6	2.4	2.5
Communication	Mean	29.7	27.2	31.6	28.8	28.5	27.9
	S.D.	2.6	3.0	2.7	3.0	2.6	2.9
Total	Mean	242.3	236.9	255.7	252.4	237.2	240.7
	S.D.	15.2	19.2	15.4	19.4	14.9	18.8

had a better command of grammatical systems no longer felt the need to rely on compensation strategies in order to communicate. Interestingly, the students who rated their grammatical improvement as 'very much' decreased the least in their use of compensation strategies. However,

Table 10.18 MANOVA: Grammar and learning strategies

Variable	Value	F	DF	P
Memory	0.89998	1.154	4, 128	0.335
Cognitive	0.92782	0.814	4, 128	0.561
Compensation	0.78937	2.678	4, 128	**0.018**
Metacognitive	0.90136	1.137	4, 128	0.345
Affective	0.82560	2.145	4, 128	0.053
Communication	0.91898	0.921	4, 128	0.483
Total strategy	0.88993	1.281	4, 128	0.271

they also used the fewest compensation strategies from the beginning of the study, indicating again that students focused on learning grammar may not increase their use of compensation strategies.

Overall proficiency
     The word proficiency has been defined in various ways in applied linguistics research. In this study, the term was chosen as one that would be familiar and have psychological reality for the learners in the study, and should be understood in this general meaning. Table 10.19 summarizes the descriptive statistics for the relationship between gains in overall L2 proficiency and language learning strategy use before and after study abroad. The results of the statistical analysis performed using these data are displayed in Table 10.20.
     Changes in overall proficiency were related to the use of cognitive strategies, metacognitive strategies and overall strategies. Students who indicated an increase in overall proficiency also reported using significantly more cognitive strategies. Students who reported only slight

Table 10.19 Overall proficiency and learning strategies

		Slightly		*Moderately*		*Very much*	
Strategy type		*Pre*	*Post*	*Pre*	*Post*	*Pre*	*Post*
Memory	Mean	43.4	41.8	45.0	40.3	44.5	43.9
	S.D.	4.9	6.7	3.0	4.1	3.6	4.9
Cognitive	Mean	93.9	74.1	82.2	84.6	83.8	90.0
	S.D.	9.5	10.1	5.8	6.2	6.9	7.4
Compensation	Mean	35.5	28.6	30.0	30.0	31.0	30.0
	S.D.	3.3	3.8	2.0	2.3	2.4	2.8
Metacognitive	Mean	56.1	56.1	54.0	45.7	57.1	50.2
	S.D.	7.4	8.1	4.5	4.9	5.4	5.9
Affective	Mean	18.0	17.1	18.6	18.2	20.9	20.8
	S.D.	3.7	3.9	2.3	2.4	2.7	2.9
Communication	Mean	34.0	29.7	33.0	30.0	36.0	31.1
	S.D.	4.0	4.5	2.5	2.8	2.9	3.3
Total	Mean	282.5	232.1	262.2	257.9	269.8	277.0
	S.D.	23.2	29.2	14.2	17.9	16.9	21.3

Table 10.20 MANOVA: Overall proficiency and learning strategies

Variable	Value	F	DF	P
Memory	0.93885	0.684	4, 128	0.663
Cognitive	0.78734	2.709	4, 128	**0.016**
Compensation	0.92758	0.817	4, 128	0.559
Metacognitive	0.75047	3.293	4, 128	**0.005**
Affective	0.95421	0.506	4, 128	0.803
Communication	0.83840	1.965	4, 128	0.075
Total strategy	0.77215	2.944	4, 128	**0.010**

gains significantly decreased their use of cognitive strategies, while students who reported moderate gains did not significantly alter their use of cognitive strategies. The general increase in the use of cognitive strategies by students who rated their overall proficiency improvement as moderate or better indicates that increased use of strategies is related to higher second language proficiency for study abroad students.

The association of metacognitive strategies with proficiency gains is somewhat complex. The three groups all had initially similar levels of metacognitive strategy use at the onset of the study abroad program. Students who fell into the 'slightly' group did not appreciably change their use of metacognitive strategies, while students in the 'moderately' and 'very much' groups significantly decreased their use of metacognitive strategies. This general decline in metacognitive strategies by the higher performing students is difficult to interpret. Possibly, these learners associated increasing their proficiency with enhancing their communicative competence, while they associated the metacognitive strategies, which deal with the organization of the learning experience, with classroom learning. If this is the case, the decline in the use of metacognitive strategies could be the result of students perceiving study abroad to be an opportunity to extend language learning from the classroom to more naturalistic settings.

The relationship between overall proficiency and total SILL scores seems to indicate that learners who perceive gains in language proficiency also increase or maintain their levels of learning strategy use during study abroad. The learners who 'slightly' improved their overall proficiency significantly decreased their use of language learning strategies. Students who improved 'moderately' also decreased their overall use of language learning strategies, but this decrease was again non-significant. Additionally, the students who increased their overall proficiency 'very much' increased their use of language learning strategies; however, this increase was not significant. It seems that students who maintain pre-study abroad levels of strategy use are better able to increase their language proficiency during study abroad.

The majority of the statistically significant results found in this study were found in the evaluation of the SILL results with reference to language proficiency gains. For the most part, these results clearly indicate that in order for students to maximize their increase in most areas of language proficiency during study abroad, they must maintain high levels of strategy use or gain more strategies. These findings underscore the importance of training students to use language learning strategies and encouraging study abroad students to increase their use of language learning strategies through direct training and through authentic communicative experiences.

In light of Ikeguchi (1996), it is interesting that the highest number of significant differences was found when reviewing the data collected on perceived proficiency. Ikeguchi found that self-evaluations were an effective method of gathering data on language proficiency for study abroad students as long as the data were collected promptly following the study abroad experience. In the current study, most information on the relevance of language learning strategies to the acquisition of second language proficiency was uncovered using self-evaluation materials. This underscores the usefulness of self-report data on language learning for study abroad students, and highlights the importance of triangulating data from multiple sources to better understand the learning experiences of study abroad students.

Conclusions

Research has indicated that language learning strategies help students to learn languages more efficiently. While there are many differences among different study abroad groups, the only program variable that this study found to be significant to the use of language learning strategies was the amount of time students spent on group travel. Students who spend more time in group travel do not improve their use of communication strategies. In order to facilitate the development of language learning strategies, group travel should be minimized, and students should be encouraged to interact in more challenging ways with native speakers of the study abroad language. While this could possibly decrease their learning of historical culture, it should also help them to increase their knowledge of socio-culture. Other program variables do not seem to hinder or encourage language learning strategy development. However, since only one type of study abroad program was evaluated here, it is possible that other program types, like international service programs or work exchanges, are more effective in helping students increase their use of language learning strategies. These types of programs could be evaluated similarly to see if it would be better to encourage serious language students to participate in them.

As with the analysis of program variables, it was found that students' backgrounds did not augment or limit their ability to learn most strategies in study abroad. In terms of language learning strategy development, study abroad seems to be as effective for beginning students as for advanced students, and for students with and without previous experience abroad. Females seem to have an advantage in affective strategies, while males use far more cognitive strategies. As there were no significant differences between genders on other factors, gender does not seem to significantly predispose learners to gain strategies in study abroad. Both males and females could probably benefit from increased opportunities to interact with native speakers in a variety of situations, and from strategy instruction during study abroad.

Indeed, the integration of strategy instruction and study abroad may be one key to promoting effective language learning. While students who had received previous strategy training had an initial advantage in their use of memory strategies, this effect diminished during study abroad. The waning effects of strategy instruction may indicate that prior instruction is insufficient. Students may need sustained focus on language learning strategies in order to continually shape their language learning experience, a possibility also raised by Paige *et al.* (2004).

Encouraging students to increase their language learning strategy use could improve study abroad as a language learning experience. Students who increased their strategy use almost uniformly indicated that they had experienced substantial gains in a variety of language learning areas including listening comprehension, writing, pronunciation, grammar, and overall language proficiency. While a range of strategies were implicated, memory, metacognitive, and affective strategies were most often related to self-reported gains in language learning success. With memory and metacognitive strategies in particular, learning was most often related to maintenance of pre-program strategies, rather than to the use of higher levels of strategies. This indicates that even minimal strategy awareness directed at preserving pre-program strategy use could positively influence study abroad as a language learning experience. The relationship between second language acquisition in study abroad and language learning strategies indicates that attention to strategies may improve learner's opportunities of benefiting from study abroad, supporting the assertion that strategy awareness has a place in the study abroad curriculum (e.g. Paige *et al.*, 2004). Helping students to be better language learners before and during study abroad could help them get the most out of study abroad. Once again, this indicates the need for strategy training for study abroad students and for making study abroad a more communicatively challenging experience.

Notes

1. Study abroad program leaders provided the students with the instruments during the final week of study abroad, and were also responsible for collecting them. Attrition occurred for several reasons. Program leaders reported that several students were overwhelmed by examinations and preparations for their return to the United States, and simply did not fill out forms. Other students missed classes because of illness, or left the program a week early for additional travel opportunities.
2. The method of analysis was identical for each variable and factor. Those included in this discussion include at least one statistically significant finding.
3. It should also be remembered that the learners in this study were all native speakers of English studying other Indo-European languages. It is possible that this limited the challenge for these students. A similar study abroad program, for example, in an Asian context, might have affected the use of cognitive and compensation strategies more.

Appendix A: Pre-Program Questionnaires

Name _____   **Gender** (circle one):   Male   Female
(*Note:* When these results are examined, your name will be replaced with an identification number for confidentiality.)

1. **Semester of study abroad program** (circle one):   Winter   Spring

2. **Study abroad country** (circle one):

    France   Dominican Republic   Spain   Russia   Austria   China
    Japan   Brazil

3. **List the BYU language classes you have completed for your study abroad language:**
   (for example, German 201, German 202, German 320, etc.)

4. **Describe any other experiences you have had using this language including length:**
   (for example, mission, high school classes, courses at another institution)

5. **a. Have you ever visited a country where your study abroad language is commonly spoken?** (circle one)   Yes   No

   b. If yes, how long were you there?

   c. While you were there, how much of your communication was in the study abroad language? (circle one)

   25% or less   26–50%   51–75%   76–100%

6. **a. Have you ever had instruction in the use of language learning strategies?** (circle one)   Yes   No

   b. If yes, please describe the instruction.

Appendix B: Post-Program Questionnaires

Name _____

(*Note:* When your responses are examined, your name will be replaced with an identification number for confidentiality.)

1. a. **Approximately how many days did you participate in group travel with your study abroad group?** (On this and other similar questions, make a mark on the horizontal line that approximates the correct answer.)

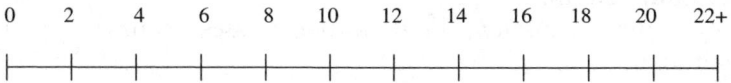

```
  0    2    4    6    8    10   12   14   16   18   20   22+
  ├────┼────┼────┼────┼────┼────┼────┼────┼────┼────┼────┤
```

   b. **Estimate the percentage of the time during these group trips that your communication was in the study abroad language.** (Mark the approximate percentage.)

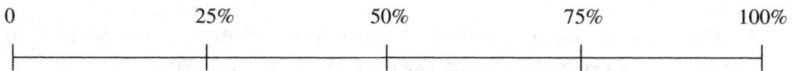

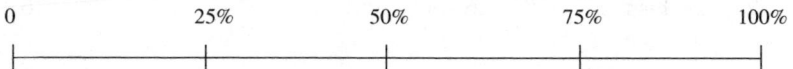

```
  0              25%            50%            75%           100%
  ├───────────────┼──────────────┼──────────────┼─────────────┤
```

   c. **Comments, if any.**

2. a. **Which classes did you complete during study abroad?** (for example, German 202, German 211)

   b. **Estimate the percentage of time in these classes that your communication was in the study abroad language.** (Mark the approximate percentage.)

```
  0              25%            50%            75%           100%
  ├───────────────┼──────────────┼──────────────┼─────────────┤
```

   c. **Comments, if any.**

3. a. **Did you live with a host family or in a dormitory?** (circle one)

   host family   dormitory   neither   both

b. Did another fluent English speaker reside there while you did? (circle one)

Yes   No

c. Estimate the amount of time that you communicated daily in your study abroad language while in your host home or dormitory. (Mark the approximate percentage.)

0 hours	2 hours	4 hours	5 hours	6 hours	more

d. Comments, if any.

4. **In what other circumstances (besides in class, in your residence, and during group travel) did you use your study abroad language often?**

5. **Estimate the total percentage of your time that you communicated in your study abroad language while in your host country.** (Mark the approximate percentage.)

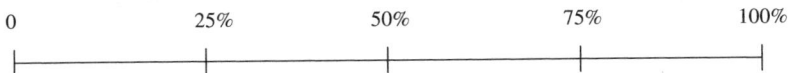

0	25%	50%	75%	100%

6. **How much do you think that your proficiency in your study abroad language improved?** (circle one for each category)

a. How much did your listening comprehension improve?

Not at all   Slightly   Moderately   Very much

b. How much did your reading comprehension improve?

Not at all   Slightly   Moderately   Very much

c. How much did your speaking ability improve?

Not at all   Slightly   Moderately   Very much

d. How much did your writing ability improve?

Not at all   Slightly   Moderately   Very much

e. How much did your pronunciation improve?

Not at all   Slightly   Moderately   Very much

f. How much did your grammar use improve?

Not at all   Slightly   Moderately   Very much

g. How much did your vocabulary increase?

Not at all   Slightly   Moderately   Very much

h. All together, how much did your ability to communicate in your study abroad language improve?

Not at all   Slightly   Moderately   Very much

References

Adams, R. (this volume) Language learning strategies in the study abroad context. In M.A. DuFon and E. Churchill (eds) *Language Learners in Study Abroad Contexts.*

Agar, M. (1994) *Language Shock: Understanding the Culture of Conversation.* New York: William Morrow & Co.

Allen, H.W. (2002) Does study abroad make a difference? An investigation of linguistic and motivational outcomes. PhD thesis, Emory University, 2002. *Dissertation Abstracts International-A* 63 (4), 1279.

Alptekin, C. (1983) Target language acquisition through acculturation: EFL learners in the English-speaking environment. *The Canadian Modern Language Review* 39 (4), 818–26.

Amendt, G. (1995) *Du oder Sie 1945–1989–1995.* Bremen: Ikaru.

American Council on the Teaching of Foreign Languages. (1986) *ACTFL Proficiency Guidelines.* New York: Hastings on Hudson.

Ammon, U. (1972) Zur sozialen Funktion der pronominalen Anrede im Deutschen. *Zeitschrift für Literaturwissenschaft und Linguistik* 2 (7), 73–88.

Aoki, H. (1986) Evidentials in Japanese. In W. Chafe and J. Nichols (eds) *Evidentiality: The Linguistic Coding of Epistemology* (pp. 223–38). Norwood, NJ: Ablex.

Armstrong, G.K. (1986) Cultural understanding, oral proficiency, and study abroad: Getting it all together. Perspectives on Proficiency: Curriculum and Instruction. (ERIC Document Reproduction Service No. ED 336 6991).

Atkinson, D. (2002) Towards a sociocognitive approach to second language acquisition. *The Modern Language Journal* 86 (4), 525–45.

Bachman, L.F. (1990) *Fundamental Considerations in Language Testing.* Oxford: Oxford University Press.

Bachman, L.F. and Palmer, A.S. (1996) *Language Testing in Practice.* Oxford: Oxford University Press.

Bachner, D.J. and Zeutschel, U. (1994) Utilizing the effects of youth exchange: A study of the subsequent lives of German and American high school exchange participants. New York: Council on International Educational Exchange. (ERIC Document Reproduction Service No. ED 410 819).

Bacon, S. (1995) Coming to grips with the culture: Another use of dialogue journals in teacher education. *Foreign Language Annals* 28 (2), 193–207.

Bailey, K. (1991) Diary studies of classroom language learning: The doubting game and the believing game. In E. Sadtono (ed.) *Language Acquisition and the Second/*

Foreign Language Classroom (pp. 60–102). Singapore: SEAMEO Regional Language Centre.

Bailey, K. and Ochsner, R. (1983) A methodological review of the diary studies: Windmill tilting or social science? In K. Bailey, M. Long and S. Peck (eds) *Second Language Acquisition Studies* (pp. 188–98). Rowley, MA: Newbury House.

Bakhtin, M.M. (1981/1935) *The Dialogic Imagination.* (M. Holoquist and C. Bakhtin, trans.). Austin, TX: University of Texas Press.

Bamberg, M. (1987) *The Acquisition of Narratives: Learning to Use the Language.* Berlin: Mouton de Gruyter.

Bardovi-Harlig, K. (1999) Researching method. In L.F. Bouton (ed.) *Pragmatics and Language Learning* (pp. 237–64). Urbana, IL: University of Illinois at Urbana-Champaign, Division of English as an International Language.

Bardovi-Harlig, K. and Hartford, B.A.S. (1996) Input in an institutional setting. *Studies in Second Language Acquisition* 18 (2), 171–88.

Barron, A. (2000) For a return to the forgotten formula: 'Data 1 + Data 2 > Data 1': The example of learners' offers and refusals of offers. *Zeitschrift für Angewandte Linguistik (ZfAL)* 33, 45–68.

Barron, A. (2003) *Acquisition in Interlanguage Pragmatics. Learning How to do Things with Words in a Study Abroad Context.* Amsterdam: John Benjamins.

Barron, A. (this volume) Learning to say 'you' in German: The acquisition of sociolinguistic competence in a study abroad context. In M.A. DuFon and E. Churchill (eds) *Language Learners in Study Abroad Contexts.*

Batstone, R. (2002) Contexts of engagement: A discourse perspective on "intake" and "pushed output". *System* 30, 1–14.

Bedell, D.A. and Oxford, R.L. (1996) Cross-cultural comparisons of language learning strategies in the People's Republic of China and other countries. In R.L. Oxford (ed.) *Language Learning Strategies Around the World: Cross-cultural Perspectives* (pp. 47–60). Honolulu: University of Hawai'i Press.

Beebe, L.M. and Cummings, M.C. (1996) Natural speech act data versus written questionnaire data: How data collection method affects speech act performance. In S.M. Gass and J. Neu (eds) *Speech Acts Across Cultures: Challenges to Communication in a Second language* (pp. 65–86). Berlin: Mouton de Gruyter.

Beebe, L.M. and Giles, H. (1984) Speech-accommodation theories: A discussion in terms of second-language acquisition. *International Journal of the Sociology of Language* 46, 5–32.

Belz, J. and Kinginger, C. (2003) Discourse options and the development of pragmatic competence by classroom learners of German: The case of address forms. *Language Learning* 53 (4), 591–647.

Benesch, S. (2001) *Critical English for Academic Purposes: Theory, Politics, and Practice.* Mahwah, NJ: Lawrence Earlbaum.

Bennett, M.J. (1986) Towards ethnorelativism: A developmental model of intercultural sensitivity. In R.M. Paige (ed.) *Cross-Cultural Orientation: New Conceptualizations and Applications* (pp. 27–69). New York: University Press of America.

Bergman, M.L. and Kasper, G. (1993) Perception and performance in native and nonnative apology. In G. Kasper and S. Blum-Kulka (eds) *Interlanguage Pragmatics* (pp. 82–107). Oxford: Oxford University Press.

Bernard, H.R. (1994) *Research Methods in Anthropology: Qualitative and Quantitative Approaches.* Thousand Oaks, CA: Sage.

Besch, W. (1998) *Duzen, Siezen, Titulieren. Zur Anrede im Deutschen Heute und Gestern* (2nd edn). Vandenhoeck/Ruprecht: Kleine Reihe V&R.

Bialystok, E. (1987) A theoretical model of second language learning. *The Modern Language Journal* 28 (1), 69–83.

Bialystok, E. (1991) Letters, sounds, and symbols: Changes in children's understanding of written language. *Applied Psycholinguistics* 12, 75–89.

Bialystok, E. (1993) Symbolic representation and attentional control in pragmatic competence. In G. Kasper and S. Blum-Kulka (eds) *Interlanguage Pragmatics* (pp. 43–57). Oxford: Oxford University Press.

Bicknese, G. (1974) Study abroad part 1: A comparative test of attitudes and opinions. *Foreign Language Annals* 7 (3), 325–36.

Billmyer, K. and Varghese, M. (2000) Investigating instrument-based pragmatic variability: Effects of enhancing discourse completion tests. *Applied Linguistics* 21 (4), 517–52.

Bion, W.R. (1975) Selections from "Experiences in Groups". In A.D. Colman and W.H. Bexton (eds) *Group Relations Reader 1* (pp. 35–42). Washington, DC: A.K. Rice Institute.

Blom, J.-P. and Gumperz, J. (1972) Social meaning in linguistic structures: Code-switching in Norway. In J. Gumperz and D. Hymes (eds) *Directions in Sociolinguistics* (pp. 407–34). New York: Rinehart and Winston.

Blum-Kulka, S. (1997) *Dinner Talk: Cultural Patterns of Sociability and Socialization in Family Discourse.* New Jersey: Lawrence Erlbaum.

Blum-Kulka, S., House, J. and Kasper, G. (1989) The CCSARP coding manual. In S. Blum-Kulka, J. House and G. Kasper (eds) *Cross-Cultural Pragmatics: Requests and Apologies* (pp. 273–94). Norwood, NJ: Ablex.

Blum-Kulka, S. and Olshtain, E. (1986) Too many words: Length of utterance and pragmatic failure. *Studies in Second Language Acquisition* 8 (2), 165–79.

Blum-Kulka, S. and Snow, C.E. (1992) Developing autonomy for tellers, tales and telling in family narrative events. *Journal of Narrative and Life History* 2 (3), 187–217.

Boa, E. (1999) AssistentInnen. Mailing on 17.12.'99 to the German-Studies mailing list. On WWW at http://www.jiscmail.ac.uk/cgi-bin/wa.exe?S1 = german-studies.

Bourdieu, P. (1984) *Distinction: A Social Critique of the Judgment of Taste.* (R. Nice, trans.). Cambridge, MA: Harvard University Press (originally published in 1979 by Les Editions de Minuit, Paris as *La Distinction: Critique Sociale de Jugement*).

Bradley, J. (2003) Formulaic language in learner discourse: How study abroad affects oral production. PhD thesis, University of Tennessee, 2003. *Dissertation Abstracts International*-A 64 (6), 2060.

Braun, F. (1988) *Terms of Address. Problems of Patterns and Usage in Various Languages and Cultures.* Berlin: Mouton de Gruyter.

Braun, F., Kohz, A. and Schuber, K. (1986) *Anredeforschung: Kommentierte Bibliographie zur Soziolinguistik der Anrede.* Tübingen: Narr.

Brecht, R.D. and Davidson, D.E. (1992) Language acquisition gains in study abroad: Assessment and feedback. In E. Shohamy and A.R. Walton (eds) *Language Assessment for Feedback: Testing and Other Strategies* (pp. 87–101). Dubuque, IA: Kendall/Hunt.

Brecht, R.D., Davidson, D.E. and Ginsberg, R.B. (1991) On evaluating language proficiency gain in study abroad environments: An empirical study of American students of Russian. Washington, DC: U.S. Department of Education, American Council of Teachers of Russian, and the National Foreign Language Center. (ERIC Document Reproduction Service No. ED 350 855).

Brecht, R.D., Davidson, D.E. and Ginsberg, R.B. (1993) Predictors of foreign language gain during study abroad. *NFLC Occasional Papers*. Washington, DC: National Foreign Language Center.

Brecht, R.D., Davidson, D.E. and Ginsberg, R.B. (1995) Predictors of foreign language gain during study abroad. In B.F. Freed (ed.) *Second Language Acquisition in a Study Abroad Context* (pp. 37–66). Amsterdam: John Benjamins.

Brecht, R.D. and Robinson, J.L. (1995). On the value of formal instruction in study abroad. In B.F. Freed (ed.) *Second Language Acquisition in a Study Abroad Context* (pp. 318–34). Amsterdam: John Benjamins.

Brock, C., Crookes, G., Day, R.R. and Long, M. (1986) The differential effects of corrective feedback in native speaker/non-native speaker conversation. In R.R. Day (ed.) *Talking to Learn: Conversation in Second Language Acquisition* (pp. 327–51). Cambridge, MA: Newbury House.

Brown, H.D. (1986) Learning a second culture. In J.M. Valdes (ed.) *Culture Bound: Bridging the Cultural Gap in Language Teaching* (pp. 33–51). Cambridge: Cambridge University Press.

Brown, J.D. (1988) *Understanding Research in Second Language Learning: A Teacher's Guide to Statistics and Research Design*. Cambridge: Cambridge University Press.

Brown, R.W. and Gilman, A. (1960) The pronouns of power and solidarity. In T.A. Sebeok (ed.) *Style in Language* (pp. 253–76). New York: Technology Press of Massachusetts Institute of Technology.

Bruner, J. (1990) *Acts of Meaning*. Cambridge, MA: Harvard University Press.

Burns, P.D. (1997) Foreign students in Japan: A qualitative study of interpersonal relations between North American university exchange students and their Japanese hosts. PhD thesis, University of Massachusetts-Amherst, *Dissertation Abstracts International-A* 57 (10), 4282.

Byrnes H. and Canale, M. (eds) (1987) *Defining and Developing Proficiency: Guidelines, Implementations, and Concepts*. Chicago: National Textbook Company.

Calvin, L.M. (1999) Culture within and around: The language learning stories of adult ESL learners in a cross-cultural, immersion setting. PhD thesis, Indiana University. *Dissertation Abstracts International-A* 60 (5), 1427.

Campbell, C. (1996) Socializing with teachers and prior language learning experience: A diary study. In K. Bailey and D. Nunan (eds) *Voices from the Language Classroom* (pp. 201–23). Cambridge: Cambridge University Press.

Canale, M. (1983) From communicative competence to communicative language pedagogy. In J.C. Richards and R. Schmidt (eds) *Language and Communication* (pp. 2–27). London: Longman.

Canale, M. and Swain, M. (1980) Theoretical bases of communicative approaches to second language teaching and testing. *Applied Linguistics* 1 (1), 1–47.

Carlson, J. S., Burn, B. B., Useem, J. and Yachimowicz, D. (1990) *Study Abroad: The Experience of American Undergraduates in Western Europe and in the United States*. Westport, CT: Greenwood Press.

Chamot, A.U. (1987) The learning strategies of ESL students. In A. Wenden and J. Rubin (eds) *Learner Strategies in Language Learning* (pp. 71–83). Englewood Cliffs, NJ: Prentice Hall.

Cholakian, R. (1992) Study abroad: Paris. *Association of Departments of Foreign Languages Bulletin* 23 (2), 20–25.

Chun, A., Day, R.R., Chenoweth, A. and Luppescus, S. (1982) Errors, interaction, and correction: A study of native-nonnative conversations. *TESOL Quarterly* 16 (4), 537–47.

Churchill, E. (2001) Co-constructing the zone in a short-term exchange. In E. Churchill and J. McLaughlin (eds) *Qualitative Research in Applied Linguistics: Japanese Learners and Contexts* (pp. 118–42). Tokyo: Temple University Japan.

Churchill, E. (2002) The effect of a short-term exchange program on request realizations by Japanese learners of English. *Kanagawa University Studies in Language* 24, 91–103.

Churchill. E. (2003a) Competing for the floor in the American home: Japanese students sharing host families. *Kanagawa University Studies in Language* 25, 185–202.

Churchill, E.F. (2003b) Construction of language learning opportunities for Japanese high school learners of English in a short term study abroad program. Doctoral Thesis, Temple University, 2003. *Dissertation Abstracts International*-64 (7), 2351.

Churchill. E. (2003c) Homestay placements and culture presentations: Who's home and whose culture? Paper presented at the annual conference of the American Association of Applied Linguistics, Arlington, VA.

Churchill, E. (this volume) Variability in the study abroad classroom and learner competence. In M.A. DuFon and E. Churchill (eds) *Language Learners in Study Abroad Contexts*.

Churchill, E. and Vivathanachai, R. (2000, November). A curriculum for student ethnography. Paper presented at the Japan Association for Language Teaching 26th International Conference, Shizuoka, Japan.

Citron, J.L. (1995) Can cross-cultural understanding aid second language acquisition? Toward a theory of ethno-lingual relativity. *Hispania* 78 (1), 105–13.

Cohen, A.D. (1997) Developing pragmatic ability: Insights from the accelerated study of Japanese. In H. Cook, K. Hijirida and M. Tahara (eds) *New Trends and Issues in Teaching Japanese Language and Culture* (Technical Report # 15) (pp. 133–59). Honolulu: University of Hawai'i Second Language Teaching and Curriculum Centre.

Cohen, A.D. (1998) *Strategies in Learning and Using a Second Language*. London: Longman.

Cohen, A. and Weaver, S.J. (1998) Strategies-based instruction for second language learners. In W.A. Renandya and G.M. Jacobs (eds) *Learners and Language Learning* (pp. 1–25). Singapore: SEAMO Regional Language Centre.

Coleman, J.A. (1995) The current state of knowledge concerning student residence abroad. In G. Parker and A. Rouxeville (eds) *"The Year Abroad": Preparation, Monitoring, Evaluation, Current Research and Development* (pp. 17–42). London: CILT.

Coleman, J.A. (1996) *Studying Languages: A Survey of British and European Students. The Proficiency, Background, Attitudes, and Motivations of Students in Foreign Languages in the United Kingdom and Europe.* London: CILT.

Coleman, J.A. (1997) Residence abroad within language study. State of the art article. *Language Teaching* 30 (1), 1–20.

Coleman, J.A. (1998) Language learning and study abroad: the European perspective. *Frontiers: The Interdisciplinary Journal of Study Abroad IV,* 167–203. On WWW at http://www.frontiersjournal.com/issues/vol4/vol4-07_Coleman.pdf.

Collentine, J. (2004) The effects of learning contexts on morpho-syntactic development. *Studies in Second Language Acquisition* 26 (2), 227–48.

Collentine, J. and Freed, B.F. (2004) Learning context and its effects on second language acquisition. *Studies in Second Language Acquisition* 26 (2), 153–71.

Condor, S. (2000) Pride and prejudice: Identity management in English people's talk about "this country". *Discourse & Society* 11 (2), 175–205.

Cook, V. (1985) Language functions, social factors, and second language learning and teaching. *International Review of Applied Linguistics* 23 (3), 177–98.

Cook, H.M. (1990a) An indexical account of the Japanese sentence-final particle *no. Discourse Processes* 13, 401–39.

Cook, H.M. (1990b) The role of the Japanese sentence-final particle *no* in the socialization of children. *Multilingua* 9, 377–95.

Cook, H.M. (1991) The Japanese sentence-final particle *yo* as a non-referential indexical. Paper presented at the Second International Cognitive Linguistics Conference. University of California at Santa Cruz, CA, July 29–August 2.

Cook, H.M. (1993) Schematic values of the Japanese nominal particles *wa* and *ga.* In R.A. Geiger and B. Rudzka-Ostyn (eds) *Conceptualization and Mental Processing in Language* (pp. 371–97). Berlin: Mouton de Gruyter.

Cook, H.M. (this volume) Joint construction of folk beliefs by JFL learners and Japanese host families. In M.A. DuFon and E. Churchill (eds) *Language Learners in Study Abroad Contexts.*

Coupland, N., Coupland, J., Giles, H. and Henwood, K. (1988). Accommodating the elderly: Invoking and extending a theory. *Language in Society* 17 (1), 1–41.

Crookes, G. and Rulon, D. (1988) Topic and feedback in native speaker/non-native speaker conversation. *TESOL Quarterly* 22 (4), 675–81.

DAAD (1999) Du oder Sie? Untersuchungen zu einem immerwährenden Konflikt. *DAAD Letter* 1, 17–18.

Day, R.R. (1985) The use of the target language in context and second language proficiency. In S. Gass and C. Madden (eds) *Input in Second Language Acquisition* (pp. 257–71). Rowley, MA: Newbury House.

DeKeyser, R.M. (1986) From learning to acquisition? Foreign language development in a U.S. classroom and during a semester abroad. PhD thesis, Stanford University.

DeKeyser, R.M. (1990). From learning to acquisition? Monitoring in the classroom and abroad. *HISPANIA* 73, 238–47.

DeKeyser, R.M. (1991) Foreign language development during a semester abroad. In B.F. Freed (ed.) *Foreign Language Acquisition Research and the Classroom* (pp. 104–19). Lexington, MA: DC Heath.

Dewaele, J.M. and Regan,V. (2001) The use of colloquial words in advanced French interlanguage. *EUROSLA Yearbook* 1, 51–67.

Dewey, D.P. (2004a) A comparison of reading development by learners of Japanese in intensive domestic immersion and study abroad contexts. *Studies in Second Language Acquisition* 26 (2), 303–27.

Dewey, D.P. (2004b) The effects of study context on the acquisition of reading by students of Japanese as a second language: A comparison of study abroad and intensive domestic immersion. PhD thesis, Carnegie Mellon University, 2002. *Dissertation Abstracts International-A*, 64 (7), 2465.

Díaz-Campos, M. (2004) Context of learning in the acquisition of Spanish second language phonology. *Studies in Second Language Acquisition* 26 (2), 249–73.

Donato, R. (1994) Collective scaffolding in second language learning. In J. Lantolf and G. Appel (eds) *Vygotskian Approaches to Second Language Research* (pp. 33–56). Norwood, NJ: Ablex.

Dörnyei, Z. (2001) *Teaching and Researching Motivation*. Essex, England: Pearson Education Limited.

Doughty, C. and Pica, T. (1986) "Information gap" tasks: An aid to second language acquisition? *TESOL Quarterly* 20 (2), 305–25.

Doughty, C. and Varela, E. (1998) Communicative focus on form. In C. Doughty and J. Williams (eds) *Focus on Form in Classroom Second Language Acquisition* (pp. 114–38). Cambridge, MA: Cambridge University Press.

DuFon, M.A. (1998) Learning the language and culture of Indonesia: A diary study of the acquisition of the tea routine in Javanese Indonesia. *Journal of Southeast Asian Language Teaching* 7, 60–96.

DuFon, M.A. (2000a) The acquisition of linguistic politeness in Indonesian by sojourners in naturalistic interactions. PhD thesis, University of Hawai'i-Manoa, 1999. *Dissertation Abstracts International-A*, 60 (11), 3985.

DuFon, M.A. (2000b) The acquisition of negative responses to experience questions in Indonesian as a second language by sojourners in naturalistic interactions. In M. Anderson, C. Klee, F. Morris, E. Tarone and B. Swierzbin (eds) *Interaction of Social and Cognitive Factors in SLA: Selected Proceedings of the 1999 Second Language Research Forum* (pp. 77–97). Somerville, MA: Cascadilla Press.

DuFon, M.A. (2003) Gift giving in Indonesian: A model for teaching pragmatic routines in the foreign language classroom with the less commonly taught languages. In A. Martínez Flor, E. Usó Juan and A. Fernández Guerra (eds) *Pragmatic Competence and Foreign Language Teaching* (pp. 109–31). Castellon: Servei de Publicacions de la Universitat Jaume I.

DuFon, M.A. (2004). Second language socialization and the acquisition of intercultural competence. Paper presented at AAAL 2004, Portland, Oregon, May 2004.

DuFon, M.A. (this volume) The socialization of taste during study abroad in Indonesia. In M.A. DuFon and E. Churchill (eds) *Language Learners in Study Abroad Contexts*.

DuFon, M.A. (in press) The acquisition of terms of address in Indonesian by foreign learners in a study abroad program in East Java. *NUSA*. Submitted for publication.

Duranti, A. (1997) *Linguistic Anthropology*. Cambridge: Cambridge University Press.

Duranti, A. and Brenneis, D. (1986) The audience as co-author: An introduction. *Text* 6 (3), 239–47.

Edmondson, W. and House, J. (1991) Do learners talk too much? The waffle phenomenon in interlanguage pragmatics. In R. Phillipson, E. Kellerman, L. Selinker, M.S. Smith and M. Swain (eds) *Foreign/Second Language Pedagogy Research: A Commemorative Volume for Claus Faerch* (pp. 273–87). Clevedon: Multilingual Matters.

Eisenberg, P. (1999) *Grundriss der Deutschen Grammatik. Der Satz* (Vol. 2) Stuttgart/Weimer: Metzler.

Eisenstein, M. and Bodman, J. (1993) Expressing gratitude in American English. In G. Kasper and S. Blum-Kulka (eds) *Interlanguage Pragmatics* (pp. 64–81). NY: Oxford University Press.

Ellis, R. (1985) *Understanding Second Language Acquisition.* Oxford: Oxford University Press.

Engel, U. (1996) *Deutsche Grammatik.* Heidelberg: Julian Groos.

Enomoto, S. and Marriott, H. (1994) Investigating evaluative behaviour in Japanese tour guiding interaction. *Multilingua* 13 (1–2), 131–61.

Erickson, F. (1990) The social construction of discourse coherence in a family dinner table conversation. In B. Dorval (ed.) *Conversation Organization and its Development* (pp. 207–38). Norwood, NJ: Ablex.

Erickson, F. (1996). Ethnographic microanalysis. In S. McKay and N. Hornberger (eds) *Sociolinguistics and Language Teaching* (pp. 283–306). Cambridge: Cambridge University Press.

Ervin-Tripp, S.M. (1971) Sociolinguistics. In J.A. Fishman (ed.) *Advances in the Sociology of Language* (Vol. 1) (pp. 15–91). The Hague, Paris: Mouton.

Faerch, C. and Kasper, G. (1984) Pragmatic knowledge: Rules and procedures. *Applied Linguistics* 5 (3), 214–25.

Faerch, C. and Kasper, G. (1989) Internal and external modification in interlanguage request realization. In S. Blum-Kulka, J. House and G. Kasper (eds) *Cross-Cultural Pragmatics: Requests and Apologies* (pp. 221–47). Norwood, NJ: Ablex.

Ferguson, C.A. (1976) The structure and use of politeness formulas. *Language in Society* 5 (2), 137–51.

Firth, A. and Wagner, J. (1997) On discourse, communication, and (some) fundamental concepts in SLA research. *The Modern Language Journal* 81 (3), 285–300.

Foster, P. (1998) A classroom perspective on the negotiation of meaning. *Applied Linguistics* 19 (1), 1–23.

Frank, V. (1997, March) Potential negative effects of homestay. Paper presented at the meeting of the Middle Atlantic Conference of the American Association for the Advancement of Slavic Studies, Albany, NY.

Fraser, C.C. (2002). Study abroad: An attempt to measure gains. *German as a Foreign Language Journal* 1, 45–65. On WWW at http://www.gfl-journal.de/1-2002/fraser.html.

Freed, B.F. (1990a) Current realities and future prospects in foreign language acquisition research. In B.F. Freed (ed.) *Foreign Language Acquisition Research and the Classroom* (pp. 3–27). Lexington, MA: DC Heath.

Freed, B.F. (1990b) Language learning in a study abroad context: The effects of interactive and non-interactive out-of-class contact on grammatical achievement and oral proficiency. In J. Atlantis (ed.) *Linguistics, Language Teaching and Language Acquisition: The Interdependence of Theory, Practice and Research (GURT 1990)* (pp. 459–77). Washington, DC: Georgetown University Press.

Freed, B.F. (1995a) Language learning and study abroad. In B.F. Freed (ed.) *Second Language Acquisition in a Study Abroad Context* (pp. 3–33). Amsterdam: John Benjamins.

Freed, B.F. (ed.) (1995b) *Second Language Acquisition in a Study Abroad Context.* Amsterdam: Johns Benjamins.

Freed, B.F. (1995c) What makes us think that students who study abroad become fluent? Predictors of foreign language gain during study abroad. In B.F. Freed (ed.) *Second Language Acquisition in a Study Abroad Context* (pp. 123–48). Amsterdam: John Benjamins.

Freed, B.F. (1998) An overview of issues and research in language learning in a study abroad setting. *Frontiers: The Interdisciplinary Journal of Study Abroad,* IV, 31–60. On WWW at http://www.frontiersjournal.com/issues/vol4/vol4-02_Freed.pdf.

Freed, B.F, Segalowitz N. and Dewey, D.P. (2004) Context of learning and second language fluency in French: Comparing regular classroom, study abroad, and intensive domestic immersion programs. *Studies in Second Language Acquisition* 26 (2), 275–301.

Gardner, R.C. (1985) *Social Psychology and Second Language Learning: The Role of Attitudes and Motivation.* London: Edward Arnold.

Gardner, R.C. and Lambert, W.E. (1959) Motivational variables in second language acquisition. *Canadian Journal of Psychology* 13 (4), 266–72.

Gardner, R.C., and Lambert, W.E. (1972) *Attitudes and Motivation in Second Language Learning.* Rowley, MA: Newbury House.

Gardner, R.C. and MacIntyre, P.D. (1991) An instrumental motivation in language study: Who says it isn't effective? *Studies in Second Language Acquisition* 13 (1), 57–72.

Gass, S. (1997) *Input, Interaction, and the Second Language Learner.* Mahwah, NJ: Lawrence Erlbaum.

Gass, S. and Varonis, E. (1984) The effect of familiarity on the comprehensibility of non-native speech. *Language Learning* 34 (1), 65–89.

Gass, S. and Varonis, E. (1985) Variation in native speaker speech modification to nonnative speakers. *Studies in Second Language Acquisition* 7, 37–58.

Gass, S. and Varonis, E. (1989) Incorporated repairs in nonnative discourse. In M. Eisenstein (ed.) *The Dynamic Interlanguage: Empirical Studies in Second Language Variation* (pp. 71–86). New York: Plenum Press.

Gass, S. and Varonis, E. (1994) Input, interaction, and second language production. *Studies in Second Language Acquisition* 16 (3), 282–302.

Gee, J. P. (2003) *What Video Games Have to Teach Us About Learning and Literacy.* New York: Palgrave Macmillan.

Geertz, C. (1960) *The Religion of Java.* Chicago: University of Chicago Press.

Geertz, H. (1961) *The Javanese Family: A Study of Kinship and Socialization.* New York: The Free Press of Glencoe.

Ginsberg, R.B. (1992) Language gains during study abroad: An analysis of the ACTR data. National Foreign Language Center Working Papers. Washington, DC: National Foreign Language Center. (ERIC Document Reproduction Service No. ED 358 717).

Ginsburg, R.B., Robin, R.M. and Wheeling, P.R. (1992) Listening Comprehension before and after Study Abroad. Washington, DC: The National Foreign Language Center. (ERIC Document Reproduction Service No. ED 358 718).

Glück, H. and Koch, K. (1998) Du oder Sie. Anredekonventionen in Deutschland und in anderen Ländern. *Der Sprachdienst* 42, 1–9.

Goffman, E. (1959) *The Presentation of Self in Everyday Life*. New York: Doubleday.

Goffman, E. (1974) *Frame Analysis: An Essay on the Organization of Experience*. New York: Harper and Row.

Goffman, E. (1981) *Forms of Talk*. Philadelphia: University of Pennsylvania Press.

Golonka, E.M. (2001) Identification of salient linguistic and metalinguistic variables in the prediction of oral proficiency gain at the advanced-level threshold among adult learners of Russian. PhD thesis, Bryn Mawr College, 2000. *Dissertation Abstracts International-A*, 61 (11), 4410.

Goodwin, C. (1979) The interactive construction of a sentence in natural conversation. In G. Psathas (ed.) *Everyday Language: Studies in Ethnomethodology* (pp. 97–121). New York: Irvington.

Goody, J. (1982) *Cooking, Cuisine and Class: A Study in Comparative Sociology*. Cambridge: Cambridge University Press.

Gumperz, J. (1982) *Discourse Processes*. New York: Cambridge University Press

Gumperz, J. and Hymes, D. (eds) (1964) The ethnography of communication. *American Anthropologist*, 66 (6), pt. II.

Gumperz, J. and Hymes, D. (1972) *Directions in Sociolinguistics: The Ethnography of Speaking*. New York: Holt, Rinehart and Winston.

Hamilton, H.E. (1994) *Conversations with an Alzheimer's Patient: An Interactional Sociolinguistic Study*. Cambridge: Cambridge University Press.

Harder, P. (1980) Discourse as self-expression – on the reduced personality of the second language learner. *Applied Linguistics* 1, 262–70.

Hashimoto, H. (1993) Language acquisition of an exchange student within the homestay environment. *Journal of Asian Pacific Communication* 4 (4), 209–24.

Hassall, T. (1997) Requests by Australian learners of Indonesian. PhD thesis, Australian National University.

Hassall, T. (2001) Modifying requests in a second language. *International Review of Applied Linguistics* 39 (4), 259–83.

Hassall, T. (2004) Through a glass, darkly: When learner pragmatics is misconstrued. *Journal of Pragmatics* 36 (5), 997–1002.

Hassall, T. (this volume) Learning to take leave in social conversations: A diary study. In M.A. DuFon and E. Churchill (eds) *Language Learners in Study Abroad Contexts*.

Heath, S. (1983) *Ways with Words: Language, Life and Work in Communities and Classrooms*. Cambridge: Cambridge University Press.

Heller, M. (1988) Strategic ambiguity: Codeswitching in the management of conflict. In M. Heller (ed.) *Code-Switching: Anthropological and Sociolinguistic Perspectives* (pp. 77–96). Berlin: Mouton de Gruyter.

Hermann, G. (1980) Attitudes and success in children's learning of English as a second language: The motivational versus the resultative hypothesis. *English Language Teaching Journal* 34 (4), 247–54.

Higa, M. (1976) Nihongo to nihonjin shakai (Japanese language and society), *Iwanami Koza Nihongo 1: Nihongo to Kokugogaku* (pp. 99–138). Tokyo: Iwanami shoten.

Higgs, T. and Clifford, R. (1982) The push toward communication. In T. Higgs (ed.) *Curriculum, Competence and the Foreign Language Teacher* (pp. 57–59). Skokie, IL: National Textbook Company.

Hisama, T. (1995) Language acquisition or language learning? *Kansai Gaidai University Journal of Inquiry and Research* 62, 1–13.

Hoffman-Hicks, S.D. (2000) The longitudinal development of French foreign language pragmatic competence: Evidence from study abroad. PhD thesis, Indiana University, 1999. *Dissertation Abstracts International*-A, 61 (2), 591.

Holliday, L. (1988) Let them talk: A study of native-nonnative interaction in conversation. *Working Papers in Educational Linguistics 4* (pp. 89–100). Philadelphia: University of Pennsylvania Graduate School of Education.

Howard, M. (2001) The effects of study abroad on L2 learners' structural skills. *EUROSLA Yearbook* 1, 123–41.

Huebner, T. (1995a) The effects of overseas language programs. In B.F. Freed (ed.) *Second Language Acquisition in a Study Abroad Context* (pp. 171–93). Amsterdam: John Benjamins.

Huebner, T. (1995b) A framework for investigating effectiveness of study abroad programs. In C. Kramsh (ed.) *Redefining the Boundaries of Language Study* (pp. 185–217). Boston: Heinle and Heinle.

Huebner, T. (1998) Methodological considerations in data collection for language learning in a study abroad context. *Frontiers: The Interdisciplinary Journal of Study Abroad* 4, 1–30.

Hymes, D. (1972) On communicative competence. In J.B. Pride and J. Holmes (eds) *Sociolinguistics* (pp. 269–93). Harmondsworth: Penguin Books.

Hymes, D. (1974) *Foundations in Sociolinguistics: An Ethnographic Approach.* Philadelphia: University of Pennsylvania Press.

Iino, M. (1993) Language-as-resource for whom? Foreign language planning in higher education: Its goal and implementation. *Japanese-Language Education around the Globe* 3, 99–119.

Iino, M. (1996) 'Excellent Foreigner!': Gaijinization of Japanese language and culture in contact situations – an ethnographic study of dinner table conversations between Japanese host families and American students. Doctoral thesis, University of Pennsylvania. *Dissertation Abstracts International*, 57, 1451.

Iino, M. (1998) Issues of video recordings in language studies: A case of remote video observation of dinner table interactions in homestay settings. Paper presented at the 1998 Annual Conference of the American Association of Applied Linguistics. Seattle, WA.

Iino, M. (this volume) Norms of interaction in a Japanese homestay setting: Toward a two-way flow of linguistic and cultural resources. In M.A. DuFon and E. Churchill (eds) *Language Learners in Study Abroad Contexts.*

Ikeguchi, C.B. (1996) Self assessment and ESL competence of Japanese returnees. (ERIC Document Reproduction Service No. ED 399 798).

Isabelli, C. (2002) The impact of a study-abroad experience on the acquisition of L2 Spanish syntax: The null subject parameter. PhD thesis, University of Illinois, Urbana-Champaign 2001. *Dissertation Abstracts International*-A, 62 (8), 2703-A-2704.

Isabelli-García, C.L. (2003) Development of oral communication skills abroad. *Frontiers: The Interdisciplinary Journal of Study Abroad*, 9, 149–173. On WWW at http://www.frontiersjournal.com/issues/vol9/vol9-07_isabelligarcia.htm.

Isabelli-García, C.L. (2004) *A Case Study of the Factors in the Development of Spanish Linguistic Accuracy and Oral Communication Skills: Motivation and Extended Interaction in the Study Abroad Context*. New York: Edwin Mellen Press.

Isabelli-García, C. (this volume) Study abroad social networks, motivation and attitudes: Implications for second language acquisition. In M.A. DuFon and E. Churchill (eds) *Language Learners in Study Abroad Contexts*.

Iwai, T. (2001, February) Family dinner conversation: Socialization of older children in Japan. Paper presented at the annual meeting of the American Association of Applied Linguistics, St. Louis, MO.

Iwakiri, M. (1993) Effects of a study abroad program on the English development of Japanese college students. *Kagoshima University Bulletin of English Education* 24, 41–60.

Jacoby, S. and Ochs, E. (1995) Co-construction: An introduction. *Research on Language and Social Interaction* 28, 171–83.

Janicki, J. (1986) Accommodation in native speaker-foreigner interaction. In J. House and S. Blum-Kulka (eds) *Interlingual and Intercultural Communication* (pp. 169–78). Tubingen: Gunter Narr Verlag.

Jay, R.R. (1969) *Javanese Villagers: Social Relations in Rural Modjokuto*. Cambridge, MA: The MIT Press.

Johnston, B., Kasper, G. and Ross, S. (1998) Effect of rejoinders in production questionnaires. *Applied Linguistics* 19 (2), 157–82.

Kaplan, M.A. (1989) French in the community: A survey of language used abroad. *The French Review* 63 (2), 290–99.

Kasper, G. (1992) Pragmatic transfer. *Second Language Research* 8 (3), 202–31.

Kasper, G. (1993) Interkulturelle Pragmatik und Fremdsprachenlernen. In J.-P. Timm and H.J. Vollmer (eds) *Kontroversen in der Fremdsprachenforschung* (pp. 41–77), Bochum: Brockmeyer.

Kasper, G. (2000) Data collection in pragmatics research. In H. Spencer-Oatey (ed.) *Culturally Speaking: Managing Rapport through Talk across Cultures* (pp. 316–41). London: Continuum.

Kasper, G. and Rose, K. (2002) Pragmatic development in a second language. *Language Learning* 52 (Monograph Supplement 1). Also published as *Pragmatic Development in a Second Language*. Malden, MA: Blackwell.

Katz, J.T. (1981) Children's second-language acquisition: The role of foreigner talk in child-child interaction. *International Journal of the Sociology of Language* 28, 53–68.

Kauffmann, N.L., Martin, J.N., Weaver, H.D. and Weaver, J. (1992) *Students Abroad: Strangers at Home: Education for a Global Society*. Yarmouth, ME: Intercultural Press.

Kinginger, C. (2004) Alice doesn't live here anymore: Foreign language learning and identity reconstruction. In A. Pavlenko and A. Blackledge (eds). *Negotiation of Identities in Multilingual Contexts* (pp. 219–42). Clevedon: Multilingual Matters.

Kinginger, C. and Farrell, K. (2004) Assessing development of meta-pragmatic awareness in study abroad. *Frontiers: The Interdisciplinary Journal of Study Abroad* 10, 19–42. On WWW at http://www.frontiersjournal.com/issues/.

Kinginger, C. and Whitworth, K.F. (2005) Gender and emotional investment in language learning during study abroad: CALPER Working Paper Series 2. University Park, PA: The Pennsylvania State University, Center for Advanced

Proficiency Research and Education. On WWW at http://calper.la.psu.edu/publications.php.

Kinoshita, A. (2001) Negotiating identities: Experiences of Japanese female students in Vancouver homestay settings. MA thesis, Simon Fraser University.

Kirsten, N. (1999) Ein ständiger Eiertanz. *Wirtschaftswoche* 42, 254–57.

Kitao, S.K. (1993) Preparation for and results of a short-term overseas study program in the United States. Bulletin of the Institute for Interdisciplinary Studies of Culture. (ERIC Document Reproduction Service No. ED 370 381).

Kline, R.R. (1998) Literacy and language learning in a study abroad context. *Frontiers: The Interdisciplinary Journal of Study Abroad*, IV, 139–65. On WWW at http://www.frontiersjournal.com/issues/vol4/vol4-06_Kline.pdf.

Knight, S.M. and Schmidt-Rinehart, B.C. (2002) Enhancing the homestay: Study abroad from the host family's perspective. *Foreign Language Annals* 33 (2), 190–201.

Kondo, S. (1997a) Longitudinal study on the development of pragmatic competence in a natural learning context – Perception behind performance. *Proceedings of Sophia University Linguistic Society* 12, 35–54.

Kondo, S. (1997b) The development of pragmatic competence by Japanese learners of English: Longitudinal study on interlanguage apologies. *Sophia Linguistica* 41, 265–84.

Krashen, S. and Seliger, H. (1976) The role of formal and informal environments in second language learning: A pilot study. *Linguistics* 172, 15–21.

Kubota, R. (1999) Japanese culture constructed by discourse: Implications for applied linguistics research and EFL. *TESOL Quarterly* 33 (1), 9–35.

Kuno, S. (1973) *The Structure of the Japanese Language*. Cambridge: MIT Press.

Kuntz, P.S. (1999) Overseas students of Arabic and their teachers: Issues in program implementation. (ERIC Document Reproduction Service No. ED 427 513).

Labov, W. (1972a) *Language in the Inner City: Studies in the Black English Venacular*. Philadelphia: University of Pennsylvania Press.

Labov, W. (1972b) *Sociolinguistic Patterns*. Philadelphia: University of Pennsylvania Press.

Lafford, B.A. (1995) Getting into, through and out of a survival situation: A comparison of communicative strategies used by students studying Spanish abroad and 'at home.' In B.F. Freed (ed.) *Second Language Acquisition in a Study Abroad Context* (pp. 97–121). Philadelphia: John Benjamins.

Lafford, B.A. (2004) The effect of the context of learning on the use of communication strategies by learners of Spanish as a second language. *Studies in Second Language Acquisition* 26 (2), 201–25.

Lantolf, J.P. and Appel, G. (1994) Theoretical framework: An introduction to Vygotskian perspectives on second language research. In J.P. Lantolf and G. Appel (eds) *Vygotskian Approaches to Second Language Research* (pp. 1–32). Norwood, NJ: Ablex.

Lapkin, S., Hart, D. and Swain, M. (1995) A Canadian interprovincial exchange: Evaluating the linguistic impact of a three-month stay in Quebec. In B.F. Freed (ed.) *Second Language Acquisition in a Study Abroad Context* (pp. 67–94). Amsterdam: John Benjamins.

Laudet, C. (1993) Oral performance of ERASMUS students: An assessment. *TEANGA* 13, 13–28.

Law, M. E. (2003) A case study of study abroad: University students learning Spanish in context. PhD thesis, University of South Alabama, 2002. *Dissertation Abstracts International-A* 63 (7), 2514.

Leech, G. (1983) *Principles of Pragmatics*. London: Longman.

Lemke, J. L. (1997) Cognition, context, and learning: A social semiotic perspective. In D. Kirshner and J.A. Whitson (eds) *Situated Cognition* (pp. 37–56). Mahwah, NJ: Lawrence Erlbaum Associates.

Lennon, P. (1990) The advanced learner at large in the L2 community: Developments in spoken performance. *IRAL* 28 (4), 309–24.

Leontyev, A. N. (1981) *Problems of the Development of the Mind*. Moscow: Progress Publishers.

Levin, D.M. (2001) Language learners' sociocultural interaction in a study abroad context. PhD thesis, Indiana University. *Dissertation Abstracts International-A* 62 (2), 498.

Li, J. (2000) Cross-culture contact: A study of factors that contribute to culture shock on ESL students' adjustment in the English Language Institute at the University of Tennessee, 1999. PhD thesis, University of Tennessee. *Dissertation Abstracts International-A*, 61 (2), 463-464.

Lightbown, P. (1985) Great expectations: Second language acquisition research and classroom teaching. *Applied Linguistics* 6, 173–89.

Liskin-Gasparro, J. and Urdaneta, L. (1995) Language learning in a semester abroad: The spring 1995 University of Iowa Universidad de los Andes program in Mérida, Venezuela. Conference manuscript. *Research Perspectives in Adult Language Learning and Acquisition-Study abroad: Research on Learning Language and Culture in Context* (pp. 138–60). Columbus, OH: The Ohio State University: National Foreign Language Resource Center.

Long, M. (1981a) Input, interaction, and second language acquisition. *Annals of the New York Academy of Sciences* 379, 259–78.

Long, M. (1981b) Questions in foreigner talk discourse. *Language Learning* 31, 135–57.

Long, M. (1983) Native speaker/non-native speaker conversation and the negotiation of comprehensible input. *Applied Linguistics* 4, 126–41.

Long, M. (1985a) Input and second language acquisition theory. In S. Gass and C. Madden (eds) *Input in Second Language Acquisition* (pp. 377–93). Rowley, MA: Newbury House.

Long, M. (1985b) A role for instruction in second language acquisition: Task-based language training. In K. Hyltenstam and M. Pienemann (eds) *Modeling and Assessing Second Language Acquisition* (pp. 77–100). Clevedon: Multilingual Matters.

Long, M. (1989) Task, group, and task group interactions. *University of Hawai'i Working Papers in ESL* 8 (2), 1–26.

Long, M. (1990) The least a second language acquisition theory needs to explain. *TESOL Quarterly* 24 (4), 649–66.

Long, M. (1996) The role of linguistic environment in second language acquisition. In W. Ritchie and T. Bhatia (eds) *The Handbook of Second Language Acquisition* (pp. 413–68). San Diego, CA: Academic Press.

Long, M. and Sato, C. (1983) Classroom foreigner talk discourse: Forms and functions of teachers' questions. In H. Seliger and M. Long (eds) *Classroom Oriented Research in Second Language Acquisition* (pp. 268–85). Rowley, MA: Newbury House.

Longcope, P.D. (2003) What is the impact of study abroad on L2 learning? A descriptive study of contexts, conditions, and outcomes. PhD thesis, University of Pennsylvania. *Dissertation Abstracts International* A, 64 (4), 1199.

Lopez Ortega, N.R. (2003) The development of discourse competence in study abroad learners: A study of subject expression in Spanish as a second language. PhD thesis, Cornell University, 2002. *Dissertation Abstracts International* 63 (9), 3171.

Loschky, L. (1989) *The Effects of Negotiated Interaction and Premodified Input on Second Language Comprehension and Retention* (Occasional Papers, No. 16). Honolulu: University of Hawai'i at Manoa, ESL Department.

Loschky, L. (1994) Comprehensible input and second language acquisition: What is the relationship? *Studies in Second Language Acquisition* 16 (3), 303–23.

Lüger, H.-H. (1993) *Routinen und Rituale in der Alltagskommunikation.* München: Langenscheidt.

Luria, L. (1976) *Cognitive Development: Its Cultural and Social Foundations.* Cambridge, MA: Harvard University Press.

Lyster, R. and Ranta, L. (1997) Corrective feedback and learner uptake: Negotiation of form in communicative classrooms. *Studies in Second Language Acquisition* 19 (1), 37–66.

MacIntyre, P.D., Clément, R., Dörnyei, Z., and Noels, K.A. (1998). Conceptualizing willingness to communicate in a L2: A situational model of L2 confidence and affiliation. *The Modern Language Journal,* 82 (4), 545-562.

Mackey, A. and Philip, J. (1998) Conversational interaction and second language development. Recasts, responses, and red herrings? *The Modern Language Journal* 82 (3), 338–56.

Maiworm, F., Steube, W. and Teichler, U. (1993) *Experiences of ERASMUS Students 1990/91.* Kassel: Wiss. Zentrum für Berufs- & Hochschulforschung der Gesamthochschule Kassel.

Makino, S. (1995) *Hoomu sutei ni okeru nihongo gakushuu kouka.* Paper presented at the Nihongo nihon bunka kouza kaki seminaa, 10 shuunen kinen kenkyuu kai, Hakodate, Japan.

Markus, H.R. and Kitayama, S. (1991) Culture and the self: Implications for cognition, emotion, and motivation. *Psychological Review* 98, 224–53.

Marriott, H. (1995) The acquisition of politeness patterns by exchange students in Japan. In B.F. Freed (ed.) *Second Language Acquisition in a Study Abroad Context* (pp. 197–224). Amsterdam: John Benjamins.

Martin, G. (1980) English language acquisition: The effects of living with an American family. *TESOL Quarterly* 14 (3), 388–90.

Mathews, S.A. (2001) Russian second language acquisition during study abroad: Gender differences in student behavior. PhD thesis, Bryn Mawr College. *Dissertation Abstracts International* A-61 (11), 4367.

Matsumura, S. (2001) Learning the rules for offering advice: A quantitative approach to second language socialization. *Language Learning* 51 (4), 635–79.

Maynard, S.K. (1997) *Japanese Communication: Language and Thought in Context.* Honolulu: University of Hawaii Press.

McDermott, R.P. (1993). The acquisition of a child by a learning disability. In J. Lave and S. Chaiklin (eds) *Understanding Practice: Perspectives on Activity and Context* (pp. 269–305). Cambridge: Cambridge University Press.

McKay, S.L. and Wong, S-L.C. (1996) Multiple discourses, multiple identities: Investment and agency in second-language learning among Chinese adolescent immigrant students. *Harvard Educational Review* 66 (3), 577–608.

McMeekin, A.L. (2003) NS-NNS negotiation and communication strategy use in the host family versus the study abroad classroom. PhD thesis, University of Hawai'i-Manoa. *Dissertation Abstracts International-A*, 64 (05), 1621.

McMeekin, A. (this volume) Negotiation in a Japanese Study Abroad Setting. In M.A. DuFon and E. Churchill (eds) *Language Learners in Study Abroad Contexts*.

Mendelbaum, D.G. (ed.) (1949) *Selected Writings of Edward Sapir in Language, Culture and Personality*. Berkeley: University of California Press.

Miles, M.B. and Huberman, A.M. (1994) *Qualitative Data Analysis* (2nd edn). Thousand Oaks, CA: Sage.

Miller, L. (1995a) Crossing ethnolinguistic boundaries: A preliminary look at the *gaijin tarento* in Japan. In J. Lent (ed.) *Asian Popular Culture* (pp.162–73). New York: Westview Press.

Miller, L. (1995b) Two aspects of Japanese and American co-worker interaction: Giving instructions and creating rapport. *Journal of Applied Behavioral Science* 31, 141–61.

Miller, L. and Ginsberg, R.B. (1995) Folklinguistic theories of language learning. In B.F. Freed (ed.) *Second Language Acquisition in a Study Abroad Context*, (pp. 293–315). Amsterdam: Johns Benjamins.

Miller, R.A. (1977). *The Japanese Language in Contemporary Japan: Some Sociolinguistic Observations*. AEI-Hoover Policy Studies, 22. Washington, DC: American Enterprise Institute for Public Policy Research.

Miller, R.A. (1982) *Japan's Modern Myth: The Language and Beyond*. New York: John Weatherhill.

Milleret, M. (1990) Evaluation and the summer language program abroad: A review essay. *The Modern Language Journal* 74 (4), 483–88.

Milroy, L. (1987a) *Language and Social Networks*. Oxford: Blackwell.

Milroy, L. (1987b) *Observing and Analysing Natural Language: A Critical Account of Sociolinguistic Method*. Oxford: Blackwell.

Milton, J. and Meara, P. (1995) How periods abroad affect vocabulary growth in a foreign language. *Review of Applied Linguistics* 107, 17–34.

Minami, M. (2002) *Culture-specific Language Styles: The Development of Oral Narrative and Literacy*. Clevedon: Multilingual Matters.

Moehle, D. and Raupach, M. (1983). *Planen in der Fremdsprache*. Frankfurt: Lang.

Morché, P. (1991) Siezt Du wohl! *Intercity* 10, 58–60.

Naiman, N., Frohlich, M., Stern, H.H. and Todesco, A. (1978) *The Good Language Learner*. Toronto: Ontario Institute for Studies in Education.

Neustpuny, J.V. (1985) Problems in Australian-Japanese contact situations. In J.B. Pride (ed.) *Cross-Cultural Encounters: Communication and Mis-Communication* (pp. 44–64). Melbourne: River Seine Publications.

Nikolov, M. (2001) A study of unsuccessful language learners. In A. Dörnyei and R. Schmidt (eds) *Motivation and Second Language Acquisition* (pp. 149–70). Honolulu, Hawaii: Second Language Teaching and Curriculum Center.

Nobuyoshi, J. and Ellis, R. (1993) Focused communication tasks and second language acquisition. *English Language Teaching Journal* 47 (3), 203–10.

Noguchi, S. (1998) Returning to the homeland: Perceptions of linguistic change among overseas Japanese instructors, *Australian Review of Applied Linguistics*, Series S, No 15, 105–22.

Noguchi, M. and Fotos, S. (2001) *Studies in Japanese Bilingualism*. Clevedon: Multilingual Matters.

Norris, J. (2001) Use of address terms on the German Speaking Test. In K.R. Rose and G. Kasper (eds) *Pragmatics in Language Teaching* (pp. 248–82). Cambridge: Cambridge University Press.

Norton, B. (2000) *Identity and Language Learning: Gender, Ethnicity, and Educational Change*. Harlow, England: Pearson Education Limited.

Norton, B. and Toohey, K. (2001). Changing perspectives on good language learners. *TESOL Quarterly* 35 (2), 307–22.

O'Malley, J.M. and Chamot, A.U. (1990). *Learning Strategies in Second Language Acquisition*. Cambridge: Cambridge University Press.

Ochs, E. (1988) *Culture and Language Development: Language Acquisition and Language Socialization in a Samoan Village*. Cambridge: Cambridge University Press.

Ochs, E. (1991) Socialization through language and interaction: A theoretical introduction. *Issues in Applied Linguistics* 2, 143–47.

Ochs, E. (1996) Linguistic resources for socializing humanity. In J. Gumperz and S. Levinson (eds) *Rethinking Linguistic Relativity* (pp. 407–37). Cambridge: Cambridge University Press.

Ochs, E. and Capps, L. (1986) Narrating the self. *Annual Review of Anthropology* 25, 19–43.

Ochs, E., Pontecorvo, C. and Fasulo, A. (1996) Socializing taste. *Ethnos* 61 (1–2), 7–46.

Ochs, E. and Schieffelin, B. (1984) Language acquisition and socialization: Three developmental stories and their implications. In R.A Shwedar and R.A. Levine (eds) *Culture Theory: Essays on Mind, Self, and Emotion* (pp. 276–320). Cambridge: Cambridge University Press.

Ochs, E., Smith, R. and Taylor, C. (1989) Detective stories at dinnertime: Problem solving through co-narration. *Cultural Dynamics* 2, 238–57.

Ochs, E. and Taylor, C. (1994) Mother's role in the everyday reconstruction of "Father Knows Best". In K. Hall (ed.) *Locating Power: Proceedings of 1992 Berkeley Women Language Conference* (pp. 447–62). Berkeley: University of California Press.

Ochs, E. and Taylor, C. (1995) The "father knows best" dynamic in dinnertime narratives. In K. Hall and M. Bucholtz (eds) *Gender, Articulated: Language and the Socially Constructed Self* (pp. 97–120). New York: Routledge.

Ochs, E., Taylor, C., Rudolph, D. and Smith, R. (1992) Storytelling as a theory-building activity. *Discourse Processes* 15 (1), 37–72.

Ogulnick, K. (1998) *Onna Rashiku (Like a woman): The Diary of a Language Learner in Japan*. Albany: State University of New York.

Ohta, A. (2001) *Second Language Acquisition Processes in the Classroom*. Mahwah, NJ: Lawrence Erlbaum Associates.

Omar, A.S. (1993) Closing Kiswahili conversations: The performance of native and non-native speakers. *Pragmatics and Language Learning* 4, 104–25.

Ortega, L. (1999) Planning and focus on form in L2 oral performance. *Studies in Second Language Acquisition* 21 (1), 109–48.

Owen, J.S. (2002) Interlanguage pragmatics in Russian: A study of the effects of study abroad and proficiency levels on request strategies. PhD thesis. Bryn Mawr College, 2001. *Dissertation Abstracts International-A*, 62 (12), 4145–4146.

Oxford, R.L. (1986) *Development and Psychometric Testing of the Strategy Inventory for Language Learning (SILL)*. Alexandria, VA: Army Research Institute for Behavioral and Social Sciences.

Oxford, R.L. (1990) *Language Learning Strategies: What Every Teacher Should Know*. New York: Newbury House.

Oxford, R.L. and Burry-Stock, J.A. (1995) Assessing the use of language learning strategies worldwide with the ESL/EFL versions of the strategy inventory for language learning (SILL). *System* 23 (1), 1–23.

Oxford, R.L. and Crookall, D. (1989) Research on language learning strategies: Methods, findings, and instructional issues. *The Modern Language Journal* 73, 404–19.

Oxford, R.L. and Nyikos, M. (1989) Variables affecting choice of language learning strategies by university students. *The Modern Language Journal* 73, 291–300.

Paige, R.M., Cohen, A.D., Kappler, B., Chi, J.C. and Lassegard, J.P. (2002) *Maximizing Study Abroad: A Student's Guide to Strategies for Language and Culture Learning and Use*. Minneapolis, MN: Center for Advanced Research on Language Acquisition, University of Minnesota.

Paige, R.M., Cohen, A. and Shively, R.L. (2004) Assessing the impact of a strategies-based curriculum on language and culture learning abroad. *Frontiers: The Interdisciplinary Journal of Study Abroad* 10, 253–76.

Parr, P. (1988) Second language acquisition and study abroad: the immersion experience. PhD thesis, University of Southern California.

Pastor, E. (1995) "SEIT WANN SIEZEN WIR UNS EIGENTLICH?" Zur Geschichte der pronominalen Anredeformen im Deutschen. Ein Streifzug durch Literatur- und Sprachgeschichte. *Germanistische Mitteilungen* 42, 3–17.

Pavlenko, A. (2001) "How do I become a woman in an American vein?": Transformations of gender performance in second language socialization. In A. Pavlenko, A. Blackledge, I. Piller, and M. Teutsch-Dwyer (eds) *Multilingualism, Second Language Learning, and Gender* (pp. 133–74). Berlin: Mouton De Gruyter.

Peirce, B.N. (1994) Using diaries in second language acquisition research and teaching. *English Quarterly* 26 (3), 22–29.

Peirce, B.N. (1995) Social identity, investment, and language learning. *TESOL Quarterly* 29 (1), 9–31.

Pellegrino, V.A. (1998) Student perspectives on language learning in a study abroad context. *Frontiers: The Interdisciplinary Journal of Study Abroad, IV*, 91–120. On WWW at http://www.frontiersjournal.com/issues/vol4/vol4-04_Pelligrino.pdf.

Philip, J. (1999) Constraints on "noticing the gap": A study of NNS' apperception of recasts in NS-NNS interaction. Paper presented at the 1999 Annual Conference of the American Association for Applied Linguistics, Stamford, Connecticut.

Pica, T. (1987) Interlanguage adjustments as an outcome of NS-NNS negotiated interaction. *Language Learning* 38 (1), 45–73.

Pica, T. (1991) Classroom interaction, participation, and comprehension: Redefining relationships. *System* 19, 437–52.

Pica, T. (1992) The textual outcomes of native speaker/non-native speaker negotiation. What do they reveal about second language learning? In C. Kramsch and S. McConnell-Ginet (eds) *Text in Context: Cross Disciplinary Perspectives on Language Study* (pp. 198–237). Lexington, MA: D.C. Heath.

Pica, T. (1993) Communication with second language learners: What does it reveal about the social and linguistic processes of second language acquisition? In J. Alatis (ed.) *Language, Communication, and Social Meaning* (pp. 434–64). Washington, DC: Georgetown University Press.

Pica, T. (1994) Review article: Research on negotiation: What does it reveal about second-language learning conditions, processes, and outcomes? *Language Learning* 44 (3), 493–527.

Pica, T. (1996) Language learners' interaction: How does it address the input, output, and feedback needs of L2 learners? *TESOL Quarterly* 30 (1), 59–84.

Pica, T. and Doughty, C. (1985) Input and interaction in the communicative language classroom: A comparison of teacher-fronted and group activities. In S. Gass and C. Madden (eds) *Input in Second Language Acquisition* (pp. 115–32). Rowley, MA: Newbury House.

Pica, T. and Doughty, C. (1988) Variations in classroom interaction as a function of participation pattern and task. In J. Fine (ed.) *Second Language Discourse: A Textbook of Current Research* (pp. 41–55). Norwood, NJ: Ablex.

Pica, T., Doughty, C. and Young, R. (1986) Making input comprehensible: Do interactional modifications help? *ITL Review of Applied Linguistics* 72, 1–25.

Pica, T., Holliday, L., Lewis, N. and Morgenthaler, L. (1989) Comprehensible output as an outcome of linguistic demands on the learner. *Studies in Second Language Acquisition* 11 (1), 63–90.

Pica, T., Holliday, L., Lewis, N., Berducci, D. and Newman, J. (1991) Language Learning through interaction. What role does gender play? *Studies in Second Language Acquisition* 13 (3), 343–76.

Pica, T., Kanagy, R. and Falodun, J. (1993) Choosing and using communication tasks for second language instruction and research. In G. Crookes and S. Gass (eds) *Tasks and Language Learning: Integrating Theory and Practice* (pp. 9–34). Clevedon: Multilingual Matters.

Pica, T., Young, R. and Doughty, C. (1987) The impact of interaction on comprehension. *TESOL Quarterly* 21 (4), 737–58.

Plough, I. and Gass, S. (1993) Interlocutor and task familiarity: Effects on interactional structure. In G. Crookes and S. Gass (eds) *Tasks and Language Learning: Integrating Theory and Practice* (pp. 35–56). Clevedon, UK: Multilingual Matters.

Polanyi, L. (1995) Language learning and living abroad: Stories from the field. In B.F. Freed (ed.) *Second Language Acquisition in a Study Abroad Context* (pp. 271–91). Amsterdam: John Benjamins.

Porter, P.A. (1986) How learners talk to each other: Input and interaction in task-centred discussions. In R.R. Day (ed.) *Talking to Learn: Conversation in Second Language Acquisition* (pp. 200–22). Rowley, MA: Newbury House.

Poulisse, N. (1997) Compensatory strategies and the principles of clarity and economy. In G. Kasper and E. Kellerman (eds) *Communication Strategies* (pp. 49–64). New York: Addison Wesley Longman Limited.

Raupach, M. (1983) *Procedural Learning in Advanced Learners of a Foreign Language.* Duisburg: Universitat Gesamthochschule Duisburg.

Regan, V. (1995) The acquisition of sociolinguistic native speech norms. In B.F. Freed (ed.) *Second Language Acquisition in a Study Abroad Context* (pp. 245–67). Amsterdam: John Benjamins.

Regan, V. (1998) Sociolinguistics and language learning in a study abroad context. *Frontiers: The Interdisciplinary Journal of Study Abroad IV*, 61–90. On WWW at http://www.frontiersjournal.com/issues/vol4/vol4-03_Regan.pdf.

Richardson, C. (1997) A study of Japanese "foreigner talk". Master's thesis, University of Hawai'i-Manoa.

Rivers, W.P. (1998) Is being there enough? The effects of homestay placements on language gain during study abroad. *Foreign Language Annals* 31 (4), 492–500.

Roberts, C., Byram, M., Barro, A., Jordan, S. and Street, B. (2001) *Learners as Ethnographers*. Clevedon, UK: Multilingual Matters.

Robinson, J.L. (1996) Second language learning in social context: An ethnographic account of an academic semester abroad in Russia. PhD thesis, University of Maryland, 1995. *Dissertation Abstracts International-A* 56 (8), 3037.

Rodriguez, S. (2001) The perception of requests in Spanish by instructed learners of Spanish in the second- and foreign-language contexts: A longitudinal study of acquisition patterns. PhD thesis, Indiana University, Bloomington, IN, 2001. *Dissertation Abstracts International-A* 62 (2), 554–555.

Rogoff, B. (1994) Developing understanding of the idea of communities of learners. *Mind, Culture, and Activity* 1 (4), 209–29.

Rose, K.R. (1994) Pragmatic consciousness raising in an EFL context. In L.F. Bouton and Y. Kachru (eds) *Pragmatics and Language Learning Monograph Series* (Vol. 5) (pp. 52–63). Urbana, IL: Division of English as an International Language, University of Illinois at Urbana-Champaign.

Ruiz, R. (1984) Orientations in language planning. *NABE Journal* 8 (2), 15–34.

Rulon, K. and McCreary, J. (1986) Negotiation of content: Teacher-fronted and small group interaction. In R. Day (ed.) *Talking to Learn: Conversation in Second Language Acquisition* (pp. 182–99). Rowley, MA: Newbury House.

Sanjur, D. (1982) *Social and Cultural Perspectives in Nutrition.* Englewood Cliffs, NJ: Prentice-Hall.

Sanjur, D. (1995) *Hispanic Foodways, Nutrition and Health.* Boston: Allyn & Bacon.

Savignon, S. (1972) *Communicative Competence: An Experiment in Foreign Language Teaching.* Center for Curriculum Development, Philadelphia.

Saville-Troike, M. (1996) The ethnography of communication. In S. McKay and N. Hornberger (eds) *Sociolinguistics and Language Teaching* (pp. 351–82). Cambridge: Cambridge University Press.

Scarcella, R.C. (1983a) Developmental trends in the acquisition of conversational competence by adult second language learners. In N. Wolfson and E. Judd (eds) *Sociolinguistics and Language Acquisition* (pp. 175–83). Rowley, MA: Newbury House.

Scarcella, R.C. (1983b) Discourse accent in second language performance. In S.M. Gass and L. Selinker (eds) *Language Transfer in Language Learning* (pp. 306–26). Rowley, MA: Newbury House.

Schatzman, L. and Strauss, A.L. (1973) *Field Research: Strategies for a Natural Sociology.* Englewood Cliffs, NJ: Prentice-Hall.

Schegloff, E.A. and Sacks, H. (1973) Opening up closings. *Semiotica* 8, 289–327.

Schell, K.A. (2001) Functional categories and the acquisition of aspect in L2 Spanish: A longitudinal study. PhD thesis, University of Washington. *Dissertation Abstracts International* A, 61 (1), 4365.

Schieffelin, B.B. and Ochs, E. (1986a) Introduction. In B.B. Schieffelin and E. Ochs (eds) *Language Socialization across Cultures* (pp. 1–13). New York: Cambridge University Press.

Schieffelin, B.B. and Ochs, E. (1986b) Language socialization. *Annual Review of Anthropology* 15, 163–91.

Schiffrin, D. (1996) Narrative as self-portrait: Sociolinguistic constructions of identity. *Language in Society* 25, 167–203.

Schlosser, E. (2001) *Fast Food Nation: The Dark Side of an All-American Meal.* Boston: Houghton Mifflin.

Schmidt, R. (1983) Interaction, acculturation, and the acquisition of communicative competence: A case study of an adult. In N. Wolfson and E. Judd (eds) *Sociolinguistic and Language Acquisition* (pp. 137–74). Rowley, MA: Newbury House.

Schmidt, R. (1990) The role of consciousness in second language learning. *Applied Linguistics* 11 (2), 129–57.

Schmidt, R. (1993) Consciousness, learning and interlanguage pragmatics. In G. Kasper and S. Blum-Kulka (eds) *Interlanguage Pragmatics* (pp. 21–42). Oxford: Oxford University Press.

Schmidt, R. and Frota, S.N. (1986) Developing basic conversational ability in a second language: A case study of an adult learner of Portuguese. In R. Day (ed.) *Talking to Learn: Conversation in Second Language Acquisition* (pp. 237–326). Rowley, MA: Newbury House.

Schmidt, R. and Richards, J.C. (1980) Speech acts and second language learning. *Applied Linguistics* 1 (2), 129–57.

Schumann, J.H. (1976) Social distance as a factor in second language acquisition. *Language Learning* 26 (1), 135–43.

Schumann, J.H. (1997) *The Neurobiology of Affect in Language.* Oxford: Blackwell.

Scollon, R. and Scollon, S.B.K. (1981) *Narrative, Literacy, and Face in Interethnic Communication.* Norwood, NJ: Ablex.

Segalowitz, N. and Freed, B.F. (2004) Context, contact, and cognition in oral fluency acquisition: Learning Spanish in "at home" and "study abroad" contexts. *Studies in Second Language Acquisition* 26 (2), 173–99.

Shaw, T., Michahelles, R., Xiangming, C., Minami, M. and Sing, R. (1994) Adapting to the U.S. classroom: Problems and strategies of Asian high school students in Boston area schools. Cambridge, MA: Harvard Graduate School of Education, Office of International Education. (ERIC Document Reproduction Service No. ED400718).

Shortreed, I.M. (1993) Variation in foreigner talk input: The effects of task and proficiency. In G. Crookes and S. Gass (eds) *Tasks and Language Learning: Integrating Theory and Practice* (pp. 96–122). Clevedon, UK: Multilingual Matters.

Shultz, J., Florio, S. and Erickson, F. (1982) Where's the floor? Aspects of the cultural organization of social relationship in communication at home and in school. In P. Gilmore and A.A. Glatthorn (eds) *Children In and Out of School* (pp. 88–123). Washington, DC: Center for Applied Linguistics.

Siegal, M. (1995a) Individual differences and study abroad: Women learning Japanese in Japan. In B.F. Freed (ed.) *Second Language Acquisition in a Study Abroad Context* (pp. 225–44). Amsterdam: John Benjamins.

Siegal, M. (1995b) Looking east: Learning Japanese as a second language in Japan and the interaction of race, gender and social context. Ph.D thesis, University of California – Berkeley, 1994. *Dissertation Abstracts International-A*, 56 (5), 1692.

Siegal, M. (1996) The role of subjectivity in second language sociolinguistic competency: Western women learning Japanese. *Applied Linguistics* 17 (3), 356–82.

Silver, R. (1999) Input, output and negotiation: Conditions for second language development. Paper presented at Second Language Research Forum 1999. Minneapolis, Minnesota.

Simões, A.R.M. (1996) Phonetics in second language acquisition: An acoustic study of fluency in adult learners of Spanish. *Hispania* 79 (1), 87–95.

Slater, P. (1966) *Microcosm*. New York: Basic Books.

Smartt, J. T. (1998) Self-repair in developing oral language of adult second language learners. PhD thesis, Witchita State University. *Dissertation Abstracts International* 59 (6),1952.

Snow, C.E., van Eeden, R. and Muysken, P. (1981) The interactional origins of foreigner talk: Municipal employees and foreign workers. *International Journal of the Sociology of Language* 28, 81–92.

Spada, N. (1985) Effects of informal contact on classroom learners' L2 proficiency: A review of five studies. *TESL Canada Journal* 2 (2), 51–62.

Spada, N. (1986) The interaction between types of contact and types of instruction: Some effects on the second language proficiency of adult learners. *Studies in Second Language Acquisition* 8 (2), 181–99.

St. Julien, J. (1997) Explaining learning: The research trajectory of situated cognition and the implications of connectionism. In D. Kirshner and J.A. Whitson (eds) *Situated Cognition* (pp. 261–79). Mahwah, NJ: Lawrence Erlbaum Associates.

Stansfield, C.W. (1975) Study abroad and the first-year student. Portland: Pacific Northwest Council on Foreign Languages (ERIC Document Reproduction Service No. ED 138 057).

Statzner, E.L. (1994) And Marvin raised his hand: Practices that encourage children's classroom participation. *Anthropology and Education Quarterly* 25 (3), 285–97.

Stevens, J.J. (2001) The acquisition of L2 Spanish pronunciation in a study abroad context. PhD thesis, University of Southern California, 2000. *Dissertation Abstracts International-A*, 62 (6), 2095.

Strong, M. (1984) Integrative motivation: Cause or result of successful second language acquisition? *Language Learning* 34 (3), 1–14.

Sugimoto,Y (1997) *An Introduction to Japanese Society*. Cambridge: Cambridge University Press.

Svanes, B. (1987) Motivation and cultural distance in second language acquisition. *Language Learning* 37, 341–59.

Swain, M. and Lapkin, S. (1995) Problems in output and the cognitive processes they generate: A step towards second language learning. *Applied Linguistics* 16 (3), 371–91.

Syed, A. (2001) Notions of self in foreign language learning: A qualitative analysis. In A. Dörnyei and R. Schmidt (eds) *Motivation and Second Language Acquisition* (pp. 127–48). Honolulu, Hawai'i: Second Language Teaching and Curriculum Center.

Talburt, S. and Stewart, M.A. (1999) What's the subject of study abroad? Race, gender, and "living culture". *The Modern Language Journal* 83 (2), 163–75.

Tamada, Y. (1996) Japanese learner's language learning strategies: The relationship between learners' personal factors and their choices of language learning strategies. Lancaster University (ERIC Document Reproduction Service No. ED 401 746).

Tan, A. (1989) *Joy Luck Club.* New York: G.P. Putnam's Sons.

Tanaka, K. and Ellis, R. (2003) Study abroad language proficiency, and learner beliefs about language learning. *JALT Journal* 25 (1), 63–85.

Tannen, D. (1985) Cross-cultural communication. In T.A.V. Dijk (ed.) *Handbook of Discourse Analysis,* (Vol. 4) (pp. 203–15). London: Academic Press.

Tannen, D. (1993) What's in a frame?: Surface evidence for underlying expectations. In D. Tannen (ed.) *Framing in Discourse* (pp. 14–56). Oxford: Oxford University Press.

Tannen, D., and Wallat, C. (1993) Interactive frames and knowledge schemas in interaction: Examples from a medical examination/interview. In D. Tannen (ed.) *Framing in Discourse* (pp. 57–76). New York: Oxford University Press.

Theophano, J.S. (1982) It's really tomato sauce but we call it gravy: A study of food and women's work among Italian-American families. PhD thesis, University of Pennsylvania.

Thomas, J. (1983) Cross-cultural pragmatic failure. *Applied Linguistics* 4 (2), 91–112.

Thomas, J. (1995) *Meaning in Interaction: An Introduction to Pragmatics.* London/NY: Longman.

Toohey, K. (1998) "Breaking them up, taking them away": Constructing ESL students in Grade 1. *TESOL Quarterly* 32 (1), 61–84.

Torres, J.P. (2003) A cognitive approach to the acquisition of clitics in Spanish: Insights from study abroad and classroom learners. PhD thesis, Cornell University. *Dissertation Abstracts International*-A, 63 (12), 4298.

Trosset, C. (1986) The social identity of Welsh learners. *Language in Society* 15, 165–92.

Trudgill, P. (1974) *The Social Differentiation of English in Norwich.* Cambridge: Cambridge University Press.

Tsunoda, T. (1978) Nihonjin no Noo: Noo no Hataraki to Toozai no Bunka (The Japanese Brain: Functions of the Brain and the Cultures of the East and the West). Tokyo: Taishukan.

Turnbull, W. (2001) An appraisal of pragmatic elicitation techniques for the social psychological study of talk: The case of request refusals. *Pragmatics* 11 (1), 31–61.

Tusting, K., Crawshaw, R. and Callen, B. (2002) 'I know,' cos I was there': How residence abroad students use personal experience to legitimate cultural generalizations. *Discourse & Society* 13 (5), 651–72.

Twombly, S.B. (1995) *Piropos* and friendships: Gender and culture clash in study abroad. *Frontiers: The Interdisciplinary Journal of Study Abroad,* 1, 1–27. On WWW at http://www.frontiersjournal.com/back/one/twom.htm.

Umesao, T. (1986) *Kokusaika suru nihongo no zahyoujiku* (On globalizing Japanese). *Kokusai Kouryuu* 41, 2–29.

Ushioda, E. (2001) Language learning at university: Exploring the role of motivational thinking. In A. Dörnyei and R. Schmidt (eds) *Motivation and Second*

Language Acquisition (pp. 93–126). Honolulu, Hawai'i: Second Language Teaching and Curriculum Center.

Uyeno, T. (1971) A study of Japanese modality: A performative analysis of sentence particles. Ph.D thesis, The University of Michigan.

Valdman, A. (1981) Sociolinguistic aspects of foreigner talk. *International Journal of the Sociology of Language* 28, 41–52.

Van Dijk, T. (1992) Discourse and the denial of racism. *Discourse & Society* 3 (1), 87–118.

Varonis, E. and Gass, S. (1982) The comprehensibility of non-native speech. *Studies in Second Language Acquisition* 4 (1), 41–52.

Varonis, E. and Gass, S. (1985a) Miscommunication in native/nonnative conversation. *Language in Society* 14 (3), 327–43.

Varonis, E. and Gass, S. (1985b) Non-native/non-native conversations: A model for negotiation of meaning. *Applied Linguistics* 6 (1), 71–90.

Visser, M. (1991) *The Rituals of Dinner: The Origins, Evolution, Eccentricities and Meaning of Table Manners*. New York: Grove Weidenfeld.

von Au, F. (1996) *Knigge 2000. Sichere Umgangsformen für alle Gelegenheiten* (3rd edn). München: Ludwig.

Vygotsky, L.S. (1978) *Mind in Society: The Development of Higher Psychological Processes*. M. Cole, V. Skip-Steiner, S. Scribner and E. Souberman (eds). Cambridge, MA: Harvard University Press.

Vygotsky, L. S. (1986) *Thought and Language*. A. Kozulin (ed.). Cambridge: MA: MIT Press.

Waldbaum, R.K. (1997) A case study of institutional and student outcomes of an educational exchange program: The University of Denver and the University of Bologna. PhD thesis, University of Denver, 1996. *Dissertation Abrstracts International-A*, 57 (7), 2908.

Walkerdine, V. (1997) Redefining the subject in situated cognition theory. In D. Kirshner and J. A. Whitson (eds) *Situated Cognition* (pp. 57–70). Mahwah, NJ: Lawrence Erlbaum Associates.

Walsh, R. (1994) The year abroad – a linguistic challenge. *TEANGA: The Irish Yearbook of Applied Linguistics* 14, 48–57.

Walsh, R. (1995) Language development and the year abroad: A study of oral grammatical accuracy amongst adult learners of German as a foreign language. PhD thesis, University College Dublin.

Warden, M., Lapkin, S., Swain, M. and Hart, D. (1995) Adolescent language learners on a three month exchange: Insights from their diaries. *Foreign Language Annals* 28 (4), 537–50.

Watanabe, Y. (1990) External variables affecting language learning strategies of Japanese EFL learners: Effects of entrance examination, years spent at college/university, and staying overseas. Lancaster University. (ERIC Document Reproduction Service No. ED 334 822).

Watson-Gegeo, K. (October, 2001) Mind, language, and epistemology: Toward a language socialization paradigm for SLA. Invited Plenary Speech presented at the 2001 Pacific Second Language Research Forum, Honolulu, Hawai'i.

Watson-Gegeo, K. and Gegeo, D.W. (1992) Schooling, knowledge and power: Social transformations in the Solomon Islands. *Anthropology & Education Quarterly* 23 (1), 10–29.

Weinrich, H. (1993) *Textgrammatik der deutschen Sprache*. Mannheim: Dudenverlag.

Wells, L. J. (1985) The group-as-a-whole perspective and its theoretical roots. In A.D. Colman and M. Geller (eds) *Group Relations Reader 2* (pp. 109–26). Washington, DC: A.K. Rice Institute.

Wenger, E. (1998) *Communities of Practice: Learning, Meaning, and Identity.* Cambridge, UK: Cambridge University Press.

Wertsch, J. (1985) *Vygotsky and the Social Formation of Mind.* Cambridge, MA: Harvard University Press.

Wilkinson, S. (1995) Foreign language conversation and the study abroad transition: A case study. PhD thesis, The Pennsylvania State University, State College.

Wilkinson, S. (1997, December) Separating fact from myth: A qualitative perspective on language learning during summer study abroad. Paper presented at the meeting of the Modern Language Association, Toronto.

Wilkinson, S. (1998a) On the nature of immersion during study abroad: Some participants' perspectives. *Frontiers: The Interdisciplinary Journal of Study Abroad, IV,* 121–38. On WWW at http://www.frontiersjournal.com/issues/vol4/vol4-05_Wilkinson.pdf.

Wilkinson, S. (1998b) Study abroad from the participants' perspective: A challenge to common beliefs. *Foreign Language Annals* 31 (1), 23–39.

Wilkinson, S. (2000) Emerging questions about study abroad. *Association of Departments of Foreign Languages Bulletin* 32 (1), 36–41.

Wilkinson, S. (2001) Beyond classroom boundaries: The changing nature of study abroad. In R.Z. Lavine (ed.) *Beyond the Boundaries: Changing Contexts in Language Learning* (pp. 81–105). New York: McGraw-Hill.

Wilkinson, S. (2002) The omnipresent classroom during summer study abroad: American students in conversation with their French hosts. *The Modern Language Journal,* 86 (2), 157–73.

Willet, J. (1995) Becoming first graders in an L2: An ethnographic study of L2 socialization. *TESOL Quarterly* 29 (3), 473–503.

Woodman, K. (1999) A study in linguistic, perceptual and pedagogical change in a short-term intensive language program. PhD thesis, University of Victoria, Canada, 1998. *Dissertation Abstracts International* 60 (3), 728.

Yamamoto, N. (1995) *Hoomu stei ni okeru ibunkakan komyunikeishon.* Paper presented at the Nihongo nihon bunka kouza kaki seminaa, 10 shuunen kinen kenkyuu kai, Hakodate, Japan.

Yashima, T. (1999) Influence of personality, L2 proficiency and attitudes on Japanese adolescents' intercultural adjustment. *JALT Journal,* 21 (1), 66–86.

Yashima, T., Zenuk-Nishide, L. and Shimizu, K. (2004) The influence of attitudes and affect on willingness to communicate and second language communication. *Language Learning* 54 (1), 119–52.

Yoshino, K. (1992) *Cultural Nationalism in Contemporary Japan.* London: Routledge.

Yuan, Y. (2001) An inquiry into empirical pragmatics data-gathering methods: Written DCTs, oral DCTs, field notes, and natural conversations. *Journal of Pragmatics* 33 (2), 271–92.

Zimmer, D.E. (1986) *Redens Arten. Über Trends und Tollheiten im neudeutschen Sprachgebrauch.* Zürich: Haffmans.

Zuengler, J. (1991) Accommodation in native-nonnative interactions: Going beyond the "what" to the "why" in second-language research. In H. Giles, N. Coupland and J. Coupland (eds) *Contexts of Accommodation, Developments in Applied Sociolinguistics,* (pp. 223–244). Cambridge: Cambridge University Press.

Index

accommodations 69, 154
acculturation 246, 256-7, 294, 314
– Bennett's model of 234, 237, 255
accuracy 8-9, 19, 76, 172, 181, 183, 198,
    231-2, 243-4, 246, 249-50, 253, 256-7, 317
– checks 17
– in agreement 239
– sociolinguistic 66
– sociopragmatic 65
achievement principle 225
acquisition viii, xiii, 1-2, 4-5, 7, 14-5, 18,
    20-1, 23, 26, 56-58, 60, 64-67, 69, 85-6, 93,
    96, 153, 177-9, 186-7, 203-4, 226, 231-3,
    237, 240, 247, 255, 257-60, 262, 264, 273,
    286, 288, 294-317
– of communicative competence 313
– of declarative knowledge 85
– folklinguistic theories of 154
– of grammar 7-8, 13, 31
– of intercultural competence 300
– of language learning strategies 264, 268, 270
– of leave-taking 31, 53
– of listening skills 3
– of literacy skills 2
– of narratives 295
– of negative responses 300
– of politeness 66, 94-6, 300, 308
– of pragmatics vii, ix, xiii, 9, 14, 31, 36, 52-3,
    58, 295
– of pronunciation 6, 300, 315
– of routines 9-10, 300
– of sociolinguistic competence v, vii, 59-60,
    67, 69, 231
– of speech acts 31
– second language vi, vii, ix, xiii, xiv, 1,
    26-7, 32, 36, 54, 85, 117, 151, 178, 186,
    231, 288, 294-316
– of terms of address 11, 65-6, 300
– of vocabulary 178
ACTFL (American Council on the Teaching
    of Foreign Languages) 4, 157, 206, 238-9,
    258, 294
Adams, R. vi, xiii, 18, 259, 294
address form/address system 59-61, 63-71,

73, 75, 77, 82-6
administrators 23, 205, 208, 224, 226, 244, 259
affective
– factors 53-4, 56, 58
– strategies 272-3, 275, 278, 280-1, 287 See
    also strategies
affinity group principle 219
Agar, M. 9, 92, 294
age 34, 37, 64, 69, 71-3, 83, 88, 91-2, 116, 119,
    127, 141, 150, 153, 157, 167, 172, 185, 238,
    261
Allen, H.W. 2-4, 15-6, 23-5, 294
Alptekin, C. 68, 294
Amendt, G. 63, 294
Ammon, U. 61, 63, 294
anxiety 1, 14, 16, 18, 26, 158, 278, 281
Aoki, H. 136, 294
appropriateness 13, 39, 54, 152-3, 159, 172
– of apology stratiegies 13
– negotiations of 165
– of pre-closings 41
– of requests 14
– sociolinguistic 166
– of strategies 261
Armstrong, G.K. 260, 294
asymmetric/asymmetrical
– input 85
– relationships 11, 162
Atkinson, D. 56-7, 294
attention
– to form 186, 189, 191
– control over 32, 53
attitudes vi, viii, 19, 172, 231-58, 296, 299,
    302-3, 305, 318
– language 166
– learner/learning 20, 170, 178, 203, 232-3,
    241, 255
– negative 20, 233
– positive 15, 233, 242, 250
– towards host culture 240, 250
– towards food 91-4, 117-8
aversion 54-5, 58
avoidance 56, 71, 73, 75, 77, 82, 87 See also
    withdrawal

319